A RHETORIC OF REFLECTION

D1220393

A RHETORIC OF REFLECTION

Edited by
KATHLEEN BLAKE YANCEY

UTAH STATE UNIVERSITY PRESS
Logan

© 2016 by the University Press of Colorado

Published by Utah State University Press
An imprint of University Press of Colorado
5589 Arapahoe Avenue, Suite 206C
Boulder, Colorado 80303

All rights reserved
Manufactured in the United States of America

 The University Press of Colorado is a proud member of
The Association of American University Presses.

The University Press of Colorado is a cooperative publishing enterprise supported,
in part, by Adams State University, Colorado State University, Fort Lewis College,
Metropolitan State University of Denver, Regis University, University of Colorado,
University of Northern Colorado, Utah State University, and Western State Colorado
University.

∞ This paper meets the requirements of the ANSI/NISO Z39.48-1992 (Permanence of
Paper).

ISBN: 978-1-60732-515-4 (paperback)
ISBN: 978-1-60732-516-1 (ebook)

Library of Congress Cataloging-in-Publication Data

Names: Yancey, Kathleen Blake, 1950– editor.
Title: A rhetoric of reflection / edited by Kathleen Blake Yancey.
Description: Logan : Utah State University Press, [2016] | Includes index. | Includes bib-
liographical references.
Identifiers: LCCN 2015044251| ISBN 9781607325154 (pbk.) | ISBN 9781607325161
(ebook)
Subjects: LCSH: English language—Rhetoric—Study and teaching (Higher) | Reflective
learning. | Reflective teaching. | Transfer of training.
Classification: LCC PE1404 .R4965 2016 | DDC 808/.042071—dc23
LC record available at http://lccn.loc.gov/2015044251

Cover photograph © littlesam/Shutterstock

A brief but heartfelt thanks to all the contributors within and to our students and colleagues. This is a story that belongs to all of us.

CONTENTS

ACKNOWLEDGMENTS

In *Reflection in the Writing Classroom*, I observed that it was a gift to have a scholarly project that was so personally meaningful; my observation today about reflection and reflective practice as a focus of scholarship, curriculum, and pedagogy is much the same, although in the interval between then and now, my thinking on reflection has continued to benefit from the contributions of many.

I begin by thanking the many, many students I've had the pleasure of teaching and learning from, students whose reflections have always taught me—whether informing, surprising, and/or puzzling me—and whose reflective practices and verbal/visual texts collectively constitute a curriculum in reflection.

I thank as well the colleagues and friends at the institutions where I've taught. I began articulating a theory of reflection when I was on the faculty at the University of North Carolina at Charlotte, where my work was supported by many, especially the Department of English, our site of the National Writing Project, and friends and colleagues Jim McGavran, Meg Morgan, and Greg Wickliff. At Clemson University, I continued learning about reflection with National Writing Project colleagues, particularly in a semester-long seminar dedicated to the topic. At Florida State University, my departmental colleagues offer an intellectual banquet situating this work: thanks particularly to Eric Walker, Andrew Epstein, Leigh Edwards, Ned Stuckey-French, Elizabeth Stuckey-French, David Gantz, David Kirby, Stan Gontarski, Diane Roberts, and David Johnson. My thinking about reflection has also been especially enriched by readings and discussions with members of our Rhetoric and Composition graduate program, including the participants in a one-credit reading course on reflection; the three intrepid graduate students—Bruce Bowles, Joe Cirio, and Erin Workman—with whom I studied reflection in an independent study; and my colleagues and friends Deborah Coxwell-Teague, Kristie Fleckenstein, Tarez Graban, Stephen McElroy, Rhea Lathan, and Michael Neal. Friends and colleagues elsewhere have likewise informed my thinking: thanks to

Linda Adler-Kassner, Matt Davis, Mary DeShazer, Teddi Fishman, Martin Jacobi, Asao Inoue, Lennie Irvin, Jessie Moore, Peggy O'Neill, Margaret Marshall, Fran Sharer, Jody Shipka, Nancy Sommers, Elizabeth Wardle, and Irwin (Bud) Weiser.

Several institutions and conferences have also welcomed and informed my thinking about reflection: thanks to friends and colleagues at Agnes Smith College, Brigham Young University, DePaul University, Fort Lewis College, Hampshire College, Illinois State University, Marquette University, Mary Washington College, Millsaps College, Queensborough Community College, Ripon College, Smith College, University of Houston, the Elon University Research Seminar "Critical Transitions: Writing and the Question of Transfer," and the International Writing across the Curriculum conference hosted at the University of Minnesota. I have also worked on reflection with colleagues in K–12: my gratitude to colleagues at Bethel, Alaska, and Virginia Beach, Virginia. And not least, I have benefited from, and thank, the many colleagues and friends participating in the Inter/National Coalition for Electronic Portfolio Research, including my co-directors Barbara Cambridge and Darren Cambridge.

This project, however, has as its centerpiece the smart thinking and generous contributions of the colleagues and friends whose chapters, here, help us understand the diversity, richness, workings, and potential of a rhetorical reflection. I wrote each of these contributors in the early Florida-sultry days of July 2013 to ask if they would share with all of us their thinking about reflection. The book before you, going to press in the early Florida-sultry days of July 2016, is the archive of their responses. Thanks, again, to Anne Beaufort, Liane Robertson, Kara Taczak, Michael Neal, Cathy Leaker and Heather Ostman, Bruce Horner, Asao B. Inoue, Tyler Richmond, Elizabeth Clark, Naomi Silver, Christina McDonald, Pamela Flash, Kevin Roozen, Jeff Sommers, and Doug Hesse. Learning about reflection from you has been a highlight of the last three years.

The reviewers—Morgan Gresham and an anonymous reviewer—extended a perfect balance of praise and help: if this book makes a contribution to our scholarship on reflection and to our curricular and pedagogical practices, they deserve thanks as well. And to Michael Spooner at Utah State University Press, whose lively encouragement, advice, and guidance has strengthened the project: *merci*.

Never least, thanks to those whose contributions to my thinking on reflection inhabit the rich space between the personal and the intellectual: David Yancey, Genevieve Yancey, Sui Wong, Matthew Yancey, Kelly Yancey—and our newest collaborator, Calder, who brings into focus the meaning and potential of a reflective life.

A RHETORIC OF REFLECTION

1

INTRODUCTION
Contextualizing Reflection

Kathleen Blake Yancey

In the summer of 2014, I offered an independent study on reflection to three doctoral students in rhetoric and composition, Bruce Bowles, Joe Cirio, and Erin Workman, each of whom brought reflection-related interests with them to the course. Bruce is very interested in writing assessment, especially response to writing. Joe was conducting a qualitative study inquiring into whether students have enough conceptual knowledge, vocabulary, motivation, and agency to participate in creating scoring guides. Erin brought with her a completed pilot project on transfer of writing knowledge and practice highlighting the role of reflection. The question: in this one-hour graduate course on reflection, what might we read?

Had we asked this question in the 1970s at the beginning of the composing-process movement, the answer would have been short and quick, the readings focusing largely on the cognitive role that reflection plays in writing. In 1979, for example, Sharon Pianko defined reflection behaviorally as the "pauses and rescannings" stimulating "the growth of consciousness in students about the numerous mental and linguistic strategies" entailed in composing and "the many lexical, syntactical, and organizational choices" made during composing (Pianko 1979, 277–78). Pianko's claim also included the idea that reflection, as a practice, distinguished able from "not-so-able" writers. And at about the same time, Sondra Perl (1980) identified two components of reflection, what she called "projection" and "retrospection," "the alternating mental postures writers assume as they move through the act of composing" (389). In brief, the emergent literature on reflection at this moment in composition's history was tightly focused on the mental activities of the composer in the process of composing.

Had we asked this question about readings on reflection in the late 1980s and into the 1990s, however, we would have had a second literature to draw on as well, much of it oriented toward *designing reflective*

DOI: 10.7330/9781607325161.c001

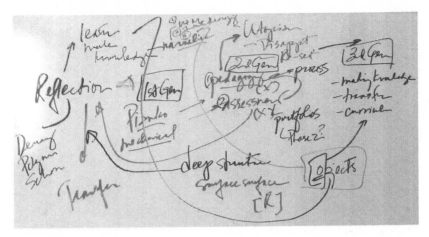

Figure 1.1.

activity to help make students' thinking external, visible, and available—for both assessment and teaching purposes. Roberta Camp (1992), for example, outlined one use of reflection, for portfolios, explaining how inside a portfolio a student could map the changing shape of a multiply drafted composition in what she called a "biography of a text"; thinking pedagogically, Bill Thelin (1994) explored how responding to writing changes, and doesn't, in the context of a portfolio and its reflection; and Jeff Sommers (1988) created a Writer's Memo allowing students, in a student's words, to go "'behind the paper'" to describe "the composing process which produced the draft" (77). Interestingly, Sommers (1988) pointed out that the memo assists both student and teacher: in Sommers's view, the memo's intent, like that of many reflective practices developed at this time, was twofold: (1) to elucidate student composing activities in students' own descriptions so as to see what was otherwise invisible and (2) to provide a context for an instructor-student conversation about the draft itself. Likewise, also addressing classroom and assessment contexts, I developed a Schonean-influenced practice-based theory of reflection in writing keyed to three related forms of reflective practice:

> *reflection-in-action,* the process of reviewing and projecting and revising, which takes place within a composing event;
>
> *constructive reflection,* the process of developing a cumulative, multi-selved, multi-voiced identity, which takes place between and among composing events; and
>
> *reflection-in-presentation,* the process of articulating the relationships between and among the multiple variables of writing and the writer in a specific context for a specific audience. (Yancey 1998, 200)

During this time, reflection was also playing a major role in assessment, first in print portfolios and later, of course, in electronic portfolios, with both portfolio models defined as the result of three processes: collecting a range of texts, selecting from among them for a portfolio composition, and reflecting (Yancey 1992)—though the reflecting on whom or what varied. In some models, the reflective text was supposed to provide a narrative of writerly development, in others an account of process or self-assessment, and in still others an introduction to the portfolio itself. Furthermore, as in the case of pedagogical practice, so too in assessment: the role reflection plays in writing assessment has been both conceptualized and reconceptualized. Early in the portfolio movement, for example, Chris Anson (1994) categorized reflection as a secondary text in dialogue with—but mostly in support of—the primary texts of a portfolio. Later, I theorized that reflective texts are primary texts in their own right, though of a different nature than "primary" writing texts, and that the relationship between these two kinds of texts was dialogic and multicontextual, not hierarchical. More recently, Ed White (2005) has suggested that the reflective text can function as a surrogate for the full portfolio in an assessment context, though earlier research such as Glenda Conway's (1994) has suggested that this cover letter is problematic, much more a performance piece than an authentic expression for students, indeed, something of a mask through which to present the best possible student self (89), which makes perfect sense given the stakes. And other research (e.g., Yancey forthcoming) has observed that the Phase 2 portfolio scoring model mistakes one construct, that of argumentative writing, for a different construct, reflective writing. In general, then, during this second period of scholarship in reflection, the field moved beyond descriptions of mental behaviors to develop and theorize new classroom and assessment practices.

Into the twenty-first century, the scholarship on reflection is in a third phase or generation, with the list of readings we might consult now both wide and varied. Seen through Perl's (1980) formation, current interest in reflection is an exercise in both retrospection and prospection, with teachers and scholars returning to earlier practices to revise them, considering those practices in larger contexts for critique and theorizing reflection in new ways and for future use. Jeff Sommers (2011), for example, has revised his Writer's Memos into a semester-long reflective project focused on students' individual and collective beliefs about writing and the ways those beliefs do, and don't, change over the course of a term; Anne Beaufort (2007) has pointed to reflection as a key component supporting transfer of writing knowledge and practice; Kara Taczak, Liane Robertson, and I have theorized reflection as part of a new writing curriculum we call *Teaching for Transfer* (TFT) (Yancey, Robertson, and Taczak 2014), and Cathy Leaker and Heather Ostman have documented the epistemological nature of reflection, demonstrating how reflection contributes to and provides evidence of knowledge developed experientially (Leaker and Ostman 2010). During this time, there has also been a different kind of return to the past, with scholars expressing concerns and raising questions. Tony Scott (2005), for instance, has raised red flags about what he perceives as a Foucaultian dimension of reflection; other scholars have questioned what they see as a presumed relationship between reflection and the unified self—or the possibility of such a self—with reflection serving as something of a flashpoint. Thus, while scholars like Pat Belanoff (2001) contend that reflection "can enable the reconstituting—if only momentarily—of a unified self, which certainly enables one to act more effectively" (421), Glenda Conway (1994) and Kimberly Emmons (2003), taking another tack, agree with Julie Jung (2011) that, in Jung's formation, reflective writing tends "to legitimize liberal constructions of the writer as a single, unified self" (629) and that "reflective writing pedagogy, which aims to help student-writers assert authority as *writers* . . . reinforc[es] some students' sense of themselves as 'only' *students*" (642; italics in original).

In higher education more generally, however, both reflection and metacognition are increasingly identified as important for learning. In writing studies, *reflection* has been the key term, while in higher-education contexts, *reflection* and *metacognition* are often used interchangeably. As constructs, reflection and metacognition have some overlap, but they also are assigned different attributes and roles in supporting learning. In *How Learning Works* (2010), for example, Susan A. Ambrose, Michael W. Bridges, Michele DiPietro, Marsha C. Lovett, and Marie K. Norman define metacognition and reflection conventionally: the first, metacognition, as thinking about thinking associated with planning, self-monitoring, and self-regulation; the second, reflection, as oriented to self-assessment activity occurring at the end of a learning cycle, though capable of prompting a new one.

Researchers have proposed various models to describe how learners ideally apply metacognitive skills to learn and perform well (Butler 1998; Pintrich 2000; Winne and Hadwin 1998). Although these models differ in their particulars, they share the notion that learners need to engage in a variety of processes to *monitor* and *control* their learning (Zimmerman 2000). Moreover, because the processes of monitoring and controlling mutually affect each other, these models often take the form of a cycle. Learners

- assess the task at hand, taking into consideration the task's goals and constraints;
- evaluate their own knowledge and skills, identifying strengths and weaknesses;
- plan their approach in a way that accounts for the current situation;
- apply various strategies to enact their plan, monitoring their progress along the way;
- reflect on the degree to which their current approach is working so that they can adjust and restart the cycle as needed. (Ambrose et al. 2010, 91–92)

Most theorists agree with this definition in that metacognition includes self-monitoring, but the role of reflection in learning, or coming to know, has received less attention from scholars in cognitive psychology. Others interested in learning writ large have focused on reflection: notable among them are John Dewey (1910) and Donald Schon (1987). Drawing on both Dewey and Schon in accounting for reflection more fully, for example, Naomi Silver (2013) agrees with the general definition of metacognition while widening reflection's scope to include "conscious exploration of one's own experiences" (1). The construct of reflection, she says, "as theorized by John Dewey is broader in its scope, and also more rigorous" (6). In his landmark book *How We Think*, Dewey defines "reflective thought" as "*active, persistent, and careful consideration of any belief or supposed form of knowledge in light of the grounds that support it, and the further conclusions to which it tends*" (Dewey 1910, 6; emphasis in original). Deweyan reflection is more sustained than a general stocktaking, then, and perhaps closer to the much broader concept of critical thought itself. Reflection, for him, constitutes a meticulous process of evidence and implication seeking, with the aim not only of understanding more fully by means of creating connections and relationships within experiences, but also of transforming experience and one's environment as a result (Dewey 1910, 1916).

In contrast, Donald Schon's approach, as Silver (2013) observes, is located more in professional practice, which allows him "to define a framework that describes how professionals' tacit knowledge of their work may be more deliberately mobilized and taught to learners in the field, ultimately resulting in a curriculum for a 'reflective practicum' to form the core of professional training" (Schon 1987).

As important for both theorists of reflection is the role of a real problem in a context of uncertainty. As Silver (2013) explains, because the thinker feels "discomfort or uncertainty, what Dewey calls 'a forked-road situation, a situation which is ambiguous,'" there is "'a dilemma, which proposes alternatives'" (Dewey 1916, quoted in Silver 2013, 11). This dilemma, according to Dewey, is fundamental. Likewise, according to Silver, Schon identifies a "confrontation with confusion or ambiguity" as the exigence for reflective thinking and the opportunity for "a professional practitioner's tacit knowledge [to be] challenged," (8) the challenge then prompting the practitioner to "name" and "frame" the problem and to begin to make explicit the tacit knowledge aligning theory and practice.

As *A Rhetoric of Reflection* demonstrates, the Deweyian-Schonian construct of reflection as a synthetic knowledge-making activity keyed to uncertainty and ambiguity is critical for scholars in writing studies focusing on reflection, as it is for scholars currently studying learning in many other contexts, including general learning contexts; preprofessional and professional contexts ranging from medicine and education to engineering; and assessment contexts, those including electronic portfolios. The research on how students learn, for example, compiled in the National Research Council volume *How People Learn* (Bransford, Pellegrino, and Donovan 2000) and documented in more reflection-specific studies like the Harvard Business School's recent working paper "Learning by Thinking: How Reflection Aids Performance," points to reflection—defined in "Learning by Thinking" as an "intentional attempt to synthesize, abstract, and articulate the key lessons taught by experience" (Di Stefano et al. 2014, 3)—as critical in helping learners secure their learning. The theory outlined in "Learning by Thinking" is particularly interesting. Building on Dewey's concept of learning by doing (1933), Giada Di Stefano, Francesca Gino, Gary Pisano, and Bradley Staats make two provocative, empirically validated arguments (Di Stefano et al. 2014). First, for learning to take hold, we must "do," engaging in experience, as Dewey said, but we must *also* think, or reflect, on that learning for it to make sense, and when we do, our performance improves. Second, such reflecting contributes to self-efficacy precisely because it helps us understand that we have learned (even if not always successfully); how we have learned; and how we might continue to learn. Likewise, in numerous professions—including medicine (e.g., Gawande 2002), teaching (Brookfield 1995; also see Pamela Flash's chapter in this volume), and engineering (as demonstrated in Virginia Tech's NSF-funded engineering project employing reflective practice to support the development of engineering faculty and researchers)—reflection provides a mechanism for professional development, for professional practice, and for the making of knowledge. The same is true for assessment: drawing on and synthesizing research sponsored by the Inter/National Coalition for Electronic Portfolio Research, for example, I have theorized reflection's potential to help students not only to *invent the university*, in David Bartholomae's telling phrase, but also, and rather, to reinvent it (Yancey 2009), a point I return to below.

In the context of large-scale national assessment efforts, reflection is also playing a role, most notably as one of the indicators of student engagement in the National Survey of Student Engagement (NSSE 2014), which has been identified as one of the (few) measures of student progress acceptable to the federal government and whose results consistently correlate with student retention and graduation. More specifically, linking reflective learning to integrative learning and to writing, NSSE results show that reflective and integrative learning "requires students to personally connect with the course material by considering prior knowledge and experiences, other courses, and societal issues. Students must take into account the diverse perspectives of others as well as their own views while examining the views of others. Reflective and integrative learning is characteristic of students who engage in deep approaches to learning" ("A Fresh Look at Student Engagement" 2013). As explained here, then, deep-learning pedagogical approaches supporting student learning as articulated in reflective writing have now been documented as fundamental to students' learning and to their advancement in college.

In other words, during the last four decades, understanding of reflection has widened and deepened in writing studies, in learning theory, in the professions, in assessment contexts, and across higher education. Moreover, reflection in writing studies, seen through the conceptual lens of a generation, seems to be entering a third generation. What we might call the *first generation of reflection*, taking its cue from more generalized work on metacognition and thinking, focused on identifying and describing internal cognitive processes assumed to be part of composing. The second generation, operating in both classroom and assessment scenes, developed mechanisms for externalizing reflection, making it visible and thus explicitly available to help writers. The emerging work of the third generation in reflection—which in writing studies has included critiques of earlier work but has focused largely on revisions of earlier work, on conceptual advances, and on an increasing appreciation of reflection in the higher-education community—creates an exigence for the essays collected here.

Perhaps most important among the work of this third generation on reflection in writing studies is our increasing appreciation of the epistemological value of reflection, of its ability to help us make new meanings, of its rhetorical power. Earlier, I referred to the distinction between a Bartholomae-ian inventing a university and a student's reinventing one, a distinction that helps us understand reflection as rhetorical. More specifically, drawing on work in portfolios, I distinguished between students' invention of our university, which is basically their replication of the given, and their reinvention of our university, which of course changes it in ways we cannot control.

> In 1985, rhetoric and composition scholar David Bartholomae coined the expression *inventing the university* to explain the basic task of the postsecondary student aspiring to success: "He must learn to speak our language." In connecting *our* language and students' invention of the university, Bartholomae highlighted a need for students to accommodate to and assimilate into *us*, into *our* institutions. Such accommodation doesn't always succeed, however, as we see in student retention and graduation rates, and as we see all too often in disengaged students who are dropouts in waiting. (Yancey 2009, 15–16)

I also pointed to portfolios as a site of such reinvention and to reflection as the practice supporting it, noting the complementary roles that portfolios and reflection play in this process, with portfolios providing a site for multiple curricula and "reflection [providing] a specific opportunity to see each [curriculum], to talk across them, to connect them, to trace the contradictions among them, to create a contingent sense of them. In this sense of reflection, it is itself a site of invention, a place to make new knowledge and to shape new selves, and in so doing, re-invent the university as well." (16)

Of course, as we have seen and as the chapters here demonstrate, reflection operates outside portfolios as well; still, the distinction between students inventing our university and their reinventing it exemplifies the epistemology of reflection and its nature as a Bakhtinian practice. In other words, I theorized reflection as a Bakhtinian rhetorical exercise through which one engages with the cultural, to draw from it and give back to it in an exercise of meaning making at once both individual and social. Such reflective meaning as it works in language, Bakhtin says, is possible

> only when the speaker populates it with his own intentions, his own accent, when he appropriates the word, adapting it to his own semantic and expressive intention. Prior to this moment of appropriation, the word does not exist in a neutral and impersonal language (it is not, after all,

out of a dictionary that the speaker gets his words!), but rather it exists in other people's mouths, in other people's contexts, serving other people's intentions: it is from there that one must take the word, and make it one's own. (Bakhtin 1981, 293–94)

Through the practice of reflection, we draw on what is culturally known and infuse, interweave, integrate it with what we as individuals know—cognitively, affectively, and socially—to make a new knowledge that draws from the extant but is not a replication of it, that is, instead, unique, a knowledge only each one of us can make as it is in dialogue with what is. Not least, that new knowledge, collectively enacted, changes the very cultures situating reflective practice. More generally, then, what we are learning in this third generation of work in and on reflection is that it offers much more to writers and teachers of writers than has previously been assumed.

What that much more might be is the focus of *A Rhetoric of Reflection*. Reading across the chapters, we can identify at least three understandings of reflection shared by the authors here. First, to think of reflection only or exclusively as a mechanism for evaluation is to waste its potential: reflection can assist with assessment, certainly, but its larger value is linked to supporting writers in a myriad of ways as they develop both writing knowledge and practice. Second, in using reflection in our instruction, we have focused on pedagogy without attending as closely to curricular and extracurricular considerations. What, we are now asking, would a curriculum in reflection look like? Perhaps more important, what would a *curriculum in reflection for writing* look like? What reflective extracurricular activities help us understand student writing development and create more facilitative curricula? Third, our current approach to reflection is more nuanced and considered; we are developing research activities seeking to document, with the help of students and faculty, how it fosters an explicitness about learning and supports all of us in articulating and claiming what we know. Increasingly, we are coming to understand the role of community in this process. Put as a general proposition, the stand-alone individual letter of reflection has become a portal for a more robust conception of reflection, one directly connected to supporting student learning and contributing to a more humane assessment.

And not surprisingly, in this process of rethinking, reconceptualizing, and reapplying what we know about reflection, the authors here are raising new questions about it and the contexts of its use—and usefulness. Thinking in terms of transfer of writing knowledge and practice, for example, Ann Beaufort speaks to the potential of reflection as a mechanism of support, while Liane Robertson and Kara Taczak articulate a theory of reflection developed in concert with the Teaching for Transfer writing curriculum. What is the role of reflection, these teachers ask, in students' transfer of knowledge and practice, and how do we design such a role into curriculum? Drawing on his years of teaching with reflection, Jeff Sommers asks about how we need to situate reflection as a pedagogical tool within the curriculum. Given the relationship of practice to theory, how do we contextualize the Writer's Memo? Elizabeth Clark, Christina McDonald, and Naomi Silver each raise several questions related to electronically mediated reflection and the affordances it can offer students. What forms, for example, does multimedia reflection take? What do we gain in a reflection linked to multimedia that may not be available in print? What difference do modality and medium make for students and for learning? Michael Neal includes teaching in his consideration of reflection, but he links it to assessment: how, he asks, does reflection operate in teaching and assessment contexts, and can these two scenes for reflection be complementary?

Approaching the question of the relationship between assessment and reflection from a different perspective, Cathy Leaker and Heather Ostman move outside the classroom to consider how reflection contributes to the making of knowledge, especially in the context of prior learning assessment (PLA). The purpose of PLA is to allow students to earn college credit for experience: in their earlier work on PLA, Leaker and Ostman carefully documented the ways that through reflection students can articulate knowledge that can be credentialed through PLA. Here, they widen their focus to ask, how can PLA and other experientially based credit-awarding practices be linked to epistemology, equity, and social justice?

Thinking of reflection as a kind of conversation, Pamela Flash and Kevin Roozen explain the reflective conversations they have staged, Pamela with faculty in the context of a writing across the curriculum program and Kevin in the context of learning from a student about her literacy trajectory. How, both ask, does a reflective conversation allow participants to explicate tacit knowledge? Taking a very different tack, Bruce Horner asks how reflection might function as an inherent resource for all language learners, while Asao Inoue and Tyler Richmond raise questions about the relationship between race, culture, and reflection: how, they want to know, can students tap the reflective resources of home cultures in the work of the academy? And not least, Doug Hesse, addressing the essay, asks about the role of reflection as genre and about the essay's distinctive features exhibiting and supporting reflection.

And yet, there are themes crossing many of these interests and questions. Thought of as *tags*, the topics addressed here include:

REFLECTION AND PORTFOLIOS
Michael Neal; Cathy Leaker and Heather Ostman; Jeff Sommers; Elizabeth Clark; Naomi Silver

REFLECTION AND FACULTY DEVELOPMENT
Pamela Flash; Christina McDonald

REFLECTION AND RACE, DIVERSITY AND LANGUAGE
Cathy Leaker and Heather Ostman; Bruce Horner; Asao Inoue and Tyler Richmond; Elizabeth Clark; Christina McDonald

REFLECTION AND CONVERSATION, ESPECIALLY AS CONNECTED TO MAKING KNOWLEDGE
Pamela Flash; Kevin Roozen; Christina McDonald

REFLECTION AND GENRE
Jeff Sommers; Elizabeth Clark; Michael Neal; Doug Hesse

REFLECTION AND COMPOSING
Jeff Sommers; Elizabeth Clark; Cathy Leaker and Heather Ostman; Doug Hesse

REFLECTION AND TEACHER CHANGE
Jeff Sommers; Elizabeth Clark

REFLECTION AND TRANSFER OF WRITING KNOWLEDGE AND PRACTICE
Anne Beaufort; Kara Taczak and Liane Robertson

REFLECTION AND SITES OF LANGUAGE AND IDENTITY
Bruce Horner; Asao Inoue and Tyler Richmond; Jeff Sommers; Elizabeth Clark; Cathy Leaker and Heather Ostman

REFLECTION AND DIGITAL MULTIMODALITY
Elizabeth Clark; Michael Neal; Naomi Silver; Christina McDonald

REFLECTION AND TENSION
Asao Inoue and Tyler Richmond; Christina McDonald; Pamela Flash; Cathy Leaker and Heather Ostman

THE CHAPTERS WITHIN
The arrangement of the chapters tells yet another narrative, invents another way to think about reflection. Beginning with the classroom,

A Rhetoric of Reflection both provides field-specific context for reflection and outlines promising practices. In "Reflection: The Metacognitive Move towards Transfer of Learning," Anne Beaufort identifies reflection in writing curricula as essential in fostering transfer of learning—but observes that by itself, reflection is not sufficient to foster transfer. Summarizing key theories on transfer of learning, including the need for repeated application of learning in addition to reflection for transfer to occur, Beaufort provides examples from her own teaching showing how she designs writing course curricula that include application and reflection. Also classroom oriented and interested in transfer of writing knowledge and practice, Kara Taczak and Liane Robertson, in chapter 3, report on the role of reflection in a specific curriculum, on the Teaching for Transfer curriculum (TFT), and on that curriculum's efficacy. In "Reiterative Reflection in the Twenty-First-Century Writing Classroom: An Integrated Approach to Teaching for Transfer," Taczak and Robertson document their claim that reflection promoting transfer is of a very specific kind: "Reflection must serve as both process and product," they say, and as "theory and practice." In addition, these authors focus on the way reflection needs to be incorporated throughout a course, a point of interest to Jeff Sommers as well—in their view, in reiterative, intentional, and systematic ways so that students become active and engaged reflective practitioners. As important, Taczak and Robertson report on two studies demonstrating that without such an approach to reflection, students are unable to identify what it is they have learned and are thus less able to tap that learning for future use.

A Rhetoric of Reflection then turns to assessment, another site of reflective practice, beginning with Michael Neal's consideration of the role of reflection in portfolio assessment. In "The Perils of Standing Alone: Reflective Writing in Relationship to Other Texts," Neal considers two issues critical to reflection on the context of assessment: (1) challenges leveled at reflective writing as a form of self-assessment and (2) the relationship of reflection to composing and to the other texts inside a portfolio. In taking up these issues, Neal is guided by two questions: What are the relationships between reflective writing and other artifacts within a portfolio? and What—if any—value remains in guiding students into specific reflective writing activities, either for teaching and learning or for the purposes of writing assessment? In considering these questions, Neal argues that reflection inside a portfolio contains a series of implicit arguments that must be supported by the accompanying artifacts in order to be valid; claims without evidence, he argues, are mere sentiments, while evidence without claims lacks self-awareness. In

"Reflecting Practices: Competing Models of Reflection in the Rhetoric of Prior Learning Assessment," Cathy Leaker and Heather Ostman also consider the relationship of reflection to the making of claims, and to the making of knowledge, in an assessment context. Building on their 2010 *College Composition and Communication* essay examining the role of reflection in the context of prior learning assessment (PLA), Leaker and Ostman provide a taxonomy of reflection operating in the PLA context, which is designed to help students receive college credit for prior learning. The first, *exchange*, is oriented to predefined standards; the second, *reflective-rhetorical transfer*, is keyed to the use of reflection to narrate and theorize experiential learning as a form of academically credited learning; and the third, the most progressive, *responsive reflection*, engages both students and assessors in a coconstruction of both knowledge and assessment. In addition, Leaker and Ostman consider the various kinds of reflective knowledge, especially that created by participants in communities of color, that the most agentive PLA practices—rhetorical reflection and responsive reflection—may be excluding.

The second section of *A Rhetoric of Reflection* addresses the relationships among reflection, language, and difference: Bruce Horner's chapter, "Reflection-Action, Cross-Language Literacy, and Language Dispositions," opens it. Drawing in part from critical pedagogy as well as from scholarship in literacy and language, Horner theorizes how cross-language work can be not only the occasion but also the model for reflection-action in writing as, simultaneously, a language disposition and an ongoing, always emergent process. In this model of reflection, translinguality is inherently reflective. Moreover, Horner argues, such a view of reflection points to possible alignments between the development of such a disposition and models of learning transfer in cross-genre and cross-disciplinary work. Also focusing on language, Asao Inoue and Tyler Richmond study the reflective practices of Hmong students, learning in particular from four young Hmong women about how and why they reflect as they do. In "Theorizing the Reflection Practices of Hmong College Students: Is Reflection a Racialized Discourse?" Inoue and Richmond also compare the differences between Hmong students' reflective practices and those discussed in the literature on reflection, in the process considering the roles that culture, gender, and race can play in reflective practice. Based on their work with these students, Inoue and Richmond advise faculty to attend to the hidden assumptions that may be informing our use of reflection, which, they suggest, tend to ignore the possible racialized nature of the discourse of student reflection assigned and expected in US writing classrooms.

The next section focuses on the relationship between reflection and media. Elizabeth Clark begins the section, noting the shift in pedagogical reflective practices that her teaching has taken, from print to digital multimodality. Clark begins her account, "From Selfies to Self-Representation in Electronically Mediated Reflection," with a meditation on the role of social media in students' lives today, in part to contrast that use of social media with a reflective use, in part to assure faculty that the two are different, that reflection is not merely a selfie exercise. What Clark appreciates about social media is their inclusion of multiple and differentiated contexts, a multiplicity she finds crucial for students' learning, and toward demonstrating what this learning looks like, she shares with us two reflective accounts explaining two very different learning situations. In presenting these, Clark is also arguing that reflection should provide for ambiguity and defer closure. Naomi Silver shares Clark's interest in the relationship of reflection and media; her focus in "Digitally Mediated Reflection: New Affordances, New Challenges" centers on what she calls a "reflective practicum," a space for new possibilities for digitally mediated reflection on writing. More specifically, in the chapter, Silver addresses and illustrates new topics for reflection and new ways to reflect in digital environments. Given that digital spaces open up many new avenues for and modes of reflection on writing—"with more genres than ever before to reflect on, more ways to compose, more tools and modes for reflection (e.g., screencasting or audio commentary), more ways to orchestrate collaborative and public reflection, and more opportunities for students and/as researchers to perform data-driven reflection on writing via versioning, histories, metadata, and the like"—there are, as Silver demonstrates, both opportunities and challenges. At bottom, however, her claim is that digitality, precisely because of its multiple affordances, offers radically new possibilities for reflective practice.

In the fourth section of *A Rhetoric of Reflection*, "Reflective Conversations outside the Writing Classroom," Christina McDonald, Pamela Flash, and Kevin Roozen help us appreciate the social, dialogic nature of reflection. McDonald, in "Toward Defining a Social Reflective Pedagogy for ePortfolios," argues that ePortfolios, used within the framework of a process-centered pedagogy of reflective learning in a general education class, facilitate students' learning about culture by enabling them to construct new meaning from their experiences. Moreover, essential to this learning is a reflective pedagogy engaging students in multiple forms of reflection (e.g., reflection-in-action, constructive reflection, reciprocal reflection), in writing reflective "tags," in posting artifacts, and in responding to each other's ePortfolios throughout the semester. Pamela Flash, also venturing outside of the writing classroom, considers the role of reflective conversations in changing teaching practices inside a writing across the curriculum (WAC) program. In "From Apprised to Revised: Faculty in the Disciplines Change What They Never Knew They Knew," Flash relies on two questions to guide her consideration of reflective practice as a mechanism for change in WAC. First, might static, habitually reinforced conceptualizations of writing and writing instruction become animated and useful were faculty groups to engage in an ongoing series of reflective discussions about both? And second, how sustainable are these reflective practices given their diverse curricular settings? In taking up these questions, Flash draws on an array of data to make her case that faculty reflection motivates new understandings about and definitions of writing and subsequent curricular reform. Kevin Roozen, in "Reflective Interviewing: Methodological Moves for Tracing Tacit Knowledge and Challenging Chronotopic Representations," returns us to the student view as he considers another context for reflection, that of the one-to-one interview with students about their literate histories and activities. As context for his own argument, Roozen outlines different forms of reflective interviewing: discourse-based interviews, process-based and practice-based interviews, and screen capture and video replay. Then Roozen outlines the fourth, reflective interviews, explaining how this methodological approach has contributed a good deal of what we currently understand about what writing, how it works, and how it might best be studied and taught.

Genre, another dimension of reflection, provides the theme of the book's last section, with its two contributions pointing in two directions. Jeff Sommers begins this section with his "Reflecting on Reflection: The Writer's Memo Twenty-Five Years Later," an essay reviewing the changing situatedness of the memo: Sommers moves from the original practice of simply assigning the memo to developing an implicit curriculum locating reflection as both a theory and a practice, including providing a rationale for reflection and the memo; sharing models of it at two points in the term; and encouraging students to see in the memo evidence they might cite in their longer reflective essays. As important, in this discussion Sommers teases out the two-pronged effects of the memo as genre: its effects on students and its effects on teachers evaluating students' writing. Then Doug Hesse, in "Reflecting and Essaying: Genre Features, Authors' Practices, and Implications for Others," considers reflection in the context of the personal essay, a reflection he identifies as "the necessary engine of the personal essay." More specifically, Hesse's chapter explores the role of reflection in the personal essay from two different perspectives: how it serves as a generative and critical force for authors and how it serves as an instructive and aesthetic force for readers. Drawing on multiple materials published in *Fourth Genre*, Hesse reminds us of the value of understanding reflection through the lens of practicing authors and of works designed for engagement and enjoyment as well as for intellectual growth. As important, he reminds us of how these writers also engage reflectively, mapping what they understand through the intersection of self, experience, and the world.

And in the last chapter, in a synthesis of what the earlier chapters have offered, I pursue the rhetoricity of reflection, the idea that reflection is rhetorical, by which I mean that a primary function of reflection is to make a kind of meaning and a kind of knowledge, one animated by attending, one located at the intersection of the personal and the intellectual, a knowledge that cannot be made without working at and inside this combination of contexts. That knowledge can take many forms: as these chapters suggest, reflection has been understood to make many, and many kinds of, contributions to writing and to learning more generally—among them, helping students transfer writing knowledge and practice from one site to another; providing students with a mechanism, in print and other media, for documenting learning; and, when prepared ethically, making available to reviewers a unique source of data for understanding how a student's learning has proceeded and progressed. At the same time, reflection is situated; it thus functions differentially according to context, purpose, and person; among those purposes are faculty development and research, and among its modalities are explicit directions and thoughtful and exploratory conversations. What we also see plotted in this third generation of reflection, however, is a widening epistemology, one encompassing, paradoxically, both clear articulation and a kind of Burkean ambiguity, with both articulation and ambiguity providing resources for a reflection that is rhetorical.

References

Ambrose, Susan A., Michael W. Bridges, Michele DiPietro, Marsha C. Lovett, Marie K. Norman. 2010. *How Learning Works*. San Francisco: Jossey Bass.

Anson, Chris. 1994. "Portfolios for Teachers: Writing Our Way to Reflective Practice." In *New Directions in Portfolio Assessment*, ed. Laurel Black, Donald A. Daiker, Jeffrey Sommers, and Gail Stygall, 185–200. Portsmouth, NH: Heinemann.

Bakhtin, M. M. 1981. *The Dialogic Imagination: Four Essays*. Ed. Michael Holquist. Trans. Caryl Emerson and Michael Holquist. Austin: University of Texas Press.

Beaufort, Anne. 2007. *College Writing and Beyond: A New Framework for University Writing Instruction*. Logan: Utah State University Press.

Belanoff, Pat. 2001. "Silence: Reflection, Literacy, Learning, and Teaching." *College Composition and Communication* 52 (3): 399–428.

Brookfield, Stephen. 1995. *Becoming a Critically Reflective Teacher*. San Francisco: Jossey-Bass.

Bransford, John D., James W. Pellegrino, and M. Suzanne Donovan, eds. 2000. *How People Learn: Brain, Mind, Experience, and School: Expanded Edition*. Washington, DC: National Academies Press.

Butler, D. L. 1998. "The Strategic Content Learning Approach to Promoting Self-Regulated Learning: A Report of Three Studies." *Journal of Educational Psychology* 90: 682–97.

Camp, Roberta. 1992. "Portfolio Reflections in Middle and Secondary School Classrooms." In *Portfolios in the Writing Classroom*, ed. Kathleen Blake Yancey, 61–80. Urbana, IL: NCTE.

Conway, Glenda. 1994. "Portfolio Cover Letters, Students' Self-Presentation, and Teachers' Ethics." In *New Directions in Portfolio Assessment: Reflective Practice, Critical Theory, and Large-Scale Scoring*, ed. Donald A. Daiker and Laurel Black, Donald A Daiker, Jeffrey Sommers, and Gail Stygall, 83–92. Portsmouth, NH: Boynton/Cook.

Dewey, John. 1910. *How We Think*. Boston: Heath.

Dewey, John. 1916. *Democracy and Education*. New York: Macmillan.

Di Stefano, Giada, Francesca Gino, Gary Pisano, and Bradley Staats. 2014. "Learning by Thinking: How Reflection Aids Performance." Harvard Business School Working Paper No. 14–093. http://dx.doi.org/10.2139/ssrn.2414478.

Emmons, Kimberly. 2003. "Rethinking Genres of Reflection: Student Portfolio Cover Letters and the Narrative of Progress." *Composition Studies* 31 (1): 43–62.

"A Fresh Look at Student Engagement." 2013. National Survey of Student Engagement. Bloomington: Indiana University School of Education.

Gawande, Atul. 2002. *Complications: A Surgeon's Notes on an Imperfect Science*. New York: Holt/Picador.

Jung, Julie. 2011. "Reflective Writing's Synecdochic Imperative: Process Descriptions Redescribed." *College English* 73 (6): 628–47.

Leaker, Cathy, and Heather Ostman. 2010. "Composing Knowledge: Writing, Rhetoric, and Reflection in Prior Learning Assessment." *College Composition and Communication* 61 (4): 691–717.

National Survey of Student Engagement (NSSE). 2014. *Bringing the Institution into Focus: Annual Results*. Bloomington, IN: Indiana University Center for Postsecondary Research.

Perl, Sondra. 1980. "Understanding Composing." *College Composition and Communication* 31 (4): 363–70. http://dx.doi.org/10.2307/356586.

Pianko, Sharon. 1979. "Reflection: A Critical Component of the Composing Process." *College Composition and Communication* 30 (3): 275–78. http://dx.doi.org/10.2307/356394.

Pintrich, P. R. 2000. "The Role of Goal Orientation in Self-Regulated Learning." In *Handbook of Self-Regulation*, ed. M. Boekaerts, P. R. Pintrich, and M. Zeidner, 451–502. Burlington, MA: Elsevier Academic Press.

Schon, Donald A. 1987. *Educating the Reflective Practitioner: Toward a New Design for Teaching and Learning in the Professions*. San Francisco: Jossey-Bass.

Scott, Tony. 2005. "Creating the Subject of Portfolios: Reflective Writing and the Conveyance of Institutional Prerogatives." *Written Communication* 22 (1): 3–35. http://dx.doi.org/10.1177/0741088304271831.

Silver, Naomi. 2013. "Reflective Pedagogies and the Metacognitive Turn in College Teaching." In *Using Reflection and Metacognition to Improve Student Learning: Across the Disciplines, Across the Academy*, ed. Matthew Kaplan, Naomi Silver, Danielle LaVaque-Manty, and Deborah Meizlish, 1–18. Sterling, VA: Stylus.

Sommers, Jeffrey. 1988. "Behind the Paper: Using the Student-Teacher Memo." *College Composition and Communication* 39 (1): 77–80. http://dx.doi.org/10.2307/357824.

Sommers, Jeff. 2011. "Reflection Revisited: The Class Collage." *Journal of Basic Writing* 30 (1): 99–129.

Thelin, William H. 1994. "The Connection between Response Styles and Portfolio Assessment: Three Case Studies of Student Revision." In *New Directions in Portfolio Assessment: Reflective Practice, Critical Theory, and Large-Scale Scoring*, ed. Laurel Black, Donald Daiker, Jeffrey Sommers, and Gail Stygall, 113–25. Portsmouth, NH: Boynton/Cook Heinemann.

White, Edward M. 2005. "The Scoring of Writing Portfolios: Phase 2." *College Composition and Communication* 56 (4): 581–600.

Winne, P. H., and A. F Hadwin. 1998. "Studying as Self-Regulated Engagement in Learning." In *Metacognition in Educational Theory and Practice*, ed. D. Hacker, J. Dunlosky, and A. Graesser, 277–304. Mahwah, NJ: Lawrence Erlbaum.

Yancey, Kathleen Blake, ed. 1992. *Portfolios in the Writing Classroom: An Introduction*. Urbana, IL: NCTE.

Yancey, Kathleen Blake. 1998. *Reflection in the Writing Classroom*. Logan: Utah State University Press.

Yancey, Kathleen Blake. 2009. "Reflection and Electronic Portfolios: Inventing the Self and Reinventing the University." In *Electronic Portfolios 2.0*, ed. Darren Cambridge, Barbara Cambridge, and Kathleen Blake Yancey, 5–17.

Yancey, Kathleen Blake, Liane Robertson, and Kara Taczak. 2014. *Writing across Contexts: Transfer, Composition, and Sites of Writing*. Logan: Utah State University Press.

Yancey, Kathleen Blake. Forthcoming. "Tagmemics *and* the Sex Pistols: Current Promising Approaches to Individual and Programmatic Writing Assessment." In *Perspectives on Academic and Professional Writing in an Age of Accountability*, ed. Shirley Logan and Wayne Slater. Carbondale: Southern Illinois University Press.

Zimmerman, B. J. 2000. "Attaining Self-Regulation: A Social Cognitive Perspective." In *Handbook of Self-Regulation*, ed. Boekaerts, M, Pintrich, P R and Zeidner, M. San Diego, CA: Academic Press.

I

Teaching and Assessment

2

REFLECTION
The Metacognitive Move towards Transfer of Learning

Anne Beaufort

Since writing teachers started identifying reflection as part of the composing process (Pianko 1979); since Flower and Hayes identified the "executive control" function (a similar act to reflection) as an essential part of expert writers' composing process (Flower and Hayes 1981); and since writing teachers and administrators started using reflective memos as tools of assessment (Sommers 1989), the reflective move has been an integral part of writing pedagogy (see also Neal, this volume). Writing studies scholars, for example, appropriated from Donald Schon's (1983) management consulting work his observation that reflection is a key to success in professions such as teaching that require a great deal of thinking and acting in ever-changing situations. And from cognitive psychology, the concept of metacognition has entered the writing studies lexicon. The writer's ability to watch their own thinking process, analogous to a painter stepping back from the canvas to see it afresh, enables the learning to deepen. Building on these core concepts, reflective teaching and reflective writing have been explored in writing studies for several decades (Yancey 1998), and now, in this book, reflective acts are examined, redefined, and applied in new ways, deepening the understanding of both similarities and differences between metacognitive and reflective thinking (see Yancey, this volume, introduction). In this chapter, the connection between reflective practices in writing pedagogy and a more recent disciplinary interest, the fostering of transfer of learning, will be explored.

Transfer of learning became a subject of research and discussion in writing studies after several studies showed little integration of learning from first-year writing courses in courses in the disciplines or in workplace settings (Beaufort 1998, 1999, 2007; McCarthy 1987). This issue

DOI: 10.7330/9781607325161.c002

matters. In today's information-rich environment, writing skill is not only marketable but essential for success in most jobs. As David Perkins and Gavriel Salomon say in a recent article, "Schools are supposed to be stopovers in life, not ends in themselves. The information, skills, and understandings they offer are knowledge to go, not just to use on site" (Perkins and Salomon 2012, 248). In other words, transfer of learning should be at the heart of education and thus at the heart of writing studies.

Reflection is one of the necessary conditions for transfer of learning from one context or problem to another. But reflection must be of a certain type to foster transfer, *and* reflection must be married with other curricular and pedagogical strategies for positive transfer of learning.

Here I briefly summarize the role of reflection in writing studies theory and practice and then discuss the recent research on transfer of learning and principles for fostering transfer, which, if enacted in conjunction with reflection, can lead to greater benefits for writers beyond a given writing course. Then I propose some ways of shaping writing curriculum and pedagogy to maximize the possibility that students will be able to take what they learn in academic writing courses into other contexts for writing—in school and beyond.

THE REFLECTIVE TRADITION IN WRITING INSTRUCTION

Reflective practice has become a standard for both teachers and students in writing classes. Kathleen Blake Yancey's (1998) text, *Reflection in the Writing Classroom*, gathered the work from writing-process theorists and Schon into a coherent theory of teaching of writing as grounded in reflective activity—for both students and teachers. She summarized three reflective moves in a writing course:

1. Reflection-in-action, the process of reviewing and projecting and revising, which takes place *within* a composing event;

2. Constructive reflection, the process of developing a cumulative, multi-selved, multi-voiced identity, which takes place *between and among* composing events; and

3. Reflection-in-presentation, the process of articulating the relationships between and among the multiple variables of writing and the writer in a specific context for a specific audience. (Yancey 1998, 200)

In the chapter on teachers' reflective practices, Yancey also included Schon's notion of reflective transfer. She said, "Reflective transfer, the procedure that enables us to learn from and thus enhance our practice requires four steps: that we (1) observe and examine our own practice;

(2) make hypotheses about successes and failures there, as well as the reasons for each; (3) shape the next iteration of similar experience according to what we have learned; when (4) we begin the cycle again" (Yancey 1998, 126–27).

This was a beginning move in writing studies toward considerations of transfer of learning in writing classrooms. And, what will become evident from examining the research in cognitive psychology and in writing studies on transfer of learning is that Yancey's conception of reflective transfer must be complemented with additional strategies on the part of both teachers and students for transfer of learning to occur.

PRINCIPLES FOR TRANSFER OF LEARNING

In the late 1980s, Perkins and Salomon, cognitive psychologists, reviewed more than two decades of research on transfer of learning and concluded, "To the extent that transfer does take place, it is highly specific and must be cued, primed, and guided; it seldom occurs spontaneously" (Mikulecky, Albers, and Peers 1994, 8). They are referring in particular to "high road transfer," those types of situations in which "mindful application of abstract concepts to new situations" is required (Perkins and Salomon 1989a, 25). They then suggested what teachers can do to facilitate transfer: "Learners are shown how problems resemble each other; learners' attention is directed to the underlying goal structures of comparable problems; . . . examples are accompanied with rules, particularly when the latter are formulated by the learners themselves (22). In another article, they refer to "mental grippers" for organizing general domains of knowledge that then can be applied in local circumstances (Perkins and Salomon 1989b, 25).

Research in cognitive psychology on transfer of learning since then has mostly confirmed and refined the earlier work on transfer of learning. In a 2012 issue of *Educational Psychologist* devoted to a review of the research on transfer of learning, Perkins and Salomon say in their overview article: "(1) The individual must '*detect*'" the *possibility of similarities* between prior tasks and the current one, (2) then '*elect*'" to *be motivated to engage in the comparative thinking* necessary for transfer and finally (3) '*connect*,'" i.e., *find a relevant relationship* between initial learning and the transfer situation" (Perkins and Salomon 2012, 252). These three mental processes can be seen as an expansion of reflective practice. Perkins and Salomon are stating, in their three-part bridging schema, that metacognition must be accompanied by a motivation to apply previous knowledge to problem solving in a new situation. And metacognition must not be a reflection only on a task just completed but also on the problem-solving tools used for completing the task, including the deep structures of the task or the broad concepts (mental grippers) that provide ways of mapping new information and new tasks using existing knowledge.

Other articles in the 2012 volume of *Educational Psychologist* point out in specific terms what a teacher's role is in fostering transfer and what the student's responsibility is. Randi Engle et al. point to a shift required in the typical "bounded" curriculum professors deliver. The teacher must create broad, instead of bounded, frames for the course content: "A teacher can frame a lesson as a one-time event of learning something that students are unlikely to ever use again, or as an initial discussion of an issue that students will be actively engaging with throughout their lives" (Engle et al. 2012, 217). This strategy sets the learner up to "detect" possible transfer situations.

Chi and VanLehn (2012), drawing from research in physics courses, propose that teachers assign students the task of finding connections among surface features of two situations in order to more easily get to the deep structures that underlie both situations—what Perkins and Salomon earmark as the third bridging strategy of connecting, via the use of broad concepts or deep structures, the new situation to previously learned skills and knowledge. Also, to lead students to the "connect" phase of transfer, Schwartz, Chase, and Bransford (2012) point out that teachers should be mindful *not to overuse* the typical tell-and-practice (T&P) format for learning, that is, tell students the day's lesson and then give students a task to practice what was just presented. While in itself not counterproductive at least to surface learning, the T&P routine does not invite open-ended inquiry, seeking new information, or examining ambiguity—activities that require use of deep structures or mental grippers to accomplish new tasks successfully (Schwartz, Chase, and Bransford 2012, 213).

In sum, what the current research in cognitive psychology suggests for facilitating transfer of learning are four moves teachers can initiate:

1. Broadly frame the course content as knowledge to go, that is, *make explicit references to broad applications for the course content* in other arenas of life. This strategy can begin to address the necessary motivation on the part of students to learn for transfer.

2. *Give multiple opportunities for practice and discovering of deep structures* similar among aspects of course content that appear on the surface to be different.

3. *Introduce reflection about deep structures, broad concepts, and process strategies* as a tools not only for getting writing done for an immediate rhetorical situation but for transfer of learning to future writing tasks.

4. *Invite application of learning to new tasks,* drawing on mental models, deep-structure knowledge, and an inquiry process for learning.

THE COMPLEXITIES OF TRANSFER THEORY AND RESEARCH

There has been one ongoing controversy in cognitive psychology about the research on transfer and assumptions underlying the research, namely, the issue of whether *any* knowledge or skill is fixed and generalizable enough to be useful in contexts other than the original site of learning. Those who argue for situated cognition (Lave 1988) cast doubt on the whole concept of transfer, disagreeing with the assumption in cognitive psychology that knowledge is "a stable mental entity, which, under the right conditions may be brought forth and applied to new situations" (Day and Goldstone 2012). Jean Lave argues that knowledge is a by-product of *activity in specific situations.* But for the most part, researchers have agreed that transfer from one context to another is possible, but that the move does require the ability of the learner to adapt prior knowledge and skills appropriately to the new context rather than simply apply previous knowledge and skills without alteration for the new situation. Samuel Day and Robert Goldstone finesse the point: "Specific prior knowledge serves as a lens for the construal of new content rather than being the direct focus of cognition itself" (2012, 165). And, in writing studies, several have offered theoretical constructs such as activity system, discourse community, and genre that can be used as mental grippers by students to analyze key differences in new contexts for writing activities (Beaufort 1997; Russell 1995).

Methodologies in transfer research are also debated. Much of the early research into transfer of learning was quantitative and laboratory based, which ignored the significant role context plays in transfer and also limited the number of variables manipulated and measured (Yancey, Robertson, and Taczak 2014). While this method does allow isolation and control of variables, without being able to know the learner's actual thinking process or what the learner might be doing that is different from the expected outcome, experimental researchers may miss transfer activity (Lobato 2012). More recently in cognitive psychology, and also in writing studies, researchers are using think-aloud protocols or interview-based research on transfer and are coding data inductively (Wardle 2007; Yancey, Robertson, and Taczak 2014). As Joanne Lobato (2012) points out, the qualitative researcher captures transfer from the actor's perspective (i.e., the learner) rather than the observer's (i.e., researcher) predetermining what transfer should look like if it occurs. But the black-box problem remains: what the learner's exact cognitive process was or is continues to be less than transparent even using the best of research methods—especially in examining the multilayered, nonlinear cognitive processes involved in complex activities such as writing.

TRANSFER OF LEARNING RESEARCH IN WRITING STUDIES

Transfer of learning first surfaced as a concern in writing studies in Lucille McCarthy's (1987) study *A Stranger in Strange Lands*, which profiled the case of one student, Dave, who did not transfer any knowledge or skills from his freshman composition course to the writing assigned in a biology course or in a literature course he subsequently took. Although McCarthy did not invoke the literature on transfer of learning to analyze Dave's problems, she nonetheless highlighted a significant transfer-of-learning problem for this student. Following upon McCarthy's work, I (Beaufort 1998, 1999, 2000), in an ethnographic study of four writers making the transition from school to work, found little positive transfer from academic writing skills to the multiple writing tasks and genres used in a nonprofit agency. In a subsequent study of a college writer, I (Beaufort 2007) found similar transfer-of-learning issues across "Tim's" four years of college. Tim had a double major in history and engineering, and in neither major was Tim given the mental grippers for writing in those disciplines nor any other cues that would have facilitated positive transfer of learning. Lack of any clear instruction or feedback on discourse-community norms, genre norms, or even appropriate frameworks for content analysis left Tim, in his words, "flapping a lot" in his writing, that is, guessing at what was acceptable writing. There was also negative transfer from his first-year writing courses because of faulty generalizations Tim made from the first-year composition (FYC) curriculum and the teacher's feedback. Other early work in transfer problems included David Russell's (1995) theoretical analysis of freshman writing as an activity system, which brought into focus one source of the transfer problem in writing courses, namely, the lack of a clearly identified subject matter situated in a specific discourse community in which the courses reside. Russell's likening FYC to a course in "general ball handling" made the point clear: in typical FYC classes, students are in a social context with no clear specificity that can enable them to discern deep structures of a discipline and its communicative practices. Russell's analysis is an apt description of part of Tim's experience in FYC. Indeed, some in writing studies debate whether the term *transfer* accurately describes the phenomenon under discussion at all, given the complexities of identifying a writer's behavior as such (Donahue 2012). But the term is still the most widely used to discuss the matter of how writers apply previous knowledge to new situations.

In the past decade the momentum has been building in Canada and the United States for continued research in writing studies on transfer of learning and exploration of the theories in writing studies that map onto transfer-of-learning theory (Artemeva 2005; Artemeva and Fox 2010; Brent 2011; Donahue 2012; Wardle 2007, 2009). The Elon University-sponsored project on cross-institutional transfer-of-learning research, several conferences in writing studies from 2011 to 2013, and a 2012 issue of *Composition Forum* were devoted to transfer. So what has recent transfer research in writing studies revealed?

Several studies have focused on the issue of genre knowledge and how that factors into writers' actions when crossing from high school into first-year composition (Reiff and Bawarshi 2011) or from first-year composition into later academic work (Driscoll and Wells 2012; Frazier 2010; Wardle 2007, 2009). Researchers found that positive transfer was limited and that students, when asked about transfer, reported either critical-thinking strategies (analyze, apply, compare, etc.) or rhetorical strategies broadly construed (argue, defend, support, etc.) (Reiff and Bawarshi 2011). Some students seemed to apply little specific genre knowledge to learning new genres or the norms for genres in new discourse communities; a few, whom Mary Jo Reiff and Anis Bawarshi labeled as "boundary crossers," did evidence using some transfer of learning from previous contexts (high school) to the new context (FYC). In another transfer study (Wardle 2009), students named broad categories of school writing such as "observation report" or "argument essay," which Elizabeth Wardle calls "mutt" genres, as they are not genres used in any particular discourse community, but rather only partially mimic "real" genres in other fields. As Angela Rounsaville (2012), drawing on rhetorical genre theory, points out, if genre knowledge is to be usefully applied in new writing situations, genres must be introduced not just as a set of formal conventions but as responses, or "uptake," to specific discourse-community values and purposes.

Other studies have focused on other types of knowledge or skill that could be transferred from one context for writing to another—process knowledge (Cleary 2013), contextual knowledge or "social capital" (Artemeva 2005; Rounsaville 2012), threshold concepts (Kassner, Majewski, and Koshnick 2012), or prior knowledge in general (Robertson, Taczak, and Yancey 2012). And aside from transfer of knowledge or skills, there is the matter of the individual learner's motivation to transfer knowledge, taken up by Driscoll and Wells (2012), also a critical factor in transfer outcomes.

In sum, the research on transfer from writing courses to other contexts for writing reveals some cases of positive transfer (Artemeva 2005; Cleary 2013; Reiff and Bawarshi 2011; Yancey, Robertson, and Taczak 2014), but more cases of negative transfer (inappropriate application of prior knowledge) or no transfer (Beaufort 1998, 2007; Brent 2012; Frazier 2010; Kassner, Majewski, and Koshnick 2012; Wardle 2007). There could be several possible explanations for repeated findings of negative rather than positive transfer: (1) the research methodology was not able to capture instances of transfer that did occur, (2) the practices that help to foster transfer had not been sufficiently employed, or (3) students were not sufficiently motivated to exercise transfer-of-learning actions.

Concerning the problem of research methodologies, in writing studies, as in cognitive psychology, the nature of the research inquiry is challenging. Self-reports of mental processes that occurred sometime in the past (surveys or interviews) are not sufficient evidence and must be triangulated with other evidence of transfer, such as a comparison of written products, use of writing logs (still a form of self-report but without such a lapse of time from action to reflection), or think-aloud protocols. One researcher (Frazier 2010) found that in focus groups rather than one-to-one interviews, students gained insights about how they had accomplished writing tasks and what prior knowledge they had used as they compared their strategies for accomplishing writing tasks. In Dan Frazier's study, surveys and interviews did not yield the same data that the comparative process of focus groups did.

But more problematic than research methodology for studying transfer of learning in writing studies is the fact that there is little consensus within writing studies about the "threshold concepts," or key framing principles and concepts for writing expertise, that should be taught in writing courses. As Wardle and Downs (2013) state, writing studies as an interdisciplinary field has some work to do in determining, first, what our core knowledge is and, next, what part of that knowledge is relevant for all students in a gen-ed course, and then what additional core knowledge is better saved for upper-level students in writing minors and majors—or even for graduate studies.

What they refer to as "core knowledge" is what in transfer literature is variously referred to as *threshold concepts* or *abstract principles* or *schemata* (mental frameworks) that enable a writer to adapt or "remix" prior knowledge to successfully perform either a new task or a familiar task that must be adapted to a new social context (Robertson, Taczak, and Yancey 2012).

There is also the matter of pedagogy and the time constraints of a quarter system (ten weeks) or even the semester system (fifteen weeks). How can teachers give both in-depth knowledge through repeated practice *and* give opportunities to foster flexibility and transfer by assigning tasks that require application of knowledge and skills to solve new problems? And furthermore, how writing situations are constructed by faculty across our campuses varies widely in terms of terminology used, genre information, and so on, which creates confusion for students. As Linda Flower (1989) noted, "In school writing the social, rhetorical context is often buried and the student is used to dealing with assignments, not problems" (20). So even if students do have some of those mental grippers—that is, the big concepts that can help them to problem solve writing tasks in new contexts—the assignments, the language used to describe the writing tasks, and the expectations can be vague, confusing, and hard for the novice to map from previous learning in writing classes (Beaufort 2004; McCarthy 1987).

WRITING CURRICULA, WRITING PEDAGOGY, TRANSFER, AND REFLECTION

No doubt there will never be universal agreement among writing studies faculty as to what and how to teach this complex subject. But the body of research on transfer of learning is substantial enough now to provide some solid guidelines for building individual writing courses or for designing writing assignments within courses in other disciplines. Following the four guiding principles I've enumerated above that summarize key principles for teaching for transfer, and drawing from my own classroom experiments, I suggest here some curriculum and pedagogy that could further our efforts at teaching writing for transfer and that extend our understanding of the important and multifaceted topics for reflective practice.

1st principle: *Broadly frame the course content as knowledge to go, that is, make explicit references to broad applications for the course content in other arenas of life.*

Seeing the need for transfer of learning is the first step toward making transfer happen. Writing studies faculty have bridled at the labeling of FYC as a *service course* because the term has come to connote a course less academically rigorous, a course that is basic, that is *only* a means to achieve higher goals. This connotation is best set aside. In fact, from the perspective of Perkins and Salomon (2012) *all* college-level courses are knowledge-to-go courses, that is, service courses. It would be prudent for writing faculty to reframe in their minds any old and derogatory associations with the label *service course* and update their knowledge of the dialogue in writing studies as it relates transfer of learning

Giving students job skills and life skills is the task of a college education. Teachers can convey what writing skill can do for (1) self-expression, (2) self-esteem, (3) success in school, and (4) success in the workplace. With creativity and forethought, teachers can find many ways to illustrate for students the efficacy of becoming better writers and the value of writing courses beyond just a grade on a transcript.

But even if teachers convey to students the intrinsic value of the course to their future success, as Driscoll and Wells (2012) point out, students may have little motivation to do the intellectual work associated with transfer of learning. Studies of motivation for learning identify key habits of mind for learning in general that are also essential to doing the intellectual work of high-road transfer. Self-efficacy, locus of control, and intrinsic motivation are the students' responsibility to cultivate (Driscoll and Wells 2012). But teachers who understand these motivational factors can support students' acquiring these frames of mind through the ways assignments are framed, the kinds of reflection they invite students to engage in, and the kinds of feedback they give students. Also essential to motivation is level of challenge (not too low, not too high) and giving students interesting problems/questions to wrestle with. As Charles Bazerman has so astutely put it, "If we want students to learn to write we must locate the kinds of writing they will want to work hard at, the kinds of writing problems they will want to solve" (Bazerman 1997, 26). These are the teacher's challenges in order to even begin setting up conditions for positive transfer of learning.

I begin any academic writing course I teach with three or four essential questions—big issues relevant to the field of study the content of the course is centered on, which have no right answers (Wiggins 1987). These are the intellectual touchstones of the course that I circle around over and over through the reading and writing assignments. They give the course content cohesion and, I hope, awaken students' curiosity and hence motivation to engage. I also challenge students in a ten-minute journaling period at the beginning of each class to connect the core issues we're studying to their personal lives—another attempt at motivating engagement and inviting them to reflect on and apply the "real-world" connection to the classroom experience. In this aspect of transfer, reflection is about seeing the wider picture beyond today's reading or lecture or writing task.

2nd principle: *Introduce reflection/metacognition about deep structures, broad concepts, and process strategies as tools not only for getting writing done for an immediate rhetorical situation, but for transfer of learning to future writing tasks.*

Here, in the context of transfer of learning, reflection becomes not just a cover memo for a writing project or portfolio, but more important, provokes vigilant attentiveness to a series of high-level questions that enable a writer to determine whether there are similarities between prior situations or problems and the current one that would benefit from transfer of prior knowledge. How is this writing task similar to others? Or different? What is the relationship of this writing problem to the larger goals and values of the discourse community in which the text will be received? These and other reflection-in-action types of questions, if part of the writer's process, will increase the ability to learn new writing skills, applying existing knowledge and skills appropriately (i.e., accomplishing positive transfer or learning). What is being added here, for the sake of transfer, is a specific topic for reflection, that is, getting writers to see the frames of analysis useful for decoding the nature of new writing situations.

The reflective memo accompanying a writing assignment that is turned in has become a standard pedagogical tool in writing studies (as Sommers, this volume, describes) and is an excellent means to begin to foster metacognition. But there are many moments in a teaching session that are ripe for the reflective move: at the beginning of a session, asking students to center themselves, become present, open their texts, and jot down their questions, concerns, interests can bring greater attentiveness and focus to the session. After a discussion, again, there is an opportunity for that reflective pause: "Jot down in your journal what you learned from our discussion. Jot down any questions forming in your mind now." And at the end of a teaching session, the same prompt can be repeated.

But reflection on what *was* learned is only the beginning for transfer of learning to occur. According to the principles of transfer of learning, a next step is necessary: the learner must be able to abstract key principles or concepts that may be applicable in other contexts for writing. However, this principle presents a conundrum in writing studies: what are the deep structures, abstract principles, mental grippers, and thresh-old concepts that will help novice writers to gain expertise and the flex-ibility of experts who can adapt to new contexts for writing with skill? The field is not in agreement on what these are.

Typically, there are two frames of reference applied to construction of curriculum for writing courses that influence what abstract concepts are taught (by implication or direct instruction): (1) a literature framework—literature having been the discipline many writing instructors earned degrees in, or (2) a rhetorical framework. The latter is more useful than a literature framework to teach writing, but rhetorical theory is also limit-ing in some ways if writing courses aim to promote transfer of learning.

Rhetoric is certainly a central aspect of most academic writing—even most nonacademic writing. But the principles for invention, for argument, and for assessing the rhetorical context do not encompass the whole of what a writer (and the curriculum designer) must con-sider. Cognitive psychology has added to rhetoric a more nuanced, robust understanding of the writing process (Flower and Hayes 1981). Linguistic anthropology has contributed a more encompassing view of rhetorical context than simply considerations of audience, purpose, kai-ros, and so forth (Heath 1983). The concept of discourse community, for example, derived from sociolinguistics, enables an understanding at deep levels of unstated but highly important social values, goals, and standards associated with written texts (Beaufort 1997; Rafoth 1990, 1988). And increasingly, the importance of subject-matter knowledge as a means of developing critical thinking, text production, and under-standing of discourse-community norms and values, previously given less attention in writing-curriculum design, has led several researchers to put forth rationales for the types of readings, intellectual questions, and themes most helpful in writing courses (Beaufort 2012; Downs and Wardle 2007; Yancey, Robertson, and Taczak 2014).

Of course, rhetorical concepts are still a core knowledge domain a writer must know. Basic principles of argument—types of persuasive appeal (ethos, logos, pathos), argument/counterargument, claims/evidence—should be defined and used over and over with students so these too become useful schemata for making textual choices. And rhe-torical context—the immediate occasion for writing and specific tar-get audience—should be a frame for any writing task. But in addition, there are other key concepts that have emerged from interdisciplin-ary research in writing studies in the past two decades that should also become part of a teacher's core curriculum. Figure 2.1 is one possible schema for representing some of the most important abstract concepts

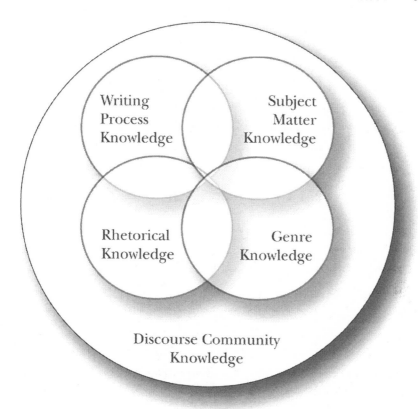

Figure 2.1.

expert writers draw upon to adapt to new contexts for writing and to accomplish writing tasks and is a framework teachers can show students to help them understand the writing task at hand in more global terms.

As Figure 2.1 illustrates, the concept of discourse community is equally important for writers to understand in order to make sense of why standards for writing change in different social contexts. It is the most abstract concept in writing theory, though, and is best introduced after the concepts of genre and rhetorical context are understood and students have been introduced to readings and writing activities that approximate those of real discourse communities the teacher is drawing from for the curriculum. As with the concept of genre, a simple rubric or operationalized definition of discourse community and a number of examples, applying the rubric, can help students begin to form a mental schema for the concept (see Appendix A in *College Writing and Beyond* [Beaufort 2007]). Midway through the course, a discussion of how the class itself is functioning as a temporary discourse community can also make the social context for learning more palpable.

In sum, the second principle for transfer of learning entails guiding learners to structure specific problems and learnings into more abstract principles so they can apply appropriate problem-solving tools to new situations. As Gick and Holyak (1987) say, "Experts shift their basis for categorizing problems from relatively surface attributes of problems to more abstract, structural attributes that cue principles relevant to the solution" (39). So, for example, teachers would not just teach the genre of the literature review but would also talk about its rhetorical purposes in particular discourse communities—that is, take a reflective pause in a discussion of a text being read or in discussing a writing assignment to introduce the big concepts students can use to accomplish the task successfully. The reflective move is one of higher-order thinking specific to the task of transfer.

3rd principle: *Give multiple opportunities for practice and discovering of deep structures similar among various aspects of course content.*

Reflection that includes continual revisiting of key concepts as they are applied to multiple tasks is a form of bridging that fosters transfer (Yancey, Robertson, and Taczak 2014). In addition, research on transfer shows that deep learning is necessary to build transfer skills. This means practice, repetition, reflection, and more practice. But how to find time for repeating tasks or variations of tasks in a single ten-week writing course? This has been a tough challenge for me. I've honed and honed and stripped down course content until I could see a few core genres that could become a genre set that allows repetition of certain analytic and rhetorical skills *and* that students will most likely encounter, in some form or another, in their other academic classes.

In my first-year and sophomore-level academic writing courses, gone is the literacy autobiography or any other personal essay. (Students spend the first ten minutes or so of class journaling to prompts that allow them to make personal connections to whatever academic subject matter we are engaging in the course—part of the reflective move of doing "big-picture" thinking.) Gone are assignments to analyze advertisements, or to write miniethnographies or essays in one or another of the rhetorical modes. In their place I now assign three tasks revolving around a research topic of the student's choice (within the parameters of the course theme) that can be considered a genre set (Devitt 1991): one, a rhetorical analysis of an article on their research topic; two, an annotated bibliography of sources for their research project; and three, a literature review of key themes or issues current in their research area. The rhetorical analysis teaches skills in finding arguments and evaluating evidence and lays a foundation for the same type of analysis and content in the annotated bibliography and literature review. A similar version of this sequence, developed by Nelson Graff (2010) to model for future high-school English teachers, offers another model for an assignment sequence that can promote the deep learning that is a first step toward positive transfer.

4th principle: *Invite application of learning to new tasks, drawing on mental models, deep-structure knowledge, and an inquiry process for learning.*

Another aspect of reinforcing learning for transfer is not only inviting students to practice skills for one assignment but also inviting them to reflect on what they learned in one task and apply it to a different task. Again, I will use my evolving academic-writing course as an example.

I have regularly assigned the reflective memo as a final "paper" in lieu of a final exam (with mixed results—some students figure out the "right" reflective claims regardless of what their actual experience was in the course). But in thinking about the fourth transfer principle, I have realized there are some simple tasks I can ask students to do as part of their end-of-course wrap-up that does not require a lot of time yet entails applying knowledge and skills from the writing projects to other tasks. Here's a sample of those tasks that require application of knowledge and skills learned in one context or form to another situation:

1. To reinforce the rhetorical power of close observation and description in academic writing, which we have been observing in others' writing but not yet incorporating into writing tasks in the course, I assign a simple one-hour activity of taking a walk in a park or wilderness area. The task is to render, with descriptive and narrative techniques they've observed in some of the course readings, one object that caught their attention. They also photograph or sketch their object. One of the essential questions in the course is, do individuals who live in urban/ suburban environments need time in the natural world in order to be "whole," or is it optional? So this mini field trip gives them an opportunity to engage the question again, directly, and respond descriptively rather than with exposition or argument.

2. To reinforce the relevance of academic research to real-world problems, I assign a letter or memo to be written to a specific, known audience of the student's choice for the purpose of persuading the audience to take action on an issue that has surfaced in the student's research project. This assignment reinforces the use of persuasive strategies but in a different genre and rhetorical context outside of school.

3. To stimulate a different mode of thinking and communicating (visual), I assign creating a visual representation of some interesting piece of information they have garnered in their research project. This can be a graph, chart, simple hand-drawn sketch, or short slide show. For example, one student, who had researched the effect of shopping malls on individuals' behaviors, sketched a diagram of a mall but with the core social behaviors malls stimulate rather than names of stores mapped onto different locations.

During the last class session, students present their work to classmates so that oral processing of information also reinforces learning. Besides requiring application of course work to new situations, these activities hopefully convey the real-world relevance of their learning. And they must process and apply their knowledge and writing skills into different rhetorical situations and different genres than the three core assignments they've completed. Students have only the last week of the course to work on these tasks because that is all the time I can give to them. Nonetheless, it is one more step toward fostering transfer of learning and deepening their reflection on what has been learned.

CONCLUSION

Here the focus has been on the place of reflection in efforts to foster transfer of learning. Transfer of learning cannot happen without reflection. But the question of transfer is a question of *what* is reflected upon—not just the task at hand but future tasks, not just *this* text but *this* text as it is part of a larger communicative system of genres, discourse communities, activity systems. Perhaps transfer is reflection of the sort that sees the world in a grain of sand.

References

Artemeva, Natasha. 2005. "A Time to Speak, a Time to Act: A Rhetorical Genre Analysis of a Novice Engineer's Calculated Risk Taking." *Journal of Business and Technical Communication* 19 (4): 389–421. http://dx.doi.org/10.1177/105065190 5278309.

Artemeva, Natasha, and Janna Fox. 2010. "Awareness Versus Production: Probing Students' Antecedent Genre Knowledge." *Journal of Business and Technical Communication* 24 (4): 476–515. http://dx.doi.org/10.1177/1050651910371302.

Bazerman, Charles. 1997. "The Life of Genre, the Life in the Classroom." In *Genre and Writing: Issues, Arguments, Alternatives*, ed. Wendy Bishop and Hans Ostrom, 19–26. Portsmouth, NH: Boynton/Cook.

Beaufort, Anne. 1997. "Operationalizing the Concept of Discourse Community: A Case Study of One Institutional Site of Composing." *Research in the Teaching of English* 31 (4): 486–529.

Beaufort, Anne. 1998. "Transferring Writing Knowledge to the Workplace: Are We on Track?" In *Expanding Literacies: English Teaching and the New Workplace*, ed. Mary Sue Garay and Stephen A. Bernhardt, 179–99. Albany: State University of New York Press.

Beaufort, Anne. 1999. *Writing in the Real World: Making the Transition from School to Work.* New York: Teachers College Press.

Beaufort, Anne. 2000. "Learning the Trade: A Social Apprenticeship Model for Gaining Writing Expertise." *Written Communication* 17 (2): 185–223. http://dx.doi.org/10.1177/0741088300017002002.

Beaufort, Anne. 2004. "Developmental Gains of a History Major: A Case for Theory-Building." *Research in the Teaching of English* (November): 136–85.

Beaufort, Anne. 2007. *College Writing and Beyond: A New Framework for University Writing Instruction.* Logan: Utah State University Press.

Beaufort, Anne. 2012. "College Writing and Beyond: Five Years Later." *Composition Forum* 26 (Fall). http://compositionforum.com/issue/26/college-writing-beyond.php.

Brent, Doug. 2011. "Transfer, Transformation, and Rhetorical Knowledge: Insights from Transfer Theory." *Journal of Business and Technical Communication* 25 (4): 396–420. http://dx.doi.org/10.1177/1050651911410951.

Brent, Doug. 2012. "Crossing Boundaries: Co-op Students Relearning to Write." *College Composition and Communication* 63 (4): 558–92.

Chi, Michelene T.H., and Kurt A. VanLehn. 2012. "Seeing Deep Structure from the Interaction of Surface Features." *Educational Psychologist* 47 (3): 177–88. http://dx.doi.org/10.1080/00461520.2012.695709.

Cleary, Michelle Navarre. 2013. "Flowing and Freestyle: Learning from Adult Students about Process Knowledge Transfer." *College Composition and Communication* 64 (4): 661–87.

Day, Samuel B., and Robert L. Goldstone. 2012. "The Import of Knowledge Export: Connecting Findings and Theories of Transfer of Learning." *Educational Psychologist* 47 (3): 153–76. http://dx.doi.org/10.1080/00461520.2012.696438.

Devitt, Amy J. 1991. "Intertextuality in Tax Accounting: Generic, Referential, and Functional." In *Textual Dynamics of the Professions: Historical and Contemporary Studies of Writing in Professional Communities*, ed. Charles Bazerman and James Paradis, 336–57. Madison: University of Wisconsin Press.

Donahue, Christiane. 2012. "Transfer, Portability, Generalization: (How) Does Composition Expertise Carry?" In *Exploring Composition Studies*, ed. Kelley Ritter and Paul Kei Matsuda, 145–66. Logan: Utah State University Press.

Downs, Doug, and Elizabeth Wardle. 2007. "Teaching about Writing, Righting Misconceptions: (Re)Envisioning 'First Year Composition' as 'Introduction to Writing Studies.'" *College Composition and Communication* 58 (4): 552–84.

Driscoll, Dana Lynn, and Jennifer Wells. 2012. "Beyond Knowledge and Skills: Writing Transfer and the Role of Student Dispositions." *Composition Forum* 26 (Fall). http://compositionforum.com/issue/26/beyond-knowledge-skills.php.

Engle, Randi A., Diane P. Lam, Senia S. Meyer, and Sarah E. Nix. 2012. "How Does Expansive Framing Promote Transfer? Several Proposed Explanations and a Research Agenda for Investigating Them." *Educational Psychologist* 47 (3): 215–31. http://dx.doi.org/10.1080/00461520.2012.695678.

Flower, Linda. 1989. "Rhetorical Problem Solving: Cognition and Professional Writing." In *Writing in the Business Professions*, ed. Myra Kogen, 3–36. Urbana, IL: NCTE and the Association for Business Communication.

Flower, Linda, and John R. Hayes. 1981. "A Cognitive Process Theory of Writing." *College Composition and Communication* 32 (4): 365–87. http://dx.doi.org/10.2307/356600.

Frazier, Dan. 2010. "First Steps Beyond First Year: Coaching Transfer after FYC." *WPA: Writing Program Administration* 33 (3): 34–57.

Gick, Mary L., and Keith J. Holyak. 1987. "The Cognitive Basis of Knowledge Transfer." In *Transfer of Learning: Contemporary Research and Applications*, ed. Stephen M. Cormier and Joseph D. Hagman, 9–46. San Diego, CA: Academic Press.

Graff, Nelson. 2010. "Teaching Rhetorical Analysis to Promote Transfer of Learning." *Journal of Adolescent & Adult Literacy* 53 (5): 376–85. http://dx.doi.org/10.1598/JAAL.53.5.3.

Heath, Shirley Brice. 1983. *Ways with Words*. Cambridge: Cambridge University Press.

Kassner, Linda Adler, John Majewski, and Damian Koshnick. 2012. "The Value of Troublesome Knowledge: Transfer and Threshold Concepts in Writing and History." *Composition Forum* 26 (Fall). http://compositionforum.com/issue/26/troublesome-knowledge-threshold.php.

Lave, Jean. 1988. *Cognition in Practice*. Boston: Cambridge University Press. http://dx.doi.org/10.1017/CBO9780511609268.

Lobato, Joanne. 2012. "The Actor-Oriented Transfer Perspective and Its Contributions to Educational Research and Practice." *Educational Psychologist* 47 (3): 232–47. http://dx.doi.org/10.1080/00461520.2012.693353.

McCarthy, Lucille Parkinson. 1987. "A Stranger in Strange Lands: A College Student Writing across the Curriculum." *Research in the Teaching of English* 21 (3): 233–65.

Mikulecky, Larry, Peggy Albers, and Michele Peers. 1994. "Literacy Transfer: A Review of the Literature." Philadelphia, PA: National Center on Adult Literacy.

Perkins, David, and Gavriel Salomon. 1989a. "Are Cognitive Skills Context Bound?" *Educational Researcher* 18 (1): 16–25.

Perkins, David N., and Gavriel Salomon. 1989b. "Teaching for Transfer." *Educational Leadership* 46 (1): 22–32.

Perkins, David N., and Gavriel Salomon. 2012. "Knowledge to Go: A Motivational and Dispositional View of Transfer." *Educational Psychologist* 47 (3): 248–58. http://dx.doi.org/10.1080/00461520.2012.693354.

Pianko, Sharon. 1979. "A Description of the Composing Processes of College Freshman Writers." *Research in the Teaching of English* 13 (1): 5–22.

Rafoth, Bennett A. 1988. "Discourse Community: Where Writers, Readers, and Texts Come Together." In *The Social Construction of Written Communication*, ed. Bennett A. Rafoth and Donald L. Rubin, 131–46. Norwood, NJ: Ablex.

Rafoth, Bennett A. 1990. "The Concept of Discourse Community: Descriptive and Explanatory Adequacy." In *A Sense of Audience in Written Communication*, ed. Gesa Kirsch and Duane H. Roen, 140–52. Newbury Park, CA: SAGE.

Reiff, Mary Jo, and Anis Bawarshi. 2011. "Tracing Discursive Resources: How Students Use Prior Genre Knowledge to Negotiate New Writing Contexts in First-Year Composition." *Written Communication* 28 (3): 312–37. http://dx.doi.org/10.1177/0741088311410183.

Robertson, Liane, Kara Taczak, and Kathleen Blake Yancey. 2012. "Notes toward a Theory of Prior Knowledge and Its Role in College Composers' Transfer of Knowledge and Practice." *Composition Forum* 26 (Fall). http://compositionforum.com/issue/26/prior-knowledge-transfer.php.

Rounsaville, Angela. 2012. "Selecting Genres for Transfer: The Role of Uptake in Students' Antecedent Genre Knowledge." *Composition Forum* 26 (Fall). http://compositionforum.com/issue/26/selecting-genres-uptake.php.

Russell, David. 1995. "Activity Theory and Its Implications for Writing Instruction." In *Reconceiving Writing, Rethinking Writing Instruction*, ed. Joseph Pegralia, 51–77. Mahwah, NJ: Erlbaum.

Schon, Donald A. 1983. *The Reflective Practitioner: How Professionals Think in Action*. New York: Basic Books.

Schwartz, Daniel L., Catherine C. Chase, and John D. Bransford. 2012. "Resisting Overzealous Transfer: Coordinating Previously Successful Routines with Needs for

New Learning." *Educational Psychologist* 47 (3): 204–14. http://dx.doi.org/10.1080/00 461520.2012.696317.

Sommers, Jeffrey. 1989. "The Writer's Memo: Collaboration, Response and Development." In *Writing and Response: Theory, Practice and Research,* ed. Chris M. Anson, 174–86. Urbana, IL: NCTE.

Wardle, Elizabeth. 2007. "Understanding 'Transfer' from FYC: Preliminary Results of a Longitudinal Study." *WPA: Writing Program Administration* 31 (1–2): 67–85.

Wardle, Elizabeth. 2009. "'Mutt Genres' and the Goal of FYC." *College Composition and Communication* 60 (4)): 765–89.

Wardle, Elizabeth, and Doug Downs. 2013. "Reflecting Back and Looking Forward: Revisiting 'Teaching about Writing, Righting Misconceptions' Five Years On." *Composition Forum* 27 (Spring). http://compositionforum.com/issue/27/reflecting-back .php.

Wiggins, Grant. 1987. "Creating a Thought-provoking Curriculum." *American Educator* 11 (4): 10–17.

Yancey, Kathleen Blake. 1998. *Reflection in the Writing Classroom.* Logan: Utah State University Press.

Yancey, Kathleen Blake, Liane Robertson, and Kara Taczak. 2014. *Writing Across Contexts: Transfer, Composition, and Sites of Writing.* Logan: Utah State University Press.

3
REITERATIVE REFLECTION IN THE TWENTY-FIRST-CENTURY WRITING CLASSROOM
An Integrated Approach to Teaching for Transfer

Kara Taczak and Liane Robertson

When I reflect back, I realize I have everything I need to understand writing better in my other classes. I know that I need to think through certain things, like the audience I'm writing for and the situation for it. I know if I think through all those things first, I can start more easily and my writing will be successful because I'm not just writing blind, I have a purpose and I can sort of see how my assignment should be at the end.

—Terry, interview

As research on writing transfer progresses and as Anne Beaufort suggests, we are increasingly aware of the integral role reflection plays in supporting students' successful transfer across writing sites, such as from one assignment to the next inside a writing course and from one course to another. Scholars such as Jeff Sommers, Dana Driscoll, Anne Beaufort, and Kathleen Blake Yancey, among others, have addressed the importance of developing reflection within the composition classroom (see, e.g., Sommers 2011). Likewise, writing studies scholars interested in transfer (Brent 2012; Dew 2003; Downs and Wardle 2007; Nowacek 2011; Yancey, Robertson, and Taczak 2014) have raised new questions about how composition should be taught and what should be taught as the content of composition. These and other researchers have identified a critical need to define the kinds of reflection we might incorporate into the teaching of writing so students can successfully transfer writing knowledge and practices across writing contexts.

In recent years, many composition instructors have drawn upon Yancey's (1998) theory of reflection, which identifies three nested types of reflective practice—reflection-in-action, constructive reflection, and

DOI: 10.7330/9781607325161.c003

reflection-in-presentation[1]—that can be included as a curricular element in writing courses. Yancey argues that reflection, when woven into a curriculum, becomes a "discipline, a habit of mind/spirit/feeling that informs what we do, always tacitly, sometimes explicitly, and that making such understanding explicit is a good" and that when students use reflection, they "learn to know their work, to like it, to critique it, to revise it, to start anew" while they also "invent [writing] identities" (Yancey 1998, 201–2). Moreover, reflection's value to students' writing processes becomes increasingly important when the need to process and apply knowledge is pivotal to a writer's development.

Yancey's definition of reflection in its attention to self-monitoring resembles the advice offered by David Perkins and Gavriel Salomon and by the researchers in *How People Learn*—we must help students become more aware of themselves as learners, which has been shown to increase the potential for transfer (Bransford, Pellegrino, and Donovan 2000b, 67; Perkins and Salomon 1992). *How People Learn* outlines three components of teaching to promote metacognition, which are similar to Yancey's three nested types of reflection: "instruction and practice with strategies that enable students to monitor their understanding; provision, initially by a teacher, of an expert model of metacognitive processes; and a social setting that enables joint negotiation for understanding" (67). These components help lead students to develop "sophisticated writing strategies . . . [by] identify[ing] goals, generat[ing] new ideas, improv[ing] and elaborat[ing] existing ideas, and striv[ing] for idea cohesion" (67).

The type of reflection theorized by Yancey (1998) and the researchers of *How People Learn* (Bransford, Pellegrino, and Donovan 2000a, 2000b) thus includes a focus on monitoring each writing context and supporting students' development of agency as they begin developing expertise by providing them with a robust understanding of their identity as writers.[2] In addition, promotion of reflective activities within the composition classroom creates an opportunity for students to theorize about their writing and identify themselves as writers who create knowledge. Reflection encourages students to put what they are learning into practice while also serving as a way to set goals and move forward in their writing ability.

However, we argue that a very specific type of rhetorical reflection helps develop the capacity for transfer: a practice that serves as process and product; theory and practice; and before-the-fact activity, during-the-fact activity, and after-the-fact activity. This type of reflection includes reflecting both inwardly—through the act of *thinking* about writing practice—and outwardly—through the act of *writing* about those writing practices. Thinking about writing gets at the *why* of a writer's rhetorical choices, which allows for deeper reflection on the act of writing than reflecting only on the *what* of a writer's actions. Likewise, when reflection is practiced as only an after-the-fact activity or as merely looking backward on what has been written, the writer focuses primarily on *what has been written*. As Lennie Irvin (2004) has suggested, more robust reflection begins with the invention or planning stages of writing and continues during the writing itself, in addition to involving a looking back after the writing is completed, or at each completed draft. It is this kind of recursive reflection, taught in intentional and systematic ways and designed so students become active reflective writing practitioners continually developing their own learning about effective rhetorical practices, that we discuss here. In this chapter, we outline a specific type of reflective framework, aimed at the deeper reflection described above that we want students to achieve, designed as part of the content for a course that explicitly encourages transfer as its goal (referred to as the Teaching for Transfer or TFT course). We first define the reflective framework developed for the TFT course and then demonstrate its integration into new contexts. Evidencing our findings with studies conducted at our respective universities, we argue that a reflective framework is most effective when integrated into a very specific kind of first-year writing course, one featuring writing as content with the intended goal of transfer.

THE INTERCONNECTIVITY OF REFLECTION AND TRANSFER: A REITERATIVE REFLECTIVE FRAMEWORK

> The transfer of knowledge is a powerful thing. It shapes our daily lives . . . [and] continue[s] to influence our development.
>
> —Maggie, "Theory of Writing"

The Teaching for Transfer curriculum was codesigned and developed for two individual research projects at a large Research I university in the Southeast.[3] Following the research findings of Perkins and Salomon (1992) that suggest we be explicit in teaching for transfer, our TFT course was developed with a primary objective: to teach students to develop as writers so they might be able to transfer knowledge and practices to other academic writing situations. From existing research in transfer (most notably the Writing about Writing approach and Anne Beaufort's conceptual writing model), we theorized that the content of such a course must focus on and be informed by writing. We translated that theory to the TFT curriculum in three representative elements, which make up the content of the course: (1) key rhetorical terms, (2) reflection, and (3) students' articulation of a theory of writing. All three of these representative elements comprise the integrated approach to the course content; none of the three alone can achieve transfer the way all three are able to accomplish it as an interconnected trio.

The key rhetorical terms are concepts about writing introduced and reiterated throughout the course, within and across multiple assignments. There are eight key terms[4] that emerged from our research as the most important for students to understand in writing across contexts: *rhetorical situation* (within which the concept of exigence is also discussed), *genre, audience, reflection, purpose, knowledge, discourse community,* and *context.* One of these key terms—*reflection*—is foundational both as a concept and a practice and is included in the course at different, deliberate points in three ways: (1) in readings about reflection, (2) in reflective assignments, and (3) through reflective activities. In these three ways, studying reflection as a key rhetorical concept while also practicing reflection, students create a reflective framework from which they develop their theory of writing—in the best-case scenario, integrating conceptions about writing they bring with them that are revised and developed further throughout the TFT course, enabling them to repurpose what they have learned in FYC for use in the various writing situations they will encounter in the future. Our use of *theory* here aligns with the definition by Downs and Robertson (2015) as "a systematic narrative of lived experience and observed phenomena that both accounts for (makes sense of) past experience and makes predictions about future experience" (110–11), which captures the way students in the TFT course understand their agency in developing their own theory of writing.

Reflection is a central and reiterative practice of the TFT course as well as a key rhetorical concept, and as such it creates the framework for transfer to occur. The ways that reflection is used throughout the course are defined through the use of the three reflective components:

- Reflective theory: students learn *about* reflection, in part, through readings in reflective theory.
- Reflective assignments: students are asked to put into practice their understanding of key terms taught in the course, and these reflective assignments are designed as integral parts of the major assignments.
- Reflective activities: students are asked to look backward, look inward, look forward, and look outward as they engage in reflection to develop their writing knowledge.

Reflection is designed as a 360-degree, reiterative approach to give students a series of opportunities to make decisions and create some understanding of their writing as a means of engaging in reflective practice in a four-part schema: (1) *look backward* to recall previous knowledge, which could include prior writing experiences, different reading assignments, and past knowledge about writing; (2) *look inward* to review the current writing situation they are working in; (3) *look forward* to project how their current knowledge about writing connects to other possible academic writing situations; and (4) *look outward* to theorize how the role of their current identities as reflective writing practitioners connects to larger academic writing situations.[5] The three reflective components are woven into the TFT course with these four ways of practicing reflection, helping students synthesize what they have learned about writing in the course. This approach allows them to theorize about their own writing overall, and it allows them to evolve not just as writers but also as thinkers *about* writing.

Reflection is a significant part of the content of the TFT course because it is so integral to the conceptual understanding about writing students are developing. Students do more than merely practice reflection about the writing they do; they engage in reflection during and outside of each class in the three contexts described above: in reflective assignments, in reflective activities, and through reflective theory. For example, reflection is frequently discussed as both a concept and a practice, it is practiced in the classroom as students engage in various reflective activities, and often it is implemented as homework to reinforce a key concept the class is learning. Reflection is the conceptual webbing students use to connect content; it is discussed and practiced in multiple ways during every class meeting. As we detail below, the reflective framework must be this deliberate and this systematic because this type of reflection is what fosters transfer. In other words, reflection matters, but its specific type and its primary role matter even more.

The content of the TFT course differs from other curricular models aimed at transfer because it centers on these interlocking pedagogical principles—key terms, reflection, and a theory of writing—specifically within the reflective frame. The theory of writing, because it is practiced reiteratively throughout the course and thus underscores the connection between opportunities for reflection, enables deliberate discussion of transfer as the primary learning goal for the course. This explicitly conveyed goal of transfer gives students the opportunity to understand that the knowledge they are gaining in the course can and should be adapted for other writing sites, but also allows them to create a conceptual model they can use *in* those other sites. Because they are using reflection to *look forward* to other writing situations, they are able to conceptualize what they might bring to the potential writing contexts that lie ahead. At the same time, the conceptual framework allows them to bring their prior knowledge to bear (as they use reflection to *look backward*) and to understand rhetorical choices from a previous context as potentially useful, or not, for a current one. Once students understand transfer as the goal and realize they can use reflection to determine conceptually what they might want to transfer, they begin to anticipate opportunities for transfer and start to expect to transfer from one situation to the next. In other words, they are motivated to transfer by a greater understanding of transfer.

THE REITERATIVE REFLECTIVE FRAMEWORK: SUCCESSES AND CHALLENGES

Since the original studies reported on in *Writing across Contexts* (Yancey, Robertson, and Taczak 2014) were completed, we've conducted additional research at two new institutions and revised the TFT course for their different student populations. The new institutions featured different writing-program goals, curricula, student demographics, and challenges, all of which have allowed us to adapt or "transfer" the TFT course design to new contexts. In addition, we have focused on particular elements of the TFT course to see whether some of its reflective framework can work as a stand-alone component within a themed-based course, arguably one of the most common content types in first-year composition courses taught across the country. What follows is the account of two case studies and their findings: one in which the reflective framework was used in a Teaching for Transfer course and compared to a first-year composition course with alternate content, and one in which the reflective framework was used in a course themed around the rhetoric of oil and water. The results of these studies indicate two important findings about reflection in teaching for transfer: (1) reflection practiced reiteratively, conceptually, and in developing a theory of writing can foster transfer, and (2) reflection helps students develop a framework for transferring their knowledge and practices about writing to new situations.

TEACHING FOR TRANSFER: CONTENT AND
THE REFLECTIVE FRAMEWORK

> I used to think good writing was just interesting to the reader and correct
> in grammar. Now I think good writing always achieves a specific goal and
> gives its audience something they need.

> —Christina, interview

In our previous research, results suggested that the effect of FYC content on transfer was significant; transfer to new contexts was more successful for those who had experienced content about writing in their FYC classroom—not only the *doing* of writing but the *study* of writing—such as the Teaching for Transfer (TFT) course provides.[6] In this research, students who had experienced non-writing-focused content in the FYC classroom experienced more difficulty in transferring knowledge and practice from that classroom to the new contexts in which they were writing just one semester afterward. Reported here are the results so far of a subsequent study, which compares the FYC content used across different sections of FYC and investigates the use of the reflective framework in those classes.

The context for this study is a racially and ethnically diverse public comprehensive four-year university in the northeast, with an undergraduate student population of approximately ten thousand, a large proportion of whom are first-generation college students and of whom roughly 50 percent graduate, often doing so within six years. Most students at this institution report spending more than twenty hours per week in the workforce, and many work a full forty hours per week because of financial need. Of utmost concern to these students is that their courses be applicable to their career choices or have future value outside of an academic context. The first-year composition program at this institution features one required course, focusing on analytical or expressive writing (for which content varies widely), and an additional course focusing on literature as the content about which writing is assigned. All students must complete the first course in the sequence with a grade of C or higher in order to pass. Writing courses are taught primarily by full-time non-tenure-track or part-time adjunct faculty.

This study, which took place from the fall semester of 2012 through the summer of 2013, included participants from two sections of the second term of FYC, one a TFT course design and one course section featuring literature as content. A total of nine participants completed the study, five from the TFT course and four from the literature-based course. The TFT course featured a reiterative reflective framework (including the three reflective components outlined above), featured sequenced major assignments, and culminated in a final theory-of-writing reflection essay in which students were required to write about the reflective knowledge and practices they had been developing all semester. The writing-about-literature course incorporated extensive reflection on assignments and writing strategies throughout the course and included an end-of-semester reflection essay.

There were several similarities between the previous content-comparison study (2009–2010) and this study, one of which was the use of reflection in FYC sections as a writing strategy. All sections in both studies used reflection as an invention technique to brainstorm ideas for assignments or ideas for revising assignments, and participants indicated both an awareness of how to use reflection as a tool for both brainstorming and revision and an appreciation of the value of reflection in revising writing to create a more polished draft. However, students in the TFT courses using a reflective framework also came to understand reflection as a concept and a practice, as a mechanism for developing knowledge rather than simply a tool for developing a process. While the literature-based composition students found reflection useful for brainstorming about *what* to write or understanding *what* they had written that might be revised, the TFT students learned to practice reflection as a means of understanding not only what to write or what to revise, but also *why* a revision was a rhetorical choice they were making and *how* they might approach a writing situation appropriately. For example, when prompted to discuss how he might approach a future writing assignment, Matt[7] reported, in his final reflection assignment, that "reflecting on my writing this semester has taught me that I can kind of reflect the other way to think about what to write before I actually start, so that way I can just start out stronger with more of a plan." Matt articulated that he understood he could *look forward* (one of the four ways of practicing reflection he learned in the course) to the writing tasks he will encounter in new contexts. He went beyond that articulation, however, when he later described how he approached writing for his psychology course:

> We had to write on one of the categories from class and we could choose whichever one we wanted. I really like abnormal psych so I chose that. We had to find other sources too, so I had to do some research. So I went to the [online] databases from the library like we did in [FYC] class and started researching stuff. Then it all came back to me, you know, how we figured out what we wanted to focus on for our research paper by writing about the ideas we found when we researched the topic. So I did that . . . I

wrote myself a note about what I wanted to find out and came up with a question and turned it into a thesis eventually.

In this interview, Matt discussed reflection as an invention technique, one in which he used writing to himself to think through his approach to the research topic. He recalled (in *looking backward* at his learning about reflection) the reflection process learned in the TFT course, and he used that process as invention, to determine his topic (what to write about), but also his approach (how to write it within the rhetorical situation), to the writing assignment in the new context of his psychology course. However, he went beyond using reflection as a process, as he articulated during the same interview:

> And then I thought about my topic, which was Borderline Personality Disorder, and who would care about it, and . . . I kind of felt like I knew how to write this even before I started, like I had an idea of how to make it happen. Anyway, the professor didn't really give us an audience so I thought about, obviously, him, but also any students who might have the disorder or their family members do or whoever. . . . So I had my audience and my purpose and then the genre was just essay. . . . And also the context, which was the other part I always think about for writing—this was just the class and the professor, but I also thought about all these people who take psych meds and how doctors just prescribe them and we don't know if people really need them all, and it's just the drug companies, you know, selling their pills, so I thought about that too, for context.

Matt demonstrated his use of the reflective framework he learned in the TFT course as a conceptual model for approaching the writing situation for his psychology assignment. Specifically, he mentioned four of the key terms from the TFT course—*audience, genre, context,* and *purpose*—as he reflected on this writing assignment, using them as cornerstones to his conceptual framework as he reflected about his writing. As he reported, in his writing approach for the psychology course, he *looked back* at his previous knowledge about writing, *looked inward* to review his current writing situation, *looked forward* to determine how to use his knowledge in the new writing situation, and *looked outward* (albeit prompted somewhat by his participation in the study) to consider himself as a writer in a situation in which writing itself was not specifically coached or directed, as it was in the writing classroom. Through reflection, Matt was able to approach the writing situation, understand his role as the writer in the specific context of the assignment, develop a conceptual map for completing the writing task, and consider the implications for his writing on an audience other than the professor assigning it. His after-the-fact reflection during this study revealed that he used his conceptual framework about writing developed in the TFT course and the four-part schema or ways of reflecting to understand the rhetorical choices he was faced with in the writing situation of the psychology course.

Jennifer also articulated her use of the reflective framework she learned in the TFT course when she was interviewed at the end of the second semester of the study.

> I always do the same thing now for all my writing, like we learned in [FYC] class about reflection and how it helps you know what to do. I just pretend I have to tell [the FYC professor] what I'm thinking of doing and hit all the important points, like audience and everything. I write it sometimes, actually just write what I'm planning to do like it's a discussion post [prompted in-class reflection assignment] and that way I can tell myself what I should do, like, how to write it.

Jennifer's simplified description indicated an internalized approach to writing based on a reflective framework. She was able not only to consider reflection as a concept she was now using beyond her FYC class, but also to comprehend it as a practice she engaged in to help herself understand what a given writing situation needed.

Other study participants who had not taken the TFT course did not demonstrate the use of reflection as did Matt and Jennifer—as a reflective framework. Their experience with reflection in the literature-based course evolved as an after-the-fact writing exercise for each assignment and focused on the writing process primarily. Taylor, a participant from this section, recalled the reflection she did in the course.

> We did reflection a lot in that class. We had to write a two-page reflection to go with every one of the essays, and then we had a big reflection essay at the end where we had to write about the whole course and the writing we did. . . . It was mostly about what we did in each draft, and how we progressed through the drafts to get to the end, and if the peer editing was helpful, and things like that. Except for the final reflection, that was more about the writing style you had worked out over the semester and what you could remember thinking about for every assignment.

Taylor's recollection focuses on the process of writing, its role in multiple drafting within assignments and as a culminating piece to the semester. When asked about reflection as a tool for thinking about current writing, Taylor reported, "It's not something I really think about, I mean, I just do the assignment, whatever is asked, and I make sure I get all the details so I know what is expected and I do okay." Taylor's use of reflection did extend to her current writing in one way. "Oh, yeah, I do use reflection if I'm doing revision on something, when I have time. I will go over the assignment and think about what I should change and what might sound better. So then I'm reflecting on it, yeah." She reported that she did not use reflection before beginning to write and not as a means of *looking backward.* "I don't really use writing from that course because those stories and [literary] terms are not useful in other classes. I mean, I guess I learned that I can do better if I revise and make sure to look over my essay, so I use that, yeah."

Taylor articulated on each occasion, as did the other study participants from her class, that there was value taken away from the FYC course in terms of understanding writing as a process—a kind of transfer that FYC in many programs has supported well (see chapter 1 in *Writing across Contexts* [Yancey, Robertson, and Taczak 2014] for a summary of this research)—which coincides with the reflection practiced in the literature-based course: it consisted of process memos students equated primarily with revision. The reflection prompts for this course asked students to focus on the writing situation they were in currently, even as they were reflecting on a finished product. However, the final reflection assignment in this course asked students to go beyond the current writing situation to reflect back on the writing they had done over the entire semester, and participants expanded their reflection to include multiple assignments in these final essays. The reflection assignment, however, only asked students to look backward: it did not ask them to *look forward* or to think about how they might use reflection in other writing situations. Students in this course practiced reflection only to *look inward* at the current writing situation, to understand only what they had done (not what they thought while doing it) within the multiple drafts, peer review, and revision processes of the assignment, and to write about it.

In their interviews, participants from the literature-based course indicated that they viewed writing as a practice rather than as both a practice and a subject of study (Adler-Kassner and Wardle 2015), and the literature they experienced as the content of their FYC course was what they perceived as the most important part of the course to take away. The reflection they practiced in the course, though, focused on their own writing rather than on the perceived course content. Perhaps not surprisingly, participants from this course in each interview often seemed to prefer offering interpretations about the literature they had studied in the course in some way, either to discuss a favorite piece of reading or to demonstrate knowledge of a literary term, even in responding to questions about writing. Later in the study, after the FYC course had been completed for some time, participants (none of whom were enrolled in an English course at the time) recalled less about the literature studied and had to be prompted to recall assignments, perhaps because the reflection in the course had been truncated to focus only on current process.

Study participants from the TFT course needed fewer prompts to recall the content of their FYC course later in the study and remembered the reflection from the course as content *and* practice, with some, like Matt and Jennifer, needing no prompting to articulate their use of reflection as a writing tool. Participants from this course saw value in reflection as a means of connecting writing situations and of assessing a situation and analyzing the writing required in order to approach it successfully; in other words, reflection was the vehicle by which they repurposed knowledge from their past writing situations to be used in a new situation. These participants understood reflection in terms of Yancey's (1998) "reflection-in-presentation" as an articulation of the relationships between writing contexts. They were also able to transfer their knowledge about writing between contexts because they had learned to develop a conceptual framework of writing knowledge (Beaufort 2007), comprised of key rhetorical terms and powered by reflection as both theory and practice. The reflective framework was evident in Juan's interview response:

> Yes, I use reflection in this course [history]. I always have to think through my assignment before I start and then while I'm writing it to make sure I don't get off track. I can get really repetitive if I don't organize and then I reflect as I go to make sure I'm thinking about the audience and purpose as I'm writing, and whatever else I learned from the last assignment so I do better on the one I'm writing now. Actually, I never really paid attention to comments on my work before [FYC] class, but now I look for what the professor wrote or I read my paper over after it has a grade to see what I can learn from that, and how I can be a better writer from that.

Juan articulated his use of reflection as a way of making sense of previous writing he had completed and using that understanding to think about new writing situations (looking backward, forward, outward, and inward) and demonstrated his understanding of reflection as more than a practice when he suggested its role in his evolution as a writer. Juan's use of the reflective framework provided him with the mechanism to transfer writing knowledge between situations.

It's also worth noting that in this study, some participants did not understand the reflective framework or were not open to learning the new way of thinking about writing required by the reflective framework (see also Driscoll and Wells 2012; Robertson, Taczak, and Yancey 2012), and some participants did not transfer between contexts effectively, regardless of institutional context or of FYC content experienced. However, what the study supports is that students have the potential to transfer writing knowledge when they experience FYC content designed for transfer, including a reflective framework that focuses on what they are writing, on why they are making choices in their writing, and on how they are using reflection to understand what they think about writing when they do so in various contexts.

THE REFLECTIVE FRAMEWORK FEATURED
INSIDE A THEMED COURSE

> As a writer, I would say my identity can be described as reflection-based, creative, witty, and always including tid-bits of my own opinion and voice.
>
> —Abby, exit survey

The second study focusing on the reflective framework took up the question of how this framework might support transfer when operating inside a theme-based FYC course—but without the course's two other curricular components: key terms and students' theory of writing. More specifically, the goal of the study was twofold: (1) to see whether or not reflection could foster the transfer of knowledge and practices about writing on its own, independent of the other two curricular parts of the TFT course and (2) to see what type of language students used to understand writing if key terms were not part of the course. The research was conducted at a private liberal arts institution with a stand-alone writing program, which includes a two-sequence first-year composition requirement students are not allowed to test out of (typically, students can use AP, IB, or dual-enrollment to opt out of the first course in the sequence, but not the second). The first course centers on argumentation and different rhetorical situations while the second is focused on types of research associated with different research paradigms. The writing program states that these courses will

> teach strategies for writing to well-educated readers in diverse academic and nonacademic situations. Students learn rhetorical principles, the analysis and use of readings and source materials, and techniques for generating, revising, and editing texts for specific situations. They also learn to present and justify positions and to produce researched writing in various scholarly traditions, including textual/interpretive (the analysis of texts or artifacts such as images or events), qualitative (the analysis of observations or interviews) or quantitative (the analysis of data from surveys or other empirical studies). (University of Denver Writing Program 2014)

So long as the program goals are met, the instructors are encouraged to teach each course in ways that speak to teaching strengths; several faculty members choose a theme-based design. The instructors engage in pedagogical and professional development through a variety of meetings and workshops throughout the year and participate in year-long teaching partnerships as ways to enhance and improve their classroom strategies and techniques. In short, the writing program, which thrives on learning more about the teaching of writing, provides a likely site of inquiry to investigate whether the reflective framework operating inside another curriculum can support the successful transfer of knowledge and practices from first-year composition to other writing contexts.

To study the reflective framework inside a themed-based course, one instructor from the writing program, Adilyn, agreed to teach the first composition course in the two-year sequence using the reflective framework alongside her theme, the rhetoric of oil and water. Aligning itself with program goals, Adilyn's course "emphasize[d] rhetorical situation and the rhetorical appeals and [the idea that] the way that we learn about rhetorical situation and rhetorical appeals is through perspectives around oil and water in contemporary society" and included as assignments a rhetorical analysis of perspectives about oil and water and a project outlining the need for critical change on campus in sustainable practices. For her three sections of this course, Adilyn also incorporated the reflective framework throughout, assigning students readings in reflective theory (e.g., students read chapter 1 from Yancey's book *Reflection in the Writing Classroom*), having them participate in reflective activities (e.g., students discussed *reflection* as a term important for their writing processes), and asking them to write reflective assignments (e.g., students attempted to respond to the four-part schema of looking forward, backward, inward, and outward).

Out of her three classes of fifteen, nine participants agreed to the study. They were interviewed three times over thirty weeks: at the beginning of the quarter in which they enrolled in the first-year composition course; at the beginning of the following quarter in which all were in enrolled in the second sequence course; and the end of that second quarter. Participants also completed an exit survey ten weeks after their final interview, and Adilyn was interviewed both before the classes began, to discuss how she would incorporate the reflective framework into her already designed course, and after the classes were completed.

Before using the reflective framework, Adilyn believed she used reflection "a lot":

> I always have them reflect on their papers before they turn them in . . . so I know what they are thinking about their paper so I can see how far off our interpretation of their work is. So I have them fill out a rubric—a self-assessment—so if they give themselves all 'excellents,' and I see some

disconnect, then I know to shape my comments accordingly. And then the portfolio, which is something I've always done since grad school.

This response suggests two things: (1) Adilyn views reflection, self-assessment, and rubric as the same thing and (2) she has a fairly typical understanding of how and where to use reflection inside a first-year composition course. Adilyn believed reflection was already integrated into her classroom, but as the term progressed, her approach became more explicit, as she observed in the postcourse interview: "I've never been as explicit [about reflection] as I was this quarter." Adilyn was also very surprised at the students' reactions to reading reflective theory, as she believed they would resist it.

> I wasn't sure how they were going to react to Yancey's paper because they aren't necessarily the audience for it, and they aren't compositionists, so I wasn't sure how they would do with it—there's a lot of comp theory packed into not a lot of pages. But in general, I think they liked it and they found it enjoyable and understand it. . . . I was kind of anticipating more pushback, but no, they found it very useful. I felt there would be resistance from the reading mostly because I was thinking about how I would react if I was a freshman, I wouldn't have known what they were talking about, and it came so early in the quarter and I wasn't sure how they would respond to it. But I felt like based on class discussion after it, many of them expressed that it was a useful way for them to think about their writing process.

The biggest change Adilyn observed concerned student engagement and their being able to see what Adilyn called "the bigger picture":

> In general, [the students] seemed much more excited about the peer review process than in the past. Another thing on the portfolio reflections, one thing they talked a lot about was how they appreciated the sequencing, which was [managed through] a discussion board which had them brainstorming [and] then a journal where they had a brainstorming and then their project, and they saw the sequencing and how it built, which is nothing new when I have designed my class, but I've had some confusion before, and I think this time with the reflection it helped them see the bigger picture.

In explaining her experience with the course with the reflective framework, Adilyn didn't note any major differences between her "normal" course and this version apart from a reduction in student "confusion." Nor did she report any difference in grades or in the ways in which the students learned. Perhaps most important, Adilyn didn't notice whether the students engaged in the reflective moves of looking backward, inward, forward, or outward. Students seemed to write about engaging in "similar" reflective practices in other courses, Adilyn said, so even though she didn't emphasize transfer, she believed that the implicit idea of transfer was apparent enough to support a student's ability to transfer knowledge and practices from her writing course to other writing contexts. Overall, Adilyn thought that the addition of the reflective framework was helpful and that she would definitely use one of the readings on reflective theory in her future writing classes because she "felt like, based on class discussion after it, many of them expressed that it was a useful way for them to think about their writing process."

One of the obstacles preventing transfer is students' inability to abstract what is taught in one course and repurpose it for another. While Adilyn *believed* the participants were able to transfer knowledge from her course to other writing situations, it became clear throughout the interview process that participants weren't able to articulate explicitly what they had learned in the course and thus what they might be transferring. For example, when participants were asked to "define writing," most were unable to put a definition to it: as one participant stated, "Wow, that's a hard answer. It's a very open question. I don't know. Define writing . . . I don't know. It could be used to . . . as kind of a way of expression through texts. It's kind of hard to define writing in a sentence." Another participant linked a definition of writing to assignments—"I guess writing has always been an assignment for me"—while another, stating, "I think of things like books, paragraphs, sentences, words," conceptualized writing in terms of component parts.

Moreover, these responses were not unusual: none of the participants was able to define writing specifically, which also suggests that the course didn't support students in developing a vocabulary about writing they could use when they entered a new writing context beyond that class. Instead, students tended to rely on previous knowledge, gained prior to Adilyn's class, to guide their writing practices. For example, one participant noted that she didn't think about key terms before writing; instead, she "mostly [thought] about the body like the intro and conclusion because [she] freaked out about them." Another said he thought about "background . . . [being] concise and getting to the point without adding too much fluff," while another stated, "I don't really . . . I just kind of just write now. I mean there are very few times where I'll outline my writing; I don't remember doing it at all this year, I just remember doing it when we had to in high school." Another student, like one of the students from the *Writing across Contexts* study (Yancey, Robertson, and Taczak 2014), cited *research* as the key term: "Hmm. I have no idea. So, I guess with writing and research I'd throw in [the term] research . . . preparation? I don't know." These responses suggest, as the *Writing across Contexts* study indicates, that if students are not pro-vided in college with specific writing terms to define writing, they revert to high-school experiences for a vocabulary.

Interestingly, the participants in this study were able to look *backward*, but they were not critically aware of how a reflective framework could help them move *forward* or even of how they could look *inward* or *out-ward*. When the participants were asked to describe their writing pro-cesses, three noted they did not think about anything before writing. For example, one participant said, "I don't think of anything specifically but I engulf myself within the prompt; I think about outside sources, what the teacher wants, which is a big part, and organize myself, which would be my biggest thing." Or as another said, "Key terms? I don't really think of key terms, I just kind of do it." Throughout the series of interviews, including the exit survey, the participants were unable to generate a list of key terms, and the ones they did identify were not well defined.

In addition, even though reflection was purposefully and intention-ally integrated into Adilyn's course, by their second interview,[8] the nine participants struggled to explain reflection as a part of their writing processes. As one participant explained, "I could definitely improve on [reflection] for sure. Do you mean reflection after the fact, like when I'm done? Definitely after the fact, but I think it's hard to think in the process to know if I've used reflection or not. Probably not as much as after writing something." Another participant understood reflection not as part of writing but rather as a possible part of an assignment: "Depending on what the assignment is, um, I mean, it depends just whenever the assignment asked me to do a reflection, but if it's an ana-lytical paper then I won't do it. Maybe like a story or something is where I'd use reflection or I don't know." Thus, even shortly after the course, the participants suggested that the reflective framework didn't take hold.

At the end of the study, participants were asked to complete an exit survey focused on their experience transferring writing knowledge and practice. One question asked specifically, "What have you transferred from [the writing course] to other writing situations?"[9] The answers, like earlier answers, ranged widely and focused on component parts, including a rhetorical strategy, "how to use transitional sentences"; part of a writing process, "the process of drafting"; and rhetorical concepts, "how to utilize ethos, pathos, and logos." One participant, Martin, was more explicit in stating what he transferred: "Simply put, I believe that utilizing my believed 3 key terms of writing [perspective, argument, audience] are all I really need moving forward. I think that it is always important to keep in mind who you are writing for and depending on the type of writing, explicating your stance on the topic at hand." However, Martin may not have learned these terms in the writing course since there the terms were merely "solidified": "I wouldn't necessarily say I learned anything new during my tenure [in the course] but rather, many ideas I learned in class were solidified." By the end of the study, one term after the conclusion of the writing course, it was clear that reflection had not become a part of the participants' writing practices and processes; students struggled to define reflection, to put writing into concrete terms, and to identify as writers. As one participant, Emily, wrote in her exit survey, "I'm not quite sure that I have a 'writing identity' yet. I guess overall I would say that I write best about ideas that I am passionate about, such as the environment. I don't believe that I have my own 'style' yet, but hopefully I will develop one in the years to come."

This study suggests that to facilitate transfer of writing knowledge and practice, the reflective framework cannot function alone in a themed course.[10] More specifically, this study provides two findings about the role of the reflective framework in a theme-based course: (1) when taught as a stand-alone framework, reflection does not aid students in developing a language or vocabulary with which they can frame new writing situations, and (2) when taught within a theme-based course, reflection becomes more of a practice of looking backward, which is not linked to creating new knowledge and does not necessarily prompt students to consider how they might reflect forward regarding either their writing processes or writing practices. What these findings mean, as demonstrated by the participants, is that reflection did help them in a composing moment to think about what they were *doing* with their writing, but it did not encourage them to become critical about what they were learning *about* writing. Thus, as a practice *in doing writing*, reflection had a limited usefulness. Some might argue that this utility is sufficient, but our research suggests that with a fuller curricular model— including key vocabulary, a reflective framework, and students' theory of writing—students *can and do* transfer knowledge and practices about writing to other writing contexts.

REFLECTION AND TRANSFER AS INTERLOCKING: A CONCLUSION

[The course] made me be able to focus on why I'm writing and how I'm writing better and also gave me a reason to write instead of just kind of blabbing on about stuff.

—Angela, one year after taking the TFT course

What we learned from our research is that there are two approaches to reflection, used in combination, that merit consideration in composition courses hoping to teach for transfer: (1) reflection as a reiterative practice that leads to a theory of writing, and (2) reflection as a framework students can use to approach new writing situations. These approaches represent the concept of reflection as both a theory and a practice, offering writers a means of framing and reframing each writing situation, and a writing activity that helps writers understand the existing frame and reimagine it as a new frame.

As the studies described here demonstrate, students who develop a reflective framework that allows them to understand writing in different contexts are able to reimagine previous writing knowledge that they can adapt to a new situation. Their understanding of how to repurpose previous knowledge is dependent on their ability to conceptualize the current context and what it calls for in terms of writing. This explicit understanding of each context also develops through the use of reflection as a practice, not just an after-the-fact practice, but one that spans the entire context and beyond so that reflection becomes embedded in the invention, arrangement, and delivery of any piece of writing.

This level of reflection also acts as a portal to understanding, or a "threshold concept" (Meyer and Land 2003) in that it allows a writer to understand writing as something beyond the crafting of words on a page, but also as a representation of a coherent set of ideas. For college writers, whose development as writers is steeped in years of formulaic writing or whose identity as writers is one of regurgitating information in our test-taking educational culture, reflection can open the door to understanding writing as something the writer structures and makes choices about. Reflection helps writers get past the idea of what they're supposed to know and move toward the idea that they can access what they know in ways of their own choosing. In other words, when reflection is treated as a rhetorical practice, reflection acts as a catalyst for learning not just how to write something, but also for knowing what to write, to whom, and to what end.

As one participant from the TFT course, Charlotte, demonstrated in reflecting about the theory of writing she developed,

> My growth in writing over this past quarter is much like the growth of a tree. In elementary and middle school I learned the basic way to form paragraphs and five paragraph essays, which are the roots of my tree. In high school I learned how to write research essays and learned how to use voice in papers, which is the trunk of my writing tree. In college, however, I learned key terms to writing that made my tree blossom. My

writing went from basic to extraordinary. . . . Along with good writing come skills like critical thinking, the understanding of how humans use language to interact, and being able to use previous knowledge to your advantage. . . . The unification of my past knowledge about writing with the key terms and writing [situations] I learned this quarter allowed my writing tree to fully blossom.

Charlotte understood reflection as a reiterative practice in which she was able to analyze her previous knowledge about writing and its evolution through her academic experience, culminating in the "blossoming" of her knowledge about writing as conceptual as well as a practice. Through the reflection about her theory of writing, Charlotte articulated the goal of the reflective framework: to theorize about writing, to understand oneself as a writer within a context, and to put into practice previous knowledge appropriate to a new context.

Notes

1. "*Reflection-in-action*, the process of reviewing and projecting and revising, which takes place within a composing event; *constructive reflection*, the process of developing a cumulative, multi-selved, multi-voiced identity, which takes place between and among composing events; and *reflection-in-presentation*, the process of articulating the relationships between and among the multiple variables of writing and the writer in a specific context for a specific audience" (Yancey 1998, 200).

2. As scholars such as Michael Carter and Nancy Sommers and Laura Saltz have shown, the transition from novice to expert is a key move in a student's ability to transfer (Carter 1990; Sommers and Saltz 2004).

3. We have published on our course design elsewhere, most notably in our coauthored *Writing across Contexts: Transfer, Composition, and Sites of Writing*, with Kathleen Blake Yancey (2014), and in our coauthored article "Case Study: Teaching for Transfer" (forthcoming).

4. In the initial design of the TFT course, we included eleven key terms, but in later iterations the eleven were adapted to the eight most important, based on research findings and classroom interaction with students (adding *purpose*, which students were already familiar with and used; deleting *circulation*, *critical analysis*, and *composing* as key terms but retaining them in course discussion as terms of lesser significance; and deleting *exigence* as a key term on its own but integrating it as part of the key term *rhetorical situation*.)

5. See also Kara Taczak 2011.

6. Details of this study and its results can be found in the Yancey, Robertson, and Taczak's (2014) *Writing across Contexts: Transfer, Composition, and Sites of Writing* (see also Robertson 2011 and Taczak 2011).

7. All participant names used in these studies are pseudonyms.

8. The second interview occurred during week one of spring quarter, which would have been two weeks after the conclusion of Adilyn's class.

9. Since transfer was explicitly discussed in Adilyn's course, transfer was defined for the participants on the exit survey as the ability to take knowledge and practices from one writing situation to another.

10.   We acknowledge the limitations of the study, one of which is that there were only nine participants from one instructor.

References

Adler-Kassner, Linda, and Elizabeth Wardle, eds. 2015. *Naming What We Know: Threshold Concepts in Writing Studies*. Logan: Utah State University Press.

Beaufort, Anne. 2007. *College Writing and Beyond: A New Framework for University Writing Instruction*. Logan: Utah State University Press.

Bransford, John D., James W. Pellegrino, and M. Suzanne Donovan, eds. 2000a. "How Experts Differ from Novices." In *How People Learn: Brain, Mind, Experience, and School: Expanded Edition*, 31–50. Washington, DC: National Academies Press.

Bransford, John D., James W. Pellegrino, and M. Suzanne Donovan. 2000b. Committee on Learning Research and Educational Practice. "Learning and Transfer." In *How People Learn: Brain, Mind, Experience, and School: Expanded Edition*, 51–78. Washington, DC: National Academies Press.

Brent, Doug. 2012. "Crossing Boundaries: Co-op Students Relearning to Write." *College Composition and Communication* 63 (4): 558–92.

Carter, Michael. 1990. "The Idea of Expertise: An Exploration of Cognitive and Social Dimensions of Writing." *College Composition and Communication* 41 (3): 265–86. http://dx.doi.org/10.2307/357655.

Dew, Debra. 2003. "Language Matters: Rhetoric and Writing I as Content Course." *WPA: Writing Program Administration* 26 (3): 87–104.

Downs, Doug, and Liane Robertson. 2015. "Threshold Concepts in First-Year Composition." In *Naming What We Know: Threshold Concepts in Writing Studies*, ed. Linda Adler-Kassner and Elizabeth Wardle, 105–21. Logan: Utah State University Press.

Downs, Douglas, and Elizabeth Wardle. 2007. "Teaching about Writing, Righting Misconceptions: (Re)Envisioning 'First-Year Composition' as 'Introduction to Writing Studies.'" *College Composition and Communication* 58 (4): 552–84.

Driscoll, Dana, and Jennifer Wells. 2012. "Beyond Knowledge and Skills: Writing Transfer and the Role of Student Dispositions in and beyond the Writing Classroom." *Composition Forum* 26 (Fall). http://compositionforum.com/issue/26/beyond-know ledge-skills.php.

Irvin, Lennie. 2004. "Reflection in the Electronic Writing Classroom." *Computers and Composition Online*. http://www2.bgsu.edu/departments/english/cconline/irvin /Introduction.htm.

Meyer, Jan H.F., and Ray Land. 2003. "Threshold Concepts and Troublesome Knowledge: Linkages to Ways of Thinking and Practicing within the Disciplines." Occasional Report 4, Enhancing Teaching-Learning Environments in Undergraduate Courses Project, University of Edinburgh.

Nowacek, Rebecca S. 2011. *Agents of Integration: Understanding Transfer as a Rhetorical Act*. Carbondale: Southern Illinois University Press.

Perkins, David N., and Gavriel Salomon. 1992. "Transfer of Learning." In *International Encyclopedia of Education*, 2–13. 2nd ed. Oxford: Pergamon.

Robertson, Liane. 2011. "The Significance of Course Content in the Transfer of Writing Knowledge from First-Year Composition to Other Academic Writing Contexts." PhD diss., Florida State University.

Robertson, Liane, and Kara Taczak. Forthcoming. "Case Study: Teaching for Transfer." In *Understanding Writing Transfer and Its Implications for Higher Education*, ed. Randy Bass and Jessie Moore. Sterling, VA: Stylus. http://dx.doi.org/10.1093/med /9780199688074.003.0035.

Robertson, Liane, Kara Taczak, and Kathleen Blake Yancey. 2012. "Notes toward a Theory of Prior Knowledge and Its Role in College Composers' Transfer of Knowledge and Practice." *Composition Forum* 26 (Fall). http://compositionforum.com/issue/26/prior-knowledge-transfer.php.

Sommers, Jeff. 2011. "Reflection Revisited: The Class Collage." *Journal of Basic Writing* 30 (11): 99–129.

Sommers, Nancy, and Laura Saltz. 2004. "The Novice as Expert: Writing the Freshman Year." *College Composition and Communication* 56 (1): 124–49. http://dx.doi.org/10.2307/4140684.

Taczak, Kara. 2011. "Connecting the Dots: Does Reflection Foster Transfer?" PhD diss., Florida State University.

University of Denver Writing Program. 2014. http://www.du.edu/writing/features.html.

Yancey, Kathleen Blake. 1998. *Reflection in the Writing Classroom.* Logan: Utah State University Press.

Yancey, Kathleen Blake, Liane Robertson, and Kara Taczak. 2014. *Writing across Contexts: Transfer, Composition, and Sites of Writing.* Logan: Utah State University Press.

4

THE PERILS OF STANDING ALONE
Reflective Writing in Relationship to Other Texts

Michael Neal

I was introduced to reflection through cover letters that accompanied student writing portfolios in the '90s when I was first entering the field. At that time portfolios, it seemed to me, were already established as a best practice in the teaching of writing, specifically as the most trustworthy and theoretically informed way of assessing student writing (Belanoff 1994; Belanoff and Dickson 1991; Black, Daiker, Sommers, and Stygall 1994; Elbow 1994; Yancey 1992). For me it wasn't a matter of *if* but *how* I would use portfolios in my composition classes, and my biggest challenge was finding a bag large enough to haul around the heavy load of binders that included multiples drafts of every paper students produced in the class—the weightiness of how much students produce in a given semester now having been largely lost in the ePortfolio era. And it went without saying that each portfolio was to be introduced by the ubiquitous reflective cover letter. In this context, reflection took on the generic conventions of an introduction of the students' writing to the reader/assessor, providing a context for the pieces included in the portfolio. In my own teaching at that time, since portfolios were used to advocate for and assess a student's writing process over the product, a reflective cover letter narrated a student's development as a writer over a period of time, usually a semester, though I did have some early exposure to program and other large-scale portfolio contexts that went beyond the time and space boundaries of a semester-long course.

As a new teacher, the idea that I could wait until the end of the semester to grade the students' writing and that I would grade the body of work as a whole rather than assess the individual pieces was exhilarating and terrifying, and I often hedged the assessment by assigning grades along the way as much to put my mind at ease as to respond to my evaluation-obsessed students. It felt like breaking the

DOI: 10.7330/9781607325161.c004

rules to respond without grading along the way. In the early days of my using portfolios, while I examined many aspects of the process and assessment mechanism, I don't remember doubting the legitimacy or value of the reflective cover letter. This letter seemed in many ways the anchor for the portfolio, and its value lay in the relationship between the reflection and the other artifacts in the portfolio. Sometimes the reflections seemed coherent with the other pieces in the portfolio, but at other times I noticed a troubling inconsistency: what some students wrote in their reflections wasn't consistent with what I read in the rest of the portfolio, which led to me to question their development as writers. This disconnect was troubling for me as a composition teacher, who had no doubts that student writers were always developing, but who also thought that articulation of their writing was a vital component of that development. Thus, I described the cover letter as a document that made specific, measureable claims about the student's writing that should be supported by evidence in the other texts. The two parts of the portfolio—and I understood them as parts at that time—were linked in the logic of their performance. At least in classroom portfolio assessment, I saw the reflection as inseparable from the other artifacts in the portfolio. Case closed.

Over the past twenty years of teaching, reading, and administrating in the field, my understanding of reflection and portfolios has evolved, as has the field's. Reflection is more nuanced and complex than I understood. It appears in written form, but it's also contemplative, visual, spatial, gestural, or multimodal. In addition, reflection is no longer inextricably linked to portfolios in my practice: I often have students reflect on multiple processes and decisions outside of portfolio work, and I don't insist on portfolios having a general cover letter . . . in fact, I discourage it, as I explain later. In part, I was helped along by Kathleen Blake Yancey's *Reflection in the Writing Classroom* (1998), which challenged me to consider reflection beyond the panacea of portfolio assessment and to theorize a practice many others in the field and I had already embraced. Building on the work of Donald Schon, Yancey delineated three types of reflection: "reflection-in-action," "constructive reflection," and "reflection-in-presentation." In my pedagogy, I'm particularly drawn to reflection-in-presentation because it acknowledges multiple potential audiences for the reflection as well as genres, contexts, and other features. To me reflection-in-presentation seems the most consistent with the kind of writing and thinking in which students engage while constructing reflective texts for portfolios. In defining and theorizing reflection in its contemporary state, Yancey draws on several key principles and foundational thinkers: John Dewey's tacit knowledge as well as Schon's distinction between reflection-on-action and reflection-in-action. In the end, through these understandings, what we have are practices that reproduce values often espoused in the field through portfolio and even ways of action, as indicated, for example, in George Hillocks's (1995) *Teaching Writing as Reflective Practice*, which encourages reflexivity for teachers of writing and for their students.

Even though reflection is not understood exclusively as a written text or a portfolio text, we have seen both the reemergence of portfolio theory and practice in terms of ePortfolios in the past several years through digital technologies and an increased emphasis on large-scale writing assessment in a time of educational accountability. The issue I thus explore in this chapter is the continued relationship—if any—between reflective texts and other artifacts in the contemporary era of portfolio assessment. Specifically, I look at two issues central in the current context: (1) challenges leveled at reflective writing as a form of self-assessment and (2) the reflective text as the single scored piece of writing, as advocated in Phase 2 portfolio assessment (White 2005). Put in the form of questions, my chapter asks:

- What are the relationships between reflective writing and other artifacts within a portfolio?
- What—if any—value remains in guiding students into specific reflective writing activities, either for teaching and learning or for the purposes of writing assessment?

In addressing these questions, my intent is to reaffirm the important relationship between reflective writing and portfolio artifacts—though not in limited, formulaic cover letters, but rather as integrated learning tools for students to make evident tacit decisions they make as writers.

A BRIEF AND SELECTIVE HISTORY OF REFLECTIVE WRITING IN PORTFOLIOS

Until Yancey's (1998) *Reflection in the Writing Classroom*, reflection in composition was frequently tied to assessment, which often included self-evaluation. As portfolios were embraced more widely at all educational levels, reflection remained a central practice and text, but it was often seen as little more than an introductory letter to the more substantial artifacts in the portfolio (Anson 1994). Educators advocated for portfolios—even in large-scale writing assessment systems—as a fix-all for a myriad of problems they associated with student writing because portfolios seemed to embody values central to the field at that time:

encouraging writing process and revision, allowing for collaboration, promoting pedagogical diversity, and challenging grade inflation and students' obsession with grades (Belanoff 1994; Belanoff and Elbow 1991; Bishop 1990; Murphy 1994; Sommers 1989).

Portfolios included three primary components—collection, selection, and reflection; each had a role, but they largely functioned in relationship to one another to make a coherent whole (Yancey 1998). The collection element, simply put, is that portfolios consist of more than a single artifact, a significant move away from assessing one piece of writing and assuming it provides a useful index to a student's abilities. Just as important, though, is that as writing outcomes and competencies require negotiating multiple contexts, portfolios allow students to include a range of work to demonstrate their flexibility and abilities to work across genres, contexts, and situations. This multiplicity also allows portfolios on a larger scale to include samples from across the curriculum and from outside the academy. A look at the WPA Outcomes Statement and the Framework for Success in Postsecondary Writing reveals how important multiplicity is to the way we understand our writing and its instruction:

FROM THE WPA OUTCOMES (EMPHASIS MINE)

- Respond to the needs of *different audiences.*
- Respond appropriately to *different kinds of rhetorical situations.*
- Write in several genres.
- Learn common formats for *different kinds of texts.*
- Use a variety of technologies to address a *range of audiences.* (http://wpacouncil.org/positions/outcomes.html)

FROM THE FRAMEWORK FOR SUCCESS IN POSTSECONDARY WRITING (EMPHASIS MINE)

- *Flexibility,* or the ability *to adapt to situations, expectations, or demands,* and
- Abilities to compose in *multiple environments,* from using traditional pen and paper to electronic technologies (http://wpacouncil.org /framework)

In order for portfolios to demonstrate such a broad range of writing situations and contexts, they must include artifacts from an equally broad range of contexts and situations. How would a student demonstrate using "a variety of technologies to address a range of audiences" with a single artifact (e.g., a Prezi) or by including multiple, word-processed assignments? Since many of the outcomes and frameworks require this type of flexibility, effective portfolios must include a variety of artifacts as well. An additional motive for collecting multiple artifacts for a portfolio is that in such a vehicle, students can create longitudinal evidence of their learning and development for their own benefit as well as to present to others (e.g., faculty, administrators, employers, graduate schools, etc.).

In addition to the portfolio's being a collection of artifacts, it is supposed to be a selection of artifacts as well. Without selection, the portfolio can become an unmanageable mass of artifacts: instead, student writers are charged with choosing from their larger body of work to demonstrate a range of competencies. Inasmuch as students understand the audiences and purposes of the portfolio, they can make informed selections and in so doing demonstrate their range of thinking, abilities, and rhetorical savvy. Not least, such students may internalize the values of the portfolio in ways that can be advantageous to them moving forward with their work.

A final piece to this traditional portfolio trifecta is reflection, which may take on a variety of forms and functions within a portfolio. As previously noted, portfolio reflection has often been understood as synonymous with a cover letter; however, this doesn't need to be case. Any type of writing that comments on a writer's processes, includes self-assessment, or provides rationale for choices either in the collection or selection principles above or about individual artifacts can be considered reflection. The question at hand in this chapter is what role reflection can and should play in the assessment of a portfolio—and whether it is even necessary in contemporary iterations of portfolios. Is a portfolio even a portfolio if it does not include a reflective element? Although I'm less convinced that a portfolio needs to include reflection, certain types of reflection can play an important role in student writing as well as its assessment.

While collection, selection, and reflection remained the foundational aspects of portfolio literature and practice, as the field became more critical of portfolio assessment, so did our view of reflection. Once portfolio assessment became so ubiquitous it was being presented as the solution for seemingly every writing situation and problem (Callahan 2000), strong voices in the field warned against the utopianism of portfolio assessment, pointing out problems, including the practice of scoring rather than reading portfolios (Broad 1994) and the drawbacks of holistically scoring a portfolio (Elbow 1994). Murphy and Grant (1996) comment on the rise of portfolio popularity in the '80s and the pitfalls that often accompany such wide-spread acceptance: "Since the mid-1980s, as educators have become increasingly dissatisfied with traditional assessment measures, there has been an escalating interest in portfolio assessment, so much so that portfolio assessment is now in danger of becoming the latest educational bandwagon. Yet bandwagons, however alluring and brightly lit, have been known to ensnare rather than transport the unsuspecting rider" (284). The same cycle brought into relief how the initial expectations for reflection were being diminished. Initially, the field's interest in reflection communicated similar high expectations; it was supposed to

- encourage metacognition;
- make pedagogy more dialogic;
- help students assume control of their own development as writers;
- enable students to develop their own voices;
- improve the quality of written assignments and students' grades;
- help students become more independent judges of their own writing;
- enable teachers to see how students read and interpret assignments and other class activities, as well as how students construct teacher expectations; and
- integrate literacy learning and authentic writing with assessment.

Anything in the field with this level of optimism is bound to be tempered to some degree in time, but I include this list to show how enthusiastic we were and how well reflective writing matched our goals with the goals of the community. It seemed a perfect fit for both our values and the problems we faced with student learning and assessment.

Perhaps most important in the rationale for portfolio reflection is the connection between reflection and self-assessment. In fact, the two became so closely related they were often used interchangeably and thus are difficult to distinguish from one another. Much of the criticism that gets leveled against reflective writing might actually be a critique of self-assessment within the context of assessment decisions. Perhaps the most significant contribution to our understanding of self-assessment in rhetoric and composition circles is Jane Bowman Smith and Kathleen Blake Yancey's edited collection *Self-Assessment and Development in Writing* (Smith and Yancey 2000). Linking pedagogy and reflection, Thomas L. Hilgers, Edna L. Hussey, and Monica Stitt-Bergh's opening chapter, "The Case for Prompted Self-Assessment in the Writing Classroom," points to targeting two specific areas to prompt reflective writing: cognitive growth and procedural skills (Hilgers, Hussey, and Stitt-Bergh 2000, 15–18). The first, cognitive growth, includes new understandings about writers and writing, writers' evaluation of their own strengths and weaknesses as writers, and even goal setting for future drafts or projects. The second area—procedural skills—prompts students to think about what obstacles they encounter and how they resolve them. In both cases, the authors argue, students need to be guided by prompts toward the most useful and significant areas to affect the pedagogical outcomes of the activity. In the same collection, Chris M. Anson writes about a writing pedagogy based on reviewing audio reflections, which indicate that the metacommentaries (or reflective self-assessment) of strong students reveal a level of control of their texts, even if those texts have other problems; in contrast, weaker students demonstrate a kind of passivity or abdication of control of their texts (Anson 2000, 69) Anson's recommendation is that in responding, faculty should not take over the decision making for the students' texts, especially for struggling writers, a concern echoed by others as well, including Irwin Weiser (1992) in "Portfolio Practice and Assessment for Collegiate Basic Writers" and Cheryl Forbes (1996) in "Cowriting, Overwriting, and Overriding in Portfolio Land Online." While reflection is certainly not the only place where such usurpation of students' texts takes place, it is one such place, and thus the motives for assigning and responding to student reflection must be carefully considered. At the same time it is important to say that just because some reflective writing situations lead to this type of takeover, it isn't necessarily the case in all models of response.

THE PORTFOLIO COVER LETTER AS A FORMULAIC PERFORMANCE

The most consistent criticism of reflective writing centers on the hollowness of the reflective writing in educational and assessment contexts (for examples, see Bower 2003; Murray 2009; O'Neill 2002; Scott 2005; Sommers 2011). For instance, Joddy Murray, in *Non-Discursive Rhetoric: Image and Affect in Multimodal Composition*, suggests that reflection—which he equates with self-assessment—does not live up to its promise: "Often touted as the panacea of assessment, self-assessment may not be as useful as some writing teachers might think, especially in terms of helping students to see the potential in the writing they do while, simultaneously, helping them to value the dynamic nature of most multimodal writing in new media today. Though reflection is for the most part a valuable exercise, it must be combined with a rigorous method of self-assessment that connects the process elements with the end product in such a way as to discourage any notions of rigidity or finality" (Murray 2009, 186). While I agree with Murray that reflective texts should be read rhetorically, evaluating their own work is difficult for many students, especially if they haven't defined or internalized criteria for making such value judgments, a point underscored in a study conducted by Joe Cirio. Interested in whether or not students could participate in devising scoring guides, Cirio (2014) found that the first-year composition students he interviewed did not have the vocabulary they would need to articulate criteria, and without those, they were unable to assess their own writing. Moreover, self-evaluation is only one form of reflective writing, one that can be the trickiest ethically, as the collection on self-assessment edited by Smith and Yancey (2000) demonstrates. Put simply, it is too easy to locate a single problem with reflection and then make a sweeping generalization about its effectiveness based on that weakness.

In fact, it's interesting to contrast Murray's approach and conclusions with how Rachel Ihara (2014), Lindsey Harding (2014), and Peggy O'Neill (2002) separately address potential problems of reflective writing being coercive or disingenuous. In a study published in *TETYC* (and as also discussed by Jeff Sommers, this volume), Ihara reports on the extent to which students feel "compelled to construct a narrative of growth" (226) in their reflective writing; Ihara finds that most of the students in the study want to be "honest" in their reflections. At the same time, Ihara is troubled that these same students have a hard time presenting textual evidence of their learning and that most fail to recognize the external audience for the reflection, instead seeing this text principally as a piece of writing more for themselves than for the reader. In that same issue of *TETYC*, Harding develops an approach guiding students to what she calls more "genuine intellectual reflection" (241–42) through a system of guided questions as a strategy to mitigate challenges of open-ended reflections leading to vague generalities. O'Neill makes the same turn in her work, pointing out the potential pitfall of putting too much weight on reflective texts but offering suggestions to make this writing more valuable: "The products and processes of reflection in these different contexts have the potential to become empty, formulaic rituals producing predictable texts that can function as a subtle means of controlling—and constructing to some extent—students. . . . Incorporating reflection ethically requires more than just adding a cover letter or a reflective essay because students need to be taught what we mean by reflection, how to generate reflective texts, and how to evaluate them as processes and products" (n.p.). For the remainder of her article, that's exactly how

O'Neill proceeds, articulating principles—much along the lines of the Smith and Yancey collection—that guide students toward productive reflective writing: reviewing the reasons for including reflective writing, avoiding using a single genre for reflection such as the reflective letter, having a number of varied reflection activities, allowing students to keep some reflection private, teaching reflective texts as a rhetorical genres, constructing prompts carefully, and being conscious of ourselves as readers of reflective texts. O'Neill's argument is leveled at a number of problems with reflective cover letters: the problem is not so much with the reflective acts or texts as it is with the forms and purposes they take on—especially as they become formulaic—and the lack of authentic context for this writing exercise. O'Neill is especially concerned, it appears, that teachers will adopt a single generic reflective prompt and genre (the cover letter) without variance, which can further encourage and enable formulaic responses to the assignment, in which case the assignment will become exactly what the goals of reflection work against: a shallow, perfunctory response that is meaningless to teachers and students alike.

That worst-case scenario of reflective writing is what Tony Scott finds in his study of high-school students' reflective-cover-letter writing (Scott 2005), which he sees as part of the bureaucratic culture of top-down educational reform in the state of Kentucky at that time. Scott critiques the genre—specifically in the context of the portfolio cover letter—as a manipulative force for writers: "Genres are therefore often not only regulative of texts, they are constitutive of activities and social orders" (9). The generic purpose he discovers through his investigation of this portfolio assessment is that the reflective cover letters—80 percent of which claim growth for the writer—keep the teachers aware of and accountable to state expectations, provide a simple formula for students to follow without spending much time or having any investment in the process, and validate the curriculum (25–26).

With these conclusions regarding the performativity of reflection in portfolio assessment, it is hard not to become cynical of or want to dismiss reflection as whole. Despite these critiques, it appears that the field isn't abandoning reflection or even reflective texts in portfolios. Many of the newer and continuing portfolio models include reflection as part of the system and assessment. Despite the challenges, reflective writing endures, including its use in large-scale assessment models. Moreover one of these models—Phase 2 portfolios—assesses the reflective writing in a portfolio exclusively, which makes it an interesting case to explore in further detail.

CONSIDERING ONLY THE REFLECTIVE COVER
LETTERS IN PHASE 2 PORTFOLIO ASSESSMENT

Taking a distinctly different position on the value of reflective cover let-ters, Edward M. White introduced Phase 2 portfolio assessment in "The Scoring of Writing Portfolios: Phase 2" (White 2005), long into the debates over the relative value of reflective writing. Citing reflection as a primary strength in portfolio assessment, White developed a large-scale assessment model in which raters score portfolios based almost exclu-sively on the reflective letter (582–83). In this system, faculty develop a list of educational goals or outcomes for students to demonstrate, and the students respond with a reflective cover letter that shows how they have exhibited these outcomes in portfolio artifacts. The portfolio arti-facts are not reviewed unless a rater chooses to engage in a "quick skim-ming" (593) of a cited piece of evidence. This model brings holistic scor-ing back to a single writing sample, which White notes was its original use; in fact, he challenges the appropriateness of using holistic scoring on a portfolio with multiple pieces of writing for the scorer to consider. As evidence of the effectiveness of Phase 2 portfolio assessment, White points to the efficiency of scoring, which in a Phase 2 model increases from two portfolios an hour to ten or more, ostensibly with substantial agreement (594). Many are familiar with claims of efficiency and reli-ability, and despite the many arguments to the contrary (see, among others, Broad 2003; Huot 1990, 2002; Williamson 1994), claims such as these appeal to pragmatists whose primary concerns are cost and sub-jectivity in scoring.

In his article explaining Phase 2 portfolio scoring, White makes a validity claim I would like to examine in closer detail: "[Phase 2 port-folio scoring] supports student learning by requiring self-assessment and responsibility, provides direct information to faculty on the out-comes of their programs, and uses existing documents in a new way that is demonstrably direct and valid" (2000, 594). Without rehashing the entire volume of scholarship on validity, I'll remind the reader that validity is a measure of degree—not a yes/no evaluation—of the accu-racy and appropriateness of decisions made based on the results of a test (Messick 1989; Moss 1994; Shepard 1993). Therefore, the question isn't, is Phase 2 portfolio assessment valid? but rather, to what degree are decisions made on the basis of Phase 2 portfolio scoring accurate and appropriate?" The answer to this question is context specific. Because educational decisions are the focus of a validity argument (not based on the test by itself), we cannot determine the degree of valid-ity outside of its use, but let's assume for a moment that the purpose of this assessment model is a course grade, a program assessment, a placement decision, an exit decision, or an admissions decision. Even with this hypothetical range, we can start to unpack the value of Phase 2 portfolio scoring.

Relative Strengths

As White points out, Phase 2 portfolio scoring is faster and thus less expensive than reading full portfolios. While this isn't the most important criterion for test validity, I'd be remiss if I didn't acknowledge that assessment models must be sustainable and that cheaper, faster models are easier to sell to administrators in a time when educational funding continues to be limited. In addition, and as White points out, Phase 2 assessment is a direct assessment (White 2005, 594): the scorers are making a decision about student writing while reading a sample of student writing. While many other writing-assessment models are indirect measures, Phase 2 portfolio assessment considers student writing, a virtue most in the field would support. In addition, *if the reflection is done well*, it can achieve some of the initial goals laid out by early proponents of reflection and reflective writing: "When a student introduces a portfolio with serious reflection about it, the student is taking responsibility for the quality of the work, the choices that were involved in the writing, and the learning that has occurred—or not occurred. It is a powerful metacognitive act—thinking about thinking—that no other assessment device includes" (583)—a point many portfolio scholars have made. Also like others, as we have seen, White is quick to concede that without proper instruction "students are likely to give a hasty overview of the portfolio contents, including much personal experience about the difficulty of writing and revising—along with some fulsome praise of the teacher—without attending to the goals of the program at all" (591). So White's conclusions, while advocating for the scoring of portfolios via reflective writing, acknowledge the misgivings about reflective letters that O'Neill (2002), Scott (2005), and others might level. His solution, to prompt students to respond to faculty-produced goals and outcomes, however, does not address Scott's findings that the letters largely become a hollow affirmation of the curriculum. The kinds of goal and outcome statements White includes in the appendices seem to be exactly the kind that Scott would find disingenuous that O'Neill would critique as being too stable and thus absent from instruction.

Relative Weaknesses

While acknowledging certain benefits of the Phase 2 scoring model, we must also account for its weaknesses when considering its degree of validity when used within particular contexts. Since validity has three main components—accuracy, appropriateness, and consequences—I'll expand on them in that order. According to White (2005), the *accuracy* of Phase 2 scoring is based on score reliability, but what reliability means isn't explained. Reliability is a measure of consistency. Is White's claim one of interrater reliability—that two people scoring the same reflective letter will give the same score—or that of consistency of scores between a whole-portfolio reading and one in which only the reflective text is read? If the former, it is not surprising that two raters with equally limited access to the full portfolio would give the same score: the simpler and more limited the text being assessed, the better chance for calibration and agreement. The latter would be more convincing if fully read portfolios were given the same scores as those given only the reflective letters, but that isn't clear. The history of writing assessment is riddled with similar claims that what is being measured is equivalent to looking at a full, authentic writing sample.

This leads to the *appropriateness* of making decisions about students based only on reading the reflective letter. To what degree is it appropriate to have students assemble a full portfolio if assessors only read and assess the opening letter? It seems duplicitous to require students to put time and effort into something assessors would spend so little time on. In addition, the educational *consequences* aren't hard to imagine. Students' understanding of how the portfolio is (or isn't) being read to score undermines the value of the portfolio itself. As students learn to beat the test, portfolio assessment is clearly one kind of assessment students could easily game and for which they would replicate hollow generic conventions, much in the way Scott suggests of the Kentucky model. In addition, in Phase 2 portfolio assessment we lose the most basic values of portfolio assessment that drew us to it in the first place. Do we really want to move back to a single writing sample when outcomes and goals for college writing have become more nuanced? I would hate to lose gains we have made in writing assessment by voluntarily retreating to a single sample of writing whose genre isn't necessarily clear and that often doesn't fulfill the same outcomes or goals as other artifacts in the portfolio.

My own experience with portfolio assessment suggests a different problem with considering only the reflective writing in a portfolio assessment. Over the past nine years I have worked with a cross-disciplinary faculty on a portfolio assessment that occurs after students' first year of college in which they submit (1) samples of writing from their coursework, (2) an essay written outside of class, and (3) a reflective letter that responds to prompts about their writing. Even though we have adjusted the description of and prompts for the reflective text multiple times, the reflective letters have remained frustratingly inconsistent and are often an anomaly compared to the other artifacts in the portfolio. For one thing, students underestimate the value and challenge of producing such a text. For another, too often students don't see composing the reflection as an integral part of the portfolio process—even though the faculty do—resulting in the letter's often being the shallowest portion of the portfolio. Moreover, since the reflective text is holistic and the portfolio isn't produced in a single class, there are limited opportunities to guide students through meaningful reflection activities and revisions that would help them effectively develop a substantial reflective text.

White has a point that holistic scoring may be difficult to use on portfolios because assigning a single judgment to a group of artifacts with varying strengths and weaknesses is often challenging. Even using a scoring guide with multiple categories for evaluation is tough when texts within the portfolio vary in quality. While the system I'm describing uses both a holistic score (pass and resubmit) and a scoring guide to explain strengths and weaknesses of the writing to students, we decided early in the process to break out categories within the scoring guide for the reflective writing because those texts were often so inconsistent with the other writing in the portfolio. Even after nearly a decade of using and revising the reflection prompts and description, we've still decided to keep those parts of the scoring separate. If I were to suggest Phase 2 portfolio scoring to this group of experienced portfolio readers, they would rightly resist: the assumption that the reflective texts in a portfolio read in isolation will mirror the other artifacts is too big a leap for those experienced in evaluating portfolio reflections. Each piece of writing is unique, and the reflective texts are especially so because they have different purposes, audiences, and exigencies than the other artifacts in the portfolio. Without stronger support, it's not clear that the reflections read alone will be representative of the other writing. Reading and evaluating multiple texts is the very essence of portfolio assessment, and without it, the theory of portfolio assessment is significantly undermined.

If we're interested in moving back to single-sample writing assessments, we need to craft an argument around that practice rather than pretending that pulling a single sample of writing out of a portfolio to assess it maintains the validity of the assessment. In many ways that's exactly what White suggests in his article: that evaluating multiple samples of writing in a single score is too difficult and that we should return to a single sample. If that's so, however, we shouldn't call that evaluation method portfolio assessment. And even were I making this argument—which I am not—I certainly wouldn't use the reflective writing sample in a portfolio as the scored single text because of how it is thus repositioned. The reflective text in a portfolio is created to situate, to be in dialogue with, and to be in response to the other portfolio texts. Thus, it doesn't make sense as a reader or assessor to isolate that text for the assessment. And of course, there is the question of the ethics of requiring students to develop a full portfolio with reflection without actually reading the full portfolio or their knowing that the full portfolio won't be read. How long will it be before students and teachers understand that the full portfolio isn't being read? What do we expect they'll do when they find out? What does that do to our ethos as teachers of writing? Stated simply, Phase 2 portfolio assessment exerts a three-pronged effect, undermining (1) the portfolio reading, (2) the value of reflection in relationship to other pieces in the portfolio, and (3) our own credibility as writing assessors.

CONCLUSIONS: THE ABANDONMENT OF REFLECTIVE WRITING?

When positioned as part of a portfolio, reflective writing is most usefully understood as a *confirmational* text (Anson 2000), one in which its dialogue and relationship with other texts is *necessary* to be meaningful. This is an important distinction in light of what I see as two disparate positions in the scholarship on reflective writing in portfolios: abandoning reflection altogether as Murray (2009) or Scott (2005) might suggest or relying on it disproportionately for the assessment as White does in his Phase 2 model. Scott's research demonstrates how disappointing reflective letters in portfolios can be since they can tend toward superficial curricular affirmation; at the same time, his study took place in a very different model than the one characterizing most in composition studies—the context of state-wide K–12 assessment, in which the political origins and implementation of the portfolio system threatened the process from the outset. To dismiss reflective writing in this context dismisses the value reflection adds to an assessment system in others. At the other end of the continuum, White's wholesale acceptance of the isolated reflective cover letters raises significant concerns. While I appreciate the nod toward portfolio assessment, scoring reflective letters alone—especially given the critiques—doesn't acknowledge or address the relationship between reflection and other texts within the portfolios, especially in cases in which the reflection is positioned to be in dialogue with the artifacts in the portfolio. Portfolio reflective texts are not intended to be read or understood in isolation, which raises questions about the propriety of any reading or scoring that strips them of their fuller context.

There is a different way to position reflective writing in relationship to portfolios and assessment that values the role reflection can play without leveraging too much on unsubstantiated claims. When evaluating portfolios, readers can consider reflection as arguments or claims students make about their writing that are substantiated when accompanied by evidence, support, examples, explications, illuminations, and so on that appear in the portfolio artifacts. Claims without evidence are mere sentiments, while evidence without claims is trivial. In either case, this relationship between reflective text and portfolio artifacts provides readers with insights into the student's writing and thinking that can be used as part of the evaluation. Thinking of the relationship between reflective writing and portfolio artifacts this way moves away from students having to self-evaluate in a context that has high stakes for them (e.g., a course grade, placement into or out of a certain course, entrance into a program, etc.) when they may not have the evaluative expertise to make the decision and when they have a vested interest in the outcome. If the task instead is making descriptive claims about their writing, their learning, or/and their development, and they are required to provide textual support for those claims, students and readers alike are put in a more tenable position in which we can inquire as to the match between the claims and the evidence students produce. The decision about the students' writing is then based on this dialogic relationship between texts rather than on the students' ability to schmooze (Weiser 1997) effectively.

I also find myself influenced by Scott (2005) and O'Neill (2002), who warn of the hollowness of generic reflective cover letters. Most of the students to whom I assign portfolios these days are preparing them for the purposes of obtaining an internship, employment, or entrance into graduate school. In most of these contexts, students are rightly concerned about the role reflection might play for these external, authentic audiences, and I no longer insist that reflection is necessary for the portfolio. At the same time reflection is playing less of a role in my students' ePortfolios, it has gained importance in my teaching, becoming the most consistent and important element of my writing pedagogy.

Repeatedly in class, I ask students to reflect on what they are thinking and on choices they are making as composers at different stages in the development of a project. Here, for example, is a set of reflective questions students addressed when turning in a grammar/usage tutorial video project; there's a clear pattern of beginning with descriptive (*what*) questions before moving to evaluative (*why*) questions.

1. What was your topic? How did you choose it? How did you narrow or expand your focus to fit the assignment constraints?

2. What did you (have to) learn or review about the topic? How nuanced or challenging are the rules? Where did you go to verify the accuracy of your work?

3. What creative element(s) did you include to try to make the topic interesting or memorable? How effective do you think you were on this point?

4. What technology platform did you use? What did it allow you to do that you liked? What couldn't you do that you might have wanted to? To what extent was it the best choice for you on this project?

5. How satisfied are you with the accessibility of your work? To what extend do you think the video will be fully accessible regardless of (dis) ability?

6. If you could start over with this project, what would you do differently?

While this video project was not part of a larger portfolio evaluation in the class (though many students were completing a professional portfolio alongside the class), I did have students complete these questions as part of the evaluation process for this assignment. And for them, the first five in the list all corresponded with content we addressed in class throughout the assignment, so none of these questions was disconnected from their curricular experiences. The way students answered these questions was useful to me as I evaluated their work as well as the effectiveness of the assignment, and much of what appeared in the reflection would have been invisible to me were I only viewing the final video. For example, one student decided to develop her video on subjunctive moods (something I could tell through the video), but what I wouldn't have known is that her original plan was to include imperative and indicative moods as well. When she included that information in her reflection with a rationale for why she selected the subjunctive over the others, it provided insight for me on one of my assessment criteria: the ability to narrow in or focus on a topic for the scope of the video. The video itself, then, served as evidence for her claims. If I had watched the video and had seen it included multiple moods, I would not have noticed the disjuncture between her claims about focus and what she completed. On the other hand, if I had only viewed the video and not read any of her reflection, I wouldn't have known to look for that focus, and I wouldn't have known if the focus were intentional, planned, or rhetorically motivated. In the end I needed to read her reflection *and* view the video with the claims from the reflection in mind.

Examples like this come up each time I read a reflection in conjunction with a project or a portfolio. Students in my writing courses often compose portfolios with professional interests beyond the academy in mind. I prompt them during the semester to write reflections on their perceived audiences and how they might tailor the content of the portfolio to the audiences' needs and interests. In the final reflections that accompany the portfolio—most often these reflections are not included in the portfolio because I am the ultimate audience for the reflection but not the portfolio—they consider their regular reflections and write a meta-reflection that situates their work and explains how the decisions they made in the collection and selection speak to their understanding of audience(s). I may not always agree with students' choices or interpretations of evoked audiences, but the reflection gives me a sense of how they are or aren't thinking rhetorically, and it gives us a starting place for dialogue. It also keeps me as a teacher from making blanket assumptions about individuals or groups of students that I might make otherwise. For example, I remember a student a few semesters ago who had developed as an editor, but in her professional portfolio, she organized her work around creative-writing genres used in our department to organize its curriculum. My initial reaction to this organization was that it was all wrong: she was looking back at her coursework before changing majors rather than forward to internships and other professional possibilities. In her reflection, though, she wrote about wanting to be a fiction and poetry editor, and she thought this arrangement was the best way to establish her credibility as a writer. While I didn't completely agree with her approach, I understood her rationale far more than if I had just seen the portfolio (and who knows what I would have thought if I had just seen the reflection but not the portfolio?). From this point we negotiated a reorganization around these recognized divisions, but she also decided to include subcategories in her portfolio that differentiated her original work from the work she edited in each generic category. We got to this point through an exchange, in part, because her tasks included making an argument about rhetorical choices in the reflection and supporting them with artifacts in the portfolio. My job was to look at *both* reflection and artifacts to help her think through the effectiveness of her strategy. While this is only one example, time and time again when I contact students after they finish my courses and/or our program—I stay in touch with many through LinkedIn and other professional networking platforms—students say that shaping the portfolio for a nonacademic audience was the key to their transition from school to their careers.

It also might be worth noting in closing that few if any of the reflective questions I have students complete during the semester ask for direct or overt self-evaluation. Rather, the prompts tend toward asking them to articulate decisions they made while writing and assume they can provide a rhetorical rationale for their choices. Questions about the effectiveness of a decision or the strengths and weaknesses of textual features move toward self-assessment, but they aren't the primary focus and self-evaluation follows their descriptions. This purposeful effort to move reflection away from self-evaluation and toward description of rhetorical decision making, not unlike Jody Shipka's (2011) design of reflection, is one of the most important shifts in my thinking about reflection in my teaching with reflection and portfolios over the past two decades. This descriptive reflection accomplishes at least two purposes: (1) it reminds students consistently throughout our time together that they should have rhetorical reasons for the decisions they are making about their texts, and (2) it provides a running record, a commentary students can access later and consider as they attempt to make meaning of their development as writers. I've been collecting and analyzing these informal reflections from students for years, and I'm amazed at how many writers in my classes still have a hard time articulating rhetorical rationales for their decisions, even though such articulation is the primary focus of the class. Their rationale too often remains author-centric, citing their own likes, dislikes, preferences, and so on instead of looking outward toward authentic audiences and purposes. However, in noticing this inward focus through the reflective writing in relation to the other texts students produce, I have a platform to engage them in more outward thinking—as well as one for my evaluation of their work. Until students make and can articulate rhetorical choices, I am not confident that I'm doing my job well, even with the writers who otherwise produce relatively high-quality texts and portfolios. The only way I can gain insight into this way of thinking is through comparing their reflections and their compositions. Each plays a vital role in the relationship, which is why I don't believe that either can be discounted or elevated above the other.

References

Anson, Chris. 1994. "Portfolios for Teachers: Writing Our Way to Reflective Practice." In *New Directions in Portfolio Assessment: Reflective Practices, Critical Theory, and Large-Scale Scoring*, ed. Laurel Black, Donald A. Daiker, Jeffrey Sommers, and Gail Stygall, 185–200. Portsmouth, NH: Heinemann.

Anson, Chris. 2000. "Talking about Writing: A Classroom-Based Study of Students' Reflections on Their Drafts." In *Self-Assessment and Development in Writing: A Collaborative Inquiry*, ed. Jane Bowman Smith and Kathleen Blake Yancey, 59–74. Cresskill, NJ: Hampton.

Belanoff, Pat. 1994. "Portfolios and Literacy: Why?" In *New Directions in Portfolio Assessment: Reflective Practices, Critical Theory, and Large-Scale Scoring*, ed. Laurel Black, Donald A. Daiker, Jeffrey Sommers, and Gail Stygall, 13–24. Portsmouth, NH: Heinemann.

Belanoff, Pat, and Marcia Dickson, eds. 1991. *Portfolios: Process and Product*. Portsmouth, NH: Heinemann.

Belanoff, Pat, and Peter Elbow. 1991. "Using Portfolios to Increase Collaboration and Community in a Writing Program." In *Portfolios: Process and Product*, ed. Pat Belanoff and Marcia Dickson, 17–29. Portsmouth, NH: Heinemann.

Bishop, Wendy. 1990. "Designing a Writing Portfolio Evaluation System." *English Record* 40 (2): 21–25.

Black, Laurel, Donald A. Daiker, Jeffrey Sommers, and Gail Stygall, eds. 1994. *New Directions in Portfolio Assessment: Reflective Practices, Critical Theory, and Large-Scale Scoring*. Portsmouth, NH: Heinemann.

Bower, Laurel L. 2003. "Student Reflection and Critical Thinking." *Journal of Basic Writing* 22 (2): 47–66.

Broad, Bob. 1994. "'Portfolio Scoring': A Contradiction in Terms." In *New Directions in Portfolio Assessment: Reflective Practices, Critical Theory, and Large-Scale Scoring*, ed. Laurel Black, Donald A. Daiker, Jeffrey Sommers, and Gail Stygall, 263–76. Portsmouth, NH: Heinemann.

Broad, Bob. 2003. *What We Really Value: Beyond Rubrics in Teaching and Assessing Writing*. Logan: Utah State University Press.

Callahan, Susan. 2000. "Responding to the Invisible Student." *Assessing Writing* 7 (1): 57–77. http://dx.doi.org/10.1016/S1075-2935(00)00016-7.

Cirio, Joe. 2014. "The Promise of Negotiation: Situating Rubrics in the Fourth Wave of Writing Assessment." MA thesis, Florida State University, Tallahassee.

Elbow, Peter. 1994. "Will the Virtues of Portfolios Blind Us to Their Potential Dangers?" In *New Directions in Portfolio Assessment: Reflective Practices, Critical Theory, and Large-Scale Scoring*, ed. Laurel Black, Donald A. Daiker, Jeffrey Sommers, and Gail Stygall, 40–55. Portsmouth, NH: Heinemann.

Forbes, Cheryl. 1996. "Cowriting, Overwriting, and Overriding in Portfolio Land Online." *Computers and Composition* 13 (2): 195–205. http://dx.doi.org/10.1016/S8755-4615(96)90009-2.

Harding, Lindsey. 2014. "Writing Beyond the Page: Reflective Essay as Box Composition." *Teaching English in the Two-Year College* 41 (3): 239–55.

Hilgers, Thomas L., Edna L. Hussey, and Monica Stitt-Bergh. 2000. "The Case for Prompted Self-Assessment in the Writing Classroom." In *Self-Assessment and Development in Writing: A Collaborative Inquiry*, ed. Jane Bowman Smith and Kathleen Blake Yancey, 1–24. Cresskill, NJ: Hampton.

Hillocks, George., Jr. 1995. *Teaching Writing as Reflective Practice*. New York: Teacher College Press.

Huot, Brian. 1990. "Reliability, Validity, and Holistic Scoring: What We Know and What We Need to Know." *College Composition and Communication* 41 (2): 201–13. http://dx.doi.org/10.2307/358160.

Huot, Brian. 2002. *(Re)Articulating Writing Assessment for Teaching and Learning.* Logan: Utah State University Press.

Ihara, Rachel. 2014. "Student Perceptions on Self-Assessment: Insights and Implications." *Teaching English in the Two-Year College* 41 (3): 223–38.

Messick, Samuel. 1989. "Validity." In *Educational Measurement.* 3rd ed. Ed. Robert L. Linn, 13–103. New York: American Council on Education and Macmillan.

Moss, Pamela A. 1994. "Can There Be Validity without Reliability?" *Educational Researcher* 23 (2): 5–12. http://dx.doi.org/10.3102/0013189X023002005.

Murphy, Sandra. 1994. "Portfolios and Curriculum Reform: Patterns in Practice." *Assessing Writing* 1 (2): 175–206. http://dx.doi.org/10.1016/1075-2935(95)90022-5.

Murphy, Sandra, and Barbara Grant. 1996. "Portfolio Approaches to Assessment: Breakthrough or More of the Same?" In *Assessment of Writing: Politics, Policies and Practices,* ed. Edward M. White, William D. Lutz, and Sandra Kamusikiri, 284–300. New York: Modern Language Association.

Murray, Joddy. 2009. *Non-Discursive Rhetoric: Image and Affect in Multimodal Composition.* Albany: State University of New York Press.

O'Neill, Peggy. 2002. "Reflection and Assessment: Resisting Ritualistic Discourse." *The Writing Instructor.* http://bsuenglish101.pbworks.com/f/ONeill+Reflection+strategies+Excerpt.doc.

Scott, Tony. 2005. "Creating the Subject of Portfolios: Reflective Writing and the Conveyance of Institutional Prerogatives." *Written Communication* 22 (1): 3–35. http://dx.doi.org/10.1177/0741088304271831.

Shepard, Lorrie A. 1993. "Evaluating Test Validity." In *Review of Research in Education,* Vol. 19, ed. Linda Darling-Hammon. Washington, DC: AERA.

Shipka, Jody. 2011. *Toward a Composition Made Whole.* Pittsburgh, PA: University of Pittsburgh Press.

Smith, Jane Bowman, and Kathleen Blake Yancey, eds. 2000. *Self-Assessment and Development in Writing: A Collaborative Inquiry.* Cresskill, NJ: Hampton.

Sommers, Jeffrey. 1989. "The Writer's Memo: Collaboration, Response, and Development." In *Writing and Response: Theory, Practice, and Research,* ed. Chris M. Anson, 174–86. Urbana, IL: NCTE.

Sommers, Jeffrey. 2011. "Reflection Revisited: The Class Collage." *Journal of Basic Writing* 30 (1): 99–129.

Weiser, Irwin. 1992. "Portfolio Practice and Assessment for Collegiate Basic Writers." In *Portfolios in the Writing Classroom: An Introduction,* ed. Kathleen Blake Yancey, 89–101. Urbana, IL: NCTE.

Weiser, Irwin. 1997. "Revising Our Practices: How Portfolios Help Teachers Learn." In *Situating Portfolios: Four Perspectives,* ed. Kathleen Blake Yancey and Irwin Weiser, 293–301. Cresskill, NJ: Hampton.

White, Edward M. 2005. "The Scoring of Writing Portfolios: Phase 2." *College Composition and Communication* 56 (4): 581–600.

Williamson, Michael. 1994. "The Worship of Efficiency: Untangling Theoretical and Practical Considerations in Writing Assessment." *Assessing Writing* 1 (2): 147–73. http://dx.doi.org/10.1016/1075-2935(95)90021-7.

Yancey, Kathleen Blake. 1992. *Portfolios in the Writing Classroom: An Introduction.* Urbana, IL: NCTE.

Yancey, Kathleen Blake, ed. 1998. *Reflection in the Writing Classroom.* Logan: Utah State University Press.

5

REFLECTING PRACTICES
Competing Models of Reflection in the Rhetoric of Prior Learning Assessment

Cathy Leaker and Heather Ostman

In 2010, in an article for *College Composition and Communication* (*CCC*), we made the claim that the potentially productive nexus between composition and prior learning assessment (PLA) enabled by reflection might herald composition's "new key," that is, a mutually supportive and renewed relationship between literate practices within and outside the academy (Leaker and Ostman 2010). In this chapter, we revisit the relationship between composition, reflection, and PLA and argue, first, that composition has a vested—and increasingly urgent—interest in current PLA discourses and, second, that reflective technologies are central to sustaining that interest. At the same time, we point out the limitations of both composition and reflection in setting the parameters of college-level learning, and we conclude by arguing for multiple alternative mechanisms with which to articulate learning and by urging compositionists to contribute to shaping such methods.

In tracing this argument, we describe three very different models of prior learning assessment and their connection to reflective practices. The first, the exchange model of PLA, dominates recent PLA policy discourses (i.e., the Gates Foundation, MOOCs, and others) and essentially asks students to exchange their knowledge, skills, and competencies for credit—they demonstrate their knowledge either through standardized tests or externally validated certificates—that meet *predefined* standards. The second, the rhetorical-reflective transfer model of PLA, invites students to combine guided reflections on their experiential learning with rhetorical strategies and documentary artifacts in order to *translate and transfer* what they have learned—demonstrated through a carefully constructed portfolio—to earn the equivalent of college course credits. The

DOI: 10.7330/9781607325161.c005

third, the reflective response model of PLA, growing out of adult education scholars' critiques (i.e., Fenwick 2006; Hamer 2010) of reflection as overly rationalist and individualist, emphasizes the co-PLA construction of both knowledge and assessment on the part of student(s) and assessor(s).

MODELS OF PLA AND ASSOCIATED REFLECTION

Much has happened since our article "Composing Knowledge: Writing, Rhetoric, and Reflection in Prior Learning Assessment" appeared in *CCC*, primarily that prior learning assessment (PLA) has assumed a much greater prominence in higher education discourses than we could possibly have imagined in 2010. *Prior learning assessment* is a broad term designating a series of practices through which students' learning acquired outside accredited colleges is assessed for, and can be awarded, college credit. The most prominent assessment mechanisms are standardized exams, certification of training programs by organizations like the American Council on Education (ACE) and the National College Credit Recommendation Service (NCCRS), and individualized portfolios. Buttressed by an enormously influential 2010 Council for Adult and Experiential Learning (CAEL) study showing a high correlation between earned PLA credits and graduation rates, interest in PLA has over the past three years exploded in higher-education policy discourses, with both government policymakers at the federal and state level and influential funding agencies trumpeting its capacity to aid college completion and contain costs (Fain 2012b). Yet while PLA's increasing prominence in national conversations might appear to vindicate the position we took in 2010, it is not at all clear that the embrace of PLA by organizations such as the Gates Foundation translates into advocacy of, or even allowance for, the kinds of reflective composing practices we outlined. Indeed, as PLA critics like Gary Rhoades are quick to point out, much of the current push for PLA is seemingly less about enhancing access, much less improving the quality of teaching and learning, than it is about "reduc[ing] accountability to simply counting more completers faster" (quoted in Fain 2012c). The fact that the push for PLA is coming from organizations like Complete College America, which are also spearheading the attack on remediation, might serve as further evidence that compositionists should be wary of wholeheartedly embracing PLA.

Still, PLA's capacity to serve dangerous agendas—among them the continued defunding of public higher education, the unbundling of teaching, learning, and assessment, and the critique of the credit hour—is not in and of itself reason to share Rhoades's conclusion that its expansion *necessarily* "prioritizes stamping students as certified over providing them with a quality education" (quoted in Fain 2012c). Although we may today assert it with greater caution, we stand by our 2010 claim that PLA practices can *both* certify legitimate college-level learning *and* enable the provision of quality education to a wider variety of students. PLA's ability to successfully do both is to some extent dependent on the particular PLA mechanism invoked and on the students' responsibility for not only documenting but actually articulating the learning for which they are seeking credit. It is not necessarily true, in other words, that PLA, as Johann Neem claims, "fails to take stock of the sophisticated thinking and original ideas that come from real college level learning" (quoted in Fain 2012a). On the contrary, as we argued in 2010, PLA processes like individualized portfolios, which encourage reflection, writing, critical thinking, and other academic competencies, thus engage with the important rhetorical work of bridging academic and workplace (or community or civic) discourses. For us, PLA practices are at their best when they function, *by design*, simultaneously to challenge and integrate traditional divisions of knowledge.

To unpack this point further, we need to first be more precise about our terms since PLA is an umbrella term for a wide range of strategies, expectations, and underlying ideological assumptions and distinguish the different levels of commitment that any version of PLA might make to reflection as an explicit part of the PLA process. So with all due caveats about the necessarily distorting function of any schematic representation, a spectrum of PLA mechanisms (linked to an almost-but-not-quite-parallel spectrum of the conceptual models we identified at the beginning of our analysis) might result in something like Table 5.1.

In this representation, the far left-hand side of the spectrum represents those PLA practices that seem to demand little to no reflection on the part of the student. Thus, while transcripted college credit may have demanded considerable reflective learning in order for credit to be *awarded*, student reflection is rarely endemic to the process of *transferring* that credit from one institutional context to another. Similarly, although assessment of training programs and certifications might well involve the kinds of "reflection-in-action" described by Schon (1984) and others, that reflective activity is performed at the level of organizational review by accrediting bodies like the American Council for Education and the National College Credit Recommendation Service; students are responsible only for presenting a certification that they have successfully

Table 5.1

Exchange				Reflective-Rhetorical Transfer			
Transfer of Transcript Credit from Accredited Postsecondary Institutions	Professional and Vocational Training Programs pre-evaluated by National Organizations	Qualifications Frameworks	Standardized Exams (CLEP, DANTExcelsior)	Non accredited Classroom learning (MOOCs; Continuing Education)	Portfolio to Demonstrate Professional Competencies	Portfolio to Demonstrate Learning Outcomes of College Course	Portfolio to Demonstrate Broad Academic Learning Outcomes or Competencies

Minimally Reflective <——> Highly Reflective

completed the program. National Qualifications Standards (or NQFs) that have gained such a purchase on educational discourses in Europe, Africa, and Latin America are more fraught. On the one hand, they are highly complicated differentiated inventories of skills and abilities, and applicants are often expected to use portfolios to document their achievements relative to the frameworks. On the other hand, NQFs nevertheless purport to offer a streamlined and simple process of assessment; as Patrick Werquin argues in his review of the literature on qualifications frameworks, "Assessment [of vocational education and training] is usually relatively straightforward, competence standards are not difficult to elaborate, and labor market needs and qualification shortages can be readily calibrated" (Werquin 2014, 98). Werquin's language here is instructive even if the claim is somewhat dubious; exchange models of PLA connected to workplace learning and training are often beholden to a human-capital theory of knowledge in which the function of the educational sector is to provide—though a "relatively straightforward" methodology—both the competencies and the credentialing that will best serve the needs of the labor market. Such assumptions underwrite the increasing significance of PLA exchange models policy discourses; in their apparent simplicity and transparency, they promise a prior learning assessment with the greatest potential for scalability, the greatest presumptive accountability, and, not incidentally, the greatest economic utility (Boilard 2011).

While we certainly agree that exchange models are necessary parts of any institution's approach to PLA insofar as they both support the transfer of learning from one context to another and facilitate the articulation of knowledge into the currency of credit, we are deeply concerned that their dominance will minimize—or worse, invalidate—other kinds of PLA practices that, for us, offer greater value to both students and institutions. Too often exchange models offer reductive evaluations of knowledge production and risk precluding the breadth and complexity of prior knowledges students may present, particularly because these models ignore the contexts in which learning has occurred. Moreover, we worry about the ways in which exchange practices buttress two common and very dangerous misrepresentations of PLA, both of which threaten to shift PLA from a tool of access and inclusion to a mechanism Judy Harris calls "alternative (maybe ultimately crueler) forms of exclusion" (Harris 1999, 132): Stephen Boilard, director of higher education for the California Legislative Analyst's Office, expresses a similar view, boldly outlining widespread but flawed assumptions in a 2011 opinion piece for *Change* magazine. He suggests that "PLA certifies learning that meets prescribed criteria and standards and rejects the rest" and that "the whole point of PLA is that the structure, nature and source of one's learning is largely irrelevant" (Boilard 2011, 57–58).

We contest the absolutism of both claims. If PLA is to provide access to a college education by legitimating alternative pathways, as we believe it should, not all criteria and standards can be determined in advance; there must be room for students to compose a case for various kinds of learning (emergent, subjugated, situated) that do not meet a prescribed set of expectations but may still, after a careful process of reflection, articulation, and assessment, be awarded credit for *college-level* learning. Equally important, while it is true that PLA affords at least the possibility of assessing learning from any source, at any time, and by any method, it does not follow from this structure, nature, and source that the contexts of learning are irrelevant. Rather, as we argued in 2010, context and a student's attention to context are fundamental to PLA practices *not* built on exchange. Indeed, the imperative for students to *compose context* while petitioning for PLA credit was the basis of our initial advocacy for portfolio-based PLA and serves as the primary feature distinguishing exchange PLA practices from PLA practices based in what we are calling *reflective-rhetorical transfer.*

PLA, CONTEXT, AND REFLECTIVE-RHETORICAL TRANSFER

When we advocated for the potential of PLA to enrich, and possibly transform, composition studies, our argument was framed through the lens of reflective practices, particularly where contextualized learning was central in the composition of the PLA petitioner's text. Context, according to Kathleen Blake Yancey, "is what allows us to understand, to interpret, to make meaning . . . the idea of context allows us to interpret, to represent, in many ways, simultaneously" (Yancey 2004, 741). Similarly, despite the claims of recent PLA converts like Boilard, researchers have known for years that context, especially social context, plays a key role in the acquisition of knowledge in adulthood. In *Learning in Adulthood*, for example, Sharan Merriam, Rosemary Caffarella, and Lisa Baumgartner stress the role social context plays in learning, particularly three main factors that shape adult learning: demographics, globalization, and technology (Merriam, Caffarella, and Baumgartner 2007, 21–26). The authors' emphasis underlines the socially developed cognitive competencies developed by adults, as seen in the following example about work with recipients of welfare: "In working with welfare recipients, for example, instructors might recognize that parents on welfare have had to learn how to take care of children on very constrained budgets, keep their families safe and healthy under difficult living conditions and in general make do with very little. Rather than asking questions about how they have learned to do this successfully, what is focused on most is their lack of formal education and skills training. Formal schooling and skills training are important, but so are the ways they have informally learned about life skills that have kept them and their families fed and clothed" (27–28).

Merriam, Caffarella, and Baumgartner (2007) foreground the welfare recipients' abilities here by outlining how they gain situated knowledge within the context of caring for families and managing budgets under very onerous circumstances. The authors challenge the primacy of "formal schooling"—and, we argue, Boilard's assumptions—by not only arguing that welfare recipients demonstrate substantial learning outside of an educational institution, but also outlining four locations where learning can occur, with formal institutions as only one of the four. The other three are nonformal settings, informal contexts, and online learning, although this last category may overlap with the others (29). Nonformal settings are "organized learning opportunities outside the formal education system," including community-based and indigenous learning (Merriam, Caffarella, and Baumgartner 2007, 30), whereas informal learning is knowledge acquired spontaneously in homes, neighborhoods, workplaces, markets, and "through the various mass media" (Coombs quoted in Merriam, Caffarella, and Baumgartner 2007, 35). We are interested here in the nonformal and informal contexts, which are where 90 percent of adults spend hundreds of hours informally learning and which host opportunities for learning that is the most challenging for adults to recognize and to articulate (Merriam, Caffarella, and Baumgartner 2007, 35). Thus, for composition scholars and adult-education researchers alike, context, far from being irrelevant, provides a necessary framework for articulating learning.

The notion of contextualized learning easily links to Yancey's categorical contexts for knowledge construction and knowledge evaluation. In 2010, we drew heavily from her work on portfolios and categorized student PLA narratives in terms of the contexts Yancey articulates, specifically within the temporal, spatial, and political realms. We knew all too well what the first context could elicit from PLA petitioners; Yancey writes that this first context of the temporal realm is a linear articulation of knowledge, one that expresses what the student first knew and then leads to what they now know (Yancey 2004, 741). For example, the first draft of "Cleaning an Antique Map," an essay by our adult student Ralph, who works at a high-end antique and map dealer in New York City, demonstrates the linear context Yancey identifies: "In this essay, I will describe the procedures for cleaning an antique map on paper. An antique map on paper is a printed image on paper that was made at least 100 years ago. When I first started at my company, I was just an art handler, which is just a glorified way of saying I was in charge of shipping all antique maps. But through my experience working with the maps, I began to learn there were special ways for cleaning paper—something I didn't even know before I started." In his opening paragraph of an essay written as part of his PLA application for college credits in the area of paper conservation, Ralph signals that he will be discussing his knowledge through a linear narrative that identifies what he did not know before and then what he knows now through his experience. The merits of such an approach include positing the students as the agents, the self-directed learners who have not necessarily set learning goals for themselves but who have acquired knowledge as needed for their work. The rhetorical approach here is narrative, but the text demonstrates little awareness of an audience, particularly one already empowered by the institution.

The second context we also often encountered occurs when students engage the spatial context, which broadens the framework for understanding a student's knowledge. In this context, knowledge does not necessarily appear to be acquired in a linear way; instead, the student uses compare and contrast to show that "what she learns in one setting, a class or a service learning setting, for example, [connects to] what she is learning in another class" (Yancey 2004, 741). Ralph's later drafts include the spatial realm, which add another rhetorical dimension of compare and contrast, but this time, his narrative demonstrates an awareness of his audience, in particular, an audience situated within the academy's walls: "In this essay, I will describe the procedures for cleaning an antique map on paper. An antique map on paper is a printed image on paper that was made at least 100 years ago. Although I read advice from paper conservation websites, much of my knowledge about map cleaning comes from experience—which is not taught in colleges. Handling the paper, cleaning it, whether it is by dry cleaning or wet cleaning or a combination of both, is something no one can teach you in a classroom. Your hands need to be acquainted with the texture of the paper, your nose needs to be familiar with the smells of paper." In this later draft, Ralph offers a contrast in the way he learned to clean antique paper, the ways he read about the process online, and the way he imagines it would be taught in a classroom. During a conference with his faculty mentor, he had indicated that his job had been a "hands-on" learning experience, so while he would look up procedures online for guidance, he came to understand that trusting his own experience of the process—also through much trial and error—emerged as his best teacher in his field. Thus, in his narrative above, he suggests that learning this process experientially is more meaningful because of the senses—here, sight and smell—that are engaged.

In addition, Ralph begins to make the gesture toward Yancey's third context, the sociopolitical realm, when he asserts the legitimacy of his knowledge in comparison to that articulated by websites and possibly institutions. His claims to knowledge demonstrate an authority his first draft omitted. In this later draft, Ralph has left out the narrative arc the linear context anticipates: what I didn't know then, and what I know now. In other words, he has avoided the representation of himself as someone who knows nothing, even though he did not know how to clean antique maps until he was faced with the actual task. As he writes,

> In my ten years as a paper conservationist, I have learned through experience the best ways for handling an antique map, and many of these techniques are best learned through "doing," as opposed to being taught in a textbook or in a classroom. As the in-house paper conservator for an antique map and book dealer, I work with antique maps, which are maps that are printed image on paper made at least 100 years ago. Although I read advice from paper conservation websites, much of my knowledge about map cleaning comes from experience. Handling the paper, cleaning it, whether it is by dry cleaning or wet cleaning or a combination of both, is something no one can teach you in a classroom. Your hands need to be acquainted with the texture of the paper; your nose needs to be familiar with the smells of paper. . . .

> In order to properly wet clean an antique map, there are certain key materials needed, including a large sink or basin, water, and a clear polyester mesh material called Remay, and then the process may begin. First, fill the basin with a half inch of water. The map must be supported from underneath before placing it into the water. To do this, I use the Remay, which should be larger than the map. This material is often used to cover the underside of sofas, chairs, and box springs. Remay is used because it is very strong but thin, water flows through it, and one has something besides the map to grab when removing the map from the bath. . . . Again, I must emphasize how important it is to be extremely careful while handling the map at this stage. Because the map is wet, it is in a very vulnerable state. It is essentially turning into pulp, and can therefore be damaged much more easily than if the sheet was dry.

In his final draft, Ralph employs several rhetorical strategies at the same time he engages the spatial and sociopolitical contexts of his actual text. Here, he primarily engages narrative, definition, comparison/contrast, and process analysis in his rendering of his knowledge of antique-map cleaning. Although he shifts from the first person to the third ("one"), his text is structurally narrative, but it has now completely abandoned the linear mode. In addition to the narrative rhetorical mode, he employs definition: Remay, he explains, is "a clear polyester mesh material." His focus is on articulating his knowledge within the social context of his work and the institutional context of the academy. To articulate the distinctions, he uses the rhetorical modes of comparison and contrast: he contrasts the acquisition of his knowledge with what he imagines can be learned by reading or in a classroom, and he deepens this contrast in the opening sentence: "In my ten years as a paper conservationist, I have learned through experience the best ways for handling an antique map, and many of these techniques are best learned through 'doing,' as opposed to being taught in a textbook or in a classroom." Again, his affirmation of learning through the senses, not only through conventional definitions of intellectual engagement, affirms the *way* he has learned, which he asserts does not occur in traditional classrooms. Finally, he employs the rhetorical mode of process analysis as he shifts the narrative focus to the procedure for cleaning a map, and throughout his rendering of the work, he continually reminds the reader of the value of his experiential knowledge with statements such as, "Again, I must emphasize how important it is to be extremely careful while handling the map at this stage. Because the map is wet, it is in a very vulnerable state. It is essentially turning into pulp, and can therefore be damaged much more easily than if the sheet was dry." Notably, Ralph's experiential knowledge has made him an expert, so his authority on the subject emerges, particularly as he is able to articulate that knowledge by using the rhetorical conventions of composition.

Of course, we were most gratified when we could help a student like Ralph—or better yet, observe him getting there himself—to manifest Yancey's third context, which also demonstrates the sociopolitical importance for our students as subordinated learners. In this context, students articulate not only their learning but also reflection about their relationship to the institution (Yancey 2004, 741). In the final example above, Ralph does this without reference to a predetermined set of criteria for map cleaning. A predetermined set of criteria found in standardized tests for prior knowledge runs the risk of precluding the full understanding and depth of a student's knowledge on a subject. Context enables Ralph to articulate his knowledge at the same time he recognizes the authority of the academy, but also—and this is key—it allows him to affirm his situated or experiential knowledge as valid knowledge within the context of the institution. In other words, it enables Ralph to assert what he knows as legitimate within a context that might not ordinarily recognize his authority as a learner. Notably, he asserts his authority in a context that, while potentially affirming, is *not* radically open ended; indeed when done effectively, rhetorical reflection sets appropriate boundaries to his learning, prompting him to focus less on revealing personal experiences or doubts and focusing instead on the production of knowledge or the acquiring of knowledge, certainly a challenging distinction. Similarly, rhetorical reflection pushes students like Ralph to engage in reflective *writing*—in which reflection denotes both content and process—as a process intrinsically linked to knowledge production and assessment of that knowledge.

PLA PRACTICE AS REFLECTIVE RESPONSE

It is tempting to rest our case here, positing Ralph as both the exemplar and the proof of our 2010 dual claim for reflective-rhetorical PLA practice, specifically that it "supports and empowers those adult and returning students who are too often excluded from our collective imagined university and whose writing needs, therefore, are not always well served by our imagined curricula. Second, whether or not institutions award experiential learning credit, PLA texts make visible the challenges all students face as they seek to acquire the kind of versatile writing expertise that will sustain them both inside and outside the academy" (Leaker and Ostman 2010, 692). And yet, our own reflections since 2010, particularly as external contexts and our own professional roles shift, have made us loathe to suggest that any one method, let alone any one student, can serve as an exemplar of ideal PLA practice. Certainly we remain confident that reflective-rhetorical PLA practices provide students and institutional agents with richer opportunities for development than practices rooted in exchange because the rhetorical reflection, as we have shown, both enables the development of academic skills *and* challenges their exclusivity. However, we now argue that to engage students fully in the latter, we might need to build a space for an approach in which a reflective response shapes knowledge claims at least as much as does guided reflection or rhetorical strategy.

In making this assertion, we have consciously decided *not* to locate reflective response on chart above and *not* to suggest that there is an optimal reflective space that can empower students, support academic development, and push the academy toward a more dialogic engagement with the communities outside its still too-delimited boundaries. Responsive reflection, as a mode, demands that we distrust a PLA schema that traces a trajectory from complicit PLA (credit exchange) to earnest PLA (rhetorical reflection) to save-the-world—or at least higher education—PLA (reflective response). Thus, we locate responsive reflection *outside* the neat chart of PLA models and reflective practices altogether in order to emphasize that *this* PLA represents less an ideal version of PLA, or even a viable alternative to other approaches, than a kind of Other(ed) space that exposes by transgressing the limits of current PLA models, pushes those practices toward more inclusive epistemologies, and forces us to confront less-than-comfortable considerations (beyond cost effectiveness and beyond academic quality) of ethics and responsibility.

In making this claim, we are heavily influenced by the work of adult educators like Judy Harris (2006) and Tara Fenwick (2006), many of whom have raised particular concerns about reflection as a regulatory practice. What haunts us most about their work, especially at this historical moment, is encapsulated in Fenwick's query: "How can alterity and care for others be understood" in a complex educational environment? (Fenwick 2006, 8). As PLA becomes more entrenched in the higher-education landscape and questions about its legitimacy, scalability, and funding surface, we worry that a question like Fenwick's too easily fades into the background. That is to say, we can become so bogged down in the transactional rhetoric of who's getting credit for what that we can no longer hear the student's too-frequent, and often too-unrhetorical, question, "How many credits is my life worth?" Undoubtedly such a question belies the complexity of PLA and fails to appropriately mark the distinction between experience and learning, even as the promotion of PLA opportunities to an untapped market of adult learners cynically begs this very question. But to dismiss the question of life and worth is to ignore the importance of alterity and care for others by refusing to explicitly engage the one question we have come to believe an ethical and responsible PLA must engage.

In an odd way, reflection (at least as we've characterized it here) distracts us from asking ourselves questions about alterity *and* care for others in the PLA context. Or rather it prompts us to ask and answer such questions in a very particular way. After all, in most PLA models, reflective technologies are mobilized at the moment(s) of a student's articulation of their experiential learning rather than at the moment(s) of institutional assessment of that learning. As such, the goal of guided reflective practice (guided by instructors, it's worth remembering) in the reflective PLA encounter is to help students develop and support the claim, whether through positivist assertions of equivalence or more sophisticated rhetorical persuasion, that one's experiential learning meets a more or less clear standard of college-level learning. Crudely put, the approach to *alterity* in this model is to encourage students to reflectively reframe it so it becomes visible as academic credit. In the same way, and because such reframing is intellectually challenging, *caring for others* is signaled by a capacity and a willingness to guide students, perhaps most especially "at-risk" students, through a winding, layered, but ultimately teleological path toward "competence," not just in a particular knowledge domain but in the realm of academic skills as well. Far be it from us to protest too much against skill development, particularly when it is embedded in a practice that can have so much material benefit and emotional resonance for students. But at the same time, we must wonder whether in our zeal to care, which in this case becomes a zeal to guide, we are less able or willing to *be guided* by the learning unfolding in the immediate and particular moment of the PLA encounter.

And here it may be useful to return very briefly to concerns adult educators have raised about reflection's role in shaping experiential leaning. As summarized by Tara Fenwick, critical accounts of reflection—particularly in the context of assessment—point to the distortions created by its "individualistic, acquisitive, psychologized and mentalist" assumptions about learning (Fenwick 2009, 230). Building on a perhaps oversimplified understanding of the Deweyan principle, this understanding argues that "raw" experience, in order to become learning, must be first processed through a cognitive mill, where dominant academic approaches to reflection (most especially David Kolb's highly influential model of reflective learning cycle) carry a "rational-ist, instrumental bias" (Jordi 2011). That unacknowledged bias is then reproduced in normative terms that have more to do with abstract models of "good thinking" than with necessarily messy and all-too-overdetermined learning processes (Jordi 2011). As a result, so the critics claim, much situated learning is actively suppressed because noncognitive sources of learning—intuitions, emotions, bodily felt sense, and so on—are either overlooked or lost in translation. Further, because the reflective encounter is represented as a moment of self-development/self-realization rather than as itself an effect of uneven sociomaterial power relations, learners are more inclined, as Fenwick's research with inservice teachers and pharmacists demonstrates, "to adapt to institutions of governance and knowledge rather than trans-forming them, and. . . focus on performing correctly rather than chal-lenging norms of performance" (Fenwick 2009, 230). To return to the final draft of Ralph's PLA petition, where he suggests his knowledge in part has been learned through the use of his senses, a less prescrip-tive use of reflection in this instance might have enabled him to bet-ter assert the primacy of bodily felt sense in the process of his learn-ing; however, it is subordinated still to the adapted articulation of that learning within the context of the academy.

Given these limitations, scholars like Fenwick advocate the cultivation of alternatives to reflection while others like Richard Jordi simply urge for more expansive and integrative reflective models. Whether they pro-pose to reject or rehabilitate reflection, however, these scholars share a conviction that educational institutions must create spaces that afford the emergence of different ways of knowing and that educators must develop the skills to recognize such knowing even if it can't easily be rec-onciled with academic norms. Drawing inspiration from disciplines like activity theory, neuroscience, actor network theory, queer theory, com-plexity science, and ecology, scholars describe these imagined spaces and skills sets in multiple ways, all of which are conceptually linked by what Fenwick (2006, 21), riffing on the work of Jerzy Grotowki, calls "poor pedagogies." That is to say, they eschew fixed trajectories, stan-dardized processes, and universal outcomes in favor of attention to the immediate, the micro, and the emergent; for Fenwick, such pedagogies are "rooted more in local needs, worries, desires and imaginings than overarching radical visions" (19). Similarly the "skills" that might enable these spaces are not so much skills per se, at least in the sense of broadly replicable best practices, as they are capacities for responsive presence: attunement, intuition, focusing, dialoguing, and listening.

It is in this latter sense that the suggestions of adult-education theorists echo Krista Ratcliffe's call for "rhetorical listening" (Ratcliffe 1999, 195). For Ratcliffe, the scholarly and pedagogical elevation of reading over listening produced an impoverished interpretive discourse, a discourse focused on textual mastery rather open dialogue. Arguing that because listening relied on "different body organs, different disciplinary and cultural assumptions and different figures of speech than reading," Ratcliffe suggests that a commitment to rhetorical listening on the part of scholars and teachers could open new spaces in which the we might "choose to hear the exiled excess and contemplate its relation to our culture and ourselves" (203). Important to note is that Ratcliffe identifies "rhetorical listening" as a tool of "cross-cultural conduct," a tool not only for negotiating but for recognizing difference. For her, the value of this tool lies in its capacity to generate understanding(s). As she explains, understanding(s) borne of this process might be different in kind than traditional academic understanding: "To clarify this process of understanding we might best invert the term and define understanding as standing under—consciously standing under discourses that surround us and others, while acknowledging all our particular and fluid standpoints. Standing under discourses means letting discourses wash over, through and around us and then letting them lie there to inform our politics and ethics" (205). Ratcliffe's advocacy of rhetorical listening thus shares a disposition of humility—of "poverty" in Fenwick's terms— with adult educators critical of reflection's grander narratives. This humble disposition includes a deliberate effort to let go as a necessary but insufficient criteria for a receptivity that in turn enables ethical response and just action.

Yet, as valid and indeed crucial as such arguments were and are for the field of composition specifically and higher education more broadly, an inclination to "stand under the discourse of others" does not easily map onto reflective practice. That mapping is even more fraught when reflection itself—of whatever variety—is situated in the high-stakes market of prior learning assessment. Nonetheless it *is* possible to imagine how such a stance might be implemented in discrete PLA contexts, and perhaps of greater importance, what new affordances might be created as a result. In order to do so, we must return to the student who, having engaged in the requisite self-reflection, is dismayed to discover that their "life is not worth any credit." As we've discussed, it's rather cold comfort to point out to the student that the academy is assessing only their learning, not their life. The very concept of experiential learning, after all, conflates the two in ways difficult to unravel. But the dilemma here is not merely an affective one of soothing bruised egos or even the pedagogical one of developing PLA protocols that first do no harm; rather, if we take Fenwick, Ratcliffe, and others seriously, we can listen to this student's voice in conscious acknowledgment of what Ratcliffe, citing Rayner, calls "the limitations of [our] own imaginary version of self and other" and thereby "fold the gaze of assessment back on itself" (Ratcliffe 1999, 207).

And it is in this context of reflection on institutional mis(sed)recognition that a humbly responsive PLA can also be also a tool of cross-cultural conduct. The oft-cited CAEL study definitively linking earned PLA credits to increased retention has played no small role in PLA's increasing prominence in government and funding circles. What is less frequently noted is that the award of PLA credit has a proportionally greater impact on women and people of color even as people of color are awarded fewer credits with less frequency than whites. These data need to be analyzed further, but we might safely draw a preliminary conclusion that those who might benefit the most from PLA have the least access to its advantages. Undoubtedly, a number of factors contribute to any given population's access to PLA processes, let alone PLA awards, but it stands to reason that access for underrepresented groups can be enhanced if PLA practices deliberately and explicitly cultivate openness to difference.

PLA, COMPOSITION, AND THE ELUSIVE PROMISE OF EQUITY

The dual hypothesis that PLA's advantages are not distributed equitably among all groups and that a more deliberately open PLA strategy might provide at least partial redress became the basis of the Women of Color and PLA workshop series that was developed and implemented with Cathy Leaker by Empire State College faculty mentor Frances Boyce in the college's two downstate locations 2013. The stated aim of the project was to create what Soloranzo et al. call a "counterspace" in which women of color could together explore their experiential learning in a context in which "deficit notions of people of color could be challenged," thus rearticulating their learning in relation not only to abstract notions of college-level standards but also to the politics of gender and race (Soloranzo et al. 2000, 70).

In the first iteration of the workshop series, the faculty/administrative facilitators (re)discovered the value of listening as a mechanism for surfacing new areas of student learning. Rhetorical practices such as storytelling, interviewing, and clustering (rather than guided reflective prompts) drew our attention to richly integrative learning that did not easily map onto a college curriculum, but that *did* map onto the kind of "outsider within" learning that Patricia Hill Collins (1986) claims is a particular and vital source of knowledge for women of color. In her now classic "Learning from the Outsider Within: The Sociological Significance of Black Feminist Thought," Collins argues that marginalized social locations create the opportunity for marginalized subjects—like women of color—in those locations to *achieve* a distinct "standpoint" with respect to dominant-knowledge claims. For Collins, that standpoint not only exposes the gaps and biases within taken-for-granted knowledge, but is itself generative of new and different knowledge. Other feminists of color, especially those working within critical race theory, have built on Collins's work to more precisely delineate the terrain of that new and different knowledge (Collins 1986). Tara Yosso (2005), for example, has developed a taxonomy of community cultural wealth among minority communities, a taxonomy that especially resonated with the learning experiences our students shared with us with us and with each other. While neither Collins (1986) nor Yosso (2005) explicitly conceptualizes these resources of knowledge in terms of outcomes and credit awards, they certainly assert their relation to academic ways of knowing, either, as in Collins's case, as correctives, or as in Yosso's case, as sites of resilience necessary for academic success. So it does not seem too far-fetched to suggest that such learning could be assessed for college credit.

What does seem far-fetched is that dominant PLA practices are equipped to see, recognize, and assess such learning because a commitment to humble listening also told us a good deal about the impediments many students—but especially students of color—experience throughout the PLA process. Listening to our students in the Women of Color and PLA project made us aware of how the PLA encounter can *feel* to students of color. For instance, while we as facilitators were eager to present PLA as an opportunity, a few of the women in the group experienced our efforts as a racially charged challenge, even a threat. Certainly many students who participate in the PLA process express anxiety about whether or not their learning will be seen and whether or not it will "count" as credit, but the women of color in the workshop acknowledged more extreme and global feelings of self-doubt in regards to their learning, while even the most confident workshop students articulated a fear that their learning might *be taken away from them.* Students also explicitly linked feelings of both self-doubt and fear to America's historicized racial politics; a few students went even further by suggesting that only such historicized understanding—and a concomitant analysis of social labels—enabled them to trust their capacity to articulate their learning in the first place.

The point here is not so much to argue the racial politics of PLA— Leaker and Boyce (2015) will be making this argument elsewhere—as it is to *stand under the student's discourse* in order to better respond to their learning and to their experiences of learning. In standing under discursive resistance of women of color to pervasive their Othering, we remind ourselves both that learning is always produced and assessed in the context of power relations according to which some people are understood as Other, and, as important, that their experience of Otherness both shapes their relationship to dominant forms of knowledge and constitutes its own rich pool of knowledge. Standing under another's discourse urges us to attend to the crucial distinction between decontextualized prescriptions to reflect on learning and listening to what is elided when a student says it's hard to claim her learning when she constantly sees herself devalued. Of course standing under—or listening to—the discourse(s) of others is not the same as awarding credit for college-level learning, but it *is* a necessary if not sufficient condition of recognizing learning that neither reflection nor rhetoric alone can perceive.

In 2010, we anticipated that reflective practice, particularly if we were mindful of Yancey's realms of context, could inform PLA practice as well as composition studies; in fact, we were very optimistic that the two disciplines might inform each other. Events in higher education and our professional experiences over the last five years have shifted our thinking. The PLA we described recognized the learning students were bringing to the college but in a context that provided an academic value added—certainly a value added to students but, on a more fundamental level, a value added to the academy. We still support portfolio PLA and advocate for its benefits, but we are more attuned to the not-so-subtle hubris in our original vision as well as to the values—such as alterity and care for others—that vision unwittingly excluded. And we are certainly aware that the context for our advocacy has expanded to include players, forces, and political agendas well beyond our capacity to predict, much less control.

At the same time, however much we might want to decry the seeming instrumentalism of those larger forces, we—and we mean *we* here to be professional academics, including those of us who specialize in composition at whatever level—share some of the blame for its ascension. More and more of the adult students we encounter lately have been persuaded that academic institutions can give them something they desperately need—a degree—but only at the price of something, like reflection, which they can't afford in either time or money. We have come to believe that the ethical response to such concerns is to take them seriously, to respond to them by saying (in multiple ways, across multiple contexts), "It may be faster and cheaper to have your learning assessed *that* way, but there are real advantages to doing it *this* way." And if, amid the hype of PLA's "disruptive" potential, we wish to reserve a space for caring for others, we would do well to begin by listening, to ask—honestly and without judgment—"tell us about what you've learned."

References

Boilard, Stephen. 2011. "Perspectives: Prior Learning Assessment Challenges the Status Quo." *Change* 43 (6): 56–59. http://dx.doi.org/10.1080/00091383.2011.618083.

Collins, Patricia Hill. 1986. "Learning from the Outsider Within: The Sociological Significance of Black Feminist Thought." *Social Problems* 33 (6): 14–32. http://dx.doi.org/10.2307/800672.

Fain, Paul. 2012a. "Ace Doubles Down on Prior Learning Assessment." *Inside Higher Ed*, March 4. www.insidehighered.com/news/2013/03/04/ace-doubles-down-prior-learning-assessment.

Fain, Paul. 2012b. "College Credit without College." *Inside Higher Ed*, May 7. www.insidehighered.com/news/2012/05/07/prior-learning-assessment-catches-quietly.

Fain, Paul. 2012c. "New Momentum for an Old Idea." *Inside Higher Ed*, Nov. 12. https://www.insidehighered.com/news/2012/11/12/lawmakers-and-foundations-push-prior-learning-assessment.

Fenwick, Tara. 2006. "The Audacity of Hope: Toward Poorer Pedagogies." *Studies in the Education of Adults* 38 (1): 9–24.

Fenwick, Tara. 2009. "Making to Measure: Reconsidering Assessment in Professional Continuing Education." *Studies in Continuing Education* 31 (3): 229–44. http://dx.doi.org/10.1080/01580370903271446.

Hamer, Jen. 2010. "Recognition of Prior Learning: Normative Assessment or Co-Creation of Preferred Identities." *Australian Journal of Adult Learning* 50 (1): 100–15.

Harris, Judy. 1999. "Ways of Seeing the Recognition of Prior Learning (RPL): What Contribution Can Such Practices Make to Social Inclusion." *Studies in the Education of Adults* 31 (2): 124–39.

Harris, Judy. 2006. *Re-theorising the Recognition of Prior Learning*. Leicester: NIACE.

Jordi, Richard. 2011. "Reframing the Concept of Reflection: Consciousness, Experiential Learning, and Reflective Learning Practices." *Adult Education Quarterly* 61 (2): 181–97. http://dx.doi.org/10.1177/0741713610380439.

Leaker, Cathy, and Frances Boyce. 2015. "A Bigger Rock, A Steeper Hill: PLA, Race and the Color of Learning." *The Journal of Continuing Education* 63: 1–6.

Leaker, Cathy, and Heather Ostman. 2010. "Composing Knowledge: Writing, Rhetoric, and Reflection in Prior Learning Assessment." *College Composition and Communication* 61 (4): 691–717.

Merriam, Sharan B., Rosemary S. Caffarella, and Lisa M. Baumgartner. 2007. *Learning in Adulthood: A Comprehensive Guide*. 3rd ed. San Francisco: Jossey-Bass.

Ratcliffe, Krista. 1999. "Rhetorical Listening: A Trope for Interpretive Invention and a 'Code of Cross-Cultural Conduct.'" *College Composition and Communication* 51 (2): 195–224. http://dx.doi.org/10.2307/359039.

Schon, Donald. 1984. *The Reflective Practitioner*. New York: Basic Books.

Soloranzo, D., Miguel Ceja, and Tara Yosso. 2000. "Critical Race Theory, Racial Microaggressions and Campus Racial Climate: The Experiences of African American College Students." *Journal of Negro Education* 69 (1/2): 60–73.

Werquin, Patrick. 2014. "RPL, Labor Markets, and National Qualifications Frameworks: A Policy Perspective." In *Handbook of the Recognition of Prior Learning: Research into Practice*, ed. Judy Harris, Christine Wihak, and Joy Van Cleef, 86–111. Leicester, UK: National Institute of Adult Continuing Education.

Yancey, Kathleen Blake. 2004. "Postmodernism, Palimpsest and Portfolios: Theoretical Issues in the Representation of Student Work." *College Composition and Communication* 55 (4): 738–61. http://dx.doi.org/10.2307/4140669.

Yosso, Tara. 2005. "Whose Culture Has Capital? A Critical Race Theory Discussion of Community Cultural Wealth." *Race, Ethnicity and Education* 8 (1): 69–91. http://dx.doi.org/10.1080/1361332052000341006.

II

Relationships

Reflection, Language, and Difference

6

REFLECTING THE TRANSLINGUAL NORM
Action-Reflection, ELF, Translation, and Transfer

Bruce Horner

Within the word we find two dimensions, reflection and action, in such radical interaction that if one is sacrificed—even in part—the other immediately suffers.

—Paulo Freire, *Pedagogy of the Oppressed*

In this chapter, I argue that Freire's concept of action-reflection, rather than representing an ideal orientation to knowledge and language, is instead the norm, and that a translingual perspective and pedagogy bring that norm to the fore. Following an analysis of the relation of Freire's concept of action-reflection to a translingual perspective on the norm of knowledge and language, I use studies of the use of English as a lingua franca (hereafter, ELF), translation, and transfer as illustrations of intensifications of that norm and therefore as demonstrating that reflection is best understood as an inevitable if not always recognized or fully realized feature of all language practice.

A translingual perspective on language, I argue, brings that reflective feature of language practice to the fore. In so doing, it represents a marked shift in conventional understandings of language, language practice, and pedagogy. Conventional understandings see language as (ideally) the conduit for the clear transfer of thought from writer to reader, speaker to listener, or at least as the common platform on which interlocutors stand and what makes interlocution, in fact, possible—Chomsky's ideal speech situation of linguistic homogeneity—hence the common equation of "clear" thinking with "clear" writing and the equally common admonitions against obfuscation—writing that is unclear, "muddy," viewed as bespeaking equally unclear, muddy thought (see Barnard 2010). In this view, reflection, coded as *thought,* is distinct from and identified with its prior expression in language,

DOI: 10.7330/9781607325161.c006

determining whether, in fact, the language has successfully communicated the thought or whether the thought itself is in need of revision—as in, "think more clearly."

Recent work exploring a translingual approach to language in writing (as well as other communicative media) calls into question such a view of language/thought relations, and, accordingly, language pedagogy, broadly understood. What such work reveals first and foremost is the containment of dominant conceptions of language within a monolingualist framework, which treats language as a singular, mass noun—as in, "clean up the language"—rather than as countable—that is, plural. Alternatively, a translingual perspective posits language as not the tool of thought or the medium of its communication but, rather, the always-emerging outcome of practices, hence always plural and fluctuating. As Louis-Jean Calvet (2006, 7) puts it, "Languages exist only in and through their speakers, and they are reinvented, renewed and transformed in every interaction, each time that we speak" (cf. Butler 1997, 8; Pennycook 2010, 115). From this alternative perspective, language is understood not so much as a tool or resource available for communicating thought, with the primary concern being the aptness of the tool to the thought ("the right tool for the right job"). Rather, language itself is the ongoing, always-emergent product of practices, as is, likewise, thought.

It's worth emphasizing that, as suggested by Calvet's formulation, while the translingual project is prompted by and incorporates practices that work across languages as conventionally demarcated—for example, practices of code-switching, code-meshing (versus code-segregation), and translation—it is not restricted to such practices, nor do such practices themselves require or define a translingual perspective on language. In fact, representations of those practices that treat codes as reified entities readily available for switching and meshing reinforce, rather than challenge, a monolingualist orientation to language (see Gilyard 2011; Lu 2009; Vance 2009). A translingual approach instead assumes that every engagement in and with any and every language entails the reinvention, renewal, and transformation of language, including engagements that appear merely to reproduce conventional language practices. As Alastair Pennycook (2008) puts it, English, for example, is a language "*always* . . . in translation" (emphasis mine).

Such a view of language might seem to increase unnecessarily the challenges writers face by including among them the challenge of having to decide whether and how and why to (re)write which language in a particular way. If, after all, writing English always engages the translation of English, that translation would appear to be more cognitively challenging than simply writing *in* English (or another language): choices, after all, pose cognitive demands, a reason that ordering coffee is, for some of us, now experienced as far more complicated (and cognitively taxing) than it was when coffee, as a mass noun, came in only one form. But note that, from a translingual perspective, the challenge of how and why to (re)write English (or any other language) in a particular way is, in fact, not one we can avoid: instead, we are all always already facing that challenge and engaged, as writers, in rewriting language with each stroke of the pen or keyboard. Thus, what a translingual perspective brings is not, in this sense, the availability of an alternative to ordinary monolingual or conventional multilingual practice—not a deviant kind of writing some of us may elect to pursue—but rather a different view of the actual norm of language practice, a norm that goes unrecognized as a consequence of monolingualist ideology.[1]

The question this translingual perspective on normal language practice then raises is, what pedagogical advantage(s), if any, might it yield? My answer is that adopting a translingual perspective brings into consciousness all language practice as action-reflection rather than, as a monolingualist perspective would have it, action about which—afterward or beforehand—one may or may not reflect. It thereby (1) enables us to recognize writerly agency and responsibility in all acts of writing; (2) points to ways to develop dispositions supportive of the best kind of academic habitus; and (3) offers a model for the vexed issue of transfer in writing studies in its focus on the necessity of the labor of reinvention to writing.

ACTION-REFLECTION AND A TRANSLINGUAL PERSPECTIVE

I anticipate that my invocation of action-reflection will have immediately prompted readers to relegate me to the status of being a Freirean, and, so far as it goes, that would be accurate. After all, Freire argues against (pedagogies) treating action and reflection as discrete. As he asserts, "Action and reflection occur simultaneously. . . . Critical reflection is also action" (Freire 1970, 128). As he explains, in "problem-posing" education, for example, "the teacher-student and the students-teachers reflect simultaneously on themselves and the world without dichotomizing this reflection from action, and thus establish an authentic form of thought and action" (83). Freire's problem-posing education "makes [students] critical thinkers" rather than "objects of assistance," helping them to "see the world not as a static reality, but as a reality in process, in transformation" (83). But while Freire avers that "the dialectical relations of women and men with the world exist independently of how these relations are perceived, . . . it is also true that the form of action they adopt is to a large extent a function of how they perceive themselves in the world" (83). Thus, as Freire explains, how students perceive themselves in the world has clear political consequences. For example, students who see themselves and the world as "fated and unalterable" are unlikely to attempt to change existing conditions, whereas seeing themselves and the world as always in process "leads people to apprehend that situation as an historical reality susceptible of transformation. Resignation gives way to the drive for transformation and inquiry, over which men feel themselves to be in control" (85).

I don't want to dismiss the political significance and problems of this framing, which have been the subject of decades of heated debate that shows little sign of ending. At the same time, Freire's alignment of problem posing with "transformation" and "revolutionary futurity," despite his cautions against conventional understandings of what these might entail, have tended to distract readers from recognizing that his discussion of consciousness, reflection, and action is an account not of what should happen, but rather of what does happen. In short, the hope he offers is founded not on seeking out an entirely different set of conditions and practices but, rather, on coming to recognize the conditions and practices in which we are already engaged—the "contradictions" to be found in the deposits banked into students, the actuality of "the dialectical relations of women and men with the world," the fact that banking education "cannot completely destroy" creativity and "the intentionality of consciousness," even the "authentic" vocation of persons "engaged in inquiry and creative transformation" (Freire 1970, 83–84).[2] In other words, chief among the limitations of banking is that it fails to "acknowledge men and women as historical beings" (84; emphasis mine). A "banking" approach is founded, in short, on a premise that is not only oppressive but also invalid.

I'm suggesting that the fervor for, or fear of, revolutionary change Freire's writings have inspired can distract us from the fact that he presents the concept of action-reflection as the norm rather than a deviation or break from ordinary cognition, however much that norm may be suppressed and, hence, remain unacknowledged. In the same way, a translingual orientation calls less for a break from ordinary language practice and more for a different understanding of what language practice entails. Thus, the political edge to arguments for a translingual orientation arises less from the language rights such an orientation demands and more from its recognition of the agency of language users operating in all language use. As Anthony Giddens puts it, "Every instance of the use of language is a potential modification of that language at the same time as it acts to reproduce it" (Giddens 1979, 220). There is, then, agency exercised in the reproduction as well as modification of language. It is monolingualism that keeps us from recognizing agency in the former and identifying it strictly with the latter. Acknowledging, insisting, and drawing upon that agency is crucial to writing (and, more generally, language) pedagogy.

Where a translingual perspective breaks from what are convention-ally understood to be Freirean dispositions toward "revolution" is in its recognition, and insistence, that reproduction (of language) itself involves difference. This becomes evident when we relocate utterances in time as well as space. By so doing, even iterations of the seemingly same carry a different valence *as* iterations produced in, and therefore contributing to, necessarily different circumstances (in time, space, etc.).[3] Freire's notion of "deposits" runs counter to this insofar as these deposits are treated as invulnerable to change when (re)iterated. This notion obscures the agency exercised and the difference produced not only in breaks from those deposits, but in their (re)production. In other words, without discounting the sharpness of Freire's critique of banking education, what the image of deposits obscures is the difference effected through their reiteration. In some ways, then, the narrative of banking Freire weaves itself grants too much power to banking and its always only partial accomplishment of hegemony.[4] Alternatively, we must recognize that it is only through iteration that such deposits can continue to hold sway: the stability banking education attempts to secure is itself an ongo-ing, and always losing, project precisely because of the invalidity of its treatment of knowledge as stable and inert. In a backhanded way, then, we might say the success of banking is dependent on its "vessels," not on the "bankers."

The difficulty we have recognizing this weakness in banking, and the common conflation of action-reflection with transformation understood as a recognizable break from the status quo, and not with iteration, are tributes to the power of dominant ideology, whether that is the ideology reifying knowledge or the monolingualist ideology reifying language. And of course, these intertwine: the latter contributes to the former in the formalism toward language and knowledge it encourages and the one-to-one model of translation it offers, whether that is a translation of thought to word or of words in one language to those in another. Difference in language is identified purely with glossodiversity (Freire's "verbalism"), eliding the semiodiversity produced in iteration.

ENGLISH AS A LINGUA FRANCA AS NORM

The preceding is meant to set markers defining translinguality not as a specific set of practices with language forms but as an orientation to language, and to identify that orientation itself with the orientation to knowledge associated with the problem-posing action-reflection of Freirean pedagogy.[5] Having set these markers, however, I now want to turn to what we might glean from studies of interactions of language practice that, in terms of conventional understandings, *are* recognizably mixed in form: cross-language work in uses of ELF and translation and work crossing the language practices associated with ostensibly different domains of knowledge production/reproduction in the phenomenon known as *transfer*. My point in doing so, despite the risk of reinforcing the identification of translinguality with such recognizable instances of engagement in cross-language work, is ultimately to enable us to see these instances not as exceptional but as representative of all language work. In other words, I am pursuing a broad strategy here of identifying the ordinary in the seemingly different (exceptional), with an eye toward then redefining the ordinary. To put it as bluntly as I can, from a translingual perspective, practices with ELF are exemplary of practices with English generally, including practices with English among people identified as English monolinguals. Translation and transfer, likewise, are the norms of language work rather than special cases.

The difference in how users of ELF engage English is, I will argue, not a difference in kind but in degree of intensity, representing an intensification of practices with English that brings to the surface features characteristic of all engagements with English. My focus on ELF as a practice rather than a distinct set of forms is consistent with a growing consensus among ELF scholars that ELF is best understood not as a specific variety of English but, rather, as a function or use of English marked by fluidity in form and pragmatics (see for example Canagarajah 2007; Friedrich and Matsuda 2010; Jenkins 2011). As Christiane Meierkord notes, "[ELF] is intersubjectively constructed in each specific context of interaction . . . negotiated by each set of speakers for their purposes" and thus "never achieves a stable or even standardized form" (Meierkord 2004, 129). Or, as Alan Firth (1996) puts it, variability is one of ELF's primary characteristics.

If ELF is not a variety but instead a function, then, as Jennifer Jenkins (2011, 931–32) observes, at least from the perspective of ELF, "A skilled English user is no longer someone who has 'mastered' the forms of a particular native variety of English, but someone who has acquired the pragmatic skills needed to adapt their English use in line with the demands of the current lingua franca situation." This is a significant break from conventional understandings of language fluency and competence, a break that, Jenkins reports, is beginning to put English monolinguals at a disadvantage, at least in their interactions with the growing majority of English speakers (who know English as an additional language).

But if we cannot distinguish ELF from, say, American or British English (or SWE) in terms of specific forms, we can distinguish ELF practice from at least some other practices with English by the orientations to language those practices bespeak. For while the pragmatic strategies in ELF, like the forms used, are variable, they nonetheless share an orientation of acceptance of variability as the norm and a concern with communicative effectiveness rather than with conformity to standards of correctness; and dispositions of patience, humility, a "focus on mutual cooperation and intelligibility," and a willingness to "let ambiguities pass" (Firth 1996; Rubdy and Saraceni 2006, 12). As Jenkins (2011, 928) observes, ELF speakers "prioritise communicative effectiveness over narrow predetermined notions of 'correctness.' . . . Their use of English is fluid and flexible, responding adeptly to the nature of the particular communicative context in ways that native English speakers, with their stronger attachment to native English norms, tend to find more challenging."

Such a practice represents an intensification, rather than deviation, from English practice generally insofar as it exhibits the actual degree of variation, change, and interlingual traffic demonstrated by the history of language(s)—including the history of that shifting, variable mongrel known as *English*. Further, except in conditions under which correctness to imposed standardized forms is the goal—for example, spelling bees and some writing courses and language tests—the orientation to language exhibited in ELF is likewise a mere intensification of orientations interlocutors commonly adopt toward language in their communicative practices. These include, it is worth noting, communicative practices of writing and reading, again except under artificial conditions like those identified above.

There is another sense in which ELF represents an intensification of ordinary language practices rather than a deviant form of practice: the greater cognitive intensity of participation in the co-construction of meaning in engagements with ELF. While a commitment to this intensity may be taken for granted as a necessary precondition for engagement in ELF, users of English unaccustomed to such intensity are likely to find it difficult to navigate ELF, such as English monolinguals accustomed to speaking only to other English monolinguals and in habitual ways and believing others ought to conform to these ways (Jenkins 2011, 934). Monolingualist ideology does not encourage dispositions of patience, tolerance for variation in form and pragmatics, humility, a willingness to let ambiguities pass, and creative co-construction of meaning in language use.[6]

I submit that the prototypical ELF situation occasions action-reflection, and insofar as that situation itself is prototypical of English generally, to the extent that we can enable all students to think of their writing of English in terms aligned with ELF, we are fostering dispositions to engage more deliberately in action-reflection. Much of such work might well accord with common practices in literacy pedagogy—questioning students' (and other writers') conventional language for what it does and doesn't allow to be thought, holding back from dismissing unconventional writing in order to consider what different way of knowing it might represent, treating ambiguous writing not simply as muddy but as potentially meaningful if and when sufficient reflection is given to its possible meanings, not allowing consensus interpretations to put an end to exploring possible meanings to be constructed from specific texts. As teachers and students engaging in such practices quickly learn, these practices, like problem- posing itself, are intense and directly at odds with dominant values of efficiency in transmission of information, goods, and services: why, for example, dominant culture asks, would anyone want to pose problems rather than solve them? The posing of problems produces resistance, friction, at odds with the ideal of a friction-free, efficient flow of information, goods, and services, and hence stands out as something to be avoided.

But as many readers will have already observed and as I have suggested, the dispositions manifested in ELF, and that I have aligned with those necessary to Freirean action-reflection, also characterize the academic habitus—or at least the academic habitus that academics tend most to admire as conducive to the best of their academic work as teachers and scholars and that they aim to encourage in their students. So, for example, academics are praised and praise their students for being challenging; for cognitive intensity resulting from engagement in considering a variety of approaches and perspectives; for responding to difficulty, difference, and ambiguity with tolerance, patience, and humility; and for letting ambiguities pass in the hope that these will be resolved with, well, patience and effort.[7] In teaching, academics commonly introduce difficulty and possible differences (in ways of interpreting texts and natural and social phenomena) where their students are initially inclined to find none and to gravitate instead toward an immediate, simple, consensus resolution. Teachers try to "interfere," as David Bartholomae (1982) advises teachers, with students' desire to close things down. The intensity such practices yield is one that academics have grown accustomed to and treat as the norm, at least for academic work. One of the difficulties students face is negotiating the difference between the academic habitus, on the one hand, and, on the other, dominant fast-capitalist culture's valuing of ideals of cool ease, speed, and efficiency, with everyone getting exactly what they want when they want it without question or reflection on either the conditions giving rise to such desires or values or the consequences of pursuing them.

A translingual perspective advances this academic habitus insofar as it rejects the givenness of language and monolingualism's relegation of language to the role of thought conduit. Such a perspective disallows the adjudication of language practice in terms of conformity to language already predetermined as right or not, appropriate or not, clear or muddy. While such adjudications seem to demand responsibility from (student) writers, the responsibility thus assigned to students is reduced to that of finding/knowing what is right/appropriate and adjusting their writing accordingly. By contrast, a translingual approach demands greater responsibility from and ascribes greater agency to writers for deciding how to use language, with the potential transformation of language, context, and the writers themselves always present. The question it asks of writers is not whether to be different from a norm of sameness but, rather, what kind of difference to make, how, and why, given difference as the inevitable norm of utterances.[8] So, for example, in my own efforts at pursuing this approach, I've asked students to explore the semiodiversity lurking in terms common to first-year composition—such as *student, education, academic, composition,* and *learning*—by considering the different ways any of these might be defined and by which any one of these terms might be translated into a different language. I then ask them to rewrite (in English) what they mean in their arguments by any one of these terms. This exercise allows them to recognize, reflect on, and select and work to distinguish among the possible meanings to be given to a term like *education* (highlighting, for example, the distinction marked in French between *éducation* and *formation*) rather than assume *education* has a singular, always-agreed-upon meaning impervious to change that the term itself communicates transparently.

TRANSLATION AS THE NORM OF WRITING

As the example just provided suggests, in the same way ELF represents an intensification of the lingua franca status of all engagements in

English, translation, as ordinarily recognized, represents an intensification of the task of writing. This proposition is of course not new, but it has circulated primarily in the areas of comparative literature and literary critical theory.[9] With the exception of scholarship in the *Journal of Second Language Writing*, composition studies has by and large not addressed translation as a writing practice. While this omission may be accounted for by the "myth of linguistic homogeneity" (Matsuda 2006) dominating composition studies for much of its history, it can also be accounted for by the (monolingualist) sense of languages as discrete: even absent that myth of linguistic homogeneity, it may be assumed that no interaction across languages occurs, even among multilingual individuals (see Grosjean 1985).

Translation or, better, cross-language work fosters action-reflection by positioning writers as having and having to make choices. Weiguo Qu (2014, 72) observes that "translation or thinking in a language that is not native de-automatizes perception and thinking." Describing Chinese students working across Chinese and English, Qu explains that the students

> confronted with different languages imbued with different cultural heritages . . . have to and are able to make decisions and choices. Critical thinking and literacy are possible only when students have more than one way of perceiving the world. . . . From being forced to make a decision and a choice, gradually students are changed to cognize the world in line with their own decisions and with what they themselves believe in. They want their own definitions, English or Chinese. It is in this way that English as a foreign language with relevant cultural heritage participates in and contributes to the cultivation of critical literacy in an alien country like China. (Qu 2014, 73)

As Qu notes, even the attempt to stay with conventional, authorized Chinese meanings represents a choice once those meanings are placed in the context of alternative possibilities (e.g., other ways of translating English to Chinese, as well as uses of English). In fact, we can see such choices as ones writers confront not only in explicitly cross-language work but in any engagement with any language, which always exists in relation to other potential engagements and languages. There is, in other words, in the writing of any language, agency and responsibility exerted as a choice, however inevitably constrained, with significance and consequences. (That these are not recognized is a consequence of material social conditions—including a prevalent monolingualist ideology—that discourage attention to the exercise of that agency and responsibility.) For example, as Yasemin Yildiz has argued, the choice of Franz Kafka, fluent in multiple languages, to write in German (only) nonetheless carried specific significance for being "German" writing in light of his Jewish identity and dominant valuations at the time of German belonging only to those deemed ethnic Germans (Yildiz 2012, 34–35*ff.*). Thus what might appear to be purely monolingual writing (only in German) can, from a translingual (or, in Yildiz's formulation, "post-monolingual") perspective be understood as still working in translation across languages to effect in an environment of language difference.

To bring in an example closer to home, it is far easier for me as a product of US schooling to write (in) English, so for me to do so seems and feels like no choice at all—unremarkable as a feature of my writing. But this sense does not mean it is not a choice, just as the fact that I now find the style in which I predominantly write (more deeply sedimented, to the point of becoming a set of stylistic tics, to readers' and my chagrin) to be easier to reproduce than some other style does not absolve me of the responsibility for deciding, however seemingly unconsciously, to continue that style. That these are not "free" choices does not mean they are not choices. Agency is not the same as mastery (Butler 1997).

The choice in what language to write and how to (re)write it that a translingual perspective brings to consciousness is explored in Rebecca Lorimer Leonard's (2014) account of the experiences of six multilingual writers. Leonard refers to the outcome of writing across languages as "rhetorical attunement," defined as "an ear for, or a tuning toward, difference or multiplicity. . . . a literate understanding that assumes multiplicity and invites the negotiation of meaning across difference" (Leonard 2014, 228). Leonard cautions that such attunement is not automatic. Instead, she avers, multilingual writers "come to know—become rhetorically attuned—over a lifetime of communicating across difference" (Leonard 2014, 228). In terms of the argument of this chapter, we can say that such (multilingual) writers' experience represents an intensification of the experiences and challenges all writers face insofar as all writers write across differences. The intensification arises from the fact that the differences of language crossed by the writers Leonard studies are those recognized within the framework of monolingualism (e.g., Hebrew, French, Spanish, Portuguese, English, Turkish, Russian, Tibetan, Kannada, Hindi, Urdu, Azerbaijani). But Leonard herself rejects the notion that attunement is restricted only to such writers or even "an entirely new concept." Instead she aligns it with other efforts to understand literate activity and defines it as "proceed[ing] from an emergent sensitivity to language" in writers that treats language difference as "an element 'at the heart' of rhetoric,' a 'mode of reasoning and decision-making which allows humans to act in the absence of certain *a priori* truth" (Leonard 2014, 230; citing Jarratt 1991, 8).

I take from Leonard's argument two points: first, being multilingual, at least in conventional terms, does not in itself produce such sensitivity, however much we might like to think so. One may be monolingualist in multiple languages. Second, and conversely, developing such sensitivity to language difference, and engaging in rhetorical attunement, do not require being multilingual in the conventional sense. It is simply easier for us to understand how such sensitivity may arise under such conditions than under those conditions we are disposed to recognize as monolingual. But that sensitivity, whether arising in a multilingual or monolingual setting, emerges through awareness of differences in language (in contingent and co-constitutive relation with, inevitably, culture, generation, region, history, profession, class, race, gender, etc.), posing the questions of how and what to say, how to position oneself in relation to how one appears to be positioned, what to attempt—questions whose (always tentative) answers rhetorical attunement addresses. In other words, that sensitivity calls on writers (and speakers) to reflect and act on these differences in the most rhetorically savvy (i.e., knowing) ways: to attempt to exercise savoir faire (literally "to know [how] to do").[10] In its conventional usage as an adopted term in English, *savoir faire* suggests a kind of elite knowledge and (hence) a characteristic of those deemed elite—knowledge, borne of elite experience, of what is "appropriate" behavior in a given situation, meaning that which the dominant has determined is "appropriate" to such a situation ("capacity for appropriate action; *especially*: a polished sureness in social behavior").[11] However, in its recuperated form, it may suggest instead knowledge-action in language use (and elsewhere) arising from knowledge of and experience with the fact of differences, knowledge-action producing an *exploration of and action upon* (action-reflection) what might be appropriate for whom, why, at this moment, for what purpose: in Freire's terms, deployments of "the word" in which the radical interaction of its two dimensions, reflection and action, are brought to the fore (Freire 1970, 87).

This recuperation suggests that writing pedagogies might aim less at producing conventionally multilingual writers—a chimera at any event in light of both the contemporary dominance of monolingualism and the invalidity of notions of language "mastery"—and instead more at encouraging in writers just such savoir faire with rhetorical attunement. They can work to bring to consciousness the possibilities of difference and engage students in explorations of ways to make rhetorically productive—not merely accommodative but transformative—use of those possibilities in writing. By posing, and giving students practice in posing, questions about what difference they might accomplish through particular engagements with language, and by engaging them in seeking out potential differences in meaning in their reading and writing, they might pursue something like the linguistic analytical approach to composition Kenneth Burke advocated.[12] Such an approach, Burke argues, entails learning and teaching "techniques for doubting much that is now accepted as lying beyond the shadow of a doubt" and making "methodical the attitude of patience" (Burke 1955, 272, 271). By directing our pedagogy toward developing patience and humility and a willingness to confront and even seek out ambiguities in language, we can encourage dispositions in accord with recognition of English as always already a lingua franca for all writers and as something inevitably "in translation" even when seeming to operate within what monolingualism teaches us to think of as a single, discrete language.

TRANSFER AND ACTION-REFLECTION IN LANGUAGE

The notion that languages are the outcome of practices rather than the medium and precondition for practices, and that they and the contexts of their engagement and the identities of the writers engaging them are in contingent and co-constitutive relation to one another and, hence, always emergent, casts a different light on the vexed issue of transfer in writing studies. The very notion of transfer has been challenged for the ways in which the model implies reification of the knowledge or skill to be transferred and the stability of the contexts the knowledge or skill is to be transferred from and to (see Beach 1999). Difficulties in demonstrating transfer following this model have led at least some writers to reject the possibility of transfer altogether or else to redefine transfer so as to enable its identification and demonstration across contexts.[13] Many of those following the latter path challenge the stability of the knowledge/skill being "transferred." Rather than assuming that, like a hammer, knowledge remains unchanged by the environment into which it is brought, in a kind of "portable" model of knowledge/ skills in which knowledge is simply "reused," theorists argue for the revision of that knowledge as it is deployed in different contexts. So, for example, DePalma and Ringer (2011) outline a theory of "adaptive transfer" that acknowledges "both the reuse and reshaping of prior writing knowledge to fit new contexts" and that refers to "the conscious or intuitive process of applying or reshaping learned writing knowledge in order to . . . negotiate new and potentially unfamiliar writing situations"

(DePalma and Ringer 2011, 135). Further, they argue that this reshaping of knowledge in new contexts changes those contexts themselves (DePalma and Ringer 2011, 142). From this perspective, they note, "students are viewed as potential contributors to an ever-changing rhetorical context rather than as passive recipients of the knowledge and conventions of a discourse of power. They are, in other words, both *users* and *transformers* of writing knowledge and writing contexts" (DePalma and Ringer 2011, 142).[14]

Michael-John DePalma and Jeffrey Ringer explicitly align their theory of "adaptive transfer" to arguments for a translingual perspective on language difference in writing (DePalma and Ringer 2011, 141). But a translingual perspective adds to theories like theirs the insistence on difference as a feature of all situations, not just those in which the question of transfer has arisen as a consequence of the apparent differences in situation. Conventionally, studies of transfer see the question of transferability as arising only when learners respond to situations we are already disposed to recognize as distinct from one another. As David Smit (2004, 119) has put it, the question transfer studies raise is, in what sense can various kinds of knowledge and skill be transferred from one situation to another, or learned in one context and applied in another? That assumption of discrete relations between situations accounts for the distinction of distance in the scholarly literature on transfer between so-called near, or low-road, transfer (across situations at least "similar"), on the one hand, and far, or high-road, transfer across situations seemingly quite different. Even in the distinction's acknowledgment of similarity, some degree of distance between situations, and hence their discrete character, is assumed to prompt the question, or problem, of transfer. Alternatively, from a translingual perspective, the question of transfer is constant rather than precipitated by special circumstances insofar as even the "same" situation is always also different as a consequence of its temporal location, the emergent product (as "the same" or "different") resulting from practices to render it "the same" or "different," and in what ways. From a translingual perspective, both sameness and difference of situation are understood as relations constructed by participants—choices—rather than as characteristics of the situations themselves participants must then adjust to in some way, or that require no such adjustment. From a translingual perspective, just as conditions conventionally understood as multilingual requiring translation represent no more than an intensification of the norm of all language work, so occasions conventionally understood as raising questions of transfer likewise represent intensifications of the norm of knowledge reproduction. For the creation of the "same" is itself a production of difference as well,[15] just as continuity of knowledge entails the reproduction of the "same" into a temporally different location, and hence its transformation. While typically the work of such reproduction goes unacknowledged, it occurs nonetheless—as evidenced by the work those suffering from memory loss must undergo in recreating, explicitly, the reconstruction of the "same" that normally goes on below the surface of consciousness.

This suggests that not only in situations that appear to pose special challenges of transfer—for example, learning to write (in) different disciplines—but also in those that appear to pose no such challenges, students should be encouraged to consider the ways in which they do and might reproduce or reshape knowledge and context and with what inevitably different consequences, in and through their writing (in terms of the writing processes and materials they engage and in terms of what they attempt to produce through that engagement). Both sameness and difference can best be understood as challenges all writers inevitably face, what they must work to accomplish a sense of for themselves and their readers in how they go about writing. The impossibility of actual generic writing of any kind illustrates, paradoxically, the inevitability of these challenges for all writers, always. If, as Freire suggests, action-reflection is an inevitable characteristic of learning and literacy, if often unacknowledged and even suppressed, action-reflection on the (re)construction of sameness and difference in writing is an inevitable characteristic of writing teachers can work with student writers to engage in more consciously and productively.

Of course, doing so inevitably slows down the process of writing, rendering visible, and thus available for more deliberate engagement (action-reflection), a process that, often enough, writers might prefer to let slide beneath the surface of consciousness—especially given contemporary demands for speed and efficiency in communication, never mind what is to be communicated, nor what prompts such demands.[16] The reshaping of knowledge thus may be more deliberate, and may be directed toward different ends, than would be the case if it were left to occur below the surface of consciousness. But this is to say that writing and learning are coterminous: the question teachers face is not simply whether to teach writing as a way of learning, as the old WAC slogan has it, but what kind of learning to encourage in writers through their language practices.

CONCLUSION

I have argued that ELF interactions, translation, and transfer represent not special cases distinct from the norm of language and learning but, rather, intensifications of the norm of action-reflection for language practice that has gone unrecognized as a consequence of the domination of monolingualist ideology. That norm of action-reflection in language practice, while typically identified only with cases designated as outside the norm, can be engaged more productively through encouragement of the longstanding academic habitus of questioning practices of language and knowledge; the dispositions of tolerance for difference, humility, and patience; and a willingness to engage ambiguity rather than using the experience of ambiguity as a reason for dismissing discourse: dispositions of seeking out the "different" in the "same" and of challenging identifications of "sameness" and "difference" for their potential consequences. While, as I have argued, action-reflection is a feature of all language practice, it is also the case that beliefs about language shape practice. As Calvet warns, "Coexisting with these [language] practices there are representations—what people think about languages . . . —representations that act on practices and are one of the factors of change" (Calvet 2006, 241).[17] To the extent that writing teachers reproduce and reinforce representations of language as, ideally, the efficient and neutral conduit of thought rather than the occasion for action-reflection, students will be less likely to take up consciously the action-reflection writing in fact occasions: less likely to see themselves as possessing agency and responsibility for producing specific kinds of difference (including the difference of continuing with the same old same old) and putting that agency and responsibility to better use. Alternatively, we can recognize, and help our students learn to recognize and engage in, writing as the occasion for just such action-reflection, posing anew the ongoing challenge of what kind of difference to attempt to make through writing, how, and why.

There is growing interest in understanding what a translingual perspective might have to offer writing studies. While much of that interest grows out of and is concerned with working with language differences that monolingualist ideology leads us to recognize as language differences, we are only beginning to explore how such a perspective can enable us to recognize difference as an inevitable outcome of all language practice, and with what consequences for ourselves and our students. One such consequence may be the recuperation of reflection as not only a crucial but also an inevitable, if often unacknowledged, constituent of the work we do in writing, one we can put to better work through our teaching.

Notes

1. I am using language ideology in the sense Pierre Bourdieu offers when he cautions that it "has nothing in common with an explicitly professed, deliberate and revocable belief, or with an intentional act of accepting a 'norm.' It is inscribed, in a practical state, in dispositions which are impalpably inculcated, through a long and slow process of acquisition, by the sanctions of the linguistic market" (Bourdieu 1991, 51).
2. I am of course invoking here Bourdieu's distinction between recognition and misrecognition.
3. For a fuller discussion of this, see Lu and Horner 2013.
4. See Raymond Williams's (1977) discussion of a living hegemony as never total.
5. Of course, that orientation also resonates, to varying degrees, with orientations to knowledge as the product of reflection articulated by other writers. See Kathleen Blake Yancey 1998, 8–15.
6. Note that I am not saying English monolinguals are incapable of or less able to develop such dispositions, only that monolingualism discourages such development in both monolinguals and multilinguals as conventionally defined and discourages recognition of these dispositions as the actual norm.
7. See, for example, David Bartholomae and Anthony Petrosky's characterization of the readings included in their popular *Ways of Reading* textbook as "rich, magnificent, too big for anyone to completely grasp all at once, and before them, it seems appropriate to stand humbly, admiringly," followed by their advice to students to respond to such challenges by adopting "a difficult mix of authority and humility" and their iteration of I. A. Richards's recommendation, presumably for English monolingual readers reading English-medium texts, that students simply "read [a difficult text] as though it made sense and perhaps it will" (Bartholomae and Petrosky 2005, 10; citing Richards 1943, 41).
8. For an extended discussion of this perspective on difference, see Lu and Horner 2013. Compare this discussion to Yancey's characterization of the reflective classroom as "interactive, oriented to agency" and its students as "*intelligent agent[s] who can engage[e] in frequent and deliberate self-awareness, theorizing and learning from their own practice*" (Yancey 1998, 8).
9. For example, in "English as a Language Always in Translation," Alastair Pennycook (2008) relies on references not to linguists or compositionists but to George Steiner, Jacques Derrida, and Gayatri Spivak to buttress and explicate his argument.
10. Compare to Daniel Coste, Daniéle Moore, and Geneviéve Zarate's distinctions, in their discussion of plurilingual (and pluricultural) competence, between *savoir* (declarative knowledge), *savoir-faire* (skills and know-how), and *savoir-être* (attitudes and values) (Coste, Moore, and Zarate 2009, 29). I am suggesting a productive conflation of these three under the category of savoir faire in grasping rhetorical attunement, however useful the distinctions among these may be for other purposes. As I discuss, *savoir faire* has a different connotation in its English use as borrowed term.
11. Merriam Webster Dictionary, ed., s.v. "appropriate."
12. Though Burke used the term *composition*, it's not clear he had the standard FYC course in mind. See the discussion of Burke's argument in Jay Jordan 2012, 88–91, on which I draw here.
13. Because transfer is a concern across disciplines in education, the literature is enormous. On the apparent impossibility of transfer, see David Smit 2004. On the need to redefine transfer altogether, see King Beach 1999. On the possibility that dominant definitions of transfer obscure its presence, see Bransford and Schwartz 1999. For recent reviews of studies of transfer in writing, see Elizabeth Wardle 2012a and Yancey et al. 2014, chapter 1.

14. Compare to Rebecca Nowacek's (2011) model of transfer as "recontextualization" and "reconstruction" and Wardle's (2012b) model of transfer as "creative repurposing."

15. A musical example illustrates: repetition of "the same" melodic phrase carries a different significance—as "repetition of the same"—that the "original" iteration of the phrase does not.

16. Wardle (2012a) points to the inculcation of "answer-getting" dispositions in pre-tertiary-level schooling that is at odds with a "problem-exploring disposition" encouraged at the tertiary level (a disposition somewhat akin to what I've been referring to as the *academic habitus*) as one explanation. Of course this raises the question of why such dispositions are inculcated. But I am also arguing that dispositions are not conditions but abstractions from practices students engage in. Thus, students can be asked what enacting either set of "dispositions" entails, and with what consequences (thereby prompting practices productive of a "problem-posing" disposition).

17. Calvet gives the example of Croats, whose belief that Croatian is different from Serbian produces language differences in what linguists would have recognized as, in fact, at least previously, the same language (2006, 245).

Works Cited

Barnard, Ian. 2010. "The Ruse of Clarity." *College Composition and Communication* 61 (3): 434–51.

Bartholomae, David. 1982. "Writing Assignments: Where Writing Begins." *Forum* 35 (Fall): 35–46.

Bartholomae, David, and Anthony Petrosky. 2005. Introduction to *Ways of Reading: An Anthology for Writers.* 7th ed. Ed. David Bartholomae and Anthony Petrosky, 1–23. Boston: Bedford/St. Martin's.

Beach, King. 1999. "Consequential Transitions: A Sociocultural Expedition beyond Transfer in Education." *Review of Research in Education* 24:101–39.

Bourdieu, Pierre. 1991. *Language and Symbolic Power.* Ed. John B. Thompson. Trans. Gino Raymond and Matthew Adamson. Cambridge: Harvard University Press.

Bransford, John D., and Daniel L. Schwartz. 1999. "Rethinking Transfer: A Simple Proposal with Multiple Implications." *Review of Research in Education* 24: 61–100.

Butler, Judith. 1997. *Excitable Speech: A Politics of the Performative.* New York: Routledge.

Burke, Kenneth. 1955. "Linguistic Approaches to Problems of Education." In *Modern Philosophies and Education: The Fifty-Fourth Yearbook of the National Society for the Study of Education, Part 1,* ed. Nelson B. Henry, 259–303. Chicago: University of Chicago Press.

Calvet, Louis-Jean. 2006. *Toward an Ecology of World Languages.* Trans. Andrew Brown. Cambridge: Polity.

Canagarajah, A. Suresh 2007. "Lingua Franca English, Multilingual Communities, and Language Acquisition." *Modern Language Journal* 91 (Supplement 1): 923–39. http://dx.doi.org/10.1111/j.1540-4781.2007.00678.x.

Coste, Daniel, Danièle Moore, and Geneviève Zarate. 2009. *Plurilingual and Pluricultural Competence: Studies towards a Common European Framework of Reference for Language Learning and Teaching.* Strasbourg: Council of Europe. http://www.coe.int/t/dg4/linguistic/Source/SourcePublications/CompetencePlurilingue09web_en.pdf.

DePalma, Michael-John, and Jeffrey M. Ringer. 2011. "Toward a Theory of Adaptive Transfer: Expanding Disciplinary Discussions of 'Transfer' in Second-Language Writing and Composition Studies." *Journal of Second Language Writing* 20 (2): 134–47. http://dx.doi.org/10.1016/j.jslw.2011.02.003.

Firth, Alan. 1996. "On the Discursive Accomplishment of Normality: On 'Lingua Franca' English and Conversation Analysis." *Journal of Pragmatics* 26 (2): 237–59. http://dx.doi.org/10.1016/0378-2166(96)00014-8.

Freire, Paulo. 1970. *Pedagogy of the Oppressed.* Trans. Myra Bergman Ramos. New York: Continuum.

Friedrich, Patricia, and Aya Matsuda. 2010. "When Five Words Are Not Enough: A Conceptual and Terminological Discussion of English as a Lingua Franca." *International Multilingual Research Journal* 4 (1): 20–30. http://dx.doi.org/10.1080/19313150903500978.

Giddens, Anthony. 1979. *Central Problems in Social Theory: Action, Structure and Contradiction in Social Analysis.* Berkeley: University of California Press. http://dx.doi.org/10.1007/978-1-349-16161-4.

Gilyard, Keith. 2011. "Rethinking the Code-Switching Paradigm." In *True to the Language Game: African American Discourse, Cultural Politics, and Pedagogy,* ed. Keith Gilyard, 112–34. New York: Routledge.

Grosjean, François. 1985. "The Bilingual as a Competent but Specific Speaker-Hearer." *Journal of Multilingual and Multicultural Development* 6 (6): 467–77. http://dx.doi.org/10.1080/01434632.1985.9994221.

Jarratt, Susan. 1991. *Rereading the Sophists: Classical Rhetoric Refigured.* Carbondale: Southern Illinois University Press.

Jenkins, Jennifer. 2011. "Accommodating (to) ELF in the International University." *Journal of Pragmatics* 43 (4): 926–36. http://dx.doi.org/10.1016/j.pragma.2010.05.011.

Jordan, Jay. 2012. *Redesigning Composition for Multilingual Realities.* Urbana, IL: NCTE.

Leonard, Rebecca Lorimer. 2014. "Multilingual Writing as Rhetorical Attunement." *College English* 76 (3): 227–47.

Lu, Min-Zhan. 2009. "Metaphors Matter: Transcultural Literacy." *JAC* 29 (1–2): 285–93.

Lu, Min-Zhan, and Bruce Horner. 2013. "Translingual Literacy, Language Difference, and Matters of Agency." *College English* 75 (6): 586–611.

Matsuda, Paul Kei. 2006. "The Myth of Linguistic Homogeneity in U.S. College Composition." *College English* 68 (6): 637–51. http://dx.doi.org/10.2307/25472180.

Meierkord, Christiane. 2004. "Syntactic Variation in Interactions across International Englishes." *English World-Wide* 25 (1): 109–32. http://dx.doi.org/10.1075/eww.25.1.06mei.

Nowacek, Rebecca S. 2011. *Agents of Integration: Understanding Transfer as a Rhetorical Act.* Carbondale: Southern Illinois University Press.

Pennycook, Alastair. 2008. "English as a Language Always in Translation." *European Journal of English Studies* 12 (1): 33–47. http://dx.doi.org/10.1080/13825570801900521.

Pennycook, Alastair. 2010. *Language as a Local Practice.* London: Routledge.

Qu, Weiguo. 2014. "Critical Literacy and Writing in English: Teaching English in a Cross-cultural Context." In *Reworking English in Rhetoric and Composition: Global Interrogations, Local Interventions,* ed. Bruce Horner and Karen Kopelson, 64–74. Carbondale: Southern Illinois University Press.

Richards, I. A. 1943. *How to Read a Page: A Course in Effective Reading.* London: Kegan Paul.

Rubdy, Rani, and Mario Saraceni. 2006. Introduction to *English in the World: Global Rules, Global Roles,* ed. Rani Rubdy and Mario Saraceni, 5–16. London: Continuum.

Smit, David W. 2004. *The End of Composition Studies.* Carbondale: Southern Illinois University Press.

Vance, John. 2009. "Code-Meshing Meshed Codes: Some Complications and Possibilities." *JAC* 29 (1–2): 281–84.

Wardle, Elizabeth. 2012a. "Creative Repurposing for Expansive Learning: Considering 'Problem-Exploring' and 'Answer-Getting' Dispositions in Individuals and Fields." *Composition Forum* 26. http://compositionforum.com/issue/26/.

Wardle, Elizabeth, ed. 2012b. "Writing and Transfer." *Composition Forum* 26. http://compositionforum.com/issue/26/.

Williams, Raymond. 1977. *Marxism and Literature*. New York: Oxford University Press.

Yancey, Kathleen Blake. 1998. *Reflection in the Writing Classroom*. Logan: Utah State University Press.

Yancey, Kathleen Blake, Liane Robertson, and Kara Taczak. 2014. *Writing across Contexts: Transfer, Composition, and Sites of Writing*. Logan: Utah State University Press.

Yildiz, Yasemin. 2012. *Beyond the Mother Tongue: The Postmonolingual Condition*. New York: Fordham University Press.

7

THEORIZING THE REFLECTION PRACTICES OF FEMALE HMONG COLLEGE STUDENTS
Is Reflection a Racialized Discourse?

Asao B. Inoue and Tyler Richmond

In this chapter, we explore reflection as a racialized discourse. To pursue this inquiry, we consider the reflective practices of Hmong students at California State University, Fresno, enrolled in a three-week summer English Bridge course designed to teach reading practices, a course intended to prepare students for their first-year writing course in the fall. Because the curriculum mostly involves daily reading and writing assignments that are reflective in nature, this course is ideal for capturing reflective writing by students. In this chapter, then, we provide context for our study; a quick survey of some findings; and a detailed textual and interview-based analysis of the reflective writing of four Hmong students. Ultimately, we explore reflection as a racialized discourse and question the conventional ways reflection has been articulated and theorized.

METHODS, STUDENTS, AND REFLECTIVE DATA

California State University, Fresno, is an Historically Hispanic-Serving Institution (HHSI) enrolling approximately twenty-two thousand students a year. In the fall of 2012 (the last semester for which we have complete data), the enrollment by racial formation included 38.8 percent Hispanic students, 28.8 percent white, 14.8 percent Asian (mostly Hmong), 4.4 percent African American, 3.0 percent International, and 0.4 percent American Indian (California State University n.d.). Like all CSU campuses, Fresno State has a large number of students whom the institution designates as remedial in English as determined by a score on a timed writing exam, the English Placement Test (EPT). The

DOI: 10.7330/9781607325161.c007

Table 7.1. Fall 2013 English remediation rates at Fresno State

Race	No. of Freshmen	No. Proficient in English	% Proficient in English	% Designated as Remedial
African American	119	61	51.3%	48.7%
Mexican American	1,298	593	45.7%	54.3%
Asian American	495	161	32.5%	67.5%
White Non-Latino	601	459	76.4%	23.6%
Total	2,913	1,274	52.2%	47.8%

remediation rates in fall 2012 for enrolled students by racial formation are shown in table 7.1, a typical distribution.[1]

One of the reasons we chose Hmong students for our focus was their unusually high frequency of EPT remediation designations. In addition, a past study (Inoue 2012, 86, 88), found that Hmong students in Fresno State's first-year writing program were on average rated higher in reflection on final program portfolios than students in any other racial formation. These two findings seem to contradict one another; either reflection as judged by the writing program is not a part of the writing construct assessed in the EPT (or is defined differently), or something else is happening.

The Summer Bridge English program at Fresno State is designed to help incoming first-year students transition from high school to college, with an emphasis on preparing them to read academic texts in productive ways. Students designated as remedial in English, and who also meet a number of other criteria that deem them "at risk," are invited to participate in the program in lieu of completing the CSU system's Early Start requirement. The most significant difference between Early Start and Summer Bridge is that participants in the latter are hand selected and provided a much larger support network, including a counselor, tutoring, and in some cases on-campus housing. In the summer of 2013, there were 4 white, 14 African American, 54 Asian (42 of whom identified themselves as Hmong), 117 Latino/a, and 3 other students enrolled (192 total), 139 of whom were female and 53 of whom were male. Our study addressed the 42 students (13 male and 29 female) specifically identifying themselves as Hmong.

Each three-week writing course consisted of approximately twenty-five students. The nongraded course met two hours a day, five days a week; students received a pass or no pass (C/NC) for one unit of elective credit.

The program's curriculum was primarily focused on academic reading practices, with three learning goals aimed at reflection: (1) demonstrating purposeful reading practices, (2) reflecting upon at least two distinct practices, and (3) demonstrating an understanding of an "academic conversation." To meet these outcomes, students read at least three academic articles and other popular cultural artifacts, practiced five different reading strategies, and engaged in a variety of reflective writing activities, all of which culminated in a final portfolio. Credit in the class was determined by a grading contract that focused on labor and absences (Inoue 2014), similar to Danielewicz and Elbow's (2009) contract.

Reflection was a large part of the course: students completed a total of three formal reflective documents in response to assignments that asked them to explicitly discuss the reading practices they learned and how they learned them. The first two reflective documents were assigned at the end of the first and second weeks, while the third was a prompted letter of reflection—similar in spirit to Kathleen Blake Yancey's (1998) "reflection in presentation"—that students included in their final portfolio; the last few days of the course were dedicated to inventing, drafting, and revising the letters. For the purposes of this study, only the third and final reflective document, the portfolio's letter of reflection, was considered. In postcourse portfolio readings conducted by teachers in the program, the Hmong Summer Bridge students' portfolios received an average score of 2.97 out of 6 in the second reflective outcome above, reflecting upon at least two distinct practices, with 3 being the lower boundary for proficient work; the portfolios of Hmong female students received an average score of 3.04, portfolios of male students a 2.86. The number of portfolios rated lower than 3 (not proficient) was also higher in male Hmong students (35 percent) than females (24 percent). Initially, then, like the practices of their white female counterparts (Black et al. 1994, 237–38), the reflective practices of Hmong females at Fresno State were valued more highly than those of males.

For our study,[2] a total of forty-two reflective letters from Hmong students were collected and read in three separate reading stages. We marked and counted instances of two features: (1) rhetorical strategies, or common ways writers structured their letters and appealed to a reader; and (2) themes, or common ideas, phrases, or sentiments writers used in the letters. In the first reading, we identified a number of rhetorical strategies and themes that emerged in the reflective samples. As we identified each, we discussed it and made two lists, one for each feature. In the second reading, we reread all the samples, paying attention only to the items on the lists of rhetorical strategies and themes identified in the first reading. We selected four provocative letters we felt best demonstrated the most popular strategies and themes in the corpus of Hmong reflection letters. In the third reading, we again reread the corpus, looking more closely at the rhetorical strategies and common themes we previously identified, paying most careful attention to the four documents that best represented those rhetorical strategies and themes, double checking our tabulations and discussing the way each letter used the strategies and themes. The two of us did these readings together and met several times more to read and discuss our findings.

The authors of the four reflection letters discussed below are Hmong females who had just graduated from high school and were seventeen or eighteen years old. We conducted short, follow-up interviews with each of these four students, asking them simply to talk to us about what they said in their letters. Although we selected portions of their letters to prompt them in the interviews, we tried very hard not to use leading questions. We simply wanted them to describe what they were thinking about or communicating in their letters, particularly in key areas, which we'll discuss below.

STRATEGIES AND THEMES IN HMONG REFLECTION

The most common rhetorical strategies and themes used in some way in reflection letters by Hmong students are indicated in table 7.2; two of these are ones most teachers might expect to find in any set of reflection letters. The first was organizing the letter around the lessons and readings from the class, often using the handout name or text name. The second, which was employed as often as the first, was using a narrative that was chronologically based, which usually amounted to a progress narrative, one identified by Tony Scott as "growth narratives" that are "a salient feature in the genre" of reflection letters (Scott 2005, 18). Glenda Conway also writes about similar progress narratives in her own classroom use of reflection letters, which she describes as letters that "pushed the right 'buttons'" and that are self-conscious demonstrations of students comparing "current selves 'against earlier, more naïve versions of themselves'" (Conway 1994, 84–85, 91).

While the most frequent theme mentioned in letters in some fashion was "I learned a lot," often coming near the opening of the letter, statements like this don't offer much substance. In addition, the statements usually seemed like a necessary salutation, or requirement of the genre for Hmong students, almost like saying "hello, how are you?" when meeting a friend. However, the second most frequent theme, "I'm

Table 7.2. Most common rhetorical strategies and themes in Hmong reflection letters

Rhetorical Strategy	Total	No. of Female	No. of Male
Names or references to lessons/readings	27	21	6
Use of chronological narrative, usually a before/after structure	21	17	4
Focus or explanation of labor, processes, or doing things in the course	11	7	4
Summary or definition of concepts learned in the course	7	5	2
Naming and/or appealing to the teacher as the reader	6	3	3
Use of personal experience to frame or illustrate	5	4	1
Descriptions of drafts included	4	3	1
Themes	Total	No. of Female	No. of Male
I learned a lot or something in the course	15	9	6
I'm glad, grateful, or lucky to take this class	11	10	1
I overcame obstacles in reading and/or writing	7	6	1
I was confident and free to write, not constrained	6	4	2
Not about reading/writing but about Summer Bridge as a whole	6	5	1
I learned annotation as a reading practice	5	5	0
Feedback as a good thing	4	2	2

glad, grateful, or lucky to take this class," was used primarily by Hmong females; the sole male who used this theme also articulated two other female dominant themes, "I overcame obstacles in reading and/or writing" and "I was confident and free to write, not constrained." These three themes were female-dominant ones, appearing almost exclusively in female-Hmong-student reflection letters, suggesting that they are sentiments associated closely with Hmong female students and their lives. Reading these common themes as statements connected to the material conditions of our Hmong students' lives, as we do below, suggests possible shared historical and material patterns in the lives of Hmong females in Fresno. For example, while the second theme, "I overcame obstacles in reading and/or writing," is a theme found in reflection letters by white, middle-class females (Black et al. 1994, 240–41), the first and third are not, suggesting these may be sentiments native to Hmong females in Fresno or more pervasive dispositions Hmong females seem

Table 7.3. Rhetorical strategies and themes found in Hmong reflection letters compared to Yancey's features in reflection-in-presentation

Identified Rhetorical Strategy/Theme	Yancey's (1998) Description of Feature
Use of chronological narrative, usually a before/after structure; I was confident and free to write, not constrained	"speaking of past selves as a way of understanding the current self" (95)
Names or references to lessons/readings; summary or definition of concepts learned in the course; I learned annotation as a reading practice; feedback as a good thing	"student works to define and address problems, and/or to summarize and interpret what she or he has learned" (70)
Focus or explanation of labor, processes, or doing things in the course; descriptions of drafts included; I was confident and free to write, not constrained	"Describe (and sometimes assess) the processes that the student used in creating texts, with specific reference to processes that explain how one draft evolved from an earlier one" (73)
Use of personal experience to frame or illustrate	"Reflective writers draw on multiple contexts to explain what they have learned" (84); "invoking other contexts voluntarily as a means of understanding and explaining" (95)
I overcame obstacles in reading and/or writing	"that learning isn't easy" (90)
Naming and/or appealing to the teacher as the reader; I learned a lot or something in the course; I'm glad, grateful, or lucky to take this class	"Shmooz is a more direct appeal, appearing in a text that plays back to us quite explicitly (quite manipulatively?) our own values" (81)
I learned a lot or something in the course	Answer the question, "What have I learned" (95)

to tap into when asked to reflect upon their learning. Likewise, most of the rhetorical strategies and themes we found in Hmong letters were similar to ones Yancey (1998) identifies in one way or another in reflection-in-presentation, as seen in table 7.3.

This accounting of strategies and themes suggests that Hmong students, particularly Hmong females at this point in their writing development, gravitate to what is a common set of rhetorical tropes for beginning college students: the use of a chronological narrative; the focus on or explanation of labor, processes, or doing things in the course; and the use of personal experience to frame or illustrate. In this case specifically, however, the strategies and themes may be a result of the curriculum (the absence of grades surely affected students' experiences and their focusing on labor), but they may also point to cultural and gendered dispositions reinforced in the material conditions of these Hmong students. For instance, reflection letters that focus on labor and personal experiences (in and out of the classroom) of the writers to explain what they have learned in a class about academic reading practices suggests that the material conditions that contextualize those students' education matter to their learning. To better understand this connection between reflection and the material lives of Fresno Hmong, we turn to a qualitative discussion of four letters.

FOUR CASES OF HMONG FEMALES' REFLECTIONS

All four reflection letters demonstrate the most common rhetorical strategies in reflections of Hmong female students, including framing their reflection letters as progress narratives or narratives that depict their selves before Summer Bridge and after it, speaking about gaining "confidence" through the lessons or work of the course, and using personal experience to frame some of the lessons learned from the course or the reading activities. Three letters speak of overcoming obstacles (Lina's, Nou's, and Maiger's), while the fourth, Celina's, does not, instead focusing on ways of working with another female student in the classroom. Collectively, these letters demonstrate that these Hmong women may be tacitly aware of the white, middle-class cultural and linguistic dispositions expected of them, used to judge them and construct them as other than a white student. While none of them names whiteness, their awareness of racialized dispositions stems from their material conditions in and around the classroom, which include their home lives.

Timothy Barnett (2000) offers a description of whiteness as a discourse of the classroom. He suggests that the writing classroom needs a vocabulary to discuss the ways race and power relations structure our language (31). Without a vocabulary to discuss whiteness, it often remains unnamed in students' rhetorical patterns and practices. Thus, when Yancey warns teachers that when we read reflections, "it may be that we are only replicating the construct of writing that was inscribed in us—that is, writing as act with intellectual, ideological, and, indeed, moral consequences linked to a unified construct" (Yancey 1998, 194), she could be warning us to be mindful of how we read and judge reflective discourse as an unmarked white discourse. Many have discussed ways academic discourses are unmarked white discourses (hooks 1994; Keating 1995), and the reflective discourse asked of students in writing classrooms is often no different from these. Yancey seems to suggest that perhaps there are false universals teachers and scholars may be working from, like whiteness, that affect how we assess students' reflective texts. These false universals, we argue, are constructs of writing that are a part of a teacher's disciplinary, linguistic, cultural, and racial dispositions.

By identifying these false universal writing constructs as constructs of whiteness, we highlight the way in which both a teacher's and a student's racialized subjectivities are implicated in a student's reflective text, how it is produced, read, judged, and so forth. Thus, as we demonstrate below, reflection is not a one-to-one correspondence between who the material writers are, what they may have learned or come to know, and who is represented on the page in their reflective texts in readers' various possible readings. The way a writer is constructed in a reflection is a consequence of a reading by a reader—an assessment—which means the discourse of whiteness embodied by the traditional reflective assignment (and teachers' reading practices) always constructs part of any student's reflective selves. And when student discourse is about their own discourse, as in reflection, there is an opportunity for students to name whiteness as a part of the standards they are attempting to meet, thus giving students of color (and other marginalized students) a vocabulary that can help them locate possible tensions in their own language use, material conditions, and writing. Reflective texts by default do not offer this vocabulary of whiteness, even if most assume a white discourse; teachers and the classroom must introduce such vocabulary, but our discussion of the four Hmong reflection letters, as demonstrated below, draws on the vocabulary of whiteness to help us show this potential.

Celina

Celina's letter, like most, opens with a signal that it will be a progress narrative, saying, "Before the dawn of Summer Bridge, I was sure that the readings of English were going to be uninteresting but, I can admit that I was wrong." She learns that her reading process is one in which she "creat[es] voices of characters" in her mind and "can live through a text." Most interesting, Celina says reading out loud allows her to "hear [her]self amongst other sounds." While she does not explain this comment, it offers an interesting juxtaposition to the previous ideas about reading and voices in her mind: she sees herself as separate or different from these other voices.

Later in the letter, Celina discusses her past embarrassment when letting others read her writing. She "assumed that [she] was not a good writer," but over time peers who read her work helped her. She explains,

> My peer Julie replied with some feedback that helped me know that I was doing something that was good and made sense. Her reply, "I like the way you mentioned the problem and I also like how you mentioned everything that's going on and how you showed the examples. I really liked how you

were informed with this information." So I also try to give positive critical feedback that can help my peers rather than bring them down to hurt them because we're all in it together wanting to succeed.

In contrast to Peter Elbow's description of reader feedback's helping a writer to move forward in a draft (Elbow 1993, 201), Celina identifies how Julie's response helped her not to write better but to participate more fully in giving her own "positive critical feedback" to others. Others' liking her writing led to her liking others' writing. The lesson Celina's reflection generates, like that for most Hmong students in the study, is not an individually oriented one but a socially oriented one, one only meaningful in a social setting. Her lesson is about feedback to others, helping others, being in a community of students who are "all in it together wanting to succeed." Later in her interview, she confirms this, saying, "It's just kind of like knowing you're not alone, writing how you would write, and knowing how others write similar to you it kind of helps. I mean, people are really not comfortable sharing their writing, but now I see they write just like me . . . you kind of get inspired by them, see a sentence and think that's really cool, so then you incorporate that into your writing."

For Celina, the letter turns into a reflection on her place within a larger community, one that scares her because of the possibility for judgment, but one that she is also eager to enter into, to "incorporate" into her own sense of self. This sentiment and lesson appears different from the typical, individually oriented lessons many reflection-letter assignments seem to promote. A focus on individualism (i.e., the Cartesian *I* epitomized in Descartes's *cogito ergo sum*) to discover or make meaning or draw conclusions is a primary aspect of white academic discourses, as discussed by many scholars (Barnett 2000, 10; Myser 2003). Celina's reflection seems to work against this autonomous, self-reliant impulse in white discourses, instead preferring a social stance.

Her reflective discourse is one about a community of students working together to overcome obstacles and find confidence, two common themes in our corpus. Does she do this self-consciously? Is she aware of her resistance to a white reflective discourse? That's harder to know, although the three other letters offer a gloss on this question. Celina does reveal to us, however, an important observation about reflective discourse that we noticed in all the letters we read; moreover, while common themes exist across racial boundaries in reflective texts, treatment of these themes differs. We see the causes stemming from the material differences that have racialized patterns in Fresno. Celina's progress narrative isn't one that culminates in the fulfillment of the individual, but in feelings of acceptance and agency within a larger group. The reflective self we read in her letter is one that consciously joins a group in order to affect that group, not an individual self struggling or achieving alone.

Lina

In Lina's letter, the orientation toward the social and material is clearer. Lina's first three and one-half paragraphs use plural pronouns (*we* and *us*) for the subjects and indirect objects of most of her sentences. Much like Celina's orientation to the lessons learned, Lina's reflection creates lessons that are exclusively social lessons: "We all grew closer with just a few conversations," and "we began to talk more in class and got to know most of the people in class." In fact, when Lina does reference herself in the singular, it is often ambiguous. For instance, when discussing a lesson on the Toulmin model, she says, "I learn how to not just annotate our notes, but a logical way for us to use in to benefit us for our college year." Lessons appear to be simultaneously social and individual. This blending of Lina's reflective self and the social community of the classroom around her becomes more problematic later in the letter when she discusses her family and what is next for her. She says,

> I have a lot of things going throughout my personal life such as family, school and work. Most of these things are just temporary, but they do impact my life a lot. For the past two years, I've been constantly keeping myself busy with school and work. Those around me usually doubt me because I usually never make time for them. Whenever I'm asked to go somewhere, knowing I'll be home super late or whatsoever, I make the decision to stay home and finish my homework or study. Most of them say, "You're working too hard with going to work straight after school and staying up late, you need to get out more," or "you're stressing too much about life when you're still so young." I've never given up on myself. I'm a hard worker even when I fail the first time, it doesn't stop me from not trying again.
>   My goal at the end of this Summer Bridge Program, I hope to achieve confident and hope. Confident to not try to doubt myself and hope to believe in myself that I'm able to do whatever I can to help me achieve and succeed.

The reflective self Lina constructs in her narrative reveals not simply how hard it has been for her to learn the previous lessons, or how difficult she knows it still will be in the year of college to come, but how the material conditions of her life, her work, relations with friends, and her family affect her progress through school.

In fact, in some ways, Lina's reflection reveals how as a Hmong woman she must succeed in school *despite* family and friends' influences, not because of them. She confirmed this reading of her story in a follow up interview when asked specifically about what she meant by this paragraph. She explained that in high school her family wasn't supportive of her education. In fact, she had to work a job in order to pay for her graduation materials (e.g., cap and gown). The youngest in a large family with five other siblings, many of whom are in college also, she explained that her mother and father didn't openly encourage her education. She wanted to "prove them wrong," prove to them that she "could do good in school." Thus, to Lina, never giving up on herself means more than struggling through homework and school; it means struggling to work and go to school, struggling to prove her academic worth to family and friends. The lessons in her reflection are more about overcoming the obstacles in the conditions of her life, which we believe are similar to the experiences of many female Hmong in Fresno, in which the emphasis often is on the sons and their educations, not the daughters and theirs.[3] Lina's reflection suggests that the three most popular themes—being grateful to be in the class, overcoming obstacles, and feeling confidence in her writing, all of which appear in Lina's letter, and especially the ways these students construct their selves in relation to these themes, the ways they interpret them in reflection—may be uniquely female Hmong discursive features because they have sources in the material conditions of Hmong females' lives outside of school. In the case of the Hmong conditions, students might feel grateful just to be in college, particularly when the obstacles the student must face are her family's disregard for her education and a need for someone to express confidence in her ability to succeed. This need may also suggest the attraction to a socially oriented reflective stance toward learning in many Hmong females' letters since lessons learned socially suggest a shared sense of confidence through working together.

Nou

Nou's and Maiger's letters reveal even more sharply the way Hmong female students may face material and cultural inconsistencies that cause the subjects developed in their reflection letters to be read as conflicting and struggling selves. Nou is most explicit about these contradictions between her own life as a multilingual Hmong woman with parents who do not speak or read English very well and the imagined life of her white, monolingual English-speaking peers. She explains,

> I remember as a child, I never got the experience of my parents reading to me before I go to sleep because my parents don't even know half of the English word that I know. Unlike most of the American parents, they tend to read to their children before they sleep; my parents gave me life lessons such as cooking, cleaning, caring for my siblings and lesson then is going to help me in the long run. I'm not saying that American parents are better or anything but what I'm trying to say is that although my parents did [sic] know English I still learn something from them and it's something that no one can take from me because I'm going to always remember those life lesson. My point is that even though your bilingual you should still be confidence in the work or whatever you do and that's what i learn from [the teacher] because we bilingual people are unique in a way because we understand two languages while other only know one language which is English.

Nou presents her reflective self as one developed by her material conditions and contrasted to an imagined ideal—white, middle-class life associated closely with the language and practices of the classroom. At the same time, Nou takes a funds-of-knowledge approach, too, resisting giving up her family's lessons. It is a complex problem-lesson in this contrast. Nou attributes the academic reading dispositions associated with the course to white middle-class parental dispositions that "American parents" embody in their bedtime reading practices with their children, a life and past that is not and was not Nou's and that presents a contradiction or barrier for her in the classroom. Instead of the white discourse of her peers, she received "life lessons" her parents taught her, which are domestic and perhaps gendered in nature—"cooking, cleaning, caring for my siblings," "something no one can take from [her]."

Furthermore, it is important to note that while the literature on whiteness provides overwhelming evidence of several attributes of whiteness, three seem most pertinent to our discussion of reflective discourse here. These three attributes of whiteness suggest that most reflective discourses expected in writing classrooms are white discourses, a point made earlier, one underscoring how difficult reflecting can be for multilingual students and students of color, like Nou, and for several reasons. First, whiteness is unspoken and unnamed in discourse, culture, and practices, that is, whiteness is always an unmarked category, whereas the racial Other and her discourse are marked in some way (Chambers 1997, 188; Dalton 2005, 16) and marked usually as deficient or remedial. If teachers are not explicit about the racialized structures in language, society, and school that influence and create their expectations for reflection and reflective texts, they leave whiteness unnamed and unexamined in reflection, which may harm students of color by neglecting their material and cultural conditions. A student like Nou might conclude that she is deficient or lacks the linguistic abilities to succeed in college, leaving her comparison above as one that only identifies a difference in family habits, not one that may identify two distinct sets of racialized dispositions stemming from material conditions in her life that have racialized trends in Fresno. Nou's reflection implicitly refers to whiteness and herself as a linguistic Other in school by being a Hmong cultural insider; however, she lacks the vocabulary of whiteness that could help her see it as more than a single instance but rather as a possible social pattern beyond her family.

Second, whiteness is associated with an individual who is detached, objective, and demonstrates abstract reasoning (Chambers 1997, 91–2; Flagg 1997, 221–22; Myser 2003, 6). If students are expected to reflect in purely detached, objective, or abstract ways, reflection can easily be a white discourse that may contradict the life and material conditions of many students. This contradiction may allow teachers to read students of colors' reflections as off topic, irrational, or too emotional to be productive, particularly if the teachers attribute ideas or lessons learned to their own racialized educational conditions. For instance, because she's nascently aware of whiteness in the teacher's readings of her writing, Nou senses she may be read irrationally, so she qualifies her own discussion of her family, saying, "I'm not saying that American parents are better or anything but." Like most students, Nou avoids naming race, even though her discussion is one about groups (us and them). She qualifies her statement as a way to assimilate a discourse of whiteness by promoting colorblindness (e.g., "Americans aren't better" meaning "we're not different from them"). Nou's awareness of her difference speaks to her awareness of the whiteness that affects her schooling.

Lina, too, seems to pull back in her conclusion about hoping "to achieve confident and hope. Confident to not try to doubt myself and hope to believe in myself that I'm able to do whatever I can to help me achieve and succeed." Underneath her declaration, we hear the words from her interview about the surely disappointing and emotionally painful feelings Lina must have felt about how her family treated her interest in school. To discuss such feelings of disappointment and pain would not be reasonable, detached, or objective, and surely, as in Nou's situation, they are conflicting.

Third, whiteness is assumed to be universal, neutral, and the norm (Dyer 2005, 10; Wildman and Davis 1997, 315–16), meaning reflection as a white discourse is assumed to be universal, done the same way by all students regardless of their linguistic traditions, cultural backgrounds, class, gender, and so on—that is, regardless of the social and economic structures that create racial or other formations in society.[4] Clearly, Nou, like all of our student examples, is writing from her conditions, ones that make it hard to have a neutral or universal stance, despite her comparisons to the American families she imagines.

In our interview with Nou, we asked about the above paragraph. She grew up in a small rural town (Easton) outside of Fresno, a place where she continues to live with her parents, her brother, and his family. She described them as very "traditional," a type of family that doesn't reflect the idealized white families she sees on television. She explained, "Watching the American movies and stuff you see their parents tucking them in bed and 'I love you' with a kiss on their cheek, none of us got to experience that because in the Hmong culture we don't really express or say 'I love you.' It just wasn't us." While she isn't necessarily embarrassed or ashamed by this difference, the tension it creates in her life—especially in the classroom—is apparent. She explained, "Now that I think of it, before when I was younger, I feel like people don't respect people who are bilingual, because my parents don't speak English, they think they're not a part of the American culture. But I do believe now that being bilingual is unique and you're not just stuck with English." Similar to the social nature of Lina's lessons, Nou's lessons about reading and language are social by definition but are contrastive. She's more aware of the whiteness that affects her schooling, even if she doesn't name it. Instead of avoiding and perhaps attempting to assimilate, as Lina's reflective self suggests, Nou's reflective self-attempts to carve out her own value against a white norm, defining her language lessons, for example, by contrasting them specifically to a white, "American" monolingual norm. She gains confidence despite her differences with the white expectations of the classroom.

Maiger

Finally, Maiger's letter is a long, mostly personal discussion of the struggles she has in class and what she forecasts will be problems in the coming year. One of the most interesting aspects of Maiger's letter is how, like Lina, she ambiguously situates her learning in social and individual terms, again suggesting the ways female Hmong racial subjectivity creates contradictory reflective selves. Maiger begins by spending some time describing herself as a "shy" and quiet student in past and present classes, in the process revealing the social and racial segregation of Fresno, particularly outside the university: "Before this program, I was never the type who gets comfortable with people who I don't know at all for the first time, even though everyone's been living in the same city as me ever since long time ago, we never talked, never seen each other, or be with each other at all. But this program changed my thought about that."

She could be talking in nonracial terms, but two observations suggest our reading of her statement as implicitly racial. First, she admits to getting to know those others in the present class, ones who are racially different from her (mostly Latino/a) and many of whom come from different areas of Fresno, economically segregated areas. Second, her reference to "living in the same city," Fresno, yet never talking or seeing "each other," suggests she's thinking in terms of wider, segregated communities, schools, and social circles. If her past experiences in high school were not experiences of racial segregation, then this class would not be so different, as it draws on three of the four main racial formations that make up Fresno. But this class's social relations were different for everyone. She also uses the plural *we* to identify how the class, or maybe her Hmong peers, have not talked, seen, or been around others in the past. Her reflective self changes because of the local diversity of the classroom and the necessary interactions in the class.

Throughout her letter, Maiger's stance as a segregated racial and social reflective self is often difficult to separate from an individual self learning in the classroom. In the next few paragraphs, she continues her discussion, revealing this ambiguity and tension:

> I was shy and I always wonder when will I stop being those kinds of people in class. A lot of people always see that as a "not so good" thing. I always think it's a normal thing. But others always say, "Oh, she is shy. Oh here comes the shy group," making me feel uncomfortable. Maybe it's because people are being rude saying stuff like that, making us have less confidence in ourselves. . . .
>
> However, overall, I'm still shy a bit, I never liked my voice, so I never liked speaking over others. . . .
>
> We've been working with other people who are strangers to us but are in the same program and in the same academy. To be honest, it's very fun to work with others in the classroom.

While it could be that Maiger is trying to use a convention in which the plural is used as the subject of her ideas, perhaps to give them more strength, this reading seems unlikely since she moves back and forth from "I" to "we." The reference to the "shy group" and its following sentence about the group's lack of confidence suggests Maiger thinks in terms of a social group she is a part of, likely her Hmong colleagues. In addition, there is the repeated use of *we* in her letter, composed in a class with daily assignments asking students to reflect and use *I*, to be personal. The letter genre itself assumes an individual author and subject, which is how the curriculum sets up this reflective assignment—it asks, what did *you* learn? So the question for us is, whom is Maiger referring to when she says "we"? Is it Hmong students, the "shy group" who "have less confidence" of which she speaks and is a member? Are these groups the same to her? Is she referring to a racially segregated group when she explains that "we've been working with other people who are strangers to us"? Whether we read these linguistic signs as ones about a racially segregated group that affects her learning or not, like those of her colleagues, Maiger's reflective practices suggest more strongly a contradiction in her reflective self and the self that others around her, or in the classroom, perceive. She sees herself as not "normal," not having white dispositions, in part because she "never liked speaking over others" like the (Hmong) group of which she is a part. Maiger valiantly looks for the silver lining but still sees herself as shy, silent, less confident, all of which she implicitly contrasts with a racialized white norm. Because Maiger appears more aware of a white discourse and its dispositions that lend themselves to particular judgments of her, one might see the theme of confidence (or a lack of it), which was a more evenly gendered theme in all the reflections, as a racialized theme in the reflective discourse of Fresno Hmong. One might thus ask, in what ways do Hmong appear as less confident or shy in their reflective writing, to themselves and to readers (teachers and peers)? And as suggested by Nou's and Maiger's reference to material conditions affecting their success in school, how might the unique material conditions of Hmong students encourage such appearance as not "normal," or deficient?

Like Lina and Nou, Maiger eventually turns explicitly to her personal struggles with education, which are associated with her material conditions as a Hmong woman in Fresno. She says,

> Every day, it's school from morning until five in the afternoon, then right after that, it's working until midnight, then come home, do homework until two in the morning, sleep, and repeat every day the same thing; that causes for me to woke up late once for class.
>
> Just like how my counselors told us, it's either work or school. I thought about that very seriously. Every day I ask myself, "If I'm like this now, and it's only math class and English class with little easy homework, how can I manage the real college, with working every day? . . .
>
> I came to think that I should try it out for a couple of days with both work and school for a while, and see how it goes. If it doesn't work out for me, I will choose my education over my work. I only get paid minimum wage only, and college gets me somewhere I get paid twice as more as that.

> Right now, I know I will not be able to work and school at the same time, because I know how much I can handle. I want to be successful; I don't want work to pull me down from school. But on the other hand, I don't know about quitting my work, because I just barely got hired three weeks ago. This is my first job and I'm scared it may look bad on my history of work. I need someone to talk to about stuff like this. I really just want to focus on my school, rather than work. I'm also scared that my family will think bad about my decisions, and not being able to help pay bills.

As in Lina's situation, Maiger's material conditions are not like those of the imagined traditional (white) college student. Maiger works. She helps her family pay bills. But she would rather go to school full time. She doesn't want to let her family down. They need her help financially and perhaps in other ways. She's also consciously thinking about and determined to go to school, despite the difficulties. There are pressures from counselors, who give her ultimatums: "It's either work or school." She knows she needs help, even if it is only someone to talk to. Again, the material conditions of family obligations and influences, which are inflected in Maiger's particular working and home conditions, have bearing on the lessons Maiger takes or can take from the course, but they are not happy or simple lessons, and they aren't really ones about academic reading or writing: they are lessons of contradictions that the conditions of her life create as she learns to read in college. It is significant, we think, that when asked to reflect on her reading practices and explain what she learned, Maiger discusses her job, family, and life outside of the classroom. To her, these things are related to her learning to read and write because they create conditions that allow her to do so, or not. Had she had a vocabulary that could name whiteness in the discourses expected of her in the class, we think she might have been able to make further insights about her learning and about these contradictions she has already exposed. Maiger might have seen how her reflection on what she has learned about academic reading practices is not just a rumination on the difficulties of being shy or not liking her own voice, or on going to school, but also is a discourse that itself resists white dispositions to interpellate her as shy or deficient or unable to succeed in school.

Because these Hmong women see themselves, and have been seen by others, as racially Other, as not the white norm in school, it is difficult for them to reflect upon their learning without references to a white norm, or an assumption of it, which causes tensions and contradictions. Through the dialectic between their material conditions and the words they use to understand and express their learning, these four Hmong women writers show how their racial and gendered subject positions form contradictions not easily resolved without identifying whiteness in reflective discourse.

RECONSIDERING *REFLECTION* IN COMPOSITION STUDIES

So is reflection a racialized discourse? While our study is too small to be conclusive, we see strong findings suggesting that yes, there are important features of Hmong female reflective discourse that seem influenced by their participation in Hmong communities in Fresno, which of course would be the case for white students, and Latinos/as, and students of other racial formations: participation in communities matters. More specifically, what we've traced are female Hmong reflective practices that attempt to enact a white discourse of reflection, one that appears to cause contradictions for the writers when they cannot name the discourse or it's not identified in the classroom in some way. The broadest tension is exhibited in the way Hmong women's reflective selves are socially oriented in the lessons they articulate. They orient themselves as inside (and outside?) social groups, and often their lessons are social in nature, benefiting those around them, not simply themselves; they present reflective selves ambiguously moving between singular and plural subject positions, perhaps suggesting the ambiguity they feel in their school selves and the social structures that contextualize their agency, or possibly suggesting their need for confidence through social acceptance or approval among peers. The continual attention to their material conditions, either tacitly or through the incorporation of personal experience, frames their lessons in reflection as a struggle to assimilate, a struggle against the conditions of their lives that make going to school difficult, or a struggle against a white norm they never seem to match up to very well, one that demands an objective, immaterial recording of their subjective, material experiences. In most cases, success in school and with writing is accomplished despite their material conditions, not because of them, revealing how the struggles they have with reading and writing in English are less about the intellectual work involved and more about finding a space for that work in their complex lives.

But let us not be fooled. While class and socioeconomic status play an important part in how the material conditions of Hmong students construct their writer selves in reflection letters, these may only be the most present set of conditions Hmong can see and discuss. Is this, then, a cultural distinction and not a racial one? Perhaps, but as many have argued, US society generally does not make such distinctions easily. Our students live in a racialized institutional topography, as much as in cultural or ethnic ones. We know whiteness was not a part of the explicit curriculum. Because one of us was the director of the program, who developed the curriculum and trained the teachers, and the other was a teacher in the program during the time these students attended it, we feel confident in concluding that very little, if any, instruction on whiteness was offered. If it had been, perhaps there might have been a stronger tendency by female Hmong in their reflections to struggle with the tensions around their confidence, or to see their material conditions as more than just obstacles to their educational success, or to see productive differences between their more socially oriented stances and the objective, individualized one white discourses promote as the norm. Identifying whiteness and how it and material conditions interpellate student writers might have helped these students who already live and work in a racializing world.

Ultimately, then, we wonder, when teachers consciously or unconsciously expect students to reproduce a dominant, white, middle-class set of dispositions in reflective texts, or do not consider the way reflection might be an invisibly white discourse, or do not account for the material conditions of students' lives (and the possible contradictions those conditions may produce in reflective selves), are they unknowingly creating hostile and unfair conditions for some students of color? Yancey points out a similar issue in her discussion by questioning whether teachers blindly reproduce themselves (Yancey 1998, 168) by expecting and assessing certain dispositions in student reflection as false universals. Part of her solution is to ask important questions in ongoing dialogue around student reflective texts: "What are the students' native languages? How do they learn? What do they already know, and how is it changed by what we want them to learn?" (166). We believe a reflection conscious of the whiteness that constructs it allows teachers (and even students) to read the reflective selves produced in reflective assignments as ones always already confronting the material conditions of students' lives, always interpellating students in uneven ways, which may account for the material conditions of local racial formations and the lessons we often focus on or expect in reflective texts. In addition, such self-conscious reflection offers ways for students to confront their existential situations as learners and to re-present that in reflective selves. We may not need to redefine reflection for students, although we might (as chapters in this volume suggest), but teachers should rethink how they read reflection, inherently reading it as a discourse of whiteness and learning to read it in alternative ways, then voicing back to students the ways this whiteness may manifest itself in students' reflective texts. In doing so, teachers can offer a potential vocabulary of whiteness to students who struggle with the contradictions discourses of whiteness prompt but who lack the language to interrogate whiteness. Doing these things may help us better account for, and be sensitive to, the ways reflection can support all student writers.

Notes

1. We use the category names *Mexican American* and *Asian American* the institution uses in its data set for this table, but in our discussion we use *Latino/a* and *Hmong*. CSU analytic studies also uses the broader description of *ethnicity* to label these categories. We follow Michael Omi and Howard Winant's critique of the ethnicity-based paradigm of race (Omi and Winant 1994, 15) in which race is relegated primarily to culture and descent, so we keep *race* as the larger description of the categories in the table. All data for table 7.1 comes from CSU analytic studies web site (Proficiency Reports of Students Entering the CSU System 2013).

2. All students identified their gender and the racial status by which they most identified in consent forms in the first week of the course, which were double-checked with institutional data from the EOP office that runs the Summer Bridge program; then those students we chose to use in our study signed a new consent form during short interviews conducted in the following fall semester of 2013 after the Summer Bridge course. We preserve all student work in this chapter as it was submitted, not changing or editing it.

3. While we both have personal experiences with Hmong students to substantiate this gender dynamic that is by no means only seen in Hmong families, one might look to John Duffy's (2007) literacy study of Hmong or see Richard Lee et al. (2009) or Mai Shoua Khang (2010).

4. We assume Omi and Winant's theory of racial formations to understand race in historical moments and places. They define a racial formation as a "sociohistorical process by which racial categories are created, inhabited, transformed, and destroyed" (Omi and Winant 1994, 55). When we discuss the Hmong racial formation at Fresno State, we mean it very specifically, historically situated in time and place, not universal or static but rather dynamic and changing, making race contingent and nonessential in nature.

Works Cited

Barnett, Timothy. 2000. "Reading 'Whiteness' in English Studies." *College English* 63 (1): 9–37. http://dx.doi.org/10.2307/379029.

Black, Laurel, Donald A. Daiker, Jeffrey Sommers, and Gail Stygall. 1994. "Writing Like a Woman and Being Rewarded for It: Gender, Assessment, and Reflective Letters from Miami University's Student Portfolios." In *New Directions in Portfolio Assessment: Reflective Practice, Critical Theory, and Large-Scale Scoring*, ed. Laurel Black, Donald A. Daiker, Jeffrey Sommers, and Gail Stygall, 235–47. Portsmouth, NH: Boynton/Cook.

California State University. n.d. Office of Institutional Effectiveness. http://www.fresno state.edu/academics/oie/index.html.

Conway, Glenda. 1994. "Portfolio Cover Letters, Students' Self-Presentation, and Teachers' Ethics." In *New Directions in Portfolio Assessment: Reflective Practice, Critical*

Theory, and Large-Scale Scoring, ed. Laurel Black, Donald A. Daiker, Jeffrey Sommers, and Gail Stygall, 83–92. Portsmouth, NH: Boynton/Cook.

Chambers, Ross. 1997. "The Unexamined." In *Whiteness: A Critical Reader*, ed. Mike Hill, 187–203. New York: New York University Press.

Dalton, Harlon. 2005. "Failing to See." In *White Privilege: Essential Readings on the Other Side of Racism*, 2nd ed. Ed. Paula S. Rothenberg, 15–18. New York: Worth.

Danielewicz, Jane, and Peter Elbow. 2009. "A Unilateral Grading Contract to Improve Learning and Teaching." *College Composition and Communication* 61 (2): 244–68.

Duffy, John M. 2007. *Writing from These Roots: Literacy in a Hmong-American Community*. Honolulu: University of Hawai'i Press.

Dyer, Richard. 2005. "The Matter of Whiteness." In *White Privilege: Essential Readings on the Other Side of Racism*, 2nd ed. Ed. Paula S. Rothenberg, 9–14. New York: Worth.

Elbow, Peter. 1993. "Ranking, Evaluating, and Liking: Sorting Out Three Forms of Judgment." *College English* 55 (2): 187–206. http://dx.doi.org/10.2307/378503.

Flagg, Barbara J. 1997. "Transparently White Subjective Decisionmaking: Fashioning a Legal Remedy." In *Critical White Studies: Looking Behind the Mirror*, ed. Richard Delgado and Jean Stefanicic, 220–26. Philadelphia, PA: Temple University Press.

hooks, bell. 1994. *Teaching to Transgress: Education as the Practice of Freedom*. New York: Routledge.

Inoue, Asao B. 2012. "Grading Contracts: Assessing Their Effectiveness on Different Racial Formations." In *Race and Writing Assessment*, ed. Asao B. Inoue and Mya Poe, 79–94. New York: Peter Lang.

Inoue, Asao B. 2014. "A Grade-less Writing Course that Focuses on Labor and Assessing." In *First-Year Composition: Theory into Practice*, ed. Debra Coxwell-Teague and Ronald Lunsford, 71–110. West Lafayette, IN: Parlor.

Keating, AnnLouise. 1995. "Interrogating 'Whiteness,' (De)Constructing 'Race.'" *College English* 57 (8): 901. http://dx.doi.org/10.2307/378620.

Khang, Mai Shoua. 2010. *Hmong Traditional Marriage Roles and the Pursuit of Higher Education for Married Hmong American Women*. MA thesis, University of Wisconsin–Stout.

Lee, Richard M., Kyoung Rae Jung, Jenny C. Su, Alisia G.T.T. Tran, and Nazneen F. Bahrassa. 2009. "The Family Life and Adjustment of Hmong American Sons and Daughters." *Sex Roles* 60 (7/8): 549–58. http://dx.doi.org/10.1007/s11199-008-9406-6.

Myser, Catherine. 2003. "Differences from Somewhere: The Normativity of Whiteness in Bioethics in the United States." *American Journal of Bioethics* 3 (2): 1–11. http://dx.doi.org/10.1162/152651603766436072.

Omi, Michael, and Howard Winant. 1994. *Racial Formation in the United States: From the 1960s to the 1990s*. 2nd ed. New York: Routledge.

Proficiency Reports of Students Entering the CSU System. 2013. California State University Analytic Studies. http://asd.calstate.edu/performance/proficiency.shtml.

Scott, Tony. 2005. "Creating the Subject of Portfolios: Reflective Writing and the Conveyance of Institutional Prerogatives." *Written Communication* 22 (1): 3–35. http://dx.doi.org/10.1177/0741088304271831.

Wildman, Stephanie M., and Adrienne D. Davis. 1997. "Making Systems of Privilege Visible." In *Critical White Studies: Looking Behind the Mirror*, ed. Richard Delgado and Jean Stefanicic, 314–19. Philadelphia, PA: Temple University Press.

Yancey, Kathleen Blake. 1998. *Reflection in the Writing Classroom*. Logan: Utah State University Press.

III

Reflection and Media

8

FROM SELFIES TO SELF-REPRESENTATION IN ELECTRONICALLY MEDIATED REFLECTION
The Evolving Gestalt Effect in ePortfolios

J. Elizabeth Clark

Oxford University Press's word of the year for 2013? *Selfie*, a self-portrait taken with a cell phone. It's probably not surprising, then, that in an age of social media saturation, students live in a world where they constantly present themselves to external audiences through status updates, photographs, videos, memes, and links. In turn, audience interaction on social networking sites encourages Likes and Favorites, which provide immediate feedback and gratification, with the result that media-savvy students have become adept at presenting carefully crafted online versions of themselves and their interests appealing to their audiences. While these selfies are representations of an individual, they offer little in the way of introspection or integration. Instead, they are the ultimate artificial moment, playing to an audience and representing a single aspect of identity.

Emerging cultural commentary on the selfie is mixed. Popular feminist media site *Jezebel*'s Erin Gloria Ryan claims "Selfies Aren't Empowering. They're a Cry for Help," while the *New York Times* recently ran a feature by actor James Franco, "The Meanings of the Selfie" (December 26, 2013). Ryan argues, "If culture were encouraging women to be smart, the word of the year would be 'diplomie' and the definition would be 'a photo of an academic achievement posted to social media.' 'Here's my face!' is not an accomplishment" (Ryan 2013). Conversely, Franco writes:

> A well-stocked collection of selfies seems to get attention. And attention seems to be the name of the game when it comes to social networking. In this age of too much information at a click of a button, the power to

DOI: 10.7330/9781607325161.c008

attract viewers amid the sea of things to read and watch is power indeed. It's what the movie studios want for their products, it's what professional writers want for their work, it's what newspapers want—hell, it's what everyone wants: attention. Attention is power. And if you are someone people are interested in, then the selfie provides something very powerful, from the most privileged perspective possible (Franco 2013).

Both Ryan and Franco agree that attention and response are the name of the game.

The point of posting selfies on social networking sites is to garner responses from an audience. While Ryan goes on to discuss the feminist implications of the selfie and the connection between body image and self-worth for young women (although one could easily expand her argument to include young men and their increasing awareness of body image), Franco argues that selfies are a central organizing mechanism in today's social media culture by which one can measure one's power, prestige, and worth. The selfie, then, is not so much about the self and a journey toward growth through introspection and self-examination as it is about performing for an audience and receiving feedback on that performance.

On one level, this cultural fascination with the self and the derision of the selfie is simply an old argument made new by the technologies that enable it. One of the complaints lodged against electronic student portfolios—and new media technology and social networking, now that we are in the throes of the digital revolution—has been a charge of narcissism and, concomitantly, relevance; critics allege that the digital medium and the easy access it allows encourage students to dwell on their lives and experiences narcissistically and without focusing on "serious" academic content.

These same critics also complain about students wasting their time on writing drivel: the meme, a disparaging epithet for personal information that goes viral, has also become a powerful dismissive in today's culture against personal writing of any kind. In "Generation Me vs. You Revisited," Stephanie Rosenbloom argues that "today's young people—schooled in the church of self-esteem, vying for spots on reality television, and promoting themselves on YouTube—are more narcissistic than their predecessors. (Heck, they join Facebook groups like the Association for Justified Narcissism.) Likewise, a study released last year by the Pew Research Center for the People and the Press continued the trend, dubbing Americans age 18 to 25 as the 'Look at Me' generation and reporting that this group said that their top goals were fortune and fame" (*New York Times*, January 17, 2008).

This all-about-me mentality is often cited as a source of resistance to ePortfolio implementation on campus; some faculty believe ePortfolios contribute to an all-about-me mentality in students. Anecdotally, faculty also share frustrations with student self-involvement and observe that reflection sometimes seems narcissistic. Understandably, they interpret this self-involvement as an interruption in their curriculum and their course goals. What they fail to understand, however, is the relationship of reflection and student self-involvement, the role meaningful reflection plays in ePortfolios, and their own responsibility to guide such reflection over time.

THE MECHANISM OF THE REFLECTED SELF: EPORT-FOLIOS AND THE EVOLVING GESTALT EFFECT

The selfie contributes to the context for ePortfolios because it speaks to the current generation's composing practices and because it presents something of a challenge to the academy's interest in a more substantive exploration of intellectual self. One mechanism supporting such substantive exploration is the ePortfolio, which has been valued precisely because it provides a critical site for self-reflection, one including both space and time, contributing to a gestalt effect whereby students examine the pieces of their lives and shape them into a connected whole. Put another way, the ePortfolio is a portable site for synthesis where students can engage with the disparate parts of their education, their varied interests, and their personal and professional goals. Because of their portability, ePortfolios support a reflected dialogue taking place longitudinally and recursively as students change over time and make meaning of those changes in conjunction with their other experiences.

As students juggle work, school, and personal lives, moreover, time is a critical factor in their studies. Gone are the days of full-time students completely focused on school. Instead, the national portrait of higher education includes accounts of students juggling multiple full-time commitments including work, family obligations, and volunteer or internship experiences, as well as academic and cocurricular activities, with the result that time is perhaps their most precious, and most limited, resource. ePortfolios are uniquely poised to meet the need for more time, as explained by Jeanne Marie Rose in "Writing Time: Composing in an Accelerated World." Rose, powerfully analyzing students' lack of time and the ways that lack creates a challenge to traditional time-intensive composition pedagogies designed to encourage learning, argues, "With students at all kinds of institutions confronting capitalism's cultural acceleration, compositionists have a shared stake in making time a central concern of writing pedagogy" (Rose 2012, 47). The promise of reflection in this context is that students can use it to make some sense and some meaning, meshing their understanding of self-presentation and audience with and through reflective writing, creating compelling narratives about their past, present, and future selves and the ways in which they understand their growth and development in multiple situations. By structuring reflection into ePortfolio assignments, instructors can create a space for students to think in more depth and with more sophistication about their emerging selves than they can in a quick selfie capturing a mood or an outfit or a moment in time.

Reflection can be assigned in many ways for many different purposes, though here, like others in this volume—Jeff Sommers, for example, and Bruce Horner—I am concerned with the form of reflection allowing students to engage with ambiguity and meaning making over time. Given that there are clear linkages between portfolio and classroom work, between personal and professional experiences and academic knowledge, reflection keyed to ambiguity is an active process in which students participate in a meaning-making ecology; in this ecology, reflection plays a primary role in their own knowledge making.

EPORTFOLIOS, REFLECTION AND ETHOS VERSUS THE RISE OF THE SELFIE

The push in ePortfolio pedagogy toward reflection is in many ways countercultural because it demands critically engaged, active learners who are making meaning of their education and (we hope) applying it to a critically engaged life in which academic lessons become part of a student's overall ethos. We might understand selfies, in contrast, as moments in time strung together, pieces of the disconnected self, whereas the ePortfolio uses many artifacts over time as evidence of the integrated self connected and made meaningful through the art of reflection. More important, the act of explicit reflection on the artifacts in the ePortfolio provides a way for students to arrive at the integrative moment: it is the vehicle for gestalt.

Through carefully crafted reflective assignments, instructors can prompt students to engage in meaningful reflection, a practice central to integrative learning. In *Integrative Learning: Mapping the Terrain*, Mary Taylor Huber and Pat Hutchings explain, "One of the great challenges in higher education is to foster students' abilities to integrate their learning across contexts and over time" (Huber and Hutchings 2005, 1). The ePortfolio becomes a working space where students and their instructors engage in incrementally more sophisticated reflective dialogue. Reflection, then, becomes a recursive process over time prompted by faculty, drafted by students, and revised through a community of faculty and staff readers who understand a student's goals through the materials and artifacts shared in the ePortfolio.

A growing digital sophistication, however, does not necessarily translate into engaging complex ideas and deeply meaningful analysis. While students are often adept at manipulating digital devices and experimenting with new social media, they are often unaware of the consequences of their online presence and their relationship to an increasingly public audience. To harken back to Shakespeare, all the world's a stage. If our social media presence involves continually playing to an audience, how then do students understand themselves in a meaningful way? Further, given the cultural pressures of time and space, where do students engage with meaningful thinking and writing?

Reflection in academic writing provides one modality in which students are able to mesh their understanding of self-presentation and audience with writing, creating compelling narratives about their past, present, and future selves and the ways in which they understand their growth and development in multiple contexts. In making such assignments, we achieve two goals: on the one hand, creating media-savvy students adept at presenting carefully crafted online versions of themselves and their interests appealing to their audiences, and on the other hand, helping students achieve a sophisticated gestalt, integrating multiple aspects of their education and personal pursuits and in the process learning how they fit together. Moreover, when reflection is dialogic—an occasion for students and faculty to focus on learning—both students and faculty learn, as Roberta Camp suggests: "When students have a real voice in the conversation about writing, as they do in portfolio reflection . . . and when teachers have the rich knowledge about students' perceptions that comes from portfolio reflection, both can be parties to a mutually satisfying dialogue about writing and learning. This dialogue can in turn create new relationships between teachers and students" (Camp 1998, 12). ePortfolios can place student learners at the center of their own experiences, encouraging them to find connections between courses and interests, but they also offer a platform for greater dialogue and connection between faculty and student; in the reflective assignments, feedback, and revision, faculty and students engage in questions of student development and learning over time.

In "Social Pedagogies in ePortfolio Practices," Randall Bass calls this the process of "learning to be": "Social pedagogies intensify the impact of ePortfolios as sites for integrative student learning. As these kinds of practices become more prevalent and developed, they will also reshape what we think of as the purpose and nature of ePortfolios, as sites of student *sensemaking* and 'learning to be'" (Bass 2014, 8). While the selfie is a sporadic and brief connection to an audience, reflective writing, in contrast, is a deeply intensive act of self-assessment and awareness mediated by faculty. In ePortfolios, that dialogue becomes wider than the concerns of a particular course and learning over a semester as a professor prompts reflective writing. Instead, the dialogue addresses student needs as a gestalt, the whole person, linking academics, vocation, and other interests. Faculty and staff come to understand students in a new way, beyond the confines of the classroom.

MAKING INTEGRATION AND GESTALT HAPPEN
EXPONENTIALLY, OVER TIME

At LaGuardia Community College in New York City, where I teach, we have a long history of ePortfolios in the classroom. Beginning in 2002 with a small pilot, our ePortfolio project has grown across disciplines and programs from eight hundred ePortfolios to almost eighty thousand. LaGuardia's work has increasingly shifted to the integrative aspects of the ePortfolio and the ways in which it can support connections across courses and across semesters, and integrating cocurricular and academic experiences and job, internship, or volunteer experiences. In such an ePortfolio, reflective writing plays a key role in helping students to make sense of their learning and tracking their trajectory over time.

In "'It Helped Me See a New Me': ePortfolio, Learning and Change at LaGuardia Community College," Bret Eynon explains how reflection supports student learning: "The process of reflection across semesters helps students surface and focus on intermediate steps in their learning, the ways that their participation in individual activities begins to add up to a larger whole. While they are learning about disciplines, the ways to be, for example, a psychologist or human services professional, at some more fundamental level the mastery LaGuardia students must first develop is what it means to be a college student" (Eynon 2009, 12). The role of reflection, Eynon argues, is critical to helping students process the experiences they have in college while also considering their future plans. Trent Batson agrees: "Situated learning brings us back to how humans actually learn and have always learned. But, for centuries, cultural knowledge changed so slowly, we moved away from expecting all learners to repeat the process of starting with experience" (Batson 2011, 113). Batson and Eynon believe education should be more than a collection of random courses in which students often memorize and regurgitate facts from seemingly unconnected courses across the curriculum. Instead, education is about making meaning and linking academic curriculum to experiences as part of a purposeful whole.

At LaGuardia, we've found that one way to combat students' lack of time for reflection and metacognitive activities is to centralize them in the ePortfolio. Our work with the ePortfolio and reflective writing, particularly in our professional-development offerings, has been heavily influenced by Carol Rodgers's 2002 article "Defining Reflection: Another Look at John Dewey and Reflective Thinking." Her article identifies reflection through multiple dimensions: reflection as connection, reflection as systematic and disciplined, reflection as social pedagogy, reflection as an attitude toward change, and reflection as connection—integration. In "Reflective Pedagogy," Bret Eynon, Laura Gambino and Judit Torok outline the ways in which this approach to thinking about reflection has influenced LaGuardia's work with reflection and the work of other campuses interested in using the ePortfolio as a student-centered learning tool (Eynon, Gambino and Torok 2014, 1–2).[1]

In their first iteration, digital student portfolios proved a powerful way to contextualize the idea of student authorship. Coming on the heels of the explosion in multicultural literary studies, the first ePortfolios in 2002 at LaGuardia Community College, a large urban community college, were characterized by a multicultural student authorship that recorded stories of immigration, cultural identity, and struggles with assimilation to a United States lifestyle and educational system. In my own earliest uses of ePortfolio in the composition classroom (2002–2006), I focused on the ways in which the ePortfolio could support my portfolio pedagogy, transitioning from paper to digital. Much like the process described by Roberta Camp, my midterm and final reflection assignments, adapted from my paper portfolio assignments, asked students to discuss what they had learned in the course and how they understood changes and progress in their writing.

As with most traditional reflective assignments, my goal was to encourage students to explore and document their own growth and development in writing over the course of a semester so they had a clear sense of their strengths and weaknesses in preparation for the next semester. Students produced interesting, rich, metacognitively appropriate essays

Hurray! You've almost finished your first college portfolio assignment! You've been working very hard on revising your essays. Through your appointments with me, your visits to the writing center, your hard work in class, and your keen attention to the revision process, you should be almost ready to hand in your ePortfolio.

As you know, the ePortfolio is your opportunity to "show off" and demonstrate the progress that you've made throughout the semester. It serves as an opportunity to both mark progress and identify the issues you need to pay attention to in the coming weeks.

Your ePortfolio Reflection Leuer should be 1-2 pages in length. When I grade your ePortfolio, I will read this first and use it as a guide to your work.

What should be in your letter?

A greeting (Dear Liz, Dear Dr. Clark, etc.)

Begin with an opening paragraph that explains what you wanted to achieve with your ePortfolio. Here, you might reflect on the differences between your pre- and current college writing. You might discuss how you view yourself as a writer. You might also consider discussing your achievements so far.

In your letter, you'll need to cover some of the following things. Use these questions as a guide to develop your reflection.

- What is your best entry? Why? Remember to be specific!
- What is your weakest entry? Why? Remember to be specific!
- How have you incorporated our discussions of good writing into your essays? (e.g. a strong thesis, rich description, focused paragraphs, understanding 101-level writing)
- What is your strength as a writer? Of what are you most proud?
- What do you need to continue to work on?
- What helped you to revise? (The Writing Center, an exercise we did in class, help from a parent or a friend, the Revision Plan, your error chart, a combination of these things?)
- What areas do you believe you need to focus on during the rest of your study at LaGuardia?
- What risks or experiments did you take in this writing?
- What kinds of writing do you look forward to doing later in the semester?
- How has your writing experience in this class informed your writing for other classes?
- How has your understanding of college-level writing changed since the beginning of the semester?

In general, your letter should give me a sense of what you think about your writing. I'm looking for an honest self-evaluation that indicates to me the ways in which you are aware of your own strengths and weaknesses as a writer. I'm also interested in knowing more about what informs your writing. I look forward to reading your letters and your ePortfolios.

Figure 8.1.

that detailed changes in their writing. Cara, for example, writes about her experiences with a first research assignment. She notes her interest in the topic as well as key skills such as quoting and citing pictures, using quotations from source material, and learning about MLA format.

This was my very first research paper written at a college level. I was required to write about revealing a moment in depth and I chose to write about the Civil Rights movement and Dr. Martin Luther King's philosophy. This particular assignment allowed me to gain more knowledge about the history of the Civil Rights Movement. This is something that I have always been very interested in. The research paper was difficult because I had never completed one before. I took this as a challenge and I completed this assignment with an A. The problems I encountered while doing this assignment was learning about MLA format, quoting and citing pictures, quotes, books, etc. The assignment introduced me to library-oriented research and learning how to choose books, use online journals for information relevant to my paper.

As a writing teacher, I am able to see what Cara learned from this assignment and others she discusses in her response, what she is taking from the course, how her skills developed, and how I might direct her to continue working on her writing. She directs me toward the meaning she finds in her work instead of relying on my assumption about what her completed paper shows. For example, I would have said that the paper demonstrated what Cara learned about the Civil Rights Movement and demonstrated her increasing sophistication with thesis statements. I thought in previous assignments she had learned the skills she instead credits to this assignment and her developing understanding of research. While these are all important teaching and learning tasks, none of them adequately explored the multimedia possibilities of the ePortfolio.

In contrast, Agata, who was in the same class, also focused her reflection on her research paper, in her case comparing her own experiences of emigrating from Slovakia to the United States to historic trends in immigration. For Agata, writing about the decision to leave Slovakia and start over in the United States was difficult. Determined to enter our college's highly competitive nursing program, she spent long hours in the writing center working on what she perceived as a significant flaw—her lack of fluency in English. In fact, Agata's written and spoken English were fluid, comparable to her counterparts in the class. However, her immigrant status made her question her authority in the classroom. As she began to find corollaries to her own story in the research she did, she became increasingly more confident in the class. When she presented her final ePortfolio, she incorporated as part of her evidence her own airline ticket to the United States and photographs she took. Her reflection focused on the importance of linking text and image in the ePortfolio to create a research paper entirely different from anything she had ever written before. Her previous academic writing included always reporting facts by authorities. She understood research as entirely external, not something that might engage her own life and experiences. Agata embodied the use of reflection and experiences, exactly as Trent Batson argues, to more fully learn and integrate the academic and the personal. While in an age of archival imagination such integration is perhaps not unusual, what was rhetorically significant about this move was her decision to cite herself, in the text, as the author of the photographs. In the space of one semester, Agata moved from understanding herself as a weak writer with significant limitations to a cultural authority and an author who was cited in her own paper, a writer who also reflected on how the visually rhetorical possibilities of the ePortfolio allowed her to change her ideas about her own writing.

While both of these examples are interesting, however, the basic assignment and scaffolding I used to guide students through reflection is no longer an effective approach in an age of digital media. These first examples of ePortfolios from composition courses asked students to use the ePortfolio as I had used paper portfolios: as a repository of work from the semester with revisions, process-based assignments to support that revision, and reflections. The multimodal aspects of my assignments were minimal: including elements of visual rhetoric and hyperlinking across assignments, pages, and sometimes research.

At the time, these nascent steps into multimodal composing, teaching with technology, and the ePortfolio were sufficient to provide my students with some of the technology they needed. Today, however, this basic approach to including technology in my classroom, and in my reflective assignments, simply isn't enough, though for many schools, incorporating technology into learning isn't easy. Some schools, for example, are attempting to bridge the gap with bring-your-own-technology (BYOT) programs that allow students to use the laptops, tablets, and smartphones they already have (Columbus 2013). A new study released by Pew finds that "more than half of teachers of the lowest-income students say children's lack of access to digital technologies is a 'major challenge' to incorporating more digital tools into their teaching" (quoted in Columbus 2013).

Against a backdrop of increasingly ubiquitous technology and a revival of the digital divide between the haves and the have-nots, then, I believe the inclusion of technology in the classroom is paramount to creating successful students. I also believe that designing conditions in which students become creators of new media, rather than just consumers, is critical for them to be able to graduate into a marketplace increasingly concerned with not only what students have learned but also how they have learned. Accordingly, we must create multimodal assignments as well as teach the skills students need to create those assignments, thus addressing the digital divide and providing access to technology students will need to show proficiency with later. The ability to move seamlessly from one technology to a new one and to be a proficient creator in that technology will be an important skill now and in the future.

One example of this shift is illustrated by a recent basic writing assignment in which students had the option to create video introductions to their ePortfolios. The prompt for the assignment was similar to the one shared above; in composing the introductions, students prepared written drafts of their videos before videoing the final version. In a course that emphasizes helping students to write in an authentic voice, I found that these video assignments were far more authentic and real than their written equivalent, in part because they literally captured students' pauses, facial expressions, and intonations. Put another way, their video voice was how I actually heard them speak and express themselves in class. Moreover, as students worked on voice in their writing, the flattening of individual expression that often occurs in initial attempts at academic writing did not characterize the video reflections: each student's reflection sounded unique. What basic writing students were still attempting to master—style, tone, and voice in an effort to create an individual writing style—they were able to better communicate using their actual voices as they presented their reflections. This was an important learning moment for me as I considered how I might continue to revise my basic writing assignment to include earlier videotaped reflective assignments as a way of teaching voice in writing: a concept that sometimes feels oblique in classroom discussion can be very transparent as we compare the written and videotaped versions of the same reflection.

For the future, I am interested in engaging students to think about the differences between their written drafts of these reflections and their videos of the same reflections. I think this is a key way to engage students in thinking about voice, tone, and style. While the basic writing curriculum at LaGuardia affords relatively little time for reflection—the reflective assignments I currently include in the ePortfolio push the curricular requirements to the extreme—I am interested in developing some low-stakes assignments that reflect on reflection, especially to help students more fully understand the concept of voice and develop multiple kinds of composed voices.

Another example of reflection supporting learning is provided in a recent assignment that asked students to reflect on their digital identities. They were to catalog how they use technology and how that use informs their digital identity. One student, who titled her essay "Digital Contagion," reflected,

I am a child of different age. The age of hardcover books, hand written letters with carefully practiced cursive and long chats with my girlfriend on a rotary phone. I am a child of a different age who was thrown into a totally different world; the world of e-books, emails and texts. I live among "digital natives" who not only embrace technology but know no other way. Although advances in technology touch my life in so many ways every day, make my life easier and more productive, I am fighting every innovation and change, full well knowing that in order to survive I need to accept and embrace them.

From the moment I wake up to the final hours of my day, technology plays a significant role in my life. It's completely changed my way of communicating, socializing, shopping and even reading.

For this student, a reflective assignment on technology proved painful to write. She recognizes the importance of technology in her life at the same time she is reluctant to embrace technology fully. It was an important reflective assignment that allowed her to grapple with the kinds of technological change swirling around her in her everyday life. Her reflection is not a neatly packaged, taut piece. Her reflection engages ambiguity and invention and as such exemplifies the evolving gestalt I am interested in for my students. Reflection allows students space to think, to engage, to evolve. Reflection allows students to look uncertainty and change in the face and find in that growth and change a continuity that will follow them over time as they learn new things, have new experiences, and engage with the unknown. Speaking to Rose's point about students and time, reflective assignments like this one, which engage the contemporary cultural moment, allow students space to think, breathe, and evaluate where they are, where they are going, and how they make sense of the world.

Both of these assignments capture something important about this critical moment of reflection and the ePortfolio: first, we must consider ways to embrace multimodal reflection and create assignments that support that kind of composing; and second, reflection and reflective assignments can play a key role in helping students to make sense of an increasingly rushed and harried world where there seems to be little time for introspection.

THE EVOLVING GESTALT, AMBIGUITY, AND
THE IMPORTANCE OF INTEGRATION

Reflective writing can also play an important role in rethinking our approach to higher education by helping students to consider the integrative elements of their education. The biggest challenges that lie ahead in the twenty-first century are not neatly bound by discipline. Solving the continuing HIV/AIDS and other public-health crises, the challenges of global warming, and the related natural disasters that accompany climate change, among others, will call for students who can do interdisciplinary work, who can make connections outside of courses from one kind of knowledge base to another. ePortfolios, in their provision for the collection of evidence and artifacts from a variety of courses, support such interdisciplinary thinking; without reflection, however, portfolios are simply a library of artifacts from different courses, a disparate collection of selfies from discrete moments in time. It's in the reflective assignment that new kinds of knowledge and connections can be made. Reflection encourages students to embrace a holistic, integrative approach to considering how these varying pieces of their education, represented in artifacts, come together to support their goals. It also allows space for students to consider how they have grown and changed over time, what they have learned in college, and how that learning will continue to follow them in future courses and schools.

Over the last five years, LaGuardia's ePortfolios have been coupled with an increased institutional focus on capstone courses, with the ePortfolio as a culminating educational practice. These capstone courses ask students to use the ePortfolio as a site for exploration and reflection as they consider their tenure at the college and their critical reflection on their learning. While there is nothing new, per se, in the use of reflection in ePortfolios, at LaGuardia the use of reflective practice allows students to chart their own progress, point to lessons learned, and demonstrate areas of strength and weakness. Moreover, as an integrative pedagogy that asks students to connect courses across the curriculum, student capstone ePortfolios often shift focus, taking on richer and more complex presentations of their academic material as students find ways to connect academic material and personal experiences in integrative reflections. Two examples from a recent capstone course show the potential of reflection.

A student who was preparing to graduate was reflecting on his journey through LaGuardia, from his first course to his capstone. This student had returned to school, leaving a career as an air-conditioning and refrigeration technician. He was driven to enroll in school because he wanted a degree, a better job, and a better life. He reflected on the challenges of being placed into basic writing in his first semester after the difficult decision to return to school. He writes, "I remember vividly the first day I went to class at LaGuardia. I was so nervous because I sensed that I was out of place. I was unsure of my writing abilities and that was what scared me the most." He goes on to talk about what he learned in that first course and what it taught him. The end of his reflection notes, "I never imagined that I would one day come home with a college degree and the thought of graduating seems surreal to me. . . . College has taught me how to be responsible, assertive, courageous, and determined to tackle any situation life throws at me. This institution may not be as fancy as others, but the diversity has shown me how to embrace many cultures." In his reflection, charting his growth over time, he identifies key factors that led to his success at LaGuardia and, more important, were outcomes of his experiences in college. He learned to be "responsible, assertive, courageous, and determined." In this case, working together, the ePortfolio and reflection provided space for him to realize those intangible lessons of college, lessons that weren't directly measured in the curriculum, like a score on a standardized exam or the grade on a paper, but rather the lessons he will carry with him, the character-building elements he discovered within himself on his first journey into higher education.

Similarly, another student in the same class reflected on her education. Her reflection took her in an altogether different direction. She traced her childhood in Trinidad and her love for her culture. She writes, "Being surrounded by various cultures for most of my life has taught me how to respect and value the social dynamics of an assortment of ethnicities. And to a great extent, the multicultural background of my country has influenced my social identity." Her reflection hyperlinks to various academic papers and projects as well as to videos showing cultural diversity. She goes on to discuss her varied coursework and how it is leading her to a degree in forensic psychology because she is concerned about the escalation of violence in Trinidad and she wants to be in a position to help. Much of her reflection wrestles with what it means to live in a multicultural society—to find ways to embrace other cultures, to celebrate one's own culture, and to mediate the differences between.

In a later part of her reflection, she wrestles with her capstone research paper. She selected the topic of Sharia law and stoning. A budding feminist interested in crime, she wanted to study this topic in detail. But she found herself at odds with her own values. How could she celebrate diversity and also disagree with Sharia law? Her reflection ends in an uncertain place where she doesn't know how to reconcile the two; it's also something she fears may play an important role in her education ahead. In other words, her reflection became a space for grappling with her own conflicting beliefs, a space for inhabiting ambiguity. Her ePortfolio was characteristic of the kind of sophisticated reflection possible for students as they deepen their learning and evaluate what they are learning against what they believe.

Reflection provides elasticity for students to grow and change and name the new and emerging shapes of their beliefs. As with the previous reflection, this student's reflection allowed her to see a clear narrative that revealed her values and the direction she wanted to head in. But it also allowed space to raise uncertainties and to think about new avenues she might need to study and explore. Bret Eynon calls this process "an elegant double helix shaping students' evolving sense of identity and personal destiny" (Eynon 2009, 12).

THE TIMELESSNESS OF THE SELFIE AND INTROSPECTION

The idea of self-documentation through imagery is not new; selfies are the latest iteration of the self-portrait, an image without self-context. Liv Constable-Maxwell compares today's selfies to the striking and now iconic self-portraits painted by Mexican artist Frida Kahlo. She argues, "Kahlo's legacy resonates strongly with modern life. The self-portraits that she so obsessively created bring to light the many conflicting motives of self-documentation that we see nowadays; motives that metamorphose between exposure, and mask-making" (Constable-Maxwell 2015). Just as with Kahlo's paintings, however, the selfie is ultimately more about the meaning the audience takes away from the composition. Laura Pappano interviewed academics studying the art of the selfie. Just as we can now argue about the greater historical context for Kahlo's work, today's selfie reveals much about our contemporary time: "It's also a political or social statement, a way to engage one's social network in real time events, says Terri Senft, a New York University professor who heads the Selfie Researchers Network on Facebook, which has a group-sourced syllabus to use for teaching" (*New York Times*, August 28, 2015).

The selfie is to contemporary culture what the single assignment or stand-alone course is to education: a one-off disconnected from the greater whole. In the same way a set of disconnected assignments across the curriculum is often a performance for a series of instructors in order to earn a grade and tells us nothing about how a student has understood and connected this learning, a collection of selfies offers little insight into a person's introspective process. There is no true element of self-reflection. Instead, as Asma Naeem, an art historian and assistant curator at the National Portrait Gallery in Washington, explains, "As with any self-portrait, no matter how candid, crafted or artfully wrought, 'the viewer of the selfie is free to interpret the work not governed by the intent of the person who took it. So you can certainly say it is the viewer who has the power and gains knowledge in the exchange'" (quoted in Murphy, *New York Times*, August 8, 2015). The selfie, then, becomes an opportunity for the audience to make meaning of the image. It is, in this sense, anti-self-reflection.

NEW PEDAGOGIES, NEW CLASSROOMS

We are not used to thinking about our curriculum as a whole. We are not used to thinking about the whole student. Often, students experience curriculum and produce assignments in the same way they do a selfie: as a single experience disconnected from the whole. The ways our courses fit together for students, the relationship between general education and the major, the relationship between personal and professional experiences, the relationship between our curriculum and students' personal lives—all call for new pedagogies that prompt us to help students integrate these different facets of their lives. ePortfolios, as spaces for synthesis, with their multimodal composing abilities, with their portability, allow students to engage in reflective dialogue over time, making meaning across courses, curriculum, and experiences. Who students are now, in a given moment, is not who they will always be. Thus, engaging students in a habit and practice they can apply long after they leave us suggests that the ePortfolio is a pedagogy of integration, an evolving gestalt with space and time for growth, change, and meaning making.

One of the most important lessons of the ePortfolio is that this new pedagogy, and the continuing role of reflection and metacognition in education, are not about the tool or the technology. It's about what kind of learning it affords and how it must keep up with a culture that changes its favorite technology every few years. The popularity of Instagram and Snap Chat today will give way to new technologies on the horizon. The ePortfolio, as a tool, must be able to morph and transform to include these new and emerging technologies. Reflection, however, and a time and space for thinking about education and the relationship between the coursework students are taking and the direction they are preparing for in their lives, assist students to embrace new technologies and to develop into savvy media creators who are able to reflect and to introspectively consider connections, relationships, and integrative aspects of the self, turning the selfie from a single candid snapshot into a deep and nuanced, integrative understanding of who they are, what they want, how all of the pieces fit together for now, and how they will effect change in the world.

Note

1.   "It Helped Me See a New Me" captures LaGuardia's ePortfolio pedagogy in 2009. LaGuardia's approach to reflection and the ePortfolio has changed over time, deepening as ePortfolio tools and technologies and softwares have influenced culture.

References

Bass, Randall. 2014. "Social Pedagogies in ePortfolio Practices: Principles for Design and Impact." *Catalyst* January 24: 1–9. http://c2l.mcnrc.org/wp-content/uploads/sites/8 /2014/01/Bass_Social_Pedagogy.pdf

Batson, Trent. 2011. "Situated Learning: A Theoretical Frame to Guide Transformational Change Using Electronic Portfolio Technology." *International Journal of ePortfolio* 1 (1): 107–14. www.theijep.com/pdf/ijep34.pdf.

Camp, Roberta. 1998. "Portfolio Reflection: The Basis for Dialogue." *Clearing House: A Journal of Educational Strategies, Issues and Ideas* 72 (1): 10–12. http://dx.doi.org/10 .1080/00098659809599377 http://www.jstor.org/stable/30189411

Columbus, Gina. 2013. "N.J. Schools Ask Students to Bring Their Own Tech." *USA Today*, September 5. www.usatoday.com/story/tech/2013/09/05/schools-ask-students-to -bring-their-own-tech/2769953/

Constable-Maxwell, Liv. 2015. "What Frida Kahlo Can Teach Us about the Art of the Selfie." *New Statesman*, July 9. www.newstatesman.com/culture/2015/07/what-frida -kahlo-can-teach-us-about-art-selfie.

Eynon, Bret. 2009. "'It Helped Me See a New Me': ePortfolio, Learning and Change at LaGuardia Community College." In *The Difference that Inquiry Makes: A Collaborative Case Study of Technology and Learning, from the Visible Knowledge Project*, ed. Randy Bass and Bret Eynon, 1–19. Academic Commons. blogs.commons.georgetown.edu/vkp /files/2009/03/eynon-revised.pdf.

Eynon, Bret, Laura Gambino, and Judit Torok. 2014. "Reflection, Integration, and ePortfolio Pedagogy." *Catalyst*, January 24: 1–19. http://c2l.mcnrc.org/wp-content/uploads /sites/8/2014/01/Reflective_Pedagogy.pdf.

Huber, Mary Taylor, and Pat Hutchings. 2005. *Integrative Learning: Mapping the Terrain.* Washington, DC: Association of American Colleges and Universities.

Rodgers, Carol. 2002. "Defining Reflection: Another Look at John Dewey and Reflective Thinking." *Teachers College Record* 104 (4): 842–66. http://dx.doi.org /10.1111/1467-9620.00181.

Rose, Jeanne Marie. 2012. "Writing Time: Composing in an Accelerated World." *Pedagogy* 12 (1): 45–67 http://dx.doi.org/10.1215/15314200-1416522.

Ryan, Erin Gloria. 2013. "Selfies Aren't Empowering. They're a Cry for Help." *Jezebel*, November 21. http://jezebel.com/selfies-arent-empowering-theyre-a-cry-for-help-146 8965365.

9

REFLECTION IN DIGITAL SPACES
Publication, Conversation, Collaboration

Naomi Silver

"Affordance" means you can do some things easily now, and you are more inclined to do these things than you were before simply because they are easier. . . . Computers make it easier. So, the new things that ubiquitous computing makes easier may not in themselves be completely new. . . . However, just because the new technology makes them easier to do, they become more obviously worth doing than they were in the past.
—Bill Cope and Mary Kalantzis, *Ubiquitous Learning*

Well, Naomi (and other Sweetland Writing Profs). You have succeeded in brainwashing me. Here I am, sitting in the library determinedly writing various papers until my computer runs out of batteries (currently at 9%—I have been here awhile), and I am writing self-reflective comments! I didn't even realize what I was doing until I had written a couple and started to rearrange some paragraphs. And then I realized that I have been using reflective commenting quite a bit lately. At work, in my internship, when reviewing friends' papers . . . and it's just so handy!
—Hannah Tasker, Sweetland Minor in
Writing student blog post[1]

THE DIGITAL DIFFERENCE

I will begin with what I take to be a truism in a book dedicated to reflection, namely, the benefits of reflective pedagogy have been pretty effectively established at this point—for student engagement, for development of student writing, and, as more and more research makes clear (including chapters in this book), for transfer of learning about writing to other contexts. But, if these rich educational experiences are possible in analog, print-based classrooms, what more do *digital* reflective spaces have to offer? How does reflection work—and does it work any differently—when it is electronically mediated? These are the questions I take up in this chapter. By way of a preliminary response, and following the

DOI: 10.7330/9781607325161.c009

line of thought sketched in the epigraph from Cope and Kalantzis (2009), recent digital technologies make student reflection on writing *easier to do*, and therefore *more obviously worth doing*, more frequently and in more diverse ways, than ever before. Here, I echo a point already made by L. Lennie Irvin in 2004: "Reflection is at the center of learning . . . . This learning cycle can happen in any context—electronic or not. However, the electronic learning environment magnifies the potentials for reflection's role within this learning cycle" (under "Conclusion").

With ubiquitous computing and ubiquitous learning, there are indeed more texts and types of texts to reflect on, more ways to reflect on them, more possibilities for social and public reflection, and more opportunities for researchers—and students as self-researchers—to perform data-driven reflection on writing by using such features as versioning, histories, metadata, and the like to study in detail changes in writing over time. But Bill Cope and Mary Kalantzis also note that "the new things that ubiquitous computing makes easier may not in themselves be completely new" (2009, 4), and, indeed, as some of the more recent literature on reflection points out, many of the genres of student reflection remain fairly stable in digital contexts, but their modes and media continue to change in ways that matter for reflective pedagogical practice. As I will suggest in this chapter, then, the integration of digital tools for reflection into writing classrooms offers, at a minimum, these affordances:

- Reflection is more easily ubiquitous, making the design of a reflective curriculum easier, and therefore a more obvious choice.
- The work of reflection can become more public and visible, allowing peers more easily to dialogue and collaborate and thus to learn from each other's reflective practice.
- More parts of the writing process can become visible, retrievable, and accurately measurable, which allows both student learning and instructor and program assessment to become more data based.
- And, last but not least, reflection can be more fun to do because it more easily offers students the opportunity to be innovative, to take new ownership of the modes and forms of their reflections, and to share those forms with multiple audiences.

I will explore these claims, first, by way of a brief review of the literature on digital reflection in writing studies and, next, discussion of a range of student examples from a course I teach at the University of Michigan.

***

In her seminal book *Reflection in the Writing Classroom*, Kathleen Blake Yancey (1998) builds on the work of Donald Schön (1987) to develop the idea of "the writing classroom as a reflective practicum," one where "reflection is woven into the curriculum" (vi). Here, she sets the stage for the idea of what we might call *ubiquitous reflection* in an analog context and delineates the ways in which students' reflective practice can permeate a writing classroom during, between, and following compositional tasks via *reflection-in-action, constructive reflection*, and *reflection-in-presentation* (see 13–14 for Yancey's initial definitions). Reflective genres such as prewriting activities, writing journals or logs, process notes, writer's memos, and portfolio letters, among others, institute reflective work both around and between each distinct writing task. At these various moments of composition, according to Yancey, reflection constitutes a kind of self-dialogue that, over time, develops into a method for self-regulated learning: "In method, reflection is dialectical, putting multiple perspectives into play with each other in order to produce insight. Procedurally, reflection entails a *looking forward* to goals we might attain, as well as a *casting backward* to see where we have been. When we reflect, we thus *project* and *review*, often putting the projections and reviews in *dialogue* with each other, working dialectically as we seek to *discover* what we know, what we have learned, and what we might understand. . . . Moreover, we can use those processes to theorize understandings that will themselves be revised through reflection" (1998, 6; emphasis in original). Taken together, these dialectical practices of projecting and reviewing enact what we might call, following Gregory Schraw (1998), an ongoing and recursive metacognitive cycle of planning, monitoring, and evaluation around the range of writing tasks students encounter. Indeed, Schraw, like other researchers of metacognition,[2] regards this process of self-dialogue as "essential to successful learning" (123). As multiple studies have suggested, a reflective curriculum of this type scaffolds and promotes reflective self-dialogue, assisting students to develop a "theory" of understanding for their writing, however nascent, that offers them a sense of self-efficacy and developing expertise (see, for example, Bandura 1989; Conner 2007; Meizlish et al. 2013; Shulman 2000; Zimmerman and Moylan 2009).

Interestingly, the earliest literature to take up the then-new idea of *digital reflection* interrogated the character and function of dialogic reflection in a "networked" environment. In 2004, when Irvin published "Reflection in the Electronic Writing Classroom" (explicitly taking Yancey's book as prompt and interlocutor), he could cite only two other publications addressing the practice of digital reflection: Steve Watkins's (1996) "World Wide Web Authoring in the Portfolio-Assessed (Inter) Networked Composition Course" and Joel English's (1998) "MOO-Based Metacognition: Incorporating Online and Offline Reflection into the Writing Process." Though Watkins doesn't explicitly use the term *dialogue*, his argument for networked electronic portfolios centers on the role of hyperlinks in enabling the imagination of an "authentic" audience for the student's artifacts and reflective letter and a consequent move from reflective self-dialogue to a reflection "oriented . . . to outside audiences" (229). English, on the other hand, constructs his argument for MOO-based writing conferences specifically around their ability to foster and support "metacognitive dialogue" between and among instructors, tutors, and students (under "Discussion of the Annotated Logs"). Irvin picks up on this idea to claim that "in a traditional writing classroom the most important 'other' a student engages with is the teacher; however, the networked environment changes this teacher-centric dynamic" and leads to an "expanded social environment for reflection" (under "Reflection in the E-Writing Classroom").

More recent literature builds on this discussion of the differences reflection in digitally mediated spaces may make for students' metacognitive processes of self-dialogue and their more social forms of reflection via the affordances of new digital tools. To take one example, as Julie Meloni notes in her August 18, 2009, *Chronicle of Higher Education ProfHacker* blog article on incorporating the versioning function in Google Docs into a portfolio-based writing class, "The Google Docs revision history allowed the students to pick specific points in their writing process and discuss the changes between these points, down to the most granular details. Although I told the students ahead of time that they would need to be aware of their writing and revision process in order to talk about it at the end of the course, students reported that the Google Docs revision history was a 'life saver.'" Meloni highlights the nuanced, self-evaluative reflection-in-presentation work the revision history made possible, and the student enthusiasm quoted here perhaps pertains primarily to this unexpected access to their previous drafts. But Meloni also speaks to another affordance of reflection in digital spaces: this tool gives students unprecedented ease of information regarding their own writing histories, down to their minute-by-minute choices, should they want to engage in such detailed self-study. In this case, the use of a digital tool may significantly alter the reflective activity of casting backward to review what we know about our own writing development.

Other publications describe remediations of existing genres of reflection—writing logs become weblogs, say, or handwritten notes in the margins of a paper move into the electronic Comments (see, for example, Irvin 2004; LaVaque-Manty and Evans 2013; Meizlish et al. 2013; Welch 1998;). These same digital tools and spaces—such as VoiceThread or blogging platforms—also bring other voices into the process, turning reflection into a much more collaborative endeavor (in an update to the benefits noted by English in 1998 in regard to the MOO) and thus building on one of the central dimensions of Web 2.0 activity. Tools like Google Docs can support social reflection as well by facilitating collaborative writing and allowing collaborators to view each other's revisions in the history and in fostering dialogue in the margins of the document via the Comments feature and push notifications to e-mail of any updates in the dialogue. Indeed, the ability to use digital forms of reflection for peer-to-peer social activities easily and regularly stimulates the important processes of affirmation and ideas testing that John Dewey (1916) and others have attributed to the work of reflection in community (see also Rodgers 2002; Vygotsky 1986).

Still other remediations of reflective genres take greater leaps. For instance, Gail Hawisher et al. (2009) describe remediating a prompt used by Prior and Shipka (2003) that asked students "to draw images of their writing processes" (Hawisher et al. 2009, 255)—itself already a remediation of an alphabetic process note—by proposing that students "attempt to capture a representation of [their] writing processes on camera" (255). The authors here comment on the meaning making enabled by this medium that is not available in the prior media: the ability, for instance, to capture time-based phenomena, such as the rhythms of writing in our everyday lives, or the opportunity to add multimedia, such as soundtracks, that may convey richer information about our writing processes. As they note, "We show how digital media can offer new images of the dispersed character of writing and learning, not as punctual events but as emergent flows" (255).

Debra Journet et al. (2008) describe a similar experiment—producing a daily reflection in "*any form: written, audio, video, still images*" (under "The Reflection Assignment," emphasis in original)—with interestingly similar results, reaching the conclusion that "what we discovered as we composed multimodal reflections was that *modality changed the nature of reflection*" (under "Home"; emphasis in original). In particular, reflecting in digital media altered these students' own sense of their writing processes and of the generative role of reflective work in these processes. For instance, in an audio reflection, one student describes becoming more aware of the ways the recursiveness of his own writing process (signified by his unedited *ums* and *ahs* as "signs of the reflective moment") challenged his attempts at linearity and clarity of purpose (under "Audio Reflection"). Another student describes, by way of multiple drafts and "takes" of her narrated final video reflection, coming to understand reflective writing itself as a form of "practice" for composition that prepares and enables it (under "Reflecting through Insecurity").

Taken together, these examples of reflection—using digital tools, often on writing in digital spaces—suggest not only that the activities of reflection have changed, but that the availability and use of these tools can change students' and instructors' expectations of what it is possible to reflect upon, of the kinds of insights and meanings that may be achieved through reflection, and of the skills and competencies that may be acquired by engaging in reflection. A brief taxonomy of this changed landscape of reflective activity might note the following multiplication of possible scenarios for reflection:

1. There are new ways of reflecting (using digital tools) on traditional ways of writing (print-based products and processes)—for example, using a webcam to record a series of brief writing-log video entries on the process of writing an argumentative essay.

2. There are also traditional, print-based ways of reflecting on new digital ways of writing (new products and processes), such as multimodal texts—for example, writing a reflective process note about composing a webpage.

3. And then there are new ways of reflecting on new ways of writing—for example, using VoiceThread to engage in a group reflection on a video essay.

In all these scenarios, core aspects of reflection, as described by Yancey (1998), persist. Yet these core aspects of reflection are augmented in various ways as they are connected to the new demands and opportunities of working with digital tools in digital learning environments, thereby enabling *ubiquitous digital reflection* within a *digital reflective practicum.*

UBIQUITOUS DIGITAL REFLECTION

But what exactly does ubiquitous digital reflection look like from the student's perspective? In the following pages, I explore the ways students take up the invitation of ubiquitous digital reflection within a classroom setting and how this experience may carry over into other later endeavors. My primary focus will be a course that tried to enact a digital reflective practicum by weaving reflective activity into every aspect of its curriculum. The Gateway course to the Sweetland minor in writing program, like the program as a whole,[3] is based upon supporting students from across the University of Michigan as they grapple with writing problems that engage them—in any mode and medium and in a variety of rhetorical situations—and as, through this process, they develop a sense of writerly identity. Students work on three major writing projects—a project examining "Why I Write," a repurposing of a previously composed argument for a new audience, and a subsequent remediation of this repurposed piece—and create an electronic portfolio.

The course has as one of its central learning goals that students "become flexible and creative writers across a range of rhetorical situations as they develop an electronic portfolio that demonstrates self-reflection and writing development" (Sweetland Center for Writing 2013). In pursuit of these goals, reflection is not simply "threaded through" the curriculum (to borrow a metaphor from Yancey [1998, 17]), an accompaniment to the three major writing projects, but in a very real sense it is the curriculum; it constitutes the warp and woof of the course. From analyses of their "go-to" sentence styles in previous writing assignments to interviews with their classmates exploring important writing experiences; from the major writing project examining "Why I Write" to planning activities, self-reflective marginal comments, and self-evaluations accompanying their Repurposing and Remediation projects; from the construction of their electronic portfolio with a reflective introduction and contextual reflections for each artifact to the blog on which all of this work is presented, shared, and dissected; and in both analog and digital media, students in the Gateway course are always reflecting on *something*. One Gateway student, sums this experience up in a December 4 , 2013, post to the *Sweetland Minor in Writing Blog*[4]: "Because of the way we have to reflect on our writing processes . . . I can honestly say I've thought and written about my writing process more in the past three months than I have in the entirety of my life, without question."[5]

The ubiquity of this reflection, however, comes not only from its frequency, but also from the fact that much of this reflective work is not necessarily identified explicitly as such but simply comprises the low-stakes writing of the class. Of course, several of the activities that surround the major projects are explicitly named *reflections*, such as the self-reflective comments students are asked to insert in the margins of primarily alphabetic texts (or in other ways in texts that don't have margins, strictly speaking) that identify areas of challenge or pride or that ask questions about a particular moment in the text, or, again, in the shorter contextualizing reflections students are asked to include in their electronic portfolios that accompany particular artifacts and provide some insight into their role in the portfolio. But, at the same time, a blog prompt may simply invite students to describe an experience trying out a new digital application they wish to employ for their Remediation project or to share some images from their planning storyboard. Here, the reflection takes place along the way, so to speak, in the act of describing, analyzing, and drawing some conclusions but not because students have been instructed to engage in some specialized activity labeled *reflection*. As a result, many students in the course stop seeing reflection as something separate from and additional to their *writing* (and perhaps, therefore, as onerous). This point about the seamless integration of reflection is highlighted by a student's commenting on the blog post cited in the previous paragraph: "Your point about reflection is definitely interesting. I hadn't really given thought to how much we do it in this class, but there's definitely a ton with the exercises we did before each project and all the reflective writing for the e-portfolio. It's definitely made me think about the choices I make during my writing process and my overall evolution as a writer."[6]

In recounting his memories of reflective writing in the course, this student identifies the *capital-R* reflection he performed but not the low-stakes reflective activities—like his own blog posts on "Scriptwriting Surprises" about his analyses of the genre of podcasting scripts as he created his own podcast; or "Admitting Defeat and Starting Anew," about deciding to use an html template for his ePortfolio rather than coding it entirely by hand; or "Writing FAST," about altering his writing and revision process out of necessity during the semester and finding it works better for him. As this student exemplifies, then, the Gateway students understand their reflection on the blog differently from their reflection in other spaces; here, they are *blogging*.[7] That is, they are engaging in a personally meaningful act of expressive communication directed at a genuine audience of their peers. And their peers respond, creating dialogue and potential collaboration. That they are also analyzing their own experience in order to share it with others is something they have learned from Andrew Sullivan (2008) and other writers on blogging to be a central feature of the genre; consequently, in this digital space, students can feel proud of their reflective writing (as demonstrated in a blog post title from this same student: "Finding My Blogging Voice . . . and Making it Look Good").[8] It is not a dead-end, school genre of writing, written only to satisfy a requirement, as less fully integrated reflective activities can feel to students.

The full integration of reflective activity I have described in the Gateway course is completely facilitated by the various digital tools and environments students use, from word-processing software to blogging platforms to audio, video, and image-editing applications to website platforms, and more. Further, student investment in these digital reflective activities is bound up with their sense that, through reflection, they are grappling with new challenges and situations introduced by the digital writing and rhetorical tasks they are taking up in the course as well as in gaining a sense of their own development as writers—and maybe more to the point, they are gaining digital skills and experiences they understand to have legs beyond the course and outside of school altogether in internships and jobs. Ubiquitous digital reflection, then, may also help circumvent what we might call *reflection burnout* resulting from the "mis-educative" experience of reflecting as a routinized activity, unconnected to genuine problem solving or meaning making (see Dewey 1916; Rodgers 2002). Scott analyzes this "mis-educative" phenomenon in connection to institutional ideologies and pressures within large-scale portfolio assessment programs that turn reflective letters into a "bureaucratic exercise" that leaves students "unengaged and resentful" and even "consciously dishonest" (Scott 2005, 26–27).[9] But even in the practices of an individual classroom, if reflective writing is perceived as routine, it may not lead students to engage the metacognitive cycle of learning so as to enable development of a "theory" of self-understanding for their writing (Schraw 1998; Yancey 1998).

Anything that can help avoid the stilted, artificial "conversion narratives" about their own writing development students often produce under such inauthentic pressures is a good thing in my book. But beyond that, as this chapter's second epigraph attests—from another Sweetland Minor in Writing student blogger, this time posting to the blog in the semester following her Gateway course—when reflection is so woven in to the writing curriculum that it becomes habit, students begin to reflect voluntarily, sometimes without "even realiz[ing] what [they are] doing," until they pause and take a look and notice they are creating, via self-reflective comments, an electronic self-dialogue in the margins of their documents. In other words, with ubiquitous digital reflection, students like this one can become self-sponsored reflective practitioners of writing.

Interviews conducted with students from several sections of the Gateway course in the semesters subsequent to their taking it bear out this idea.[10] Students reported overwhelmingly that they found the course's number and variety of reflective activities "productive," "useful," and "valuable." Further, in response to the question "Are you still using reflection in your current writing?" a majority described both continuing their reflective practices in one form or another and also internalizing them, as suggested in the epigraph. For instance, as one student remarked, "Yeah, just reflecting on . . . how I want it to say and what I want it to say. Then examine it. Does this actually do what I want to do? . . . My whole process of writing now is kind of self-reflective, in maybe not such an explicit way as we did in the course." And another:

"I think doing it [reflecting] out loud [i.e., in writing] like that makes me do it in my head now all the time, like why am I making this choice and then what is my choice saying?" These students are clearly engaging in the self-dialogue fundamental to effective metacognition, and in so doing, I argue, they describe a genuine transfer of reflective learning: they apply ubiquitous reflective strategies to new writing situations, and, further, they employ a metacognitive language of projection and review to describe their ongoing reflective practice. This connection of conscious, scaffolded, and reiterative reflective practice to student transfer of learning is consistent with what is reported in other studies (see, for example, Clark and Hernandez 2011; Jarratt et al. 2009; Yancey, Robertson, and Taczak 2014) and is the subject of ongoing research.

THE DIGITAL REFLECTIVE WRITING PRACTICUM

At this point it makes sense to turn to some student artifacts to illustrate some of the reflective work I have discussed. All of the artifacts presented below, produced by students in sections of the Gateway course for the Sweetland minor in writing program, were selected because they are typical of student work for the course, both in quality and in the range of genres of digital reflection represented, and I offer examples from the full cycle of metacognitive work—planning, monitoring, and evaluation—students engaged in.

Planning

Students in the Gateway course undertake a range of planning and discovery activities for their major writing projects throughout the semester in a variety of modes and media: interviews with their classmates, pen-and-paper storyboarding, low-stakes writing in Word documents and on the class blog, and more. Students also share their planning work on the blog as a way of presenting their project ideas and receiving additional feedback and comments from their classmates (beyond their more extensive writing workshops). These three blog posts show students presenting the storyboards they drew for their Remediation projects in response to this brief prompt: "This week, post some images from your storyboard to the blog and comment on them." We can see these students reflecting on the medium of the storyboard (markers, colored pencils, butcher paper) as well as that of their Remediation platform (iMovie, Tumblr, Twitter); we see their varied responses to the helpfulness of the storyboard form as a prewriting activity—it aided one student

My Drawn Out Storyboard

I just figured out how to get this drawing to be the right size in here, that was a small tech challenge in itself. But this is my storyboard, which is very subject to change. I learned that you have to ask yourself a lot of questions to simply create the storyboard, so I'm glad it forced me to think through the details more thoroughly. I hope I will have the proper amount of time to create this video and make it the way I am imagining it, but if I do not, it will definitely be a simpler version of this. I need to spend some more time coming up with good questions and considering how I will phrase the argument, but it should be fun.

Some questions I am currently considering are, "What do you think the overall message in pop music is?", "Do you think the message in Pop Music matters?", "What Pop song do you like most?", "What do you think the message is?" and more. I am hoping to show that Pop Music does have a message and if people are aware of it, than what do they think of it? Songs have different messages of course, but there are definitely some common styles and patterns that are used to make Pop Music that creates some overarching messages. I am a Communications major so I am interested in this ha.

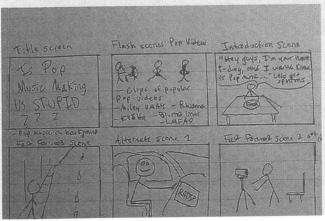

Figure 9.1. Student blog post reflecting on usefulness of storyboard for video planning.

in thinking through the details of the project of making a movie (see fig. 9.1 and Appendix 9.1); it led another to a realization about the limitations of her initial choice of platform for the Remediation (see fig. 9.2 and Appendix 9.2); to a third, it seemed less applicable to a Remediation platform that isn't intrinsically narrative (see fig. 9.3 and Appendix 9.3). We see these students talking through their storyboard images with their classmates and receiving comments and further advice that affirm their Remediation ideas and in some cases indicate peer learning or "inspiration" already from these initial plans (see fig. 9.4 and Appendix 9.4). A key benefit of the digital platform for this sort of planning exercise is the opportunity for students to externalize a set of ideas and share it with an interested audience, to turn "writer-based prose" into "reader-based

Storyboarding Part 2

I wrote before about loving the storyboard experience (mostly after the fact) of the e-portfolio, so I was actually looking forward to storyboarding my Re-Mediation project. For this project, I was going to create a collection of animated GIFs, on the topic of gender socialization.

I planned to make a Buzzfeed-type article about breaking gender stereotypes, with most of the information presented visually through animated photos or video clips. Creating my storyboard was pretty straightforward – I typed a list of what images or clips I wanted to find (ex: a female gamer, a boy playing with dolls). I even had a title, "(#) People Valiantly Breaking Gender Stereotypes."

But when I looked at my completed storyboard, I realized it lacked depth and context. I felt that viewers would not get anything out of this project. It left much open to interpretation and did not take a clear stance on the issue of gender stereotypes.

So, I changed my platform. Instead of creating a single, static list, I will compile my animated GIFs into a Tumblr. While many of the posts will still be visual, using Tumblr should give me more room to explain the issue, how the GIFs relate to each other, and will give my topic more of the depth and seriousness it deserves.

Figure 9.2. Student blog post reflecting on how storyboard helped her rethink her choice of project platform.

prose" (to borrow Flower's [1979] terms). These students accomplish this move with varying degrees of polish and detail; sometimes the key ideas come out in the Comments section in an exchange with a peer or in the thoughtful rephrasing and extension of an idea other readers give them. In allowing the publication of the storyboard in the first place, the digital space makes this dialogic reflection possible, and, additionally, preserves the exchange for later reference and further reflection.

Monitoring

For every draft of each major writing project, students are asked to include self-reflective monitoring comments—using the Comments tool in their word processing or PDF-creation program for alphabetic and multi-modal print documents[11] or tools like VoiceThread or a screencasting

My First Storyboard

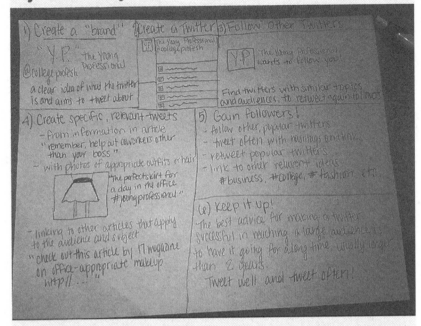

For my remediating project, I plan on taking the advice and information I have learned through my repurposing project (a magazine spread on being a young professional) and turning it into an anonymous advice twitter. I have experience many of these as an avid twitter user and find them a successful medium for getting information across to girls of my age.

Creating a storyboard for this kind of project is a little bit difficult. Twitters don't exactly tell a story, rather a string of 140 character blurbs that all apply to the same topic. Argues about our

Figure 9.3. Student blog post reflecting on limitations of storyboard planning for nonnarrative projects.

program for websites or time-based digital media projects—that indicate bottlenecks, breakthroughs, or anything else they wish to draw to their readers' attention. The prompt for these comments was developed out of a study of metacognitive strategies in upper-level writing-in-the-disciplines courses (see Appendix 9.5 for the full prompt).[12] Students practice using these comments all semester and receive feedback on the form of the comment as well as its specific content, helping to scaffold their use of comments and leading students to become more precise and push deeper in their queries and observations.

As the examples included here suggest, students' self-reflective monitoring comments—which function as a kind of embedded

3 thoughts on "My First Storyboard"

November 4, 2013 at 9:53 pm

It looks like you have a pretty good plan for creating a successful twitter! I like how you addressed the less obvious things that can influence the success of a twitter, like the description, background, and twitpic. Do you plan on updating the twitter even after the semester is over? It would be interesting to see its progress months/years from now.

Excited to see your final product!

Log in to Reply

November 5, 2013 at 12:05 am

Dang, your storyboard looks really good! I really like how you are branding YP and plan to provide lots of links/pictures/etc. in your tweets. This is definitely a unique and interesting project to be working on, and I can't wait to see more in class!

Log in to Reply

November 6, 2013 at 8:08 pm

This is such a cool idea! As Sophia said, your storyboard does a great job of showing all the different components that make a twitter successful. I also like how your project has the potential to be very interactive. Since the discussion of Web 2.0 in the Lev Manovich reading, I have been looking for ways to make my own remediation project more open to the public, probably through social media. Your storyboard reminds me that social media success takes more than simply posting a few photos or links. You have to join conversations that are already happening and actively invite others to check out your brand or thoughts. Thank you for the inspiration, and I can't wait to see how your project turns out!

Figure 9.4. Students' reflective dialogue in comments on blog post.

reflection-in-action—provide an excellent means of creating a reflective dialogue in the margins between writer and reader (whether instructor or peers). Readers get a "back story" on the writer's paper, enabling responses that speak directly and efficiently to the writer's central questions and concerns. Further, over time, these small acts of self-monitoring become integrated into students' composing processes—become a kind of self-dialogue as well—such that in the act of noticing and formulating a comment, students often become able to supply their own response and enact an appropriate revision. One of the Sweetland Minor in Writing student-interview respondents explains the process in this way: "You insert little comments. If you, as a writer, have a question or you're not sure about something, you'd say, 'I wasn't sure if this was

Your Brain, The Muscle

Like the early stages of Alzheimer's Disease (AD), the early physiological changes are nearly as subtle. It is only at the severely progressive stages of the disease that changes become noticeable. The changes occur in the frontal and temporal lobes of the brain which are the two lobes primarily responsible for executive functioning tasks such as decision-making, the ability to adapt in novel situations, multi-tasking, working memory, and planning. A loss of volume in these areas is an indicator of AD onset. The loss of volume occurs because neurons die. Why these neurons die is still being investigated. These lobes show the fastest rate of age-related cognitive decline, therefore physical activity (PA) has the greatest chance to be of benefit there.

However, the neurological benefits from PA are not global, they are specific to brain structures associated with executive functioning. Exercise exerts a *unique* protective role in not only preserving, but maintaining cognitive functioning. A 2006 study found that aerobic training actually increased brain volume for previously sedentary individuals. When you engage in aerobic exercise (walking, jogging, anything that increases heart rate), your body releases a growth factor that induces angiogenesis, or the birth of new blood vessels, in your brain. Increased blood vessels in your brain means increased blood flow and increases in cerebral blood flow are a measure of cognitive processing. Increased cerebral blood flow allows for neurogenesis, or the birth of new neurons which in turn increases brain volume. Furthermore, PA stimulates the release of brain derived neurotropic factor (BDNF) that maintains neural integrity. This entire process can take place in as little as three months post workout. Importantly however, for this processes to occur, the exercise must be aerobic in nature.

Comment [1]: Student: New lines of research suggest that plaques and tangles are the culprits of AD—is this worth mentioning here or do you think it is too much of a tangent from the exercise focus?

NS: I think a quick and casual reference could be useful. Also, avoid the passive voice in this sentence ('still being investigated') – it reads too formally.

Comment [2]: Student: I didn't know if I should spend this paragraph explaining all the background stuff...what Alzheimer's is, what's known, etc. or if I should assume a reader of TIME would be familiar...the articles I read varied on the level of detail they went into explaining or not explaining general knowledge topics

NS: As a reader, I felt the broader background info was sufficient (though adding a bit about plaques, etc. would be good, I think), but I'm a bit confused by your last sentence, because it's less clear to me why physical activity has an impact on neuron life or death... Another connective sentence would be useful here. (I see that you get into the explanation below, but it doesn't come quite quickly enough – perhaps a bit of reorganization here, or a preview phrase or sentence?)

Figure 9.5. Student self-reflective monitoring comments.

the best argument here.' I really like that. I think that really strengthened my writing, because it made me ask questions. Then sometimes after just seeing that question, I was able to answer it on my own, and then sometimes the teacher or students would answer those questions."

The two excerpted examples of self-reflective monitoring comments I've included here are drawn from the major Repurposing project, in which students are asked to select "a piece of writing you've already completed on a topic that's dear to your heart and/or mind, a topic you'll want to continue living with this semester" and "repurpose it for a new audience and with a new or extended argument." Both students are grappling with repurposing an academic argument into one directed at a popular audience (fig. 9.5 and Appendix 9.6 show how a kinesiology research paper on the effects of exercise on the development of Alzheimer's disease was repurposed as a *Time* magazine article, and Appendix 9.7 shows how political science and philosophy research papers on global feminism and universal human rights were repurposed as a *Foreign Policy* journal article). These students' comments speak to struggles with balancing their depth of subject knowledge against what might be expected from their audience, striking an appropriate tone for the target publication venue and refining their argument to convey the complexity of their ideas appropriately. My responses aim to address their question or concern directly and to strike a balance between offering a readerly response of impressions and more specific advice for revision.

Evaluation

As they did for all of their final project drafts during the semester, alongside the polished draft of the Remediation project students were asked to submit a reflection accounting for their response to feedback on the earlier drafts, and they were also asked to comment specifically (1) on the extent to which they were able to reach their ideal version of the project, given the constraints and learning curve of the medium or platform in which they chose to work, and (2) on the "behind-the-scenes" rhetorical choices they made working within this medium/platform, a reflective activity not unlike Michael Neal's "rhetorical rationale" (this volume). Students could use any medium they chose for this reflection, and most used print. But some students chose to make videos instead for a variety of reasons—because they had made videos for projects in the class and felt comfortable with the medium, because videos afforded the ability to narrate their process dynamically, because videos can convey affect in ways print cannot always (as Elizabeth Clark notes, this volume),[13] and because videos can approximate a reader's experience of a project (navigating a website, say) in a way print text cannot easily.

The video reflection presented here (see fig. 9.6) was composed by a student for whom the Remediation project video was her first foray into video making. For her Repurposing project, this student had chosen to rework an analysis of a girls' health website into an APA-style research paper, and she remediated this paper into a video, "Female Body Image and Sexuality." She incorporated survey data and interview footage she collected as research for the two projects. Her video reflection is essentially a frame-by-frame screencast commentary—from within the "back end" or workspace of the iMovie software program—on her choices and her revisions as she pulled all of these elements together and moved closer to the version of the project she had in mind. Among many topics addressed in the fifteen-minute video, this student talks in detail about how she learned to use the iMovie software and the video tutorials that helped her; she responds to feedback I had given her in a one-to-one conference, concerning transitions, for instance, and also discusses the rhetorical choices behind certain transition effects she ended up using; she discusses her aesthetic and organizational choices in the service of impact of argument, parallelism, and uniformity of effect; and she closes by noting her satisfaction at having taken on the challenge of the project.

Video reflections can take a range of forms, from the "talking head" speaking to the camera, to more narrative forms documenting and portraying writing processes (as in some examples from Hawisher et al. 2009), to more experimental and impressionistic collages (as in some

Figure 9.6. Student reflective video evaluation of remediation project. (http://deepblue .lib.umich.edu/handle/2027.42/113197)

examples from Journet et al. 2008). This student's choice to offer a frame-by-frame reflective narration on the video was completely her own and is unlike any other video reflection I've encountered. In a sense, this video commentary has much in common with—is perhaps a kind of remediation of—self-reflective marginal comments in that it takes the viewer into the text of the video production itself to engage in fine-grained annotation. It is also reminiscent of the work Meloni (2009) describes her students doing with the Google Docs revision history in that the iMovie software workspace, captured in a screencast, offers unprecedented access to moment-by-moment rhetorical choices. It is a very long video—almost three times the length of the original 6:18-minute video on which it comments (http://deepblue.lib.umich .edu/handle/2027.42/113196)—and one could offer a critique here that it essentially constitutes a narration rather than an edited composition in itself;[14] yet (for this viewer), it is a fascinating look at a student's account of her rhetorical processes in creating a complex composition and, in that way, beautifully fulfills the reflective genre of the (video) process note.

Reflective Essay

As part of the final electronic portfolio they create for the Sweetland Minor in Writing Gateway course that collects their work in the course and tasks them with constructing and presenting a provisional writerly self-identity, students include a reflective essay presenting their process of working through their Repurposing project and its subsequent Remediation. A brief prompt (part of a larger prompt for the portfolio as a whole) directs students to compose "a reflective essay on our big two-part project that leads your reader through the steps from 'source' text to 're-purposing' essay to 're-mediation' project—it should say something about your motivations and your choices and also include links to your 'source' and 'model' texts." This essay requires students to make a number of moves quickly: charting the pathway of texts from point A to point B and so on, making these texts (and, if they choose, also their drafts) available to the reader, accounting for the choices made and the understanding gained in the process of remaking an idea in new genres and media in a style that invites readers in and makes them care about this process. It's a complex rhetorical situation in any event, made more so by its being embedded in the high-stakes assessment scenario of a final course portfolio that counts for a quarter of the course grade.

I juxtapose two examples of this reflective essay to demonstrate different possibilities for taking up the prompt and to highlight some subtle intertextual connections between them. Josh, who hand coded his site, makes expert use of thumbnail screenshots, hyperlinks, text interspersed with images, and arrows and other diacritical markers that indicate connectivity and movement and foreground the visual rhetoric of his own work of repurposing and remediating (see fig. 9.7 and Appendix 9.8). His linear top-to-bottom format narrates the temporal progression of his conceptual relation to the topic of zombies over a few semesters and specifically his "exploration of the undead and the cultural implications of our culture's obsession over them." It also narrates and demonstrates changes in his relation to the modes and media in which it is possible to explore the topic, as we see in the shift from traditional alphabetic essay to multimodal magazine article to website.

Beixi takes a different approach, essentially creating a miniwebsite within a website that illustrates not only the evolution from Repurposing to Remediation but also the evolution of each of those projects in itself (see fig. 9.8 and Appendix 9.9). In its use of arrows to point the way from topic to topic, her reflection in some ways draws inspiration from Josh's—a very real possibility in that Josh's reflective essay is published on a publicly accessible website (it is housed in the ePortfolio showcase on the Sweetland Minor in Writing blog [http://writingminor.sweetland.lsa.umich.edu/portfolios/]) and was used as a model of this reflective genre in Beixi's Gateway class two years later, which allowed Beixi

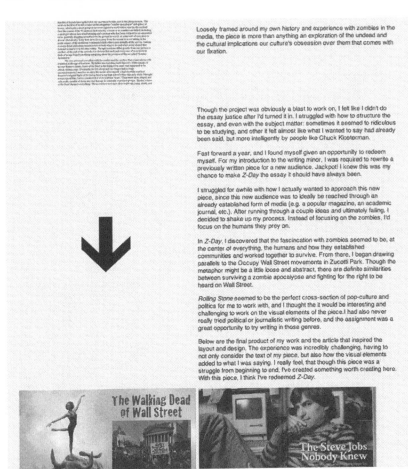

Figure 9.7. *Student reflective essay portraying linear temporal development of repurposing and remediating projects.*

to view it, reflect upon it, and learn from it on her own time. This asynchronous form of peer-to-peer learning extends the model of dialogic reflection afforded by the digital space of the public website. The shift in Beixi's essay, from the single large arrows pointing downward we see in Josh's, to clusters of arrows pointing first right and then left, signify in some sense the complex hyperlinking of her miniwebsite. Buttons naming the source texts (Memoirs), repurposed texts (Short Stories), and remediated text (Ann Arbor Awesome) lead us to webpages that present those artifacts along with brief contextual reflections for each item. The text of the reflective essay itself also includes hyperlinks to each individual artifact, and sidebar columns include links to drafts of the

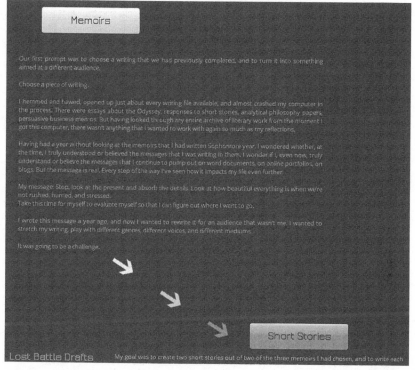

Figure 9.8. Student reflective essay portraying networked development of repurposing and remediating projects.

Repurposing project short stories as well as brief reflections on topics related to the development of the Remediation project: the choice of a platform, rhetorical choices behind the image captions in the final version of the project, and ways she understood her writing style to change over the project's creation.

These reflective essays, which constitute a kind of middle ground between the writerly identity-building work of constructive reflection, made public and explicit, and reflection-in-presentation offer a rich sense of how students take up real choices among complex rhetorical situations and the investments they have in both subject (or content) and medium. In so doing, they enact a remediation of the *essay* form.[15] Josh describes knowing from the outset that he wanted to make a website about zombies, but then feeling frustrated when constraints on his composing process did not allow him to achieve his aim as he had envisioned it, despite his previous experience building websites; he also describes his excitement at deepening his work with the topic by incorporating the visual rhetoric of his magazine article. Beixi, on the other hand, describes wanting to try out a genre she had never explored in order to return to some ideas about growing up she wanted to think through more fully and the challenges this genre posed for her, particularly in regard to craft; she also describes the leap in collaborating with a classmate to create the *Ann Arbor Awesome* website (http://beixili.wix .com/livelaughloveshare#!listen/c3c1), a process that combined a wide range of analog and digital media, from in-person interviews and digital photography to writing and website building. The rich multimodal and multimedia dimensions of these two reflective essays are central to the conceptual, aesthetic, and metacognitive work they do—for their writers and readers alike—work that fully depends upon the affordances of the digital spaces in which they live.

DIGITAL REFLECTION AND DIGITAL RHETORIC PEDAGOGY

In response, then, to the questions with which I began—how does digital reflection work and how does it differ from nondigital reflection?—the literature and the examples I've presented suggest that digital spaces present both new challenges and new opportunities. We see these challenges and opportunities

- in the relative "ease" (to return to Cope and Kalantzis's [2009] term) of designing a reflective curriculum using digital tools and thereby cultivating students' capacity to become reflective practitioners of writing;
- in the new and varied forms of dialogic reflection and collaborative possibilities these tools make possible;
- in the increased visibility of aspects of writing development and writing processes enabled by these tools that can alter our sense of what we're doing when we write; and
- in the creativity, engagement, and sense of ownership of their reflective writing students exhibit when given the freedom to explore these tools and use them to make authentic composing choices.

But beyond these student experiences of reflection in digital spaces, of course, as Yancey reminds us, "teachers are also reflective practitioners" (Yancey 1998, 15). I want to conclude, then, by taking a look at how teaching ubiquitous digital reflection may have effects on instructors' own reflective and pedagogical practices. Does pedagogy work differently in digital reflective spaces, and does reflection work differently in digital pedagogical spaces (such as a Google Doc or student website)? Just as we saw that there are multiple possible scenarios combining digital and print-based tools for writing and for reflection, there are also various ways of incorporating digital reflection into writing classrooms. Indeed, some instructors may wish to introduce their students to multimodal composition in a primarily low-stakes way and so may use forms of digital reflection in curricula based around analog forms of major writing assignments. In this way, then, the use of tools for digital reflection need not entail a more general digital pedagogy.

Yet, I want to suggest that there are significant benefits to teaching digital forms of reflection in classrooms where students are also engaging in other genres of multimodal and multimedia composition. And beyond that, once we have taken the plunge, so to speak, into teaching certain digital genres, it can be hard to resist transforming the writing classroom into a fully digitally mediated space. Journet et al. (2008) describe their efforts "to move the [multimodal reflective] work [they] were doing into [their] own undergraduate teaching" and their sense that their teacher experience of the affordances and constraints of reflecting in digital spaces ended up facilitating deeper insight into their students' digital *and* analog print-based writing experiences, in terms of students' apprehension and resistance to reflection but also opportunities for "play" and new composer/audience relations (under "Home"; see also Rogers, Trauman, and Kiernan 2010). In part, it may be the case that teaching and cultivating student reflection with digital tools and in digital environments may feel different because there are so many elements to be figured out—more variables to juggle and more permutations possible in all aspects of the rhetorical situation for a particular piece of writing. In these scenarios, the instructor does not have all the answers and may play the role of codiscoverer. Indeed, instructors may themselves be reflecting in ways more urgent and deep than usual on the pros and cons of their pedagogical choices with the tools at their own disposal.

In my own experiences with teaching in the digital reflective practicum of the Sweetland Minor in Writing Gateway course, I have found that students' explorations of (and growing confidence and expertise in) digital rhetoric in their major writing projects (particularly the Remediation and ePortfolio) and on their blogs creates a kind of synergy with their uses of digital tools for purposes of reflection, leading to digital reflections that are unexpectedly innovative, nuanced, and thoughtfully conceived. Here, then, working with students as they discover the rhetorical affordances and constraints of various digital tools for their writing, as part of digital rhetoric pedagogy, supports as well the development of a digital reflective curriculum. On the other hand,

I have found that my students' digitally mediated reflections on their own and their classmates' writing have also changed the ways I respond to their writing, such that much of my own commentary and feedback has become multimodal—almost as a means of keeping up with them. One example of this change can be found in the dialogue initiated by my students' self-reflective monitoring comments, but I have also found myself needing tools like VoiceThread and screencasting software to respond to my students' videos, podcasts, websites, and the like. Most recently, I have screencast my one-to-one conferences with my students; we sit at my computer and they lead me through the questions and comments they have about their multimodal compositions in progress. After the conference, I send them the link to the video so they have a record of our conversation, in what might be a kind of time-based remediation of the alphabetic record English (1998) describes students taking away from their conversations in the MOO.

Teacher and student, then, we both become aware that there is now much more to reflect on, that our digital composing work has us crossing into new and unexpected compositional and rhetorical spaces, and that there is therefore real exigency and scope for our work of reflection. At the same time, we both understand that our digital tools for reflection are themselves part of these spaces and that in wielding these tools with increasing precision and know-how, we may glean important new insights into the significance for writing, learning, and teaching of a reflective curriculum.

Notes

1. Hannah Tasker, February 2, 2012, "PSA on Self-Reflective Comments," *Sweetland Minor in Writing Blog*, http://writingminor.sweetland.lsa.umich.edu/author/hazita/page/2/.

2. The literature on the role of metacognition in self-regulation of learning is vast. Some key texts include Flavell 1976; Palinscar and Brown 1984; and Dunlosky and Metcalfe 2009. See also Matthew Kaplan et al. 2013 for an overview of strategies for teaching metacognition across the disciplines.

3. According to the program website, "Students in the Minor experiment with writing in numerous ways, including (but definitely not limited to!) multi-modal projects, traditional papers, professional writing, and creative work. They can make use of what they have learned in their major and other courses within their writing projects for the minor, as well as explore new ways of writing that they might not otherwise encounter" (under "Minor in Writing," University of Michigan Sweetland Center for Writing, https://lsa.umich.edu/sweetland/undergraduates/minor-in-writing).

4. Sweetland Minor in Writing students are required to post to this blog (http://writingminor.sweetland.lsa.umich.edu/) during enrollment in their Gateway and capstone courses for the minor program and are invited to post in the semesters in between and subsequent to their completion of the program.

5. Dylan Baig, December 4, 2013, "My Blogging Voice," *Sweetland Minor in Writing Blog*, http://writingminor.sweetland.lsa.umich.edu/2013/12/my-blogging-style/.

6. Joseph Ostrow, comment on Baig, "My Blogging Voice."

7. Toby Fulwiler (1987) notes an interesting similarity in *The Journal Book*, describing an analog form that has much in common with the blog genre in what he lists as its language features, cognitive activities, and formal features that facilitate students' free rein in expression and conceptual exploration (see, e.g., 2–3). One key feature this form lacks in relation to the blog, however, is its built-in availability to other readers and its promotion of easy dialogic reflection.

8. The student blog posts mentioned in this paragraph all appear on the *Sweetland Minor in Writing Blog* and can be found on Joseph Ostrow's author page: http://writingminor.sweetland.lsa.umich.edu/author/jstro/.

9. Kathleen Blake Yancey, Stephen McElroy, and Elizabeth Powers note this problem, too, writing, "There is a line of research, small but growing, suggesting that asking students to perform [reflection] . . . (as 'proving' they have learned) might in fact be counterproductive because in such a context, ironically, they can be required to dissemble in order to succeed, with the result that portfolio-as-site-for-authentic-assessment becomes another platform for the game of grades" (Yancey, McElroy, and Powers 2013, under "The Take-Away").

10. These interviews comprise one dataset from an ongoing longitudinal study of student writing development conducted by the Sweetland Center for Writing at the University of Michigan, on which I am a coinvestigator. I cite only a tiny fragment of interview language coded as *Reflection*. I am grateful to the study research team for permission to make use of this material here.

11. The Insert Comment tool in the student's word-processing platform is so commonplace as to be almost "low-tech," but it does provide a digital space, which enables a level of detail in both student comment and instructor or peer response, as the examples suggest, that would be quite difficult to achieve with handwriting in the margins.

12. I have been asking my students to insert self-reflective comments in the margins of their working and final drafts regularly since 2008, when I and colleagues from UM's Center for Research on Learning and Teaching proposed their use as one intervention in this study, titled "The Impact of Metacognitive Strategies within Writing in the Disciplines," funded by the Spencer and Teagle Foundations. The study found overwhelmingly that students and instructors are engaged by and learn from use of these comments: "Our analysis suggests that the [self-reflective] monitoring comments had the largest impact. They were the most highly rated of our interventions, both by instructors and by students. In fact, between 83% and 95% of students agreed or strongly agreed that the monitoring comments were useful" (Meizlish et al. 2013, 11; see also LaVaque-Manty and Evans 2013, particularly their discussion of the dialogic function of these comments, 135–36 and 138–39).

13. J. Elizabeth Clark also notes a similar effect in her comments on student ePortfolios at LaGuardia Community College, as cited in Cambridge, Cambridge, and Yancey 2009.

14. See Yancey et al. 2013 for a critique of excessive length in video reflections as well as important questions regarding establishment of the genre conventions for video and audio reflections (199–200).

15. This chapter was completed prior to the publication of *On Multimodality: New Media in Composition Studies* by Jonathan Alexander and Jacqueline Rhodes. Nonetheless, I want to acknowledge their important contribution to a new theory of "the essay" in a multimodal, multimedia compositional world as well as their critique of the field of composition studies' "fetishization" of this form (Alexander and Rhodes 2014, 43).

APPENDIX 9.1.

My Drawn Out Storyboard

📅 November 4, 2013 (http://writingminor.sweetland.lsa.umich.edu/2013/11/my-drawn-out-storyboard/) 👤

I just figured out how to get this drawing to be the right size in here, that was a small tech challenge in itself. But this is my storyboard, which is very subject to change. I learned that you have to ask yourself a lot of questions to simply create the storyboard, so I'm glad it forced me to think through the details more thoroughly. I hope I will have the proper amount of time to create this video and make it the way I am imagining it, but if I do not, it will definitely be a simpler version of this. I need to spend some more time coming up with good questions and considering how I will phrase the argument, but it should be fun.

Some questions I am currently considering are, "What do you think the overall message in pop music is?" , "Do you think the message in Pop Music matters?" , "What Pop song do you like most?" , "What do you think the message is?" and more. I am hoping to show that Pop Music does have a message and if people are aware of it, than what do they think of it? Songs have different messages of course, but there are definitely some common styles and patterns that are used to make Pop Music that creates some overarching messages. I am a Communications major so I am interested in this ha.

APPENDIX 9.2.

Storyboarding Part 2

📅 November 7, 2013 (http://writingminor.sweetland.lsa.umich.edu/2013/11/storyboarding-part-2/) 👤

I wrote before about loving the storyboard experience (mostly after the fact) of the e-portfolio, so I was actually looking forward to storyboarding my Re-Mediation project. For this project, I was going to create a collection of animated GIFs, on the topic of gender socialization.

I planned to make a Buzzfeed-type article about breaking gender stereotypes, with most of the information presented visually through animated photos or video clips. Creating my storyboard was pretty straightforward – I typed a list of what images or

APPENDIX 9.3.

My First Storyboard

📅 November 4, 2013 (http://writingminor.sweetland.lsa.umich.edu/2013/11/my-first-storyboard/) 👤

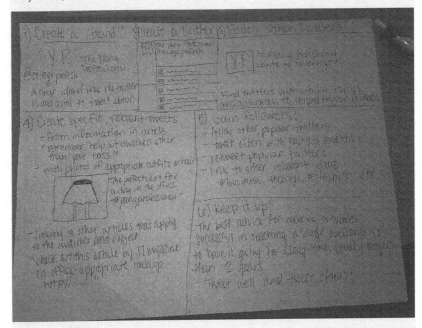

For my remediating project, I plan on taking the advice and information I have learned through my repurposing project (a magazine spread on being a young professional) and turning it into an anonymous advice twitter. I have experience many of these as an avid twitter user and find them a successful medium for getting information across to girls of my age.

3 thoughts on "My First Storyboard"

It looks like you have a pretty good plan for creating a successful twitter! I like how you addressed the less obvious things that can influence the success of a twitter, like the description, background, and twitpic. Do you plan on updating the twitter even after the semester is over? It would be interesting to see its progress months/years from now.

Excited to see your final product!

REPLY (/2013/11/MY-FIRST-STORYBOARD/?REPLYTOCOM=1890#RESPOND)

Dang, your storyboard looks really good! I really like how you are branding YP and plan to provide lots of links/pictures/etc. in your tweets. This is definitely a unique and interesting project to be working on, and I can't wait to see more in class!

REPLY (/2013/11/MY-FIRST-STORYBOARD TOCOM=1893#RESPOND)

APPENDIX 9.5.

Appendix 1: Inserting Self-Reflective Comments in Essay Drafts Handout

Asking students to comment on their own writing in progress and identify bottlenecks and areas that are working well promotes the kind of metacognitive self-assessment that supports writing development. Responding directly to student comments promotes focused dialogue about writing, and aids overall writing assessment. This handout is adapted from a study of successful writing strategies being conducted by the Sweetland Writing Center and the Center for Research on Learning and Teaching. The study is funded by the Spencer and Teagle Foundations.

Instructions
Once you've written your draft, take a step back and think about any questions or comments you have about what you've achieved in your writing. Use the "comment" function in Word to insert 3 to 5 questions or comments in the margins of the paper. This is your opportunity to communicate with me "backstage" about the choices you've made. You might note places where:

- you've tried to draw on key concepts from the readings or course materials,
- you think you've expressed an idea or posed an argument particularly well,
- you feel uncertain about whether you've gotten your point across,
- you are struggling with or confused about a particular concept,
- you've incorporated suggestions for revision from me or your peers.

Make sure your questions and comments offer enough information to allow the reader to know how to respond to you—e.g., explain *why* you're confused (not just that you're confused), or why you've used the concepts you've chosen; refer to specific ways you think you've expressed something well; and so on.

Here are two examples – one of an appropriately specific question for this activity and one of an overly broad question:

Specific Question
Here's an example of an appropriately specific question: "I originally had this section, and a few others later in the paper, in italics. I wanted to differentiate the lines that are more of an inner monologue from the primary narrative of the piece, but thought the italic style might take the reader's focus away from the content of my paper. As a reader, do you think several interjections in italics would enhance the flow of the piece? Or would it be too much of a distraction from my main ideas?"

Overly Broad Question
Here's one that is too broad: "Does this make sense? Or should I go deeper into that idea? Or leave it out completely?"

Note: To use the "comment" function in Word, use your mouse to select the portion of your text you want to comment on. Then select "insert" from the menu at the top of your screen. This will open a drop-down menu; select "comment" from the list of options you find there.

Danielle D Lavaqu... 5/18/2014 12:03 AM
Comment [1]: Once you've selected "comment," Word will place a bubble like this one in your margin. Type your comment or question there. When you've finished, use your mouse to click anywhere in your main document; this will allow you to exit the bubble.

APPENDIX 9.6.

Your Brain, The Muscle

Like the early stages of Alzheimer's Disease (AD), the early physiological changes are nearly as subtle. It is only at the severely progressive stages of the disease that changes become noticeable. The changes occur in the frontal and temporal lobes of the brain which are the two lobes primarily responsible for executive functioning tasks such as decision-making, the ability to adapt in novel situations, multi-tasking, working memory, and planning. A loss of volume in these areas is an indicator of AD onset. The loss of volume occurs because neurons die. Why these neurons die is still being investigated. These lobes show the fastest rate of age-related cognitive decline, therefore physical activity (PA) has the greatest chance to be of benefit there.

However, the neurological benefits from PA are not global, they are specific to brain structures associated with executive functioning. Exercise exerts a *unique* protective role in not only preserving, but maintaining cognitive functioning. A 2006 study found that aerobic training actually increased brain volume for previously sedentary individuals. When you engage in aerobic exercise (walking, jogging, anything that increases heart rate), your body releases a growth factor that induces angiogenesis, or the birth of new blood vessels, in your brain. Increased blood vessels in your brain means increased blood flow and increases in cerebral blood flow are a measure of cognitive processing. Increased cerebral blood flow allows for neurogenesis, or the birth of new neurons which in turn increases brain volume. Furthermore, PA stimulates the release of brain derived neurotropic factor (BDNF) that maintains neural integrity. This entire process can take place in as little as three months post workout. Importantly however, for this processes to occur, the exercise must be aerobic in nature. Studies that compared anaerobic to aerobic exercises, found that no neurological effects correlated with the anaerobic workout groups.

Though the above findings are encouraging, studies by Bixby and Lytle further corroborate and give more clout to the results. One important factor to consider in analyzing brain volume is IQ. Higher IQ is associated with more education which in turn is indicative of more neurons and dendrites and therefore a higher brain volume at baseline. However, the Bixby study rigorously controlled for IQ, socioeconomic status (SES), and education level and a positive association still remained between PA and increased cognitive functioning. Furthermore, the Lytle study looked at rural populations in Pennsylvania that reported cognitive functioning problems at younger ages, were of lower SES status, lower IQ levels, and fewer years of completed formal education. This was an atypical population for scientific studies and the fact that a correlation still remained for PA preventing the onset of dementia really lends to the generalizability of these results.

According to the research, keeping your wits about you may be as simple as taking a 30 minute walk each day, five days a week...if you're following the guidelines set forth by the American College of Sports Medicine. What about standing, taking the stairs, or even cleaning the kitchen? You burn more calories engaging in these activities than sitting or watching TV.

Naomi Silver 5/18/2014 11:57 PM

Comment [1]: Student: New lines of research suggest that plaques and tangles are the culprits of AD—is this worth mentioning here or do you think it is too much of a tangent from the exercise focus?

NS: I think a quick and casual reference could be useful. Also, avoid the passive voice in this sentence ('still being investigated') – it reads too formally.

Naomi Silver 5/18/2014 11:57 PM

Comment [2]: Student: I didn't know if I should spend this paragraph explaining all the background stuff...what Alzheimer's is, what's known, etc. or if I should assume a reader of TIME would be familiar...the articles I read varied on the level of detail they went into explaining or not explaining general knowledge topics

NS: As a reader, I felt the broader background info was sufficient (though adding a bit about plaques, etc, would be good, I think), but I'm a bit confused by your last sentence, because it's less clear to me why physical activity has an impact on neuron life or death... Another connective sentence would be useful here. [I see that you get into the explanation below, but it doesn't come quite quickly enough – perhaps a bit of reorganization here, or a preview phrase or sentence?]

Naomi Silver 5/18/2014 11:53 PM

Comment [3]: Student: Is the association between IQ and brain volume and why it matters to make these results legitimate clear? I don't think I did a good job of explaining the correlation, but again, I don't know how much to assume a reader knows. I feel like I should explain things more thoroughly

NS: this section feels too academic, really. In some ways, I wonder if you need it, or if you could paraphrase the key idea more quickly? I'm not clearly getting the correlation you want to convey... H[...] [l]

Naomi Silver 5/18/2014 11:58 PM

Comment [4]: Student: Are you clear on what exactly the new research is? Did I make it explicit enough what the correlation/benefits of exercise and cog functioning are?

NS: Yes, for the most part, though I think it can be clarified some, as I mention above. The main point has been conveyed, though.

Page 1: [1] Comment [3]   Naomi Silver   5/18/14 11:58 PM

Student: Is the association between IQ and brain volume and why it matters to make these results legitimate clear? I don't think I did a good job of explaining the correlation, but again, I don't know how much to assume a reader knows. I feel like I should explain things more thoroughly

NS: this section feels too academic, really. In some ways, I wonder if you need it, or if you could paraphrase the key idea more quickly? I'm not clearly getting the correlation you want to convey... How do your model articles handle this kind of thing?

APPENDIX 9.7.

Appendix 3: Student Self-Reflective Monitoring Comments noting strengths and weaknesses in the paper's argument and style

But not so fast. There is something too simplistic about the causal relationship between investment and improvement, and perhaps too narrow. How, exactly, does one tangibly and sustainably *invest* in women, actually? In developing nations in the midst of severe economic crises, prolonged civil unrest, and environmental disasters, investments made be the Western world, or lack thereof, is perpetuating the development crisis. The World Bank, the UN and the IMF have, albeit unsuccessfully, have strategized loan systems and other various economic strategies to uplift the developing. Needless to say, development is not a simplistic issue, and the benefits and failures of current strategies have not yet been realized—we are still trying to figure out the most effective policies. Drawing the conclusion that investment in women is the answer to this crisis is not only a vague and an abstract rhetorical ploy, but it completely undermines the complexity of strategies currently being assessed.

It is easy to pinpoint where and to what degree vulnerable populations of women are suffering throughout the world, and perhaps even easier to recommend strategies that would elevate the level of political participation, economic independence and social empowerment. The United States of America has figured it out, after all. Is it not our duty as a developed country that reaps the benefits of a three-wave movement to spread our knowledge, our insight, and our resources to those women who aren't as fortunate as us!

You see what I'm getting at here? There is a sentiment vaguely demonstrative of imperialistic superiority that we are applying to our understanding of global women's rights. There is a fundamental conflict in approaching global gender inequality as we do humanitarian aid—with a paternalistic concept that our values as a Western democracy are inherently more developed and legitimate.

Naomi Silver 5/16/2014 11:56 PM

Comment [1]: Student: Again, another sweeping conclusion that I haven't justified enough! I need to talk a little bit more about current economic development strategies, and how focusing JUST on women may not be the most effective way to create foundational and sustainable change for a county.

NS: Yes, sounds good. It seems like one of the issues may be teasing out the economic from the empowerment issue? When activists like Clinton claim that investing in women is good for the economy, is this a way of kind of dressing up the call for women's equality in language that will appeal more broadly (to men)? I.e., 'you men with power probably wouldn't want to bother with women just for the principle of it, but see, you can get something from it too...' I guess for me as a reader the question comes down to what the main aim is – if it's 'foundational and sustainable change for a country,' then yes, you're probably right – though I guess the argument could be made that greater social equality in general should be (needs to be) part of that equation, no?... Lots of really great food for thought here!

Naomi Silver 5/16/2014 11:56 PM

Comment [2]: Student: Okay so my argument is not NEARLY as refined and specific as I need it to be. There is a lot more thought, evidence and specific examples that I need to elaborate on in this essay before I can make this a compelling argument. However the tone and style of this is what I'm going for...resembling an argumentative journal article.

NS: I like this last paragraph a lot. It states a main point clearly and contentiously, and it opens up room for debate. What if you were to lead with something like this before circling back to Clinton and that background?

APPENDIX 9.8.

Josh Kim
student. writer. nerd.

Contact

Portfolio

Writing as Process

About

Home

I've always believed that writing was more of an action than a thing, a verb rather than a noun. Over these last few months, I've really been exposed to writing as a process and how self-reflection leads to clearer, more expertly composed pieces.Here's an example of what I'm talking about.

The piece to the left started as a creative-nonfiction piece, written for an English class I took in the Fall of 2010. Though creative-nonficiton oriented, the assignment required me to do a significant amount of independent research. I was however allowed to choose any topic that suited us.

At the time, I was pretty enamored with zombies and the idea of surviving a zombie apocalypse scenario like that which is presented in various forms of media-movies, television, video games, and even books-so they were the obvious choice to write on. The presence of zombies across such a variety of media got me thinking about why it was they were such a prominent force in our pop cultural identity.

Loosely framed around my own history and experience with zombies in the media, the piece is more than anything an exploration of the undead and the cultural implications our culture's obsession over them that comes with our fixation.

Though the project was obviously a blast to work on, I felt like I didn't do the essay justice after I'd turned it in. I struggled with how to structure the essay, and even with the subject matter: sometimes it seemed to ridiculous to be studying, and other it felt almost like what I wanted to say had already been said, but more intelligently by people like Chuck Klosterman.

Fast forward a year, and I found myself given an opportunity to redeem myself. For my introduction to the writing minor, I was required to rewrite a previously written piece for a new audience. Jackpot! I knew this was my chance to make Z-Day the essay it should have always been.

I struggled for awhile with how I actually wanted to approach this new piece, since this new audience was to ideally be reached through an already established form of media (e.g. a popular magazine, an academic journal, etc.). After running through a couple ideas and ultimately failing, I decided to shake up my process. Instead of focusing on the zombies, I'd focus on the humans they prey on.

In Z-Day, I discovered that the fascincation with zombies seemed to be, at

the center of everything, the humans and how they established communities and worked together to survive. From there, I began drawing parallels to the Occupy Wall Street movements in Zucotti Park. Though the metaphor might be a little loose and abstract, there are definite similarities between surviving a zombie apocalypse and fighting for the right to be heard on Wall Street.

Rolling Stone seemed to be the perfect cross-section of pop-culture and

APPENDIX 9.9.

From Memoirs to Blogs

The major project for our Writing 220 semester was a multi part project that asked us to start with a source piece, and then adapt it for other mediums and other audiences. My source writing was a series of memoirs written during Sophomore year of college that reflected on rushing through life and not living in the moment.

The first part of my project focused on repurposing these originals into works presented in a different light. I chose to turn my memoirs into two short stories that would make my story anybody's story. By casting it into a plot with characters other than the narrator, I hoped to bring these stories to life and to show people how relatable the message could be to everyone.

The second part of the project was called remediation, using a different medium to illustrate our writing. For this part, I worked with Emily Schell and we developed a blog, Ann Arbor Awesome. The goal of this blog was to meet strangers on the street and to ask them two questions to see the variety of answers that we got.

From this project, I've seen so many changes in my perspective, in my writing, and in how I reflect on myself. It's tested me beyond self constructed borders, and has asked me to be creative in communicating with writing. Through ups and downs, successes and challenges, it's been a journey from memoirs to blogs.

Memoirs

Our first prompt was to choose a writing that we had previously completed, and to turn it into something aimed at a different audience.

Choose a piece of writing.

I hemmed and hawed, opened up just about every writing file available, and almost crashed my computer in the process. There were essays about the Odyssey, responses to short stories, analytical philosophy papers, persuasive business memos. But having looked through my entire archive of literary work from the moment I got this computer, there wasn't anything that I wanted to work with again so much as my reflections.

Having had a year without looking at the memoirs that I had written Sophomore year, I wondered whether, at the time, I truly understood or believed the messages that I was writing in them. I wonder if I, even now, truly understand or believe the messages that I continue to pump out on word documents, on online portfolios, on blogs. But the message is real. Every step of the way I've seen how it impacts my life even further.

My message: Stop, look at the present and absorb the details. Look at how beautiful everything is when we're not rushed, hurried, and stressed.
Take this time for myself to evaluate myself so that I can figure out where I want to go.

I wrote this message a year ago, and now I wanted to rewrite it for an audience that wasn't me. I wanted to stretch my writing, play with different genres, different voices, and different mediums.

It was going to be a challenge.

Short Stories

Lost Battle Drafts

My goal was to create two short stories out of two of the three memoirs I had chosen, and to write each story in a different voice so that it would also seem like they came from two separate authors.

References

Alexander, Jonathan, and Jacqueline Rhodes. 2014. *On Multimodality: New Media in Composition Studies*. Urbana, IL: NCTE.

Bandura, Albert. 1989. "Regulation of Cognitive Processes through Perceived Self-Efficacy." *Developmental Psychology* 25 (5): 729–35. http://dx.doi.org/10.1037/0012-1649.25.5.729.

Cambridge, Darren, Barbara L. Cambridge, and Kathleen Blake Yancey, eds. 2009. *Electronic Portfolios 2.0: Emergent Research on Implementation and Impact*. Sterling, VA: Stylus.

Clark, Irene, and Andrea Hernandez. 2011. "Genre Awareness, Academic Argument, and Transferability." *WAC Journal* 22:65–78. http://wac.colostate.edu/journal/vol22/.

Conner, Lindsey N. 2007. "Cueing Metacognition to Improve Research and Essay Writing in a Final Year High School Biology Class." *Research in Science Education* 37 (1): 1–16. http://dx.doi.org/10.1007/s11165-004-3952-x.

Cope, Bill, and Mary Kalantzis, eds. 2009. *Ubiquitous Learning*. Urbana: University of Illinois Press.

Dewey, John. 1916. *Democracy and Education: An Introduction to the Philosophy of Education*. New York: Macmillan.

Dunlosky, John, and Janet Metcalfe. 2009. *Metacognition*. Los Angeles, CA: SAGE.

English, Joel A. 1998. "MOO-Based Metacognition: Incorporating Online and Offline Reflection into the Writing Process." *Kairos* 3 (1). http://english.ttu.edu/kairos/3.1/features/english/bridge.html.

Flavell, John. 1976. "Metacognitive Aspects of Problem Solving." In *The Nature of Intelligence*, ed. Lauren Resnick, 213–35. Hillsdale, NJ: Erlbaum.

Flower, Linda. 1979. "Writer-Based Prose: A Cognitive Basis for Problems in Writing." *College English* 41 (1): 19–37. http://dx.doi.org/10.2307/376357. http://www.jstor.org/stable/376357.

Fulwiler, Toby, ed. 1987. *The Journal Book*. Portsmouth, NH: Boynton/Cook.

Hawisher, Gail E., Paul Prior, Patrick Berry, Amber Buck, Steven E. Gump, Cory Holding, Hannah Lee, Christa Olson, and Janine Solberg. 2009. "Writing (2): Ubiquitous Writing and Learning: Digital Media as Tools for Reflection and Research on Literate Activity." In *Ubiquitous Learning*, ed. Bill Cope and Mary Kalantzis, 254–64. Urbana: University of Illinois Press.

Irvin, L. Lennie. 2004. "Reflection in the Electronic Writing Classroom." *Computers and Composition Online* (Spring). http://www2.bgsu.edu/departments/english/cconline/irvin/Introduction.htm.

Jarratt, Susan, Katherine Mack, Alexandra Sartor, and Shevaun E. Watson. 2009. "Pedagogical Memory: Writing, Mapping, Translating." *WPA: Writing Program Administration* 33 (1–2): 46–73.

Journet, Debra, Tabetha Adkins, Chris Alexander, Patrick Corbett, and Ryan Trauman. 2008. "Digital Mirrors: Multimodal Reflection in the Composition Classroom." *Computers and Composition Online* (Spring). http://www2.bgsu.edu/departments/english/cconline/Digital_Mirrors/index.html.

Kaplan, Matthew, Naomi Silver, Danielle LaVaque-Manty, and Deborah Meizlish, eds. 2013. *Using Reflection and Metacognition to Improve Student Learning: Across the Disciplines, Across the Academy*. Sterling, VA: Stylus.

LaVaque-Manty, Mika, and Margaret Evans. 2013. "Implementing Metacognitive Interventions in Disciplinary Writing Classes." In *Using Reflection and Metacognition to Improve Student Learning: Across the Disciplines, Across the Academy*, ed. Matthew Kaplan, Naomi Silver, Danielle LaVaque-Manty, and Deborah Meizlish, 122–46. Sterling, VA: Stylus.

Meizlish, Deborah, Danielle LaVaque-Manty, Matthew Kaplan, and Naomi Silver. 2013. "Think Like/Write Like: Metacognitive Strategies to Foster Students' Development as Disciplinary Thinkers and Writers." In *Changing the Conversation about Higher Education*, ed. Robert J. Thompson, 53–74. New York: Rowman and Littlefield.

Palinscar, Annemarie Sullivan, and Ann L. Brown. 1984. "Reciprocal Teaching of Comprehension-Fostering and Comprehension-Monitoring Activities." *Cognition and Instruction* 1 (2): 117–75. http://dx.doi.org/10.1207/s1532690xci0102_1.

Prior, Paul, and Jody Shipka. 2003. "Chronotopic Lamination: Tracing the Contours of Literate Activity." In *Writing Selves, Writing Societies*, ed. Charles Bazerman and David Russell, 180–238. Fort Collins, CO: WAC Clearinghouse.

Rodgers, Carol. 2002. "Defining Reflection: Another Look at John Dewey and Reflective Thinking." *Teachers College Record* 104 (4): 842–66. http://dx.doi.org/10.1111/1467 -9620.00181.

Rogers, Scott L., Ryan Trauman, and Julia E. Kiernan. 2010. "Inquiry, Collaboration, and Reflection in the Student (Text)-Centered Multimodal Writing Course." In *Teaching with Student Texts: Essays toward an Informed Practice*, ed. Joseph Harris, John D. Miles, and Charles Paine, 200–9. Logan: Utah State University Press.

Schön, Donald. 1987. *Educating the Reflective Practitioner: Toward a New Design for Teaching and Learning in the Professions*. San Francisco, CA: Jossey-Bass.

Schraw, Gregory. 1998. "Promoting General Metacognitive Awareness." *Instructional Science* 26 (1/2): 113–25. http://dx.doi.org/10.1023/A:1003044231033.

Scott, Tony. 2005. "Creating the Subject of Portfolios: Reflective Writing and the Conveyance of Institutional Prerogatives." *Written Communication* 22 (1): 3–35. http://dx.doi.org/10.1177/0741088304271831.

Shulman, Lee. 2000. "Teacher Development: Roles of Domain Expertise and Pedagogical Knowledge." *Journal of Applied Developmental Psychology* 21 (1): 129–35. http://dx.doi .org/10.1016/S0193-3973(99)00057-X.

Sullivan, Andrew. 2008. "Why I Blog." *Atlantic*, November. http://www.theatlantic.com /magazine/archive/2008/11/why-i-blog/307060/.

Sweetland Center for Writing. 2013. "Writing 220: Introduction to the Minor in Writing, Course Goals and Objectives." Ann Arbor: Sweetland Center for Writing.

Vygotsky, Lev. 1986. *Thought and Language*. Cambridge, MA: MIT Press.

Watkins, Steve. 1996. "World Wide Web Authoring in the Portfolio-Assessed (Inter) Networked Composition Course." *Computers and Composition* 13 (2): 219–30. http://dx.doi.org/10.1016/S8755-4615(96)90011-0.

Welch, Nancy. 1998. "Sideshadowing Teacher Response." *College English* 60 (4): 374–95. http://dx.doi.org/10.2307/378908.

Yancey, Kathleen Blake. 1998. *Reflection in the Writing Classroom*. Logan: Utah State University Press.

Yancey, Kathleen Blake, Leigh Graziano, Rory Lee, and Jennifer O'Malley. 2013. "Reflection, ePortfolios, and WEPO: A Reflective Account of New Practices in a New Curriculum." In *Using Reflection and Metacognition to Improve Student Learning: Across the Disciplines, Across the Academy*, ed. Matthew Kaplan, Naomi Silver, Danielle LaVaque-Manty, and Deborah Meizlish, 175–202. Sterling, VA: Stylus.

Yancey, Kathleen Blake, Stephen J. McElroy, and Elizabeth Powers. 2013. "Composing, Networks, and Electronic Portfolios: Notes toward a Theory of Assessing ePortfolios." In *Digital Writing Assessment & Evaluation*, ed. Heidi A. McKee and Danielle N. DeVoss. Logan: Computers and Composition Digital Press/Utah State University Press. http://ccdigitalpress.org/dwae.

Yancey, Kathleen Blake, Liane Robertson, and Kara Taczak. 2014. *Writing across Contexts: Transfer, Composition, and Sites of Writing*. Logan: Utah State University Press.

Zimmerman, Barry J., and Adam R. Moylan. 2009. "Self-Regulation: Where Metacognition and Motivation Intersect." In *Handbook of Metacognition in Education*, ed. Douglas J. Hacker, John Dunlosky, and Arthur C. Graesser, 299–315. New York: Routledge.

IV

Reflective Conversations outside the Writing Classroom

10

TOWARD DEFINING A SOCIAL REFLECTIVE PEDAGOGY FOR EPORTFOLIOS

Christina Russell McDonald

Midway through the semester in Rhetorical Traditions, a course in historical rhetoric I had agreed to pilot using WordPress as a new platform for VMI's ePortfolio Project, a first-class cadet (a senior) asked in class one day, "Ma'am, I had to create an ePortfolio last semester for my civilizations and cultures course in history. And this semester, I'm making one for your course and another in biology. What is with the ePortfolio at VMI all of a sudden?" The same semester, a colleague who was using the ePortfolio, which was adopted initially as an instrument of assessment in core curriculum civilizations and cultures courses, asked me a related question: "Can't I incorporate reflective learning into my course without using the ePortfolio?"

Although in somewhat different ways, both wanted to know why reflective learning using the ePortfolio had been embraced at VMI. "Why teach (or learn) this way, and why now?" they seemed to be asking. More practically, neither cadet nor colleague seemed to know whether the goal of the initiative was reflective learning (as a process) or the ePortfolio (as a product). More than five years after VMI's adoption of ePortfolios and despite a robust, sustained series of faculty-development workshops and cadet-orientation sessions, there remained much work to do to clarify the purpose and value of VMI's ePortfolio Project. As one who advocated the adoption of ePortfolios on my campus, I wanted to know why the educational, theoretical, and pedagogical underpinnings of ePortfolios so lacked transparency, especially to the primary audiences for which they were intended.

Our experience, I've learned from colleagues involved with ePortfolio initiatives on other campuses, is not unique. In fact, one of the greatest challenges for those interested in, or already involved with, an ePortfolio initiative is trying to understand how local institutional

DOI: 10.7330/9781607325161.c010

goals and constraints align (or not) with the vastly different goals, contexts, purposes, and quite simply *kinds* of ePortfolios in use on college campuses today. Students are creating reflective ePortfolios in first-year composition (U of Georgia), assessment ePortfolios for general education (Clemson U), professional ePortfolios for a writing minor (U of Michigan), reflective capstone ePortfolios for the major (IUPUI), and career ePortfolios in preprofessional programs such as theater, education, and nursing (Florida State U), among countless others. Depending on the local context, purpose, and intended audience(s) for a given ePortfolio, the role of reflection can vary widely. And while reflection is central to the "working portfolio," which documents the process of learning over time, the "presentation portfolio" emphasizes the "portfolio as product," which tends to minimize attention to the process of reflection necessary for students to present "the results of their learning" (Barrett and Richter 2009). These dichotomies—between process and product, ePortfolios *for* learning and *of* learning, pedagogy and assessment—can easily derail productive conversations about reflective learning using ePortfolios by framing reflection as one option among many rather than as the key affordance of this digital space for teaching and learning.

The widespread adoption of electronic portfolios has created a new context for learning that requires practitioners to define reflection for an increasingly broad, cross-disciplinary audience. Articulating a pedagogy of reflective learning using ePortfolios is one way to push against these dichotomies and to translate theories of reflective learning to encourage and support ePortfolio practice in different disciplines. To suggest how we might best initiate and facilitate those conversations, I will draw on results from a study of reflective learning and ePortfolios in civilizations and cultures courses, a cross-disciplinary requirement of a new core curriculum at my institution, which help to define a process-centered pedagogy of reflective learning using ePortfolios across the curriculum.

DISEQUILIBRIUM AS RHETORICAL CONTEXT

A writing curriculum is shaped by the mission of the university which houses it, and the larger cultural and political milieu shapes the goals of educational institutions by defining what it means to be an educated citizen.

—Marie Secor and Davida Charney, *Constructing Rhetorical Education*

The exigence for revisiting the general education curriculum, which hadn't been substantively revised for some thirty years, was VMI's reaccreditation by the Southern Association of Colleges and Universities (SACS). In 2005, a faculty committee was formed and charged with redesigning the core curriculum as VMI's Quality Enhancement Plan (2006) (QEP). One of the more ambitious components of the new core curriculum was the development of a group of cross-disciplinary courses for the study of cultures and civilizations, which would be developed and offered by every department. In the new core curriculum, cadets are required to take two such courses, which seek to cultivate in them a "global consciousness" in order to prepare them to serve as "citizen-soldiers," able "to anticipate, to respond, and to lead" in an increasingly complex world ("Quality Enhancement Plan: The Core Curriculum: The Nucleus of Effective Citizenship and Leadership" 2006, 14). Confronted by the need to assess cadets' learning—one of the signal obligations of the QEP process—in this rich array of courses taught in different disciplines, an ePortfolio was chosen as a vehicle for teaching, learning, and summative assessment. For the purposes of assessment, the ePortfolio offered the ability to compare authentic forms of evidence of cadets' learning without standardizing learning experiences across different disciplines. Pedagogically, the digital space encouraged active, engaged, and reflective learning—a guiding principle of VMI's core curriculum as an integrative, four-year student experience. As carefully considered as the rationale was for adopting the ePortfolio, it wasn't transparent enough to assuage concerns about the implementation of this new tool in a moment steeped in change, from new courses and pedagogies to new technologies and assessments.

The conversation about reflective learning using ePortfolios was quickly engulfed by two overriding concerns: fulfilling the requirements of the assessment and learning to use a new form of technology. At the time, there was considerable tension between faculty members' efforts to develop meaningful assessments for each component of the core curriculum and the prevailing approach in the Office of Institutional Research and Assessment, which favored a quantitative, outcomes-driven, summative model with little room for negotiation. In civilizations and cultures courses, it was decided, cadets would self-select demonstrations of their learning to include in the ePortfolio, then respond to a common writing prompt for a reflective essay in which they would make the case that they had achieved the learning outcomes by drawing on artifacts to illustrate their claims (Appendix 10.A). The unit of analysis for assessment, then, was not the full portfolio but rather the reflective essay. Not surprisingly, concerns about the requirements and expectations for the assignment quickly dominated the attention of faculty members, who understandably wanted their students to earn acceptable ratings. These practical concerns, however, supplanted their interest in exploring reflective teaching and learning in a broader context—one grounded in the educational philosophy of John Dewey (1933) and Donald Schön's (1983) theory and practice of reflection. In the absence of a culture of reflection among faculty and students, introducing the ePortfolio as a site for reflective learning *and* assessment posed unanticipated challenges for those leading the initiative.

To compound matters further, teaching with technology was not yet prevalent on post, though there certainly were some practitioners who had adequate resources to support their efforts in the classroom. These early adopters shared models of multimodal assignments to illustrate the potential of the ePortfolio, but those examples were lost on faculty who were preoccupied with learning the new software. In fact, and perhaps not surprisingly, both faculty members' and cadets' interests were dominated by anxieties about meeting the basic requirements of the assessment. Indeed, the stakes were high. The assessment data presented in the five-year report to SACS would determine whether or not the civilizations and cultures courses, a key global learning component of VMI's new core curriculum and QEP, would be considered a success. Efforts to recover the discussion about reflective learning, then, took place during a high-stakes period marked by considerable disequilibrium—a state of being Dewey would consider, in fact, an essential motivation for reflective inquiry.

CONNECTING RESEARCH AND PRACTICE

Faculty members who taught civilizations and cultures courses and participated in the early assessments found initial results disappointing. Using Edward M. White's (2005) Phase 2 model for scoring portfolios by rating students' reflective essays, faculty readers used a five-point holistic rubric to assess the degree to which cadets demonstrated their achievement of two learning outcomes: (1) "identify cultures of the world and the components and practices that distinguish them from others," and (2) "appreciate a culture's distinctiveness either through texts or experiential contact" (Appendix 10.B). The first samples of randomly selected reflective essays (drawn across sections and departments) revealed the very dichotomies identified earlier: by and large, these early ePortfolios functioned as electronic repositories for completed assignments that had been uploaded at the end of the course as a showcase and were accompanied by a descriptive rather than reflective essay. Put another way, cadets were able to describe learning experiences illustrated by certain artifacts, but seldom wrote about their significance or how the work prepared the students for what lay ahead. Cadets whose reflective essays were more successful, though, seemed to have exploited a feature of the ePortfolio software that required a description when posting an artifact, which we termed a "reflective tag" (Dellinger, Koons, and McDonald 2013, 4). When invited to use this space within the ePortfolio as opportunity for reflection, cadets responded to three fundamental reflective questions: *What* is the artifact? *So what*, or why was this a meaningful learning experience? *Now what*, or what do I need to know or do for the learning that lies ahead? (Barrett and Richter 2009).

To investigate the significance of this practice, a faculty research team was assembled to participate in the Inter/National Coalition for Electronic Research's sixth cohort in hopes of generating both quantitative and qualitative data that would inform teaching and learning in civilizations and cultures courses. In particular, we wanted to examine the quality of reflection in cadets' ePortfolios in order to determine how "spaces for reflective learning [could] be cultivated by a process-centered pedagogy using the ePortfolio" (Dellinger, Koons, and McDonald 2013, 1). From personal experience, we had discovered that prompting cadets to "tag" the artifacts they posted to their ePortfolios helped them to adopt a reflective stance from which they could consider their work and begin to make meaning of their development as learners. The goal of our research was to gather evidence that this practice was indeed valuable so we could help other instructors design opportunities for learning through the reflective tagging of artifacts within the ePortfolio. Through our examination of cadets' ePortfolios, we hoped to discover what a process-centered pedagogy might look like.

METHODOLOGY

Toward that end, a random sample of 162 ePortfolios was selected from thirty-eight of the civilizations and cultures courses taught during the 2011–2012 academic year. Five reflective essays were drawn from each course. The sample represented cadets' ePortfolios in the humanities (48.2 percent), the natural sciences and mathematics (22.8 percent), the social sciences (17.3 percent), and engineering (11.7 percent). In pulling this sample, special care was taken to avoid overrepresenting courses that were taught in multiple sections (Dellinger, Koons, and McDonald 2013, 2, 3).

Readers used a five-point holistic rubric to assess the quality of reflection (table 10.1). Trained faculty raters scored each essay independently.

Table 10.1. Rubric to measure reflection in cadet reflective essays.

Quality of Reflection	
5 rating	Meaningfully reflects on the relationship between what the writer learned about the target culture(s) and how the writer came to learn it through the ePortfolio process
4 rating	Thoughtfully reflects on the relationship between what the writer learned about the target culture(s) and how the writer came to learn it through the ePortfolio process
3 rating	Adequately reflects on the relationship between what the writer learned about the target culture(s) and how the writer came to learn it through the ePortfolio process
2 rating	Describes learning experiences
1 rating	Does not discuss relevant learning experiences

A third reading was required in cases in which these ratings differed by more than two points. Readers also catalogued ePortfolios for "the presence or absence of reflective tags to accompany artifacts" (Dellinger, Koons, and McDonald 2013, 3). If a reflective essay was rated highly by readers and the ePortfolio contained artifacts accompanied by reflective tags, those examples were examined more closely to determine how the reflective tags were used in the ePortfolio to prepare cadets to write the final reflective essay.

FINDINGS

As anecdotal evidence had suggested, quantitative analysis showed that "cadets whose ePortfolios contained reflective tags produced final reflective essays that were rated [more] high[ly] for the quality of reflection" (Dellinger, Koons, and McDonald 2013, 4). While the correlation between the presence of reflective tags and the quality of reflection in the reflective essay was positive and high, it was also preliminary (Appendix 10.C). During the early stages of implementing civilizations and cultures courses and ePortfolios, practices varied widely enough that evaluating the quality of reflection in the reflective tags would not have been meaningful. Some cadets wrote reflective tags that corresponded to Barrett and Richter's (2009) three reflective questions, while others wrote tags that served as titles for the artifact (e.g., "Reading Response #1"). Some wrote reflective tags each time they posted an artifact during the semester, while others posted all the artifacts and tags at once near the end of the term. These differences in classroom practice frequently (and fairly obviously) led to notable differences in the quality of reflection in cadets' reflective essays and posed a significant challenge for faculty raters. And while student performances on the assignment still were comparable, the finer distinctions between performances called for in the rubric, especially for the 5, 4, and 3 ratings, proved difficult to make with some of the earlier essays.

Faculty raters' collective understanding of the differences between a meaningful, thoughtful, and adequate reflection "on the relationship between what the writer learned about the target culture(s) and how the writer came to learn it through the ePortfolio process" grew slowly over the course of several assessment cycles and as a result of a series of faculty-development activities. In the earliest stages of those conversations, faculty members grappled with their own differing interpretations of the learning outcomes for civilizations and cultures courses as well as with differences in their disciplinary approaches to teaching culture. They also recognized the need to establish a mutual understanding of the nature of reflective learning in this context and the role the ePortfolio might play in facilitating cadets' understanding of the culture they were studying. In addition, since the genre of the reflective essay was not commonly used by those outside of the field of English, defining the characteristics of an effective reflective essay initially proved to be quite challenging. Collecting and discussing sample essays that served as benchmarks for each of the ratings in the holistic rubric crystallized readers' collective understanding of the distinctions the rubric enabled them to make with regard to the quality of reflection in cadets' essays.

To investigate whether the quality of reflection in cadets' essays was enhanced by a process of composing reflective tags, we conducted interviews with them, inviting them to describe their experiences as research-team members and cadets viewed the ePortfolios together. Uniformly, the cadets told us they "felt better prepared to write the final reflective essay," as one cadet put it, when they engaged in "a process of reflection that entailed posting reflective tags and artifacts through the semester." In the absence of this process, however, another cadet candidly told us he chose to analyze just the most recent artifacts to discuss in his reflective essay because, quite frankly, he remembered them better than assignments completed earlier in the semester. The reflective tag, he argued, was "almost more important than the artifact itself" in facilitating his work on the final reflective essay (Dellinger, Koons, and McDonald 2013, 7). Moreover, the reflective tags, he explained, functioned as a chart or map of his learning over the course of the semester from which he could more easily identify significant themes, "ah-ha" moments, or uncertainty: "After reflecting back using my ePortfolio on

WordPress on the works I created and the research I conducted, I discovered the cultural practice I had been focusing on all along." In sum, the reflective tags were a site of invention for composing his final reflective essay. And as important, cadets' experiences helped us understand the purpose of a process-centered pedagogy of reflection and, in general terms, how it should function.

COMPOSING A PROCESS-CENTERED PEDAGOGY OF REFLECTION

Bridging the gap between the "delivered curriculum," evident in statements regarding the common requirements of these courses, including the final reflective essay, and the "experienced curriculum" (Yancey 1998, 18), illustrated by local assessment results, research findings, and cadets' reflections in civilizations and cultures courses, depended on our ability to accomplish a couple of related tasks. First, the ePortfolio had to be disassociated from assessment and promoted instead as a tool for teaching and learning in other courses beyond those designated as civilizations and cultures courses. Faculty volunteers were recruited to pilot the ePortfolio in courses they were teaching, using a new web-based platform. In the context of these other courses—in which the ePortfolio was not a vehicle for assessment—it was possible to redefine reflection not as synonymous with the reflective essay (narrowly framed as reflection-in-presentation for assessment in Civilizations and Cultures courses), but as a way of cultivating students' awareness of their learning in any course, on any subject (Yancey 1998, 14). By facilitating the conversation beyond the civilizations and cultures courses, we were better able to understand the challenges of using the ePortfolio for reflective learning.

Second, we needed to help both instructors and students articulate their largest concerns about the ePortfolio so they could be addressed. The challenges we discovered might best be described as arising from a "knowledge problem," a "rhetorical problem," and/or a "language problem" (Flower and Hayes 1981, 34, 40). Instructors and students alike confronted a knowledge problem in the sense that they needed to learn (quickly and often through trial and error) new theories and practices about reflective learning and ePortfolios. Then, they had to decide how it fit with what they already knew about teaching and learning. In addition, instructors and students confronted a closely related language problem" since new terms, symbols, and concepts accompanied both theories of reflective learning and ePortfolios, making it difficult to discuss teaching and learning in ways that were familiar. They also grappled with a sticky rhetorical problem, first as they confronted questions of audience, occasion, purpose, and message in writing the reflective essay for assessment and later as the rhetorical context shifted (moving beyond reflection-in-presentation for assessing learning in civilizations and cultures courses), leaving them to try to decode the purpose of reflective ePortfolios in different types of courses. Often using reflective tags from cadets' ePortfolios as examples, we worked with faculty members to address these related concerns by exploring ways to define reflection as a process rather than simply as the culminating product of learning (e.g., the reflective essay). These reflective tags helped to reveal the learning that was (or was not) taking place when cadets posted an artifact in their ePortfolios. Based on their observations, instructors had the opportunity to discuss what sort of awareness they hoped cadets might exhibit in these moments of reflection and then design sequences of assignments that would help students engage the process(es) of reflection.

Drawing on theories of reflection (articulated by Dewey 1933; Schön 1983, 1987; Yancey 1998; and others), a process-centered pedagogy involved a sequence of assignments to compose reflective tags that engaged students in distinct stages and forms of reflection. Using examples from cadets' ePortfolios in different courses, I'll describe the process-centered approach to reflection we developed, paying special attention to how instructors might capitalize on students' expectation that reflective learning in this digital space is (and should be) public and social, not private and solitary.

INVITING REFLECTION-ON-ACTION

Cadets reflect on their knowing in practice when they compose reflective tags to accompany artifacts, recently completed assignments cadets post to their ePortfolios, by writing about how the work facilitated learning (Schön 1983, 61). "We reflect *on* action," Schön explains in his work, *Educating the Reflective Practitioner*, "thinking back on what we have done in order to discover how our knowing-in-action may have contributed to an unexpected outcome" (Schön 1987, 26). The template assignment for a reflective tag, then, invites reflection-on-action. Cadets respond to Barrett and Richter's (2009) three reflective questions, adapted to ePortfolios: *What* is the artifact? *So what* (is its significance)? *Now what?* The following reflective tag posted to a cadet's ePortfolio in a course titled Shakespeare: Power and Politics is typical of a response to these questions early in the semester:

This is my response paper on *Henry IV, Part One.* In this paper, I analyze one of the most intriguing characters in the play, Prince Henry. My analysis focuses on the unorthodox yet successful approach that he took in establishing his authority and regaining the trust of his father, King Henry IV, and the larger British population. In writing this paper, I have become interested in looking further into this event and other instances where a Prince approached his position of authority in an unorthodox manner.

Early in the semester, students may seem more comfortable describing the artifact (What is it?) than they are commenting on its significance (So what?) or knowing what to do next (Now what?). In the first two sentences, for example, this writer describes the approach he took in the paper without really commenting on the significance of his focus on Prince Henry's "unorthodox yet successful approach" to "establishing his authority and regaining the trust of his father." A bit later in the semester, we might expect the student to be in a better position to answer the question "So what?" Why, or how, does this example touch on an important theme (or themes) in the larger context of the course? But early in the semester, he may not have enough information about the course either to discuss its significance or to do more than predict the possibility that he'll continue to be interested in "this event and other instances where a Prince approached his position of authority in an unorthodox manner." At the beginning of a course, students often still look to the teacher to discover what they need to know or do next. Consequently, a key ingredient of a process-centered pedagogy of reflective learning is response, a point also made by Naomi Silver (in this volume).

Cadets we interviewed said they regarded the ePortfolio as an inherently social space and reflection as a more public than private enterprise (Dellinger, Koons, and McDonald 2013, 7). They expected to engage in dialogue with others about their own learning and to comment on the artifacts they posted to their ePortfolios during class, as well as afterward. In a digital space, these processes would be "both individual and social" (Yancey 1998, 72). Instructors, however, frequently viewed the purposes of reflection using ePortfolios differently. Many faculty regarded students' reflections on learning as largely for the students' own benefit. Together with their collection of work in the ePortfolio, their reflections would serve as a product that would be valuable to them at some time in the future as a digital archive. As a result, the instructors' pedagogical approach to courses in which cadets were using ePortfolios actually changed very little. For example, during the early phases of the ePortfolio initiative, some required students to engage in two parallel processes: to post artifacts and reflective tags to their ePortfolios and to submit assignments in hard copy to receive comments and grades. When this was the case, cadets viewed the ePortfolio as a kind of "busy work," a task they were required to complete but that wasn't central to their learning in the course because it wasn't a space to interact with anyone other than the teacher, and, in some cases, there was only the self as audience. When asked to make observations about their own learning in isolation, they often found it difficult. In fact, one cadet said interaction was a necessary condition for his learning. He came to know and understand more about himself and the course material, he told us, when given the chance to talk about his work with others than when he worked alone. As Kathleen Blake Yancey reminds us, "To be meaningful, reflection must be situated: the writer creates meaning in context, in community" (Yancey 1998, 63). In the digital space of the ePortfolio, cadets expect to join a community. And they expect the ePortfolio to be a site in which they interact and learn together, even when they meet in a physical classroom. A social pedagogy of reflective learning capitalizes on these expectations by sequencing and scaffolding interactions among students and teachers in both the classroom and the digital space of the ePortfolio.

One such sequence, drawn from a capstone course for the English major at VMI, embeds in the course syllabus assignments to write reflective tags designed to move cadets through different phases of reflection as they draft and revise components of their capstone paper. Definitions of reflection are established through readings including Carol Rodgers's (2002) essay "Defining Reflection: Another Look at John Dewey and Reflective Thinking" and excerpts from Yancey's (1998) *Reflection in the Writing Classroom*, which help to provide a foundation for a process-centered approach to reflection using ePortfolios. Drawing on these theories and adapting them for the purposes of the capstone course, the class developed this overview.

> *Reflection-on-action*: the act of writing about a recently completed assignment posted as an artifact to the ePortfolio, answering four reflective questions:
>
> - What did I learn from this assignment?
> - How did I learn it?
> - Why is this new knowledge significant as it contributes to my learning in (or beyond) this course?
> - What do I need to know, or do, next? And why?

Recursive reflection: the act of reflecting on reflective tags (or reflective artifacts) to revise the evolving narrative of your own processes of learning (e.g., "what you have come to know" and "how you came to know it").

Constructive reflection: the act of drawing connections among existing and previous artifacts and their accompanying reflective tags.

Reflection-in-presentation: the act of reflecting about your "self" and/ or your learning for an external audience (e.g., a reflective essay, a showcase ePortfolio), illustrated by self-selected evidence to support observations.

As a quick reference document, especially early in the semester, this overview helped to prepare them for the different kinds of reflective tags they would be asked to write to accompany artifacts they posted to their ePortfolios and to respond both to their own work and their classmates' work throughout the semester.

Cadets first engaged in reflection-on-action when they composed a reflective tag to accompany each draft they posted to their ePortfolios and again when they responded to classmates' comments in a reflective tag that moved them to articulate a plan for their approach to revision. The schedule of assignments below outlines the first iteration of a process-centered approach to reflection:

Tuesday   Complete draft of Project Proposal with reflective tag **due** (uploaded to ePortfolio)

Workshop: Peer Consultation, Global Concerns

ePortfolio Post (in class): *Write* a reflective tag in response to draft and priorities for revision. *Respond* to a classmate's draft (one who was not in your peer consultation group) by posting a comment to his or her ePortfolio.

Thursday   Revised draft of Project Proposal with reflective tag **due** (uploaded to ePortfolio)

Workshop: Peer Consultation, Local Concerns (Writers bring three copies to class.)

ePortfolio Post: In-class reflective tag in response to draft and priorities for revision

Tuesday   Project Proposal with reflective tag **due** (uploaded to ePortfolio); in-class presentations

ePortfolio Post (in class): *Read* your previous drafts of the proposal and the accompanying reflective tags. *Write* a "constructive reflection," drawing on those materials and posting it to your ePortfolio. *Respond* to one classmate's project proposal by posting a comment to his or her ePortfolio.

To illustrate the way in which cadets responded to the prompts for reflective tags, I selected examples from an ePortfolio composed by Michelle, one of the students in the course. The first assignment asked Michelle to post a complete draft of her research proposal to her ePortfolio and compose a reflective tag that was a reflection-on-action. Michelle's reflective tag read as follows: "Research Proposal Draft: This is the first draft for my research proposal where I have started exploring the ideas I am interested in, but haven't yet written a formal proposal." Like the earlier example of a reflective tag written at the beginning of the semester, this cadet identifies the artifact (e.g., research proposal draft) and minimally describes the work (e.g., an exploratory draft) rather than discussing its significance. A classmate responds to her proposal, "Healthy Eating as a Lifestyle: How Communities Can Enable Individual Change," by assuring her that she has found a clear focus in this discovery draft while also encouraging her to consider more carefully the scope of the "ways of influencing the decisions that individuals make" about "food and lifestyle."

> This looks great so far. You have clearly defined the problem and demonstrated you have a grasp on the initial research for the project. The few sources you mentioned are solid and seem to fit perfectly with your argument. When trying to influence the decisions of individuals make sure to focus on realistic changes. You can make it apparent that changing the way Americans eat may force the individuals to change their way of life completely but make sure to show whether this can even be accomplished or not.

As her instructor, I also encouraged her to interrogate the argument, which seemed to focus primarily on individual responsibility for change.

> I'm still very excited about the path you've taken to argue that communities can provide the network necessary to encourage and facilitate an individual's choice to change their lifestyle in order to be more healthful. In the third paragraph, this line of argument emerges but sort of as a concession to the "individual responsibility" argument. See if you can frame it so that the community responsibility is the vehicle by which individuals are encouraged to make more healthful choices in lifestyle. If it's true that communities can play a key role in this effort, then how? What have some communities already achieved in this regard? Pollan is arguing for a change in the American lifestyle writ large. How can community organizations (which ones?) contribute to that effort? Once you frame these ideas more specifically, I think it will provide a context within which to explore the relationship between food and lifestyle (the next section) in a way that gives you even more to say (and do) with the ideas presented by your sources. How can communities, for example, help address what Berlant argues is Americans' "tiredness"? If obesity is

the result of unhealthy eating, which is a symptom of a larger societal problem (e.g., the go, go, go American lifestyle), then which community organizations are in the best position to be able to provide opportunities for its citizens to make a different choice? If specialization has led to a lesser quality of food, as Pollan argues, then how might community organizations respond to this problem?

In Michelle's revised draft, she includes a more detailed discussion of the barriers—social, cultural, economic, educational—that might make change more difficult. "The most effective way to change someone's behavior long term seems to be through education and providing them the means to continue that new behavior on their own" she contends. "It is also important to understand why people eat and the live the way that they do, whether it be because of a lack of knowledge, resources, time, money, or some other reason. When these things are considered, it enables the cause of the problem to be treated rather than merely the symptoms." And while her ideas about the responsibilities and actions of the community in effecting meaningful change took a bit longer to emerge, the reflective tag that accompanies this second artifact in her ePortfolio acknowledges the significance of her classmate's observation, echoed by the instructor, in shaping her revisions.

In Michelle's constructive reflection, the culminating assignment in this sequence, she draws on "previous drafts of the proposal and the accompanying reflective tags." "Constructive reflection," according to Yancey, "is the *cumulative effect* of reflections-in-action on multiple texts," which we can invite through questions such as 'How does this [what you've learned] connect with what you already knew?'" (Yancey 1998, 51, 61). The act of reflecting on reflection, which this assignment invites by asking students to revisit (and sometimes to revise or extend) the reflective tags they have written, is what Schön calls "reciprocal reflection" (Schön 1983, 304). In her reflective tag that accompanied the final draft of her proposal for the capstone paper, Michelle locates this project in the larger context of research she already has done, a summer undergraduate research project, as well as ongoing research for her institute honors thesis:

> When I wrote the first draft of this proposal, I knew I wanted to explore an area of my thesis that I did not have enough time or space to do with that project. At first I think it was difficult to fully understand my idea because I was so immersed in the material for my thesis research, that I had a hard time relating this project clearly in the context of the other work I have done. But I think after several revisions, there is a thorough, yet concise background for this project and it is beginning to take a clear shape. I am still not entirely sure of how my writing should look based on

my audience, and how to it should be written for the people that actually need to change. But I think this will become clearer as the project develops. Overall I am pleased with the topic and excited about how my work for both my thesis and this project will work and build off of each other.

She also identifies the challenges that lie ahead, such as defining a suitable target audience for this paper. Through a process of reflection, she collected artifacts (in this case, drafts and revisions of her capstone-course research proposal), reflected on each stage of the composing process in accompanying reflective tags, connected this project in relation to her other research on this subject, and projected a plan of action for the next stage of the project. During this process, she and other cadets in the class were regularly in conversation with one another (about their evolving texts and their learning) in the workspace of the ePortfolio, creating the community that would fuel and support them throughout the semester-long project as well as prepare them for the final reflection-in-presentation in which they would share their research with the faculty (Yancey 1998, 69).

REFLECTIVE TAGS AS SITES OF (AND FOR) LEARNING

Reflective tags play an important role in preparing cadets for this moment in several ways. A thoughtfully composed reflective tag has immediate value. It gives students a voice in the conversation about their own learning by systematically engaging in reflection as "a meaning-making process that moves the learner from one experience into the next with deeper understanding of its relationships with and connections to other experiences and ideas" (Rodgers 2002, 845). Tagging artifacts prompts them to reread, and thus *resee*, not only the artifacts in their ePortfolios and thus in another context, but also the earlier reflections-on-action and constructive reflections that accompany them. Engaging in this iterative process—in community and in the digital space of the ePortfolio—also helps students address the problem of distance. As one cadet put it, writing reflective tags prompted him to "step away from the experience" of creating the artifact in order to try to understand it, for himself and with his classmates, in a wider context. At the same time, working inside the ePortfolio diminishes the distance between students and their evolving body of work. Even if he kept all of his work in hard copy in a single folder, another cadet confessed, he would not be likely to revisit it as often as he does when an artifact is just one click away from view. And increasingly, as digitally multimodal assignments begin to emerge to take full advantage of the affordances of the ePortfolio, cadets' work takes various forms—printed texts, images, and video. Writing reflective tags moves cadets through different stages of reflection, considering and reconsidering artifacts of their learning, so that when they arrive at the moment of reflection-in-presentation, they are better prepared for such a culminating assignment.

Perhaps even more powerfully than the voices of administrators and teachers, cadets' broader experience with, and perspectives on, reflective learning using the ePortfolios speaks to the value of this approach to learning across disciplines. Cadets in the class of 2015 were among the first to engage in reflective learning using the ePortfolio throughout most of their academic careers at VMI, albeit in various ways and in a range of different courses. Early adopters in this student cohort, though perhaps unknowingly at first, helped to articulate and promote a model for a social reflective pedagogy for use of the VMI ePortfolio across disciplines. Some employed this approach even when it wasn't required by assignments in a course, in part because they had discovered for themselves its inherent value and wanted to continue to use it in order to build a rich, personalized ePortfolio. Along the way, they provided feedback to faculty members that in many cases helped to solidify our understanding of how to use VMI's ePortfolio and to refine how we implemented it in our classrooms. In their efforts, these cadets were far less prone to the dichotomous thinking that often plagued ePortfolio discussions among faculty. Instead, when working in this digital space, cadets felt they were engaged in coincident, mutually reinforcing practices. A process-centered approach to reflective learning, they understood, was a necessary pathway toward a product (e.g., reflection-in-presentation as a reflective essay or a showcase ePortfolio). But so too was each stage of the process a significant product made visible by an artifact and accompanied by a reflective tag. They regarded ePortfolios as vehicles *for* learning and as representations *of* learning simultaneously, continuously.

Cadets, we decided, were the key to supporting the continued use of ePortfolios in civilizations and cultures courses (especially after the ePortfolio was no longer used as an instrument of assessment in these courses) and to expanding its use in other courses across the curriculum. The way forward seemed clear: capture the enthusiasm, practical experience, and digital skills of those cadets who had taken ownership of their own ePortfolios and let them advocate its use to other cadets. To make this possible, the institute writing program created positions for cadets to train and work as ePortfolio consultants in the VMI Writing Center. Under the supervision of the writing center coordinator, cadets create informational content about the ePortfolio (e.g., reflective tagging, posting artifacts, working in multimodal genres) and meet in one-on-one consultations with cadet clients in the writing center. This team of cadets also works with the developer of ePortfolio research and resources, an adjunct instructor who designs similar materials for faculty members and consults with those who wish to use, or are currently using, the ePortfolio in any course. Although the initiative is still young, perceptions of the VMI ePortfolio, especially among cadets and new members of the faculty, are noticeably beginning to shift.

WHAT WE WANT TO KNOW (AND DO) NEXT

Those advocating or implementing a process-centered pedagogy of reflection using ePortfolios would be well advised to devote a substantial period of time to exploring answers to the tough questions with which this essay began: Why teach and learn this way (toward a set of learning outcomes in a particular course or courses using the digital space of the ePortfolio to facilitate reflective learning)? Why teach and learn this way *in this place* (in light of institutional missions, disciplinary conventions, curricular goals, course content)? And why teach and learn this way *now* (in the twenty-first century, in response to regional accreditation requirements, state mandates, curricular revision)? Administrators, faculty, and students should be prepared to explain the rationale on their campus in a comprehensive way and the process by which they arrived collectively at answers to these essential questions. Though the evolution of this conversation at VMI was shaped differently by the expectations and requirements of the larger QEP process, through reflection we have come to understand not only where we have been (and why), but also where we have an opportunity to go next.

We now know, for example, that a process-centered pedagogy of reflection using ePortfolios is not simply a matter of scaffolding a process of reflection in a course syllabus. As with any process approach, the curriculum must be dynamic, responsive, and often highly individualized. Cadets need help, as we saw in earlier examples, developing more fully the tags in which they engaged in reflection-on-action and constructive reflection. Writing prompts for reflective tags can be useful in this regard. However, if those prompts become generalized templates for every reflective tag, students' responses tend to become formulaic as well—vague, repetitive answers to open-ended questions rather than thoughtful, detailed reflections. More discrete prompts tied to individual assignments that generate artifacts can often elicit more substantive reflective tags, as can responses to these posts from classmates and the instructor. Similarly, the reflective essay as a culminating assignment, through sheer repetition, can be reduced unintentionally to a standardized form (e.g., state three things you learned, illustrated by an example from three different artifacts), especially when students are asked to complete this assignment repeatedly. Having reached the point of saturation, one cadet who had written *four* reflective essays at the end of one semester jokingly observed, "We think *a lot* about what we've been thinking about [as English majors]." Another cadet, naively but quite practically, asked permission to write the reflective essay in one course *early* so he stood a better chance of finishing the other two that also were due on the last day of class. Taking their sentiments to heart, we are beginning to consider what forms, in addition to the reflective essay, reflection-in-presentation might take. As ePortfolios slowly begin to be used by others on our campus, we are discovering with our students how to resist the temptation to rely on more familiar *products* of learning and instead remain *in process* when working within the newer context of the ePortfolio. The genre of the reflective tag encourages this state of being. Tags are snapshots that capture moments in students' emerging metacognitive awareness and make the processes of learning visible, to themselves and others. Whether in core-curriculum courses, research-and-writing-intensive experiences, or senior capstone courses, the practice of reflective tagging in ePortfolios invites students to compose new knowledge by engaging in an iterative process of looking backward and forward, individually and collectively.

APPENDIX 10.A

As part of the Civilization and Cultures Core Curriculum, students in this course will use an ePortfolio on wordpress.com (through sites.vmi.edu) to organize and publish their assignments/artifacts. Each artifact must be tagged with a brief description of its scope and purpose. At the end of the semester, all students must create a **3–5 page reflective essay**, in which they look back on their work produced, reflecting on the assignments and how those helped them learn best about the target culture.

Learning Outcomes. As part of the Civilization and Cultures Core Curriculum, by the end of the course, students should be able to

1) demonstrate knowledge of characteristic products or practices of the world's communities, civilizations, or cultures.

2   reflect on their learning about a culture or cultures.

CIVILIZATIONS AND CULTURES COURSES

Writing Prompt for the Reflective Essay Common Assignment

Write a three- to five-page reflective essay in which you identify some of the significant products or practices of the culture(s) you have studied. To develop and illustrate your focus for the essay, you should discuss the ways in which the activities and assignments you've selected as artifacts have informed and shaped your learning by making specific reference to them. Use the style of documentation (e.g., MLA, APA, or *The Chicago Manual of Style*) suggested by your instructor to clearly document references.

Requirements:

- The reflective essay should develop from a clear, compelling focus that is organized, thoroughly developed with relevant examples drawn from ePortfolio artifacts, cohesively structured, and expressed in clear, carefully edited sentences.
- For the reflective essay, you will draw on artifacts from a rich assemblage of work that you have created over the course of the semester. Though no minimum number of artifacts is required to be placed in

the "showcase" ePortfolio and discussed in the reflective essay, you should have a sufficiently large number of completed assignments and activities in the "workspace" ePortfolio so that you may choose from among them to select those that help you advance and develop your thesis most effectively.

- The reflective essay will contribute to your final course grade. (The weight of the assignment will be determined by your instructor but must count a minimum of ten percent in all Civilizations and Cultures courses.) The assignment must be submitted by the last day of classes, which is the Institute's deadline for submission of written work.

CIVILIZATIONS AND CULTURES COURSES

Instructions for Students: Preparing to Write the Reflective Essay

As a student in a Civilizations and Cultures course, you have been asked to reflect on your learning experiences periodically throughout the semester. The goal of this approach—a theory of reflective learning advanced by 20th century educational philosopher, John Dewey—is to cultivate a habit of mind that enables you to articulate not only *what you know*, but also *how you came to know* it. In this culminating assignment, you are invited to **write a reflective essay that will lead you to contemplate the connections between what you have done (e.g., assignments in the course) and what you have learned—and ultimately how both have influenced you or your thinking about the culture you have studied.**

***

As you undertake the process of this final reflection, you'll find it helpful to spend some time responding to the questions below which are designed to help you generate and discover a compelling and viable thesis/focus to develop in the reflective essay.

Step 1: As you reflect on the cultural communities you have been studying, take time to generate specific examples in response to each question below. Some might find it useful to make lists, map clusters of ideas, or write short paragraphs.

- What are the various cultural products, practices, and/or perspectives of this community (or communities)?
- What activities and assignments in the course have facilitated your learning about the culture(s)?

Step 2: Once you have generated some ideas in response to the questions above, now identify some of the more salient products or practices of the target culture(s) you have studied. Which products or practices best represent the target culture(s) and why? Your goal is to articulate *what you have come to know* about the culture(s) that you can present as significant in some way.

Step 3: With these products and/or practices in mind, identify the course activities and assignments (that you've collected as artifacts) which have informed and shaped your understanding of the culture(s). Consider their relationship to one another. These are the artifacts that you'll present and analyze as you discuss the process of your learning, or *how you came to understand* the products and practices of the culture you studied.

Step 4: By this point, you should have some sense of the ideas you'd like to present in the essay. After reading the formal writing prompt for the reflective essay assignment, try to express in a nutshell what you want to say in the essay, and why it's worth saying. You could do this by writing down a couple of sentences or by talking with a classmate or your instructor. After you get some feedback to the ideas, you're probably ready to start writing the initial draft of the essay.

Suggested timeline for composing the Reflective Essay (to be completed by instructor):

Date: Complete steps 1–4, "Preparing to Write the Reflective Essay"

Date: Full draft due for response

Date: Revised draft due for response

APPENDIX 10.B

REVISED REFLECTIVE ESSAY RUBRIC (JANUARY 2014)

Table 10.2.

	Understanding of Cultural Components	Analysis of ePortfolio Artifacts	Reflection on Learning
"5" Rating	Advances a complex, insightful thesis/ focus for the essay that demonstrates knowledge of the products/ practices of the target community(ies), civilization(s), or culture(s)	Presents a complex, insightful analysis of a selection of substantive, varied, and revealing artifacts which fully support and develop the essay's thesis/focus.	Meaningfully reflects on the relationship between *what the writer learned* about the target culture(s) and *how the writer came to learn* it through the ePortfolio process
"4" Rating	Advances an effective thesis/focus for the essay that demonstrates knowledge of the products/ practices of the target community(ies), civilization(s), or culture(s)	Presents an effective analysis of a selection of relevant and varied artifacts which effectively support and develop the essay's thesis/focus.	Thoughtfully reflects on the relationship between *what the writer learned* about the target culture(s) and *how the writer came to learn it* through the ePortfolio process
"3" Rating	Advances a clear thesis/ focus for the essay that demonstrates knowledge of the products/ practices of the target community(ies), civilization(s), or culture(s)	Presents a clear analysis of an election of appropriate and varied artifacts, which loosely support and develop the essay's thesis/ focus.	Adequately reflects on relationship between *what the writer learned* about the target culture(s) and *how the writer came to learn it* through the ePortfolio process
"2" Rating	The thesis/ focus for the demonstrates knowledge of the products/ practices of the target community(ies), civilization(s), or culture(s), but may be simplistic or stereotyped in thought.	A weak analysis, which may be attributed to a poor selection of artifacts either in terms of relevance, diversity, or quality.	Describes learning experiences
"1" Rating	Thesis/ focus for the essay does not demonstrate knowledge of the products/ practices of the target community(ies), civilization(s), or culture(s) and is unclear or fails to address the prompt.	Fails to include or discuss artifacts.	Does not discuss relevant learning experiences

APPENDIX 10.C

From Mary Ann Dellinger, Ken E. Koons, and Christina R. McDonald, "ePortfolios and the Study of Civilizations and Cultures," Inter/National Coalition for Electronic Portfolio Research, Cohort VI, Final Report, 2013.

Table 10.3. Tau-c Scores to Measure Association among Tags, Artifacts, and Reflection

	Total Sample (n=162)		Humanities Classes (n=78)	
	Reflection-Tau-c Scores	Percentage of Sample ePortfolios	Reflection-Tau-c Scores	Percentage of Sample ePortfolios
Tags	0. 48**	29	0. 50**	51
Movies	0. 25**	16	0. 35**	28
Journals	n. s.	15	n. s.	21
Blogs	n. s.	5	n. s.	9
PowerPoint Presentations	n. s.	22	n. s.	19
Essays	n. s.	76	n. s.	73
Drawings/ Graphics	n. s.	10	n. s.	18
Humanities Classes	0. 54**	48		

For all statistical analyses reported in Table 10.3, Kendall's Tau-c, a common measure of association, was used to test the strength of relationships between variables. This measure is designed for cross-tabulations between ordinal variables with a different number of categories, i.e., rectangular tables. The range of values for this measure is from -1 to 1, where -1 is a perfect negative relationship, 1 is a perfect positive relationship, and 0 is perfectly independent. "Rough guidelines" for interpreting Tau-c scores are as follows: less than .1 is "very weak"; between .10 and .19 is "weak"; between .20 and .29 is "moderate"; and .30 or above is "strong." A detailed discussion of Kendall's Tau-c as a measure of association may be found in Le Roy and Corbett, 192–194. Stata software was used to calculate the coefficient and conduct the test of statistical significance. We use "**" to signify statistical significance at the .01 level and "n.s." to denote the lack of statistical significance.

References

Barrett, Helen, and Jonathan Richter. 2009. "Recipes for Reflection." Reflection4Learning. https://sites.google.com/site/reflection4learning/recipes-for-reflection.

Dellinger, Mary Ann, Ken E. Koons, and Christina R. McDonald. 2013. "ePortfolios and the Study of Civilizations and Cultures." Inter/National Coalition for Electronic Portfolio Research, Cohort VI, Final Report.

Dewey, John. 1933. *How We Think*. Boston: D. C. Heath.

Flower, Linda, and John R. Hayes. 1981. "A Cognitive Process Theory of Writing." *College Composition and Communication* 32 (4): 365–87. http://dx.doi.org/10.2307/356600.

"Quality Enhancement Plan: The Core Curriculum: The Nucleus of Effective Citizenship and Leadership." 2006. VMI. http://www.vmi.edu/Administration/Superintendent/VMI_Mission/Mission___Vision/.

Rodgers, Carol. 2002. "Defining Reflection: Another Look at John Dewey and Reflective Thinking." *Teachers College Record* 104 (4): 842–66. http://dx.doi.org/10.1111/1467-9620.00181.

Schön, Donald A. 1983. *The Reflective Practitioner*. New York: Basic Books.

Schön, Donald A. 1987. "Teaching Artistry through Reflection-in-Action." In *Educating the Reflective Practitioner: Toward a New Design for Teaching and Learning in the Professions*, 22–40. San Francisco: Jossey-Bass.

Secor, Marie, and Davida Charney. 1992. *Constructing Rhetorical Education*. Carbondale: Southern Illinois University Press.

White, Edward M. 2005. "The Scoring of Writing Portfolios: Phase 2." *College Composition and Communication* 56 (4): 581–600.

Yancey, Kathleen Blake. 1998. *Reflection in the Writing Classroom*. Logan: Utah State University Press.

11

FROM APPRISED TO REVISED
Faculty in the Disciplines Change What
They Never Knew They Knew

Pamela Flash

Writers have long found that routine reflection upon their practices and products can increase senses of agency, intentionality, and rhetorical agility. Here, working analogically, I ask whether routinized reflective dialogues—conducted by departmental faculty members about writing and writing instruction—can yield increased senses of *pedagogic* agency, intentionality, and agility.

To address this question, I propose that we move to the excitable (and often cranky) realm of the departmental faculty meeting, an atypical venue in writing-across-the-curriculum (WAC) circles, and even in writing-in-the-disciplines (or WID) circles. To this setting, faculty members arrive to find that typical meeting fare (tenure decisions, photocopier service contracts, requests for reduced fiscal modeling, enrollment reports . . .) has been jettisoned, that the entire meeting is dedicated to deliberating upon this question: what specific writing abilities should students in your majors be able to demonstrate by the time they graduate?

This scenario depicts exactly what the WAC program at the University of Minnesota has been up to for the past decade under the auspices of its comprehensive writing-enriched curriculum program, or WEC. The reflective process at its heart begins something like this, from a meeting of biological-science faculty that took place in 2008.

PROF A: One thing we haven't talked about yet is objectivity . . .

PROF B: That's one of the things I certainly respond most vitriolically to, when I get something to read and it's all, "I did this . . ." and "I thought that . . ." I mean it's all very touchy feely in the way it's presented and that just . . .

PROF A: Ugh . . . it makes your skin crawl.

DOI: 10.7330/9781607325161.c011

PF: Huh. So, how would you describe what you're after? You can ask for "objective" writing, but no one really knows what that means . . . do they?

PROF A: They don't? Really? Why don't they?

PROF B: Remove the writer out of it! . . . They either talk about themselves, or they say, like, "Shaw et al said this, Shaw et al said that," and the emphasis is on Shaw et al rather than the result or the finding . . .

PF: Which is an approach that may have been introduced in a literature or theory course . . .

PROF C: *That's* why they do that? Because people in other departments teach them to?

PROF D: Right, that's, uh . . . more like historical narrative; not what we expect of scientific writing . . .

PF: So, you ask students to focus on presenting the science, not the scientist?

PROF B: I think that's right. We want it to be replicable; see what I mean? So that if someone else came along and did the exact same study that Shaw et al. described, they should get the exact same results. That's the point. Scientific writing is not egotistical . . . it's contributive.

PF: If I were a student in your class, I might find it useful to learn that writing here is expected to emphasize scientific procedure and findings and that this is because the emphasis is on replication. That scientific writing contributes to collective science . . .

PROF A: Right, right. Until right now that seemed so obvious. Uh . . . I've never really spelled that out. Does anyone? (Ecology, Evolution, and Behavior Faculty 2008)

And here's a second scenario, this one from the political science faculty in 2007:

PROF W: Writing in political science is *analytical.* We want *clear analysis.*

PF: Right, that makes sense. And what does clear analysis look like here? When they come up with clear analysis in their writing what are they doing?

PROF W: Uhhh . . .

PF: Because they may have been exposed to different kinds of analysis, right? Break something apart, examine the pieces closely, interpret using a series of theoretical lenses. . . . It could be that when a writing prompt asks students to do something they don't really get, they'll find it safer to just keep on describing . . .

PROF X: Exactly. Exactly! In my class, I must continually emphasize that papers should not be merely descriptive and derivative. . . . So, really? We have to explain to them what "analytical" means?

PROF W: Nah. They know. Can't we expect that they know this already?

PROF Y: It suddenly occurs to . . . me that we may be expecting our undergraduates to be like our graduate students. And that that may be a mistake. We train our graduate students in rigorous analysis, yet we expect it from our undergraduates without training them.

PROF Z: Yeah—we don't teach analytical methodology to undergraduates like they do in, for example, economics. In political science classes, we always start with the big questions like how do you get a democracy? and then expect them to look at specific situations in the light of this big question.

PROF X: But they don't! We would like students to write as intuitive scientists but they come to us as intuitive lawyers. They are used to partisan political arguments, like on TV.

PROF W: Right, they ingest glib arguments that rarely involve analysis. TV doesn't teach them what we want. We don't teach them what we want. So, okay—by "analyze" what do we mean? (Political Science Faculty 2007)

What's going on in these meetings? On the face of it, two groups of departmental faculty members are complaining conversationally about the kinds of writing students are doing in their courses. Nothing new there. But when we look closely, we see a line of productive deliberation threading through the conversation. Initial characterizations of writing—possibly long-held and socially reinforced characterizations— "Objective!" "Clearly analytical!"—are voiced, explained to me (the outsider) and loosened ("What do we mean?"). Participants in this discussion are revealing presumptions about generic discourse norms ("Can't we assume that they know this already?") and beginning to poke at inconvenient truths ("We may be expecting our undergraduates to be like our graduate students"). In these public moments, ideas informing teaching practice can change, and because the collective faculty composes and creates curricular systems, airing these ideas can promote pedagogic and curricular transformation. Creating situations in which these transformative moments can emerge is a central objective of the WEC model.

But do most departmental faculty members want their impressions of writing and writing instruction to undergo transformation? Won't they resist? It is incontrovertible that WAC programs encounter faculty resistance. Faculty audiences routinely resist the appearance of meddling or efforts that seem intent upon replacing familiar practices with imported content. Many WAC programs operate in spite of this resistance, viewing it as an inevitable but ignorable corollary to the kinds of change they are trying to effect. While pragmatic, the impulse to downplay or ignore faculty resistance may unintentionally restrict the reach of WAC initiatives.

By contrast, the WEC model positions faculty members' attitudes about writing and writing instruction as critical pivot points of change. Instead of working around resistance, I tease it out. I'm interested in working directly with resistant reactions, and more important, with the core-level assumptions that give rise to these reactions. Over the course of developing, implementing, and assessing the WEC program, an effort entirely structured around discussions like those excerpted above, I have become convinced that the sustained integration of relevant writing instruction into disciplinary curricula relies on ongoing, locally situated faculty reflection about writing and about writing instruction. Absent this reflection, the long-held WAC goal of integrating meaningful writing instruction into diverse curricula will remain uneven, intermittent, and vulnerable.

In what follows, I draw upon transcript, survey, and assessment data collected over the past decade to illustrate the powerful role reflective discussion plays in changing the way faculty members think about and teach writing within their disciplinary homes. The ideas I bring forward here, and the faculty members who voice them, can inspire us to expand the context in which we study reflection and will provide WAC/WID practitioners a method for productively addressing and transcending faculty resistance to cross- and intradisciplinary writing initiatives.

Reflection-in-Action. While structured reflection may be a relatively new focus in the WAC/WID world, it is not new to educational philosophers like Donald Schön and Steven Brookfield, who advocate the use of "reflection-in-action" (Schön 1983) and "critical reflection" (Brookfield 1995) in order to engender increased senses of *pedagogic* efficacy on the part of individual instructors. According to Schön, instructors' increased agency, intentionality, and agility is proportional to their willingness to investigate their own epistemologies and tacitly held values. In *Reflection in the Writing Classroom*, Kathleen Blake Yancey characterizes Schön's use of analytical reflection as rhetorical (Yancey 1998), highlighting his assertion that by analyzing our own thinking patterns, by considering the ways these patterns align with or diverge from our intentions, we can adjust and refine the ways we think and work.

The excerpt of political science faculty discussion provides an instantiation of rhetorical reflection when Professor W asks, "So, okay . . . by 'analyze' what do we mean?" Here, a seasoned professor is questioning a concept he'd thought, until that moment, was obvious. In the act of trying to explain it to me, someone without the same set of tacit understandings, he stumbled. Schön would sympathize. "Often we cannot say what it is that we know," he asserts. "When we try to describe it we find ourselves at a loss or we produce descriptions that are obviously inappropriate. Our knowing is ordinarily tacit, implicit in our patterns of action and in our feel for the stuff with which we are dealing" (Schön 1995, 49). Professor W's understanding of what he meant by *analysis* had become loosened, made strange to him. Upon further reflection, he recognized he didn't really know how to describe what he'd meant.

Likewise, in the first excerpt, Professor A reached a similar point in trying to explain why scientific writing should be framed around research, not researchers. In her response, "Until right now that seemed so obvious. Uh . . . I've never really spelled that out. Does anyone?" she looks to her peers for affirmation or contradiction. She was questioning her approach and, at the close of the meeting, told me she was piqued by this moment in the discussion because, as a conscientious instructor, she didn't like the idea that she might be unwittingly disadvantaging her students by withholding what was now revealed as useful information. In the course of a few more discussions, she and her colleagues hammered out some language to describe their expectations of "objectivity." Their current list of writing outcomes includes these two items: "Directly communicates a scientific narrative using an overt logical structure: moves from problem, to procedure, data, conclusions, and back to target problem" and "Describes significant gaps in scientific knowledge by articulating a target question or problem and describing its significance" (University of Minnesota College of Biological Sciences 2013). As Professors A and W found out, these in-depth reflective discussions that uncover uncertainty can be unsettling. What they may not have suspected is that this unsettling is an initial goal of these conversations. When faculty members engage in active, dialogical reflection—when they effectively make the familiar strange—these discussions can catalyze a dismantling of entrenched and unproductive pedagogical thinking. Gratifying realizations can result. "Oh!" exulted a political-science professor at the completion of the analysis discussion excerpted above, "Now, for the first time, I know how to answer a student who asks me, 'What do you want?' without having to spell the whole thing out like a recipe" (Political Science Faculty 2007).

DEVELOPING THE WEC MODEL

Aware of the role reflection can play in making instructional and curricular change, and equally aware of faculty members' likely resistance to engaging in reflective analysis of their individual or collective values and practices, I set about creating a model that would capitalize on reflection and divert resistance. To subvert resistance, the model would need to be owned by internal stakeholders. To instigate change, it would need to offer a reflective process aimed at uncovering and working through issues and assumptions that may be blocking it. What sort of mediating moves might keep the process progressing while simultaneously posing no threat to local faculty ownership?

This was my question in 2006 after five years of convening departmental faculty focus groups to assess the University of Minnesota's then eight-year-old writing-intensive course requirement. Discussions with faculty groups from dozens of departments had made it apparent to me that resistance to incorporating writing instruction into departmental curricula was largely based in a narrow set of assumptions about what was meant by *writing* and by *writing instruction*. Effective writing was clear writing; student ability was declining; writing instruction therefore must be remedial, must emphasize clear structures and inevitably take time away from important discussions of content. Sympathy was offered to those recruited to teach the writing-intensive courses, and resistance was aimed at the bureaucratic procedures required to certify them, but little consideration was given to developing alternative methods for ensuring that students graduated as able writers. Faculty members within departments had not identified harmonious or divergent writing values or outcomes they expected students in their majors to be able to demonstrate by the time they graduated and had only the sketchiest of ideas about who was requiring what in which course down the corridor. Until we found a way of getting at and potentially loosening the grip of unproductive assumptions and inconsistent practices, the writing-intensive initiative would have limited success in transforming curricula or writing pedagogy.

Focus on individual instructors and/or individual courses (in workshops and consultation, for example) was thus having limited impact on the goal of integrating writing into departmental curricula or on faculty satisfaction with graduation-level student writing. In developing our WEC model, I changed points of contact. This shift, illustrated by figure 11.1, shows that instead of positioning instructional practices as the primary point of intervention, the WEC model takes primary aim at faculty conceptions of writing and writing instruction. These become the *trigger points for change* rather than the inevitable and ignorable *reactions to change*. Understanding that faculty conceptions of writing and writing instruction shape their instructional practices, and, in turn, the extent to which students conceptualize (and are motivated by) the relevance of writing to their coursework, makes broader change possible. When faculty members see writing as highly relevant to their instructional goals,

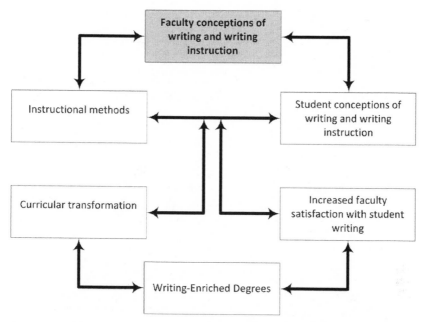

Figure 11.1. The WEC model positions faculty conceptions of writing and writing instruction as a preliminary point of contact. Changes in faculty perceptions trigger changes in instructional methods, curricular sequencing, and student perceptions and ultimately allow students to graduate with degrees that have been writing enriched.

they are more likely to see its intentional integration into departmental curricula and graduation outcomes as advantageous.

WEC METHODS

Since 2007, faculty members from fifty-five undergraduate departments have enrolled in the WEC program, and each year, five additional units (primarily departments, but also, where appropriate, schools or entire colleges) are added to the roster. Enrolled units engage in a recursive process of generating, implementing, and assessing multiple iterations of comprehensive documents called *undergraduate writing plans,* and although they are provided with a boilerplate for organizational purposes (see fig. 11.2), the content of these five-section plans is faculty authored and is generated by the sorts of reflective discussions I've been describing. Although WAC team members prime discussions by providing faculty discussants with a variety of data collected from within their departments and follow meetings with thorough summaries, an appointed member for the faculty, the WEC liaison, is ultimately

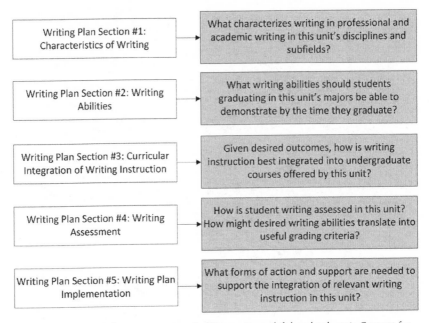

Figure 11.2. Writing plans are composed of five sections (left-hand column). Content for each section is generated by faculty in response to critical questions (right-hand column) related to the shape and role of writing in specific departments and disciplines.

responsible for cofacilitating the meetings and for weaving colleagues' ideas together into comprehensive writing plans.

Throughout the process of creating and assessing editions of writing plans, members of the WAC team collect various forms of writing-related data. When a unit enrolls, we collect and catalog samples of writing assignments and samples of student writing. We administer an online survey that asks unit faculty, students, and professional affiliates to characterize discipline-relevant writing abilities and offer baseline assessments of writing and writing instruction. To prompt curricular perspective, we create visual representations (maps, matrices, flow charts) of key courses comprising the curricula, and to ensure that the various perspectives voiced in meetings are incorporated into the writing plan, we circulate thorough summaries of faculty discussions, which we tape. These departmentally derived data are all offered back to faculty for their interpretation over the course of four faculty meetings within two semesters. Ultimately, armed with meeting summaries, survey data, curricular maps, and writing samples, faculty liaisons draft first-, second-, or third-edition writing plans. Plan drafts circulate intradepartmentally and, once revised, are ultimately granted approval by the Campus

Writing Board, a subcommittee of the university's faculty senate. From there, fiscal requests are approved by the provost's office, and service requests (for workshops, consultations, material development, etc.) are approved by the WAC team.

In a nutshell, the WEC model equips a departmental faculty with an elective, funded, and faculty-driven method for critically reflecting upon assumptions related to the kinds of writing they assign students in their undergraduate curricula and for intentionally implementing and assessing context-specific activities warranted by these reflective processes. The model, designed to capitalize on reflection and divert resistance, has resulted in sustainable changes in the ways writing and writing instruction are conducted at our research university.

CHANGES YIELDED BY WEC'S REFLECTIVE PROCESSES

Reflective processes involved in the creation, implementation, and assessment of writing plans can result in three areas of change: changes in attitudes about writing and writing instruction, changes in instructional methods and in language used in describing writing to students and colleagues, and changes in the rate at which student writing meets faculty expectations. These results are documented in the evolving editions of plans themselves, in transcripts of meetings held to create those plans, in annual liaison surveys (in which we pose the question, "What effect has the WEC process had on practices and attitudes related to writing instruction in your unit?"), and in the longitudinal ratings of student writing. To evidence these changes in approaches to teaching, I will excerpt responses to our annual liaisons survey and discussions from meeting transcripts. To demonstrate changes in student writing, I will provide data yielded by our panel ratings of student writing.

Changes in Faculty Attitudes and Assumptions

Changes in attitudes about writing and writing instruction are evident throughout our data. "The big impact has been attitudinal," notes one faculty liaison who goes on to say, "This is the first time in my six years in this unit that our department has ever had a discussion about what we actually do as teachers, in the classroom, across our different programs. Many of my colleagues who have been here for much longer tell me that they have never seen interest in this dimension of their work before" (WEC Liaison Survey 2009). Another liaison recounts changes in attitude by noting that as a result of the reflective discussions, colleagues

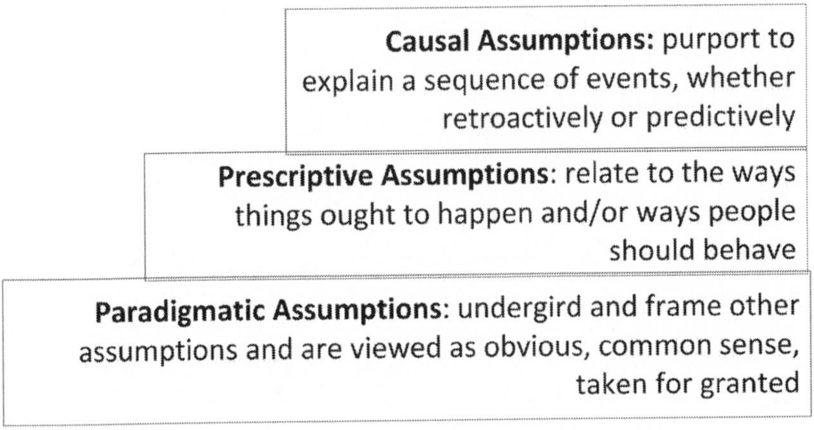

> **Causal Assumptions:** purport to explain a sequence of events, whether retroactively or predictively

> **Prescriptive Assumptions:** relate to the ways things ought to happen and/or ways people should behave

> **Paradigmatic Assumptions:** undergird and frame other assumptions and are viewed as obvious, common sense, taken for granted

Figure 11.3: An illustration of Stephen Brookfield's typology of assumptions informing instructional practices.

"are more accepting that they are the 'experts' regarding writing instruction in their discipline" (WEC Liaison Survey 2013). A third liaison credits the necessarily slow pace and ongoing, discursive nature of the WEC process with its ability to build buy-in among her colleagues, writing that "with WEC, the Department has been engaged in a slow but very substantial process of consensus-building and consciousness-raising regarding the role of writing in our pedagogical mission and curriculum, resulting in a high level of faculty 'buy in' to the WEC process" (WEC Liaison Survey 2011).

Useful in describing and tracking attitudinal shifts triggered during WEC discussions is a classification system introduced by Stephen Brookfield (1995). Interested in understanding assumptions that inevitably underlie, shape, and give direction to teaching practices, Brookfield organizes assumptions about teaching into three stepped levels as illustrated in figure 11.3.

Causal assumptions, at Brookfield's top level, are explanatory and predictive ideas that guide our understanding of how actions and reactions do (and might) play out. Prescriptive assumptions, one level below, relate to the ways things *should* work and how stakeholders *ought* to behave. At the deepest and most tacit level are paradigmatic assumptions, which Brookfield considers foundational to the extent that those who hold them may not see them as assumptions at all, but as facts (Brookfield 1995).

WEC meeting transcripts reveal that causal and prescriptive assumptions about writing and writing instruction typically arise in the course of the first of four faculty meetings. At the surface, or causal level, one of the first assumptions voiced in WEC discussions is this: "If we have to devote class time to writing instruction, we won't get through the content teaching we are actually hired to do." An example at the prescriptive level would be, "Students ought to enter our courses with higher levels of writing proficiency." As WEC discussions progress, assumptions lurking at the paradigmatic level can surface. I've found that these include the assumption that effective writing can be broadly and generically defined across all disciplines, that it is reasonable to expect writing skills to be mastered prior to students' matriculation to post-secondary institutions, and the parent assumption from which these emerge: that teaching writing and teaching content are fundamentally discrete activities. Beneath these core assumptions may reside the most influential—and the most cloaked—assumption of all, namely that these faculty members suspect that they don't know how to go about teaching writing.

Happily, WEC meeting transcripts are also filled with hints of shifting attitudes. When faculty members deliberate accurate ways of describing desired writing abilities (as the two faculty groups are doing in the opening excerpts), an assumption that writing can be generically described and that students can be expected to understand what is meant by such commonly used grading criteria as logical, substantive, or clear—two assumptions that have previously been unchallenged—begin to shift. When Professor A says, "Right, right. Until right now that seemed so obvious," a shift is hinted.

Changes in instruction

Asking faculty members again and again over the course of four meetings to explicitly describe for and with each other the characteristics and function of relevant, effective student writing is changing the ways they in turn teach and talk to students about writing. "Whenever we talk about writing now," writes one liaison, "we are . . . using our WEC language" (WEC Liaison Survey 2011). Along those lines, another writes, "I think [WEC] has helped many of our faculty be more thoughtful and self-reflexive about their teaching. It has helped others find language to talk with students about what they are doing in writing assignments" (WEC Liaison Survey 2013). A third notes, "We have learned better ways of helping students do what all along we hoped they would do. There are far more faculty discussions about writing in classes" (WEC Liaison Survey 2009). This faculty member goes on to reflect that "the idea that

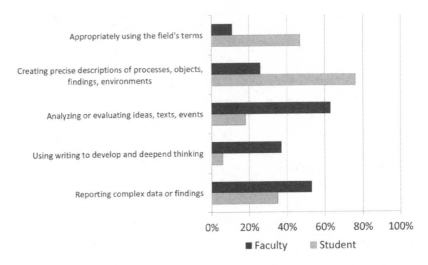

Figure 11.4. Data yielded in a science department by the WEC survey question, What are the three most important writing abilities majors in this unit should be able to demonstrate by the time they graduate?

pedagogy, especially writing pedagogy, can be improved by a process of breaking down and more clearly describing the tasks you are asking students to perform . . . is a huge revelation. The practices and attitudes of those faculty who have engaged with the WEC process have been transformed." (WEC Liaison Survey 2012).

Changes in the language these instructors use to talk about and assess student writing are triggered by reflective review of survey data during the first WEC discussion we hold. On their surveys, both faculty and students are asked to rank critical writing abilities. Data reveal that abilities ranked highly by faculty are often not the most obvious to students. An excerpt of survey data drawn from a science department (see fig. 11.4) includes a provocative juxtaposition of perceptions related to high-priority writing abilities.

Reflecting upon the contrasting perspectives illustrated by these data, faculty members were compelled to consider the source of students' impressions.

PROF E: But why are they so hung up on creating precise descriptions? That's . . . *easy* compared to analysis.

PROF F: Not for them, maybe.

PROF C: I mean, what the students think we want from them is . . . the more technical information, but what we really want in most cases, at least for me, is the ability to synthesize.

PROF A: Yes, we are emphasizing synthesis but what do we grade them on? I realize from these discussions that what we want is synthesis, but when I when I told students in my course that's what I wanted, they didn't know what it meant. They'd never heard that before, so when I graded them on their ability to synthesize I had to figure I was ahead of where I guess I should be.

PROF B: Well, unless we all tell them that's what we want, right? So by the time they get to you, they know what we're talking about.

(Ecology, Evolution, and Behavior Faculty 2008)

At least two important ideas are raised in this excerpt, and the first is that writing abilities develop over time. Professor F responds to Professor E's exasperation by suggesting that creating precise descriptions, an old hat routine for faculty, might get a high ranking from students to whom it is a new or challenging ability. The second is that if they want to see an increase in students' ability to synthesize information, faculty will need to describe it explicitly to students throughout courses in the major so that by the time students get to the capstone course (taught by Professor A), they know what we're talking about.

Curious about the degree to which valued writing abilities were being explicitly described to students, this department's faculty hired a research assistant to collect and code writing assignments and grading schemes from every one of its undergraduate courses, scouting for explicit language that correlated with the faculty-generated abilities list. As figure 11.5 illustrates, this investigation revealed that explicit mention of writing abilities faculty prized (the ability to synthesize information from disparate sources to draw logical conclusions and to analyze for cause and effect) was rare. Instead, assignments and grading criteria gave explicit mention to "accurate description of results," "grammatically accurate writing," and "use of scientific templates." Reviewing these results, Professor A looked around at her colleagues asking, "Is it any wonder that our students think we prioritize accurate description of results?" Acting on these data, this faculty group set about developing, workshopping, and cataloguing a variety of writing assignments, activities, and supplemental resources they could use to focus explicit instruction on developing students' abilities to demonstrate effective synthesis in their writing.

As the excerpt reveals, WEC discussions involve faculty reflection and the purposeful eliciting of candid attitudes and insights. Essential to the model's success has been a steadfast interest in working *with*, not *in spite of*, attitudes of resistance.

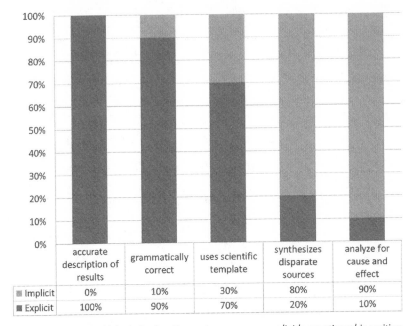

	accurate description of results	grammatically correct	uses scientific template	synthesizes disparate sources	analyze for cause and effect
Implicit	0%	10%	30%	80%	90%
Explicit	100%	90%	70%	20%	10%

Figure 11.5. Rate at which desired writing outcomes were explicitly mentioned in writing assignments in a biological sciences department.

Changes in Curricula

Deliberating over terms that more accurately describe expected writing can trigger multiple shifts in faculty thinking about what is meant by *writing*, but also by *writing instruction*. When the biology faculty agreed that "synthesizing information from disparate sources to draw logical conclusions" is an act of writing, they became less likely to see writing instruction as irrelevant to their curricula; the relevance was obvious. It became equally obvious to them that they could not reasonably expect undergraduates to enter the major already able to demonstrate proficiency in this area. If majors are expected to demonstrate these discipline-relevant writing abilities by the time they graduate, it became apparent to faculty discussants that explicit instructional attention should be incorporated into courses throughout the major.

Incorporating formal curricular changes can have productive systemic benefits. After an interdisciplinary humanities unit made structural changes to its curriculum to ensure that more explicit writing instruction was situated in courses majors took prior to their final year, the unit's WEC liaison noted that "the backlog for enrollment in senior paper courses has vanished" (WEC Liaison Survey 2008). Elsewhere, in a performing arts department, the liaison described ways in which discussions about writing were helping to smooth over previously troublesome curricular fractures. "We have seen several really promising innovations within specific sectors of the curriculum that bridge artistic practice and writing instruction," she wrote, adding that she had also noticed "a greater level of awareness of the importance of clarity and rigor in communicating writing expectations to students amongst a broad range of faculty" (WEC Liaison Survey 2011).

Discussions about perspectives on writing as they relate to individual subfields and to disciplinary clusters can also have a positive effect on the curriculum, as the preceding comments indicate, and can trigger a sense of community among those who teach the component courses. Illustrating this sense, another liaison had this to say about the initial effects of the WEC process: "This has engendered a new respect and understanding of my colleagues' work that goes beyond the question of writing to embrace our disciplinary philosophy as a whole. I think this process truly has the potential to help us reshape and integrate what we do as a department. This is especially the case in my unit, as so many of our faculty are adjunct and practitioners, and not well integrated into the communications mechanisms of the [university] as a whole" (WEC Liaison Survey 2009).

Likewise, reviewing simplified visual representations of curricular structure can provoke realizations about needed adjustments. This was true in mechanical engineering, a department that routinely uses a schematic to represent its curricular mechanism and student-path circuitry (see fig. 11.6). In 2007, when the department began the WEC process, we highlighted courses that included explicit writing instruction by circling them with black rings. Before students' senior year, when they took a measurements lab and a senior design course, the only explicit writing instruction they experienced was in the required introductory physics labs and a first-year writing course. Both of these courses are situated outside departmental offerings, and both courses are waived for students with in-range AP scores. Once faculty had generated their list of writing outcomes and determined that they were largely dissatisfied with students' ability to demonstrate those outcomes, it didn't take them long to identify the problem when we projected their curriculum. The problem was obvious. As they described in the their first-edition writing plan, mechanical engineering instructors from six additional courses (indicated in the 2009 diagram) agreed to include explicit writing instruction in their courses, as indicated by the revised curricular map.

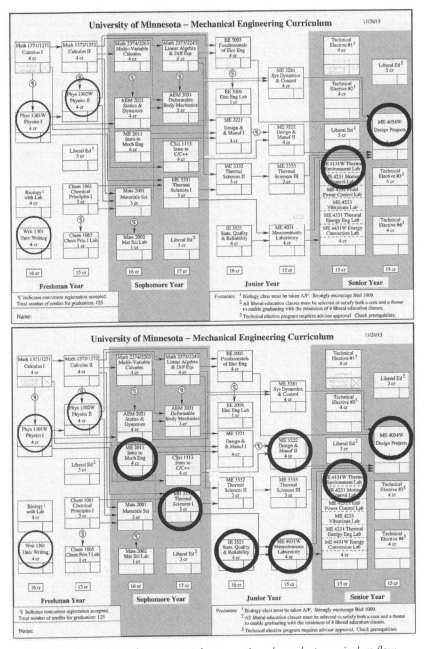

Figure 11.6. The mechanical engineering department's undergraduate curriculum flow-charts from 2007 (top) and 2009 (bottom).

Transcripts of a similar discussion in the geography department reveal complications that can occur when students' curricular paths are less prescribed than those required for mechanical engineering degrees. In geography, a department composed of diverse subfields ranging from cartography to urban studies, significant skepticism was expressed about even guessing at common writing abilities. Facilitating the meeting, I met this skepticism by reminding faculty participants that the lists of desired writing abilities they generated could be as diversified and exhaustive as they wished them to be, that no need for curricular or pedagogic change was assumed, and that their developing a meaningless list of homogenized writing standards was not a goal of the WEC program. This line of rebuttal had a generative effect. In the following excerpt we see that once the faculty accepted that *they* were in a position to make curricular decisions about the extent to which writing instruction was going to be offered in their courses, they had some issues to talk about.

> PROF H: But are you saying that . . . we can choose how much writing concentration we want for [students]? *We* can figure out how to put writing into the majors so that we catch them all?
>
> PROF I: It seems there are two ways of thinking about how writing works here. One of them is . . . saying that if students spend enough seat time in a class that's Writing Intensive then they'll have learned how to write. The other way . . . takes a look at what students are able to do and what we want them to do. It's harder, but it is really the only effective way to find out if they've learned how to write . . . Right now, we evaluate the senior project at the end and don't like the results, but by then it's too late.
>
> PROF J: The number one complaint is that [students] are not prepared for the senior project experience. Can we unify some components of writing at the gateway level so that they are in place by the time students tackle the project?
>
> PROF I: It's important to remember that students rarely take the Gateway courses before they take their other courses. So, either we change that situation, or we incorporate writing into as many courses as possible. Which way do we want to go?
>
> (Geography Faculty 2008)

Here we see faculty deliberating between permitting apathy and committing to action, between maintaining strategies that reinforce the disappointing status quo and strategies that might require work. When doing nothing is presented as an explicit choice, it can become less viable.

Changes in Student Writing

Changes in faculty assumptions and adjustments to curricular architecture are significant achievements for any educational initiative. Still, a sense of obligation to faculty and students involved with the WEC process propelled us to investigate WEC's effect on the quality of student writing. To this end, my team and I developed a longitudinal assessment process that is initiated by the approval of a unit's first-edition writing plan and reprised every three years. The assessment involves a panel's rating of capstone-level student writing against sets of faculty-generated criteria and engages unit faculty and panel raters in formative reflective on assessment results. Like all components of the WEC model, the process used to rate student writing is faculty driven. They generate rating criteria, identify a capstone-level course from which rated samples are collected, nominate raters, and interpret results. Rating reports comprise aggregated ratings on each individual criterion by year, but they also contain excerpts of comments made by raters during reflective debriefing sessions. In these sessions, raters discuss patterns of writing strength and weakness found in the samples they rated, and they comment on the utility of individual criteria.

Meetings held to discuss rating reports encourage their context-specific interpretation. In these meetings, the faculty discusses the ratings in reference to their criteria, and where merited, come up with strategies for targeted support. Certainly advances and regressions of these scores are affected by multiple variables, including changes in course faculty, writing assignments, and student populations. However, because the criteria were generated by faculty to describe cumulatively developed writing abilities, and because the results are provided to faculty for their interpretation and recommendations, these variables do not obscure the formative value of the assessment exercise.

Across WEC units, rating reports indicate movement in students' ability to demonstrate or achieve the standards set by faculty criteria. Although this movement is often positive (as seen in table 11.1), negative trends also occur; in most situations it is the negative ratings that lead to the most constructive faculty discussions and ensuing action. Movement is also seen in the criteria themselves. If raters report finding a criterion difficult to use, the faculty may choose to make slight wording adjustments. Adjusted wording of criteria can initially result in decreased scores (as seen in table 11.2). However, when unit faculty begin to integrate revised wording into their instructional artifacts (assignments and grading schemes), chances are good that these decreases will be temporary.

Table 11.1. Upward-trending scoring excerpts from departmental WEC rating reports

Unit Name	Criterion: the text . . .	2010 Score	2012 Score	+
History	Demonstrates an awareness of the particular nature, value, limitations, and incompleteness of historical sources	.29	.53	+ .24
Horticulture Science	Interprets and applies data by making connections between academic and real-world situations	.67	.91	+ .24
Mechanical Engineering	Summarizes key points	.40	.94	+ .54

Table 11.2. Scoring excerpts from a department's WEC rating reports including adjustments in criterion wording

Unit Name	Original wording	Revised wording	2010 score	2013 score	+/−
Political Science	Contributes to discussions of questions central to the field (2010)	Explains why these questions are germane to the study and practice of politics (2013)	.60 (2010)	.36(2013)	−.24
Geography	Analyzes observations (2010)	Evaluates and interprets the meanings and effects of visual and/or numerical information (2013)	.71 (2010)	.54(2013)	−.17

CRITICAL REFLECTION ON PEDAGOGIC ASSUMPTIONS

In WEC meetings, I've found that posing direct questions about how writing is being defined, and about the stability and implications of those definitions, can provoke revision of those definitions and the instructional approaches they inspire. I regularly encounter assumptions at all three levels of Brookfield's typology; it is thus my especial goal to unearth obstructive assumptions residing at the paradigmatic level, sensing that until these deep-seated, often unconscious ideas are brought out for examination and possible revision, sustainable pedagogic change is unlikely. Instead, the recursive swirl of causal and prescriptive assumptions, both residing closer to the surface, will continue to be affirmed and reinforced within departmental meeting rooms and hallway discussions.

Although Brookfield assures us that critical reflection on teaching will lead to confidently informed, intentional actions that can be embraced and explained rationally to students, self, and colleagues, Robert P. Yagelski isn't so sure. In his essay "The Ambivalence of Reflection: Critical Pedagogies, Identity, and the Writing Teacher," Yagelski acknowledges having mixed feelings about reflective instructional practice, describing "a troubling space between doubt and committed action that writing teachers often inhabit, a space of both possibility and paralysis that we rarely acknowledge directly in our discussions about teaching writing" (Yagelski 1999, 32). Yagelski suspects that this sense of ambivalence, this tension between possibility and practice, can lead to counterproductive regressions. "If we try to change practices that grow out of assumptions, conventions, and institutional structures to which we have become accustomed," he warns, "then we are inevitably unsettled and feel a tendency to retreat to the familiar" (Yagelski 1999, 35).

To Schön, however, the progressive possibilities engendered by reflection-in-action depend upon achieving precisely the sort of space Yagelski characterizes as troubling. The challenge in all this is to steer reflective ruminations—in our case, reflections about writing and writing instruction—away from all this self-conscious autobiographical scrutiny, to divert the temptation of retreating to the familiar, and to increase the likelihood of collective and progressive curricular transformation.

Breaking away from the cyclical traps of self-scrutiny may require external intervention, or, at the very least, movement into an interpersonal venue. Lev Vygotsky's zone of proximal development, a theoretical construct popularized by the 1978 translation of his *Mind and Society*, seems an apt way to describe what is wanted here. In its most essential translation, the zone of proximal development can be understood as increased developmental potential that can be achieved when independent problem solving is mediated by external instructors or peers (Vygotsky 1978). Vygotsky saw learning, or change, as a socially mediated process occurring first on a social, interpersonal level and later on an internal, intrapersonal level. In other words, where one lone reflector might struggle to spark new insights, external interlocutors and thinking partners who engage in joint reflection may affect the critical distance necessary to do so.

Schön acknowledges that collective negotiation about thorny issues like writing, writing instruction, and assessment of writing require descent from the "high hard hill" (Schön 1987, 3) of technical rationality and research-based theory in order to negotiate the "swampy lowlands" (1983, 42) of messy problems that have no technical or easy solutions. "The practitioner is confronted with a choice," he writes. "Shall he remain on the high ground where he can solve relatively unimportant problems according to his standards of rigor, or shall he descend to the swamp of important problems where he cannot be rigorous in any way he knows how to describe?" (Schön 1983, 43).

Schön's analogies help us understand why faculty members might feel some reluctance at finding their monthly meetings devoted to trips down from the high hill of their intellectual expertise and into swampy curricular murk they did not elect to plumb or traverse. Nobody, including Brookfield, said such processes would necessarily be either easy or fun. "Becoming aware of the implicit assumptions that frame how we think and act is one of the most challenging intellectual puzzles we face," he acknowledges. This awareness is also "something we instinctively resist. . . . Who wants to clarify and question assumptions she or he has lived by for a substantial period of time, only to find that they don't make sense?" (Brookfield 1995, 2).

WEC AND MEDIATIONAL REFLECTION

Why, then, does the WEC model, which is based upon choreographed reflection, yield such encouraging evidence of change related to writing instruction? The most immediate answer is that the model doesn't stop at provoking instructional reflection. It establishes long-term alliances with departmental faculty, providing them with a sustained and sustaining partnership as they act on their new convictions. Forging this partnership is the WAC consultant.

If WEC discussions can be described as productively disruptive, it is the WAC consultant who both instigates that disruption and maintains convivial and constructive rapport with the disruptees. Ever present at each step in the process of creating, implementing, and assessing writing plans, the WAC consultant works behind the scenes to enable and mediate productive reflection. This work starts with preliminary research into the unit's curriculum and stakeholder populations and a series of advance meetings with critical departmental stakeholders. Once meetings with the unit faculty are underway, the consultant delivers digestible amounts of locally sourced data (from faculty and student surveys, student writing samples, unit ratings sessions) and persistently engages the faculty with clarification questions. Consultants record all meetings in order to provide liaisons with thorough summaries of each discussion and partner with the unit faculty as it crafts, implements, and assesses its writing plan. Without the involvement of this departmental and disciplinary outsider, discussion would likely be yanked into unproductive directions by intrafaculty politics and members' inability to step outside collectively reinforced sets of assumptions. In this way, the consultant—a cultural outsider—evokes Vygotsky's zone of proximal development and takes on the role of mediator.

The role of the mediator points us as well in another direction for analysis, activity theory. Activity theorist Aleksei Leont'ev used the analogy of the hunt, for example, to describe activity theory's emphasis on mediators and mediational tools (Leont'ev 1981). From a primeval perspective, hunting was an activity motivated by basic human needs for food and clothing and was aided by the work of beaters, individuals who moved out in advance of the hunters to flush the prey. In isolation, Leont'ev explains, the beater's actions, while essential, did not lead directly to procuring game (Leont'ev 1981, 210). The beater was a mediating tool in the dynamic process, the activity. In the WEC process, where a goal is effective pedagogic change rather than procuring game, the WAC consultant serves a mediational role similar to that of beaters by flushing out obstructing attitudes and assumptions.

What the WEC model exemplifies about activity systems is that mediational activity can proceed despite diverse stakeholder objectives. These objectives may vary, conflict, and even change in the course of the reflective discussions the model organizes. The objects or goals held by individual faculty members participating in WEC meetings might at any time include graduating more effective undergraduate writers, working around college governance to obtain funding from the provost's office, evidencing superior pedagogy and instructional commitment to external accreditors, or simply surviving (and outlasting) another university initiative. Goals held by the WAC consultant may also differ from those of faculty participants. These include uncovering and dismantling unproductive assumptions about writing and writing instruction; increasing the sense of relevance, intentionality, and faculty agency with regard to writing instruction; increasing the rate at which student writing meets faculty expectations; and so forth. The WEC model proceeds and succeeds despite this babelesque group of goals, fueled by the belief that objectives and objections are all relevant to change making and that slow change processes often result in sustainable change.

As we continue to implement the WEC model at our home site, and as adaptations of our model are implemented elsewhere, activity theory will help us address questions of longitudinal worth and programmatic sustainability. We will be looking, specifically, at the degree to which economic and technological exigencies challenge faculty control over curricula and thus impact the extent to which faculty reflection and pedagogic insights can be put to work. We will ask, in other words, whether change within the departmental activity system can be sustained when concerns relevant to the larger, institutional activity system threaten local pedagogic agency.

References

Brookfield, Stephen D. 1995. *Becoming a Critically Reflective Teacher*. San Francisco : Jossey-Bass.

Ecology, Evolution, and Behavior Faculty. 2008. Writing-Enriched Curriculum Program. University of Minnesota, October 28. Meeting transcript.

Geography Faculty. 2008. Writing-Enriched Curriculum Program. University of Minnesota, November 7. Meeting transcript.

Leont'ev, Aleksei N. 1981. *Problems of the Development of the Mind*. Moscow: Progress.

Political Science Faculty. 2007. Writing-Enriched Curriculum Program. University of Minnesota, March 27. Meeting transcript.

Schön, Donald. 1983. *The Reflective Practitioner*. New York: Basic Books.

Schön, Donald. 1987. *Educating the Reflective Practitioner*. San Francisco: Jossey-Bass.

Schön, Donald. 1995. "Knowing-in-Action: The New Scholarship Requires a New Epistemology." *Change* 27 (6): 27–34. http://dx.doi.org/10.1080/00091383.1995.105 44673.

University of Minnesota College of Biological Sciences. 2013. University of Minnesota Writing Plan. http://undergrad.umn.edu/cwb/writing_plans.html.

Vygotsky, Lev. 1978. *Mind and Society*. Cambridge: Cambridge University Press.

WEC Liaison Survey. 2008–2013. Writing-Enriched Curriculum Program. University of Minnesota.

Yagelski, Robert P. 1999. "The Ambivalence of Reflection: Critical Pedagogies, Identity, and the Writing Teacher." *College Composition and Communication* 51 (1): 32. http://dx.doi.org/10.2307/358958.

Yancey, Kathleen Blake. 1998. *Reflection in the Writing Classroom*. Logan: Utah State University Press.

12

REFLECTIVE INTERVIEWING
Methodological Moves for Tracing Tacit Knowledge and Challenging Tacit Chronotopic Representations

Kevin Roozen

As one of its enduring objectives, writing studies has continually sought richer, fuller accounts of how persons act with texts. Lee Odell, Dixie Goswami, and Anne Herrington, for example, cite a need to know "the assumptions that writers made or what background knowledge they had concerning the audience, the topic, and the strategies that might be appropriate for achieving their assigned purpose with a given audience" (Odell, Goswami, and Herrington 1983, 222). Arguing that scholarship had been focused too heavily on a few dominant "scenes of writing," Linda Brodkey argued for researchers to "see writing anew" by "look[ing] at it from different vantage points" (Brodkey 1987, 57). Only a few years later, Stephen Witte called for "a conceptualization of writing that is predicated on broader and, I believe, more realistic understandings of text and writing than have generally informed writing research to date" (Witte 1992, 238). Informed by Witte's work, Dorothy Winsor argued for "expanded notions of writing and text" (Winsor 1994, 859). Focusing on the bounded notions of literate activity that had informed studies of disciplinary writing, Paul Prior encouraged researchers to adopt "perspectives that are longer in term, more diverse in settings, and, not incidentally, less grounded in dominant institutional perspectives" (134), and more recently, Kathleen Blake Yancey has argued persuasively that the complexity of literate life in the early twenty-first century demands increasingly expansive notions of the contexts in which persons write and otherwise act with texts (Yancey 2004).

Responding to such calls is no easy matter. Researchers have repeatedly identified two key challenges to enriching our understanding of literate action: accessing persons' tacit writing-related knowledge, abilities, and dispositions (Odell, Goswami, and Herrington 1983; Prior

DOI: 10.7330/9781607325161.c012

2004) and productively challenging the tacit representations of writing and literate activity that drive research designs and data collection and analysis (Brodkey 1987; Prior 1998; Prior and Shipka 2003; Winsor 1994; Witte 1992) as well as pedagogy, as Pamela Flash has just demonstrated in this collection. As one strategy for meeting these challenges, this chapter argues for reflective interviewing, a methodological approach that creates a discursive space in which writers can both develop an understanding of themselves as writers and the wealth of literate activities they are engaged in and communicate that understanding to themselves and others, given its ability to make visible the tacit knowledge persons bring to bear on their literate activities and to complicate the chronotopic scenes that mediate what researchers attend to and the questions they ask.

In this chapter, I first elaborate what I see as the two key challenges to enriching our understanding of literate action and discuss reflective interviewing as a means of productively addressing those challenges. I then employ excerpts from a series of reflective interviews conducted during a case study of one writer to demonstrate how reflection as a methodological approach makes visible the resources one writer tacitly brings to bear on her literate engagements and productively complicates one researcher's understanding of the writer's literate activity. Ultimately, I argue that in addition to its pedagogical functions, reflection as an epistemological practice can also serve as a powerful methodological move.

CHALLENGE 1: MAKING VISIBLE PERSONS' TACIT TEXTUAL KNOWLEDGE

In her opening chapter of *Reflection in the Writing Classroom*, Yancey (1998) argues that reflection proved an effective way for teachers of writing to address what had become a considerable challenge: accessing students' tacit writing-related knowledge, abilities, and dispositions. Facing a similar challenge, researchers of writing also turned to reflection as a way to generate richer, fuller understandings of how persons come to invent and act with texts. As Odell, Goswami, and Herrington (1983) point out, getting a full understanding of the writer's perspective is not easy largely because much of the writer's knowledge is "tacit." Drawing upon the work of Michael Polanyi, these authors state that much of the knowledge a writer uses is "inexplicit functional knowledge" that is "not consciously formulated" (221). Writers "derive it through repeated experience, writers can use it without having to formulate it consciously each time they write" (222–23). This knowledge includes "what assumptions writers made or what background knowledge they had concerning the audience, their topic, and the strategies that might be appropriate for achieving their assigned purpose with a given audience" as well as "detailed, useful information concerning the occupational and rhetorical context for their writing" (222). Prior, echoing what these authors have to say about much of writers' knowledge being below a conscious level of awareness, acknowledges that "writers themselves are only partially aware of the many debts they owe to these intertextual and intercontextual influences" (Prior 2004, 171).

The tacit nature of writing-related knowledge raises considerable methodological challenges. Mature practices and abilities, those that persons have developed a considerable facility with through regular and repeated use, can be difficult for persons to understand and talk about. As a way to address the tacit nature of mature practice, a basic methodological principle of sociohistoric research involves studying practice in its genesis, when persons are just learning to engage in given practices or when routine practice is disrupted for some reason. During these moments of genesis and disruption, knowledge that was tacit comes to conscious awareness.

CHALLENGE 2: CHALLENGING RESEARCHERS' TACIT REPRESENTATIONS OF LITERATE ACTIVITY

A second key barrier to generating richer conceptions of how persons act with texts is researchers' own tacit representations of writing that drive research designs and data collection and analysis. Prior states that the dominant representations that tend to inform situated studies of textual activity tend to simplify literate activity and thus reduce its complexity. He writes that "usual representations of writing collapse time, isolate persons, and filter activity" (Prior 1998, xi). Prior argues that dominant representations of literate action tend to be grounded in our understanding of three key chronotopic scenes: school, the professional workplace, and academic disciplines (141). The dominant perspectives offered up by each of these scenes "filter out most of the sociohistoric contexts, resources, and processes involved in textual production and reception (and use)" (141). These representations, these picturings of writing, are powerful in that they suggest what researchers expect to see and thus inform what researchers attend to and what they ignore. They also inform what researchers ask about and the kinds of questions they pose.

REFLECTIVE INTERVIEWING

Odell, Goswami, and Herrington ask, "How can researchers get at the tacit knowledge of people who write in nonacademic settings? What methodology will enable writers to make explicit the knowledge or strategies that previously may only have been implicit?" (Odell, Goswami, and Herrington 1983, 223). Reflective interviewing, I argue, can serve as an effective approach to both making visible the tacit knowledge persons bring to bear on their literate activities and complicating the chronotopic scenes that mediate what researchers attend to and the questions they ask. At its heart, reflective interviewing is an approach designed to occasion what Yancey (1998) refers to as "constructive reflection," an epistemic process through which writers generate and communicate knowledge of their writing and how they have invented, and continue to invent, themselves as literate persons in the world. Initially forwarded by Yancey as a pedagogical approach to better understand student writers and their writing, constructive reflection invites writers to look back at specific experiences with composing with an eye toward attaining some insight into what they see themselves doing, and why, and what background knowledge they bring to those engagements. For the writer, such reflection occasions a space in which sense can be made of the complexity of writing and how acts of composing contribute to the production of a writerly self. For others, it affords a view of literate activity from the writer's perspective rather than from the dominant perspective offered up by the social space in which writing occurs.

Constructive reflection centers around the use of open-ended questions, typically about specific writing tasks, that invite writers to considering their purposes, goals, and practices for writing and what they see themselves learning through participating in those composing activities. The open-ended nature of the questions engenders responses oriented toward what Yancey refers to as "story making," narrative accounts that generate knowledge rather than brief responses that tend toward communicating something the writer already knows (Yancey 1998, 53). Such questions also invite writers to adopt a stance toward response that is tentative and exploratory rather than grounded in certainty. As Yancey states, asking writers to think about and talk about their purposes and goals and what they have learned through their writing provides a formal and structured occasion in which writers can do the work of figuring out those aspects of their writing (57).

The open-ended questions at the center of reflective interviewing are especially effective in terms of making visible the tacit, implicit knowledge that develops as writers engage in multiple literate activities over lengthy spans of time. While the questions are grounded in particular literate activities, their open-ended nature invites writers to forge connections across what might seem like disparate activities widely separated by space, time, and genre. In this sense, writes Yancey, "constructive reflection is thus cumulative, taking place over several composing events. As it takes place, of course, and as response to composings are provided, such reflection has a shaping effect; it thus contributes to the development of a writer's identity, based in the *multiple texts* composed by the writer, in the *multiple kinds of texts* composed by the writer, and the *multiple contexts* those texts have participated in"(Yancey 1998, 14). Ultimately, Yancey views the cumulative nature of reflection as resulting in writers "developing a cumulative, multi-selved, multi-voiced identity, which takes place between and among composing events and the associated texts" (14).

KINDS OF REFLECTIVE INTERVIEWS

It might be easiest to consider two basic categories of reflective interviewing. The first category includes interviews that do not rely on texts the writer has produced. I am thinking especially here of approaches that invite writers to look back on their histories with literacy using established sets of interview questions or semistructured interviews. The in-depth reflective interviews Deborah Brandt conducted for *Literacy in American Lives*, for example, come most readily to mind. Informed by life-story research, the interviews Brandt conducted were designed to trace participants' memories of learning to read and write and their motivations for doing so from birth to the present. Brandt's interviews worked to focus people's attention on the past by asking them to remember concrete activities and material scenes of literacy learning in their near and distant pasts. It's also important to note that Brandt made a conscious decision not to collect participants' writing or even have participants show her their writing, in part because Brandt did not want her study to center around the analysis of texts and in part because she did not wish to force into her relationship with her eighty research participants "the long shadow of the teacher ready to uncover shameful inadequacies of expression" (Brandt 2001, 13).

The second category includes reflective interviews that focus on the writer's writing or action with a particular text or set of texts. These kinds of interviews involve using texts or artifacts to stimulate the writer's recall. Prior sees clear advantages to reflective interviews involving texts or artifacts: "The more relevant texts you are able to collect, the fuller the view you can develop of the process and its contexts" (Prior 2004, 172). There are many kinds of texts or artifacts used in these kinds of interviews: texts writers have produced or otherwise acted with, diaries or logs writers have kept, screen-capture replays, or other kinds of technologies or artifacts writers act with in accomplishing literate activity. I also include in this category interviews that involve having writers depict their writing processes and then using those depictions as the basis for interview questions (see, for example, Prior and Shipka 2003; Shipka 2011).

Both of these approaches to reflective interviewing provide researchers with a means of viewing literate activity from the writer's perspective and of making visible the writing-related knowledge, practices, identities, and dispositions writers bring to bear on their literate engagements. They also offer researchers a means of understanding persons' experiences with texts and textual practices from other times and places, from their near and distant pasts and projected futures, that might be shaping literate action in the immediate here and now of the ethnographic present.

"SEEING THE WHOLE PATIENT": REFLECTIVE INTERVIEWING IN ACTION

Yancey argues that the ultimate benefit of reflection as a pedagogical practice is that "it enables us to make sense" (Yancey 1998, 187) of writers and their writing. The same, I argue, is true for reflection as a methodological approach. As a way of showing readers what such sense making looks like in action, both for the interviewee and the writing researcher as interviewer, I draw here from a series of reflective interviews conducted during a case study of one writer. After describing the approach to reflective interviewing I employed during the study, I turn to some telling excerpts from those interviews to make visible the interviewee's sense of the relationship between her writing as a nurse and a number of her everyday literate engagements. I also make visible my own emerging sense of how narrowly I, as the interviewer, had initially conceptualized the texts and activities informing her writing and literate identity as a healthcare professional.

These reflective interviews were conducted during a case study with Terri Ulmer (a pseudonym). I initially met Terri when she was a graduate student enrolled in a GTA preparation course I taught at a large public university in the southeastern United States. The semester after the class had ended, Terri and I began talking briefly at a departmental function, and she mentioned she had been a healthcare professional in a number of capacities for about twenty years. She had for example, worked as a nurse in a variety of institutions and had served in a number of administrative capacities in healthcare as well. I had recently received approval through the university's Internal Review Board to conduct studies of persons' disciplinary literate activities, and while reading a series of articles and chapters focusing on the textual practices animating medical practice, I had developed a curiosity about the literate activities that texture healthcare settings. I asked Terri if she would be interested in doing some interviews about her work and literate activities as a healthcare professional, and she agreed to participate.

The interviews didn't go precisely as planned. Our two initial interviews, conducted in my office at the university, focused mainly on Terri's wealth of experiences as a healthcare professional and were driven by a series of relatively close-ended questions such as these: What kinds of work did you do in healthcare? What positions have you held and where were you employed? What kinds of responsibilities did you have? What did your training entail? and What kinds of writing and reading did those positions involve? The second interview also touched briefly on her history with reading and writing, but although I had intended the entire second interview to be devoted entirely to Terri's literacy history, her recollections of her early experiences with reading and writing tended to lead back to talk of her healthcare work, and I was reluctant to keep directing the interview away from Terri's desire to talk about that topic. I was very unfamiliar with the topics covered during those initial interviews, but rather than interrupt Terri's responses, I decided to listen back to the interviews a few hours after they were completed and then email Terri with any follow-up questions I might have. Perhaps sensing my confusion about the activities involved with healthcare, Terri indicated that she was willing to respond to my follow-up questions when time in her schedule permitted her to do so. And one other change: I had intended the initial interviews to cover fairly broad, general topics, so I didn't ask Terri to bring any sample texts. Still, two texts found their way into those interviews: a copy of Terri's resume and a blank sample of a chart she'd used extensively as an intensive-care-unit nurse. Terri brought the copy of her resume as a way to help me keep track of her complex employment history and the sample chart in response to my lack of familiarity with this kind of text and subsequent confusion about both its nature and how it was used.

While listening back through the audiotapes of both of those initial interviews and reading through Terri's responses to my follow-up questions, I was immediately struck by two things. First, I was amazed at the

Table 12.1. Types of interviews conducted during the case study with Terri

Type of Interview	Focus
Initial interviews (2)	Terri's experiences as a healthcare professional and her experiences with literacy during her childhood
Formal reflective text-based interviews (7)	Terri's experiences acting with texts associated with • work in healthcare • writing poetry • writing her autobiographical memoir • writing a science-fiction novel • writing a religious devotional • writing short stories

detailed knowledge of texts that informed Terri's activities as a healthcare professional, especially regarding the various functions they served depending on which department in the hospital (i.e., patient care, administration, legal, etc.) was using them. Second, I realized Terri frequently talked about "seeing" patients and especially about the importance of "seeing the whole patient," a phrase Terri evoked when talking about understanding patients from medical and personal perspectives simultaneously. I became curious about how Terri had developed such an approach given that the many texts she mentioned seemed only to afford a strictly medical perspective of patients' illnesses and diagnoses. Although I was curious about how Terri might have developed this approach, I did not attempt to steer the remainder of the interviews in this direction. Rather, I decided to let Terri's responses go wherever she wished to direct them.

At the time of the study, Terri was not currently serving as a healthcare professional, so I could not conduct any observations of her literate activities while doing healthcare, but I wanted to learn more. As a way to gain a deeper insight into Terri's writing as a nurse, I decided to conduct a series of reflective interviews centered on sample texts Terri had used. In some of my previous case studies (Roozen 2009, 2010), I had employed what I referred to as "process tracing interviews" (Emig 1971; Flower and Hayes 1981; Prior 2004; Prior and Shipka 2003), reflective interviews that involved participants creating retrospective accounts of the processes involved in the production of a particular text or writing project, which provide a means to generate detailed accounts of discursive processes and practices used for specific tasks. Rather than have participants draw pictures of their writing processes, as Prior (2004) and Prior and Shipka (2003) have done, I asked participants to explain the process involved in the invention and production of various literate tasks by showing me how various texts and materials were employed. In addition to helping trigger and support participants' memories of the processes and practices they employed in the production and use of these materials, some of which had occurred decades before, this form of "stimulated elicitation" (Prior 2004) during the interviews also helps to make visible participants' tacit knowledge of text invention and production.

For the case study with Terri, I decided to focus the text-based reflective interviews less on the processes she used to invent and produce the texts she acted with in healthcare contexts, since many of the texts she'd mentioned during the initial interviews were produced during fairly brief episodes (e.g., filling in a chart at the patient's bedside, filling out an incident report at the end of her shift, etc.), and more on her practices for using and acting with texts, how she learned to act with texts in these ways, and the role of texts in accomplishing particular activities. In keeping with Yancey's argument "that [persons] should reflect on writings they care about, that they must be allowed to exercise some authority over their material" (Yancey 1998, 201), I invited Terri to identify significant texts she acted with to serve as the focus of our reflective interviews. As she brought samples of those texts (and often other related texts) to our sessions, I used the following kinds of more open-ended questions to make her textual knowledge visible: What kinds of activities were these texts used for? What functions do these texts serve? How did you use these texts? How did you learn how to act with these texts? What other kinds of texts were used in conjunction with this text? Who else used these texts and for what purposes?

Over the next eighteen months, Terri and I conducted seven text-based reflective interviews, each lasting between one and one-half and two and one-half hours, which resulted in just over fifteen hours of video- and audiotaped data. The lengthy time span provided opportunities for the kinds of "longer conversations" and "cyclical dialogue around texts over a period of time" Teresa Lillis (2008, 362) identifies as crucial for understanding practice within the context of the participant's history. It was frequently the case that we delayed scheduling interviews in order to give Terri time to locate and retrieve materials she had stored in her home or in a storage space she rented close to her home. These reflective interviews centered on the wealth of texts she brought to the interviews or had sent me in advance; these included a variety of blank texts Terri used when interacting face to face with patients at their bedside, reports or forms of varying lengths that documented patient behavior, articles from medical journals, and protocols for stocking supplies or cleaning equipment—and some forms we discussed were those Terri had designed for use at the institutions where she was employed. As the text-based reflective interviews progressed, I found it useful to keep copies of the sample texts Terri provided from previous interviews on hand in my office in the event that she referred back to them during later interviews.

These formal practice- and activity-based interviews were supplemented with dozens of follow-up questions I developed while listening to and/or viewing the interview recordings, reading back through my notes, and examining texts Terri had brought to the interviews or had provided at other times. As with the two initial interviews, I emailed these follow-up questions to Terri after the formal interviews, and she responded via email or by placing handwritten responses in my campus mailbox. Her email responses usually arrived within the week and were printed and archived; her handwritten responses usually arrived within ten days and were also archived. I also supplemented practice- and activity-tracing interviews with dozens of informal conversations throughout the data-collection period when Terri happened to drop by my office or when we happened to talk when we ran into each other on campus. I kept notes on seven of these informal conversations, which occurred during chance meetings on campus or when Terri stopped by my office, and all information identifying Terri was removed from these data after they were collected. In total, I read approximately seven hundred pages of inscriptions (collected texts, key sections of transcripts of audio and video recordings of interviews, interview notes, and analytic notes) and listened to and viewed more than seventeen hours of audio and video recordings.

Terri's reflections on the texts she used during her nursing activities contained a wealth of references to how they mediated her perspective of her patients. For example, while reflecting on her use of what she referred to as a "flowsheet," a chart-like document that recorded the progression of an ICU patient's vital signs during ten-minute intervals, Terri stated,

> You learn how to do your assessment according to the [flow]sheet so that you do it in the same order and it's not difficult. . . . So you come in and your shift starts and you do an assessment and you assess the patient completely and you document it on the flowsheet: vital signs; if they had special equipment, all the readings from the equipment go on here; their intake and outputs; heart rhythm and what it looks like; if they had drains, tubes, it all goes on here. You've got your criteria neurological assessment down here and that gets documented up here as well. . . . So you put the date and the time, then you do level of consciousness, then you do orientation, and then you do Glasgow coma scale, like that.

Table 12.2. Data inscriptions from the case study with Terri

Type of data inscription	Number of pages
Transcripts of ten audio and/or videotaped interviews	137 pages
Sample texts collected	
• healthcare	212 pages
• poetry	35 pages
• autobiographical memoir	44 pages
• family video	30 minutes
• science-fiction novel	39 pages
• religious devotional	190 pages
• short stories	15 pages
Follow-up questions emailed to Terri	3 pages
Terri's emailed responses	10 pages
Notes from seven of our informal conversations	9 pages
My own analytic notes	27 pages

Terri's reflections about the flowsheet indicate her understanding of how this document offers a strictly medical perspective of the patient she is attending to. In addition to directing her vision and attention to features such as the patient's vital signs, level of consciousness, heart rhythm, and the readings from any monitoring equipment, the flowchart also suggests the order in which Terri needs to look at those features.

And yet, as our reflective interviews progressed, they also revealed Terri's tacit knowledge of the other kinds of texts that encouraged her to see the whole patient. Apparently, Terri's ability to see the whole patient was a product of acting with texts commonly associated with healthcare, such as the flowsheet, and of acting with texts that she created and completed for a wide range of other purposes. For example, while reflecting on the articles from medical journals she regularly located and read and on the kinds of tasks she used the knowledge from those articles to accomplish, Terri mentioned that in addition to informing her work in the intensive-care unit, information from those articles also found its way into what she referred to as her "cancer video," a video presentation she had created as a Christmas gift for members of her extended family based on some of the reading she did about cancer and with interviews she did of females in her family who had survived cancer. The video, as Terri described it, was "a blending" of what she had learned while doing research on cancer and "the life stories" of her mother and three of her mother's sisters. Reflecting further on how she created the video, Terri stated,

> I took photographs of them, and then I took their stories, I interviewed them, all four of them sitting around the table at my aunt's house talking about their different experiences with cancer. And so it [the video] was just them telling their stories, but specifically directed to, like, what will you tell your children? . . . What will you tell anybody else? You've been through this experience, what would you say to somebody else that may be facing it or that doesn't know, or whatever? So it's kind of that with the science that I know blended in using the Powerpoint slides, like, you know these are the risk factors. Like when aunt [name omitted] says, "well I found this knot," then there is a slide after that that says, you know, "most lumps are discovered by women during a self-exam." You know, just kind of a blending of the science that I know and their story.

In addition to the enormous amount of agency Terri demonstrates in arranging the slides and in giving advice to others, what strikes me so powerfully about Terri's reflection on the cancer video is how it essentially offers a view of her mother and aunts as "whole patients." The women represented in the video, then, are not merely cancer survivors but are also Terri's family members.

I am also struck by how Terri's understanding of her family members as patients, and of patients as family members, developed over time across multiple, seemingly disconnected composing activities, how it came into focus from her work at the intersections of multiple composing events. Essentially, Terri's knowledge of patients and of her work as a writer emerged from the enduring connections she forged across composing as a nurse and for members of her family. Perhaps the extended duration of Terri's integrative work accounts for the depth, detail, and eloquence with which she communicated this knowledge during our interviews. I also argue that Terri's response articulates the continuity she came to recognize between the literate self she composed as a nurse and the one she crafted as she composed videos for her family members. She is realizing, in other words, that her identity as a writer is woven from participation in both of these engagements rather than one or the other.

Successive reflective interviews with Terri would reveal even more of the tacit textual knowledge Terri brought to bear on her perspective of patients. When I asked Terri during a later interview if she could say more about the kind of "blending" she did in the cancer video, Terri offered as an example a number of poems she had written focused on the personal facets of the patients she had cared for while working as a nurse. Below, I include one such poem from a stack of fifteen Terri placed in my campus mailbox the following week. The poem is titled *Sonia*, after the patient of Terri's it describes.

> By the time I came
> speech had left you
> moaning at my touch,
> helping hands mauling,
> probing, insulting. Pieces of you
> assail me, photos
> of a dignified vibrant woman,
> vigorous, alive, amid
> images of Mother Teresa,
> Christ, children,
> and yet,
> I am your companion
> for death's vigil.

Reflecting on *Sonia* during our next interview, Terri stated that it was about a patient who had passed away on her shift at a convalescent home where she was working as a wound-care nurse. Terri stated that she was very taken by "those few framed photos strewn about [Sonia's] room with the intention of representing a life, rendering the comfort of familiarity, making a home" for Sonia during her stay in the nursing home where Terri was working at the time. Talking further about the poem, Terri stated,

> So you could take an incident report, or you could take the nursing notes, because it would have charted in the nurse's notes what explicitly was the condition that I found her in, and what her vital signs were and what not because she was a hospice patient so she was dying. We knew she was dying. So all I would have documented would have been her level of consciousness, her response, and her vital signs, her response to me, and then whether there was any family present or not. Those are the things that would have been appropriate to document in her chart. But, what I saw when I walked in the room was [that] this is a woman who had this rich life as depicted in the pictures around her bed.

Much like the cancer video, Terri's *Sonia* poem recognizes the whole patient. The poem offers a perspective of the patient as a woman with a "rich life," a perspective Terri notes is sadly lacking in the "incident report" or the "chart" or the "nursing notes," the official institutional genres that animate the work of healthcare.

This opportunity for constructive reflection creates a space for Terri to develop a perspective of Sonia, and of her patients more broadly, across the many forms of composing she participates in for her profession and as a poet. It also creates a space for Terri to consciously consider the affordances and constraints of various institutional genres she acts with both as a nurse and a poet and to voice her knowledge to herself and to me over the course of our interviews. As with her reflections on composing the cancer video for her family members, it also affords an opportunity for Terri to understand how she composes herself as a writer at the intersections of these multiple activities, that there is no textual space in which she is ever only a nurse or only a poet.

Terri's reflection on another of her poems, one titled *The Nurse's Prayer* that she wrote and distributed to the other nurses that worked in her unit, illuminates the tight linkage between her poetry and her work in the unit. Reflecting on writing the poem, Terri stated, "I gave it to the nurses who were working with me when I was Director of Nursing. So they got a Christmas present and it [the poem] was stuck down in there. . . . I would like give them silly stuff too, you know, like limericks on Valentine's Day or something. . . . This [the prayer] was probably the only 'serious' thing I gave them." I include Terri's *The Nurses Prayer* poem below.

> Help me remember as I start each day
> I've chosen to serve with my life in this way
> Help me to listen and comfort and care,
> Your perfected love, my actions to share.
> Help me to faithfully serve those you send,
> Those broken and twisted with your love to mend.
> Help me to see them through your loving eyes,
> To hear them and know how to quiet their cries.
> Help me remember, dear Lord, how to give,
> To be an example, to know how to live.
> Help me remember as I walk this road
> Your love has the strength to lighten each load

Reflecting on the poem and the functions it served her as a nurse, Terri indicated it was something that helped her to get through some of the emotional challenges of working in healthcare, stating "It would be in my desk. . . . I would look at it frequently, because sometimes the unit got pretty bad. But [also] sometimes when I would get extremely frustrated." Terri indicated that she had written it many years before she gave it to her nurses as a Christmas present. Elaborating, she stated,

> This was written in response to a particular discussion at LPN school, but it was written much later. The very first instructor I had in LPN school

was, she graduated from Vanderbilt and she was great. She was really smart and she was very compassionate, and she was very, she was a patient advocate, and that's where, I think, the big difference in my approach to patient care came from, was her insistence that you see that patient as a human being.

Here again, Terri's reflective comments reveal some of the tacit knowledge that informs her perspective of patients. What is also of interest with the *Nurse's Prayer* poem is how it is shaped by the compassion demonstrated by the instructor Terri encountered as a nursing student. As Terri indicates in her reflective response, her understanding of nursing as being primarily about serving as an effective patient advocate developed over time across multiple composing events, including a classroom discussion during one of her early LPN classes, her later work as a nurse, writing the *One Nurse's Prayer* poem, reading that poem to herself during challenging moments in the unit, sharing the poem with the other nurses she worked with, and likely others as well. Her reflective response also communicates Terri's developing understanding of how her multiple experiences with multiple kinds of texts over a lengthy span of time have contributed to her blended identity as nurse and poet.

WHAT EMERGES: WHAT REFLECTION TEACHES

In the final chapter of *Reflection in the Writing Classroom*, Yancey writes that "fragments and disconnects inhabit out daily lives every bit as much as the connects. Sometimes we can reconnect the disconnects, thread the fragments. Sometimes we can't. But identifying them is every bit as important as forging connections, sometimes more valuable because unless and until they are acknowledged, we rely on a detached and clean though ultimately false and much less human sense of: *what is*" (Yancey 1998, 194). What emerged from these reflective interviews was a sense that Terri's perspective of the whole patient was occasioned by the connections she had forged among seemingly disconnected texts. Some of those texts, of course, were those readily associated with patient care, like the flowchart Terri used while recording at a patient's bedside. Other texts, though, included texts such as the cancer video she created for her family members and the many poems she wrote about patients and her experiences as a nurse. Further reflective interviews with Terri revealed that in addition to the cancer video and her poetry, a number of other texts she regularly acted with also foregrounded a more personal view of patients. By the time our interviews had ended, Terri had revealed that she had acted with an extensive and variegated network of genres that reached across multiple composing events to blend medical perspectives of patients with more personal perspectives, including portions of a memoir she had been working on in fits and starts over the previous decade that described her friends and members of her family in terms of healthcare discourse. In one section of her memoir, for example, she writes about her best friend's dying in ICU while she was an ICU nurse. Terri also mentioned portions of a religious devotional she had written and published ten years before, which regularly included her experiences working in a trauma unit or emergency room in light of specific passages from the Bible. She also mentioned portions of a science-fiction novel she had been working on for some time about a surgeon who loses all perspective of his patients' humanity.

For Yancey, the ultimate value of reflection is that "it allows us to make sense" (Yancey 1998, 187), particularly in regard to writers' identities as literate persons in the world. This is particularly the case with what she terms as "constructive reflection," "the process of developing a cumulative, multi-selved, multi-voiced identity, which takes place between and among composing events" (200). The shift from interview questions that demanded knowledge already made toward reflective queries that invited knowledge in the making, from knowledge telling to knowledge generating, afforded multiple occasions for Terri and me to make sense of her literate life. For Terri, these interviews afforded her the chance to understand and articulate the close-knit relationship between her multiple literate engagements, between the "official" world of the professional healthcare workplace and the various "unofficial" worlds she inhabited. These occasions for reflection as rhetorical practice also provided her with a sense of how the literate activities that animate her work as a healthcare professional had come to texture her other textual engagements, and, in turn, how those other engagements had come to mediate her seeing and understanding of patients. Paul Prior acknowledges that "writers themselves are only partially aware of the many debts they owe to these intertextual and intercontextual influences" (Prior 2004, 171). My sense is that through this series of reflective interviews, Terri grew increasingly aware of the many debts she owed to her everyday literacies as a sources of agency and identity for her work as a nurse.

This series of reflective interviews also allowed me as the researcher to make sense of Terri's identity as a literate person in the world. As the interviews progressed, and as I immersed myself in her responses to my follow-up questions and read and reread the sample texts she provided, it became increasingly difficult for me to consider any single facet of her textual activity and identity without considering the others. Whereas initially I could imagine Terri as a nurse charting at a patient's bedside, what emerged from the reflective interviews productively complicated that scene. While I could still imagine Terri as a nurse acting with a flow-chart, that setting was also animated with and connected to a lengthy historical trajectory that reached through other texts that included the poems she'd written, the cancer video she'd created, the religious devo-tional she'd written and published, the memoir she'd been drafting, and the science-fiction novel she'd been drafting. There was, it seemed, no point at which Terri was only a nurse, only a creative writer, only a mem-ber of a family of cancer survivors, only a religious practitioner.

Ultimately, my sense is that our series of reflective interviews proved much more instructive to me as the researcher than they did for Terri. Prior to the interviews with Terri, I had spent a number of years study-ing the disciplinary writing and learning of students at multiple levels of higher education and how such activities were linked into their other lit-erate engagements. And yet, despite coming to understand disciplinary activities as being intimately connected to persons' everyday literacies, I initially failed to recognize Terri's writing as a healthcare professional in the same manner. Dominant representations of writing for the profes-sional workplace position it "worlds apart" (Dias et al. 1999, 223) from the writing students encounter in school and even farther removed from per-sons' more informal literacies. Terri's reflective revelations complicated the chronotopic scene of writing I had initially formed regarding Terri's seeing of patients. Without thinking about it or meaning to, I had initially understood Terri's seeing of patients as a product of her acting with the genres most readily associated with her work in a hospital. And yet, Terri's reflections of her cancer video, her poetry, and her many other literate activities forced me to look anew at my own tacit assumptions that Terri's seeing of patients was only facilitated by healthcare genres.

Odell, Goswami, and Herrington ask, "How can researchers get at the tacit knowledge of writers? What methodology will enable writers to make explicit the knowledge or strategies that previously may have been only implicit?" (Odell, Goswami, and Herrington 1983, 223). For writ-ing researchers such as Sondra Perl and Janet Emig through Paul Prior, Jody Shipka, and Kathleen Yancey, reflective interviewing has offered one productive approach to doing so. In addition to making explicit the wealth of tacit knowledge writers bring to bear on their literate activities, reflective interviewing can also productively challenge the dominant chronotopic representations of writing that powerfully inform research design and inquiry.

References

Brodkey, Linda. 1987. *Academic Writing as Social Practice.* Philadelphia, PA: Temple University Press.

Brandt, Deborah. 2001. *Literacy in American Lives.* Cambridge: Cambridge University Press. http://dx.doi.org/10.1017/CBO9780511810237.

Dias, Patrick, Anne Freedman, Peter Medway, and Anthony Pare. 1999. *Worlds Apart: Acting and Writing in Academic and Workplace Contexts.* Mahwah, NJ: Erlbaum.

Emig, Janet. 1971. *The Composing Processes of Twelfth Graders.* Urbana, IL: NCTE Press.

Flower, Linda, and John Hayes. 1981. "A Cognitive Process Theory of Writing." *College Composition and Communication* 32 (4): 365–87.

Lillis, Teresa. 2008. "Ethnography as Method, Methodology, and 'Deep-Theorizing': Closing the Gap between Text and Context in Academic Writing Research." *Written Communication* 25 (3): 353–88. http://dx.doi.org/10.1177/0741088308319229.

Odell, Lee, Dixie Goswami, and Anne Herrington. 1983. "The Discourse-Based Interview: A Procedure for Exploring the Tacit Knowledge of Writers in Nonacademic Settings." In *Research on Writing: Principles and Methods,* ed. Peter Mosenthal, Lynne Tamor, and Sean Walmsley, 221–36. New York: Longman.

Prior, Paul. 1998. *Writing/Disciplinarity: A Sociohistoric Account of Literate Activity in the Academy.* Mahwah, NJ: Erlbaum.

Prior, Paul. 2004. "Tracing Process: How Texts Come into Being." In *What Writing Does and How It Does It: An Introduction to Analyzing Texts and Textual Practices,* ed. Charles Bazerman and Paul Prior, 167–200. New York: Erlbaum.

Prior, Paul, and Jody Shipka. J. 2003. "Chronotopic Lamination: Tracing the Contours of Literate Activity. In *Writing Selves, Writing Societies,* ed. Charles Bazerman, and David Russell, 180–238. Fort Collins, CO: WAC Clearinghouse. http://wac.colostate.edu /books/selves_societies/.

Roozen, Kevin. 2009. "Fanfic-ing Graduate School: A Case Study Exploring the Interplay of Vernacular Literacies and Disciplinary Engagement." *Research in the Teaching of English* 44 (2): 136–69.

Roozen, Kevin. 2010. "Tracing Trajectories of Practice: Repurposing in One Student's Developing Disciplinary Writing Processes." *Written Communication* 27 (3): 318–54. http://dx.doi.org/10.1177/0741088310373529.

Shipka, Jody. 2011. *Toward a Composition Made Whole.* Pittsburgh: University of Pittsburgh Press

Witte, Stephen. 1992. "Context, Text, Intertext: Toward a Constructivist Semiotic of Writing." *Written Communication* 9 (2): 237–308. http://dx.doi.org/10.1177/0741088 392009002003.

Winsor, Dorothy. 1994. "Invention and Writing in Technical Work: Representing the Object." *Written Communication* 11 (2): 227–50. http://dx.doi.org/10.1177/07410883 94011002003.

Yancey, Kathleen Blake. 1998. *Reflection in the Writing Classroom.* Logan: Utah State University Press.

Yancey, Kathleen Blake. 2004. "Made Not Only in Words: Composition in a New Key." *College Composition and Communication* 56 (2): 297–328. http://dx.doi.org/10.2307 /4140651.

V

Reflection and Genre

13

PROBLEMATIZING REFLECTION
Conflicted Motives in the Writer's Memo

Jeff Sommers

Sometimes I think these memos help me as much as they help you.
    –Student comment on the Writer's Memo (Sommers)

INTRODUCTION: THE WRITER'S MEMO AS IDYLL

The Writer's Memo is a self-reflective communication from a student writer to an instructor that accompanies a submitted draft. I adapted and developed this concept (see Beaven 1977), and I subsequently published four articles on reflective memos in the 1980s. As we see in this volume and elsewhere, as Michael Neal suggests (this volume), the practice of reflection has grown fairly common in the teaching of composition in the days since then. Indeed, in recent years, *Teaching English in the Two-Year College* has published three pieces on reflective writing in first-year composition courses (Harding 2014; Ihara 2014; Parisi 2014). But more than one generation of students has come and gone since I began assigning reflective writing, so I have had the opportunity to reflect on the Writer's Memo. In this essay I want to problematize the genre of the Writer's Memo and examine how recognizing the problematic nature of the genre has necessitated changes in my teaching practice. The student comment in the essay's epigraph actually poses the question I want to tackle: just who is supposed to be "helped" by the Writer's Memo, the student-writer or the teacher-evaluator? That is an important complication, but I cannot claim to have been very cognizant of it in the early days of assigning the Writer's Memo.

Over the years, however, I have recognized that the Writer's Memo, or any similar reflective writing intended to accompany a draft, is an unfamiliar genre to students, one that requires an introduction. I have also realized that the Writer's Memo may in fact have conflicting motivations,

DOI: 10.7330/9781607325161.c013

both for me and for student writers: ostensibly, its purpose is to encourage students to become more aware of their composing processes and of the choices they have made and might make in the drafting and revising of a work in progress, based on the premise that a more self-aware writer can become a more effective writer. But there has always been an equally important additional motivation—the memos are intended to assist me in responding productively to the students' drafts so they can produce an improved final product. In short, I want my students to think about their thinking, but I also want them to take an active role in the response process, providing me with insights and questions so I can offer them more helpful feedback on their drafts. I plan to interrogate these multiple motivations out of my concern that the focus on response may in fact overwhelm the hope for metacognition by encouraging a reductive classroom dynamic of the student attempting to please the instructor that trumps the metacognitive activity of writing the memos. And these considerations no doubt make the Writer's Memo a more complex genre that I once believed.

Over the years of assigning students the Writer's Memo, I grew increasingly aware that its results were inconsistent. Recently, Lindsey Harding has expressed her related dissatisfaction with students' reflections, concluding her analysis of a number of end-of-term reflective essays by noting that they "seemed to lack metacognition" and blaming "an inadequacy in the assignment prompt itself to provide students with the opportunity to step back from their writing and think about the thinking they had done throughout the semester" (Harding 2014, 240). Laurel Bower has similarly critiqued portfolio cover letters, concluding that "because metacognition is a complex skill, . . . reflection should be integrated into the classroom from beginning to end, progressing from simple to more complex reflective problem-solving questions" (Bower 2003, 64), and in Rachel Ihara's analysis of portfolio cover letters, she observes that "the general movement in the field . . . seems to be away from a romanticized notion of reflection as something students should be able to do intuitively and on their own to an understanding of reflection as socially situated, dependent on particular ways of writing about writing that must be practiced and honed" (Ihara 2014, 223–24). These assessments are congruent with the argument advanced by Sarah Ash and Patti Clayton that add a "critical reflection process that generates, deepens, and documents learning does not occur automatically—rather, it must be carefully and intentionally designed" (Ash and Clayton 2009, 28). I must confess now that my earliest work on the Writer's Memo, in retrospect, does seem to present a somewhat "romanticized notion of reflection," as a review of my own published work on the Writer's Memo substantiates.

When I review those publications, designed to encourage others to adopt the strategy, I see a relatively idealized version of the memos being described. The language I used in writing about the memos is at once both assertive and definite, presenting a rather uncomplicated teaching strategy: "My job has become easier simply because I am listening . . . no tears, no threats, no shouts—just listening and communicating. The great mysteries about how my students manage to produce their papers also tend to dissolve if I listen to the . . . memos" (Sommers 1984, 30). Later in this same essay, I claimed that "one of the most important values of listening to students [is that] the more I listen, the more they 'talk'" (33). Apparently no scaffolding was needed to introduce students to reflection. I simply presented the concept once, assigned the questions, and watched the reflections proliferate. In retrospect, I think the novelty of the strategy, and my enthusiasm about sharing it with colleagues, resulted in a rather "romanticized" (Ihara 2014, 223) representation of this reflective activity. In reality, of course, not all students talked more, and not all memos were as revealing as I would have wished.

My later published work on the Writer's Memo continued to rely upon direct statements that admitted of no problems or complications. Note my use of the verb *compel*: "Questions about pre-writing, organizing, and projected re-writing compel each student to explore her composing process, a new experience for many students" (Sommers 1988, 78). Of course, I have since learned that the memo assignment does not *compel* students to explore their composing process so much as it *invites* them do so. Completing the assignment may take the students "behind the paper" (77), but it does not guarantee they will discover anything significant unless they believe the activity has value for them. But in those days I simply assumed my classes would recognize the memos' value once I had provided an explanation and assigned them. I also seemed oblivious to the competing motivations behind the memos and how they might make the students' task in writing them more challenging.

I persisted in later publications in avoiding any nuance at all in presenting the strategy. I made the argument that encouraging metacognition would lead students to develop their own voices and to write "reader-based prose," harking back to Linda Flower's research on the writing process (Flower 1981, 62). I discussed the kinds of questions I asked students to answer and described the impact of those questions, using the verb *compel* again to describe the power of the questions to induce reflection. Later I asserted that the students' metacognition "leads to discovery" (Sommers 1989, 180) rather than noting that it *might lead* to discovery. This definitive diction continued as I claimed that "in writing their memos, students *become* real writers writing to a real audience" (182; my emphasis) as if there were an automatic cause-effect relationship involved. The same confident tone appears a few pages later: "Since the memos vividly present the authentic voices of student writers, they invite the teacher to respond in his or her own authentic voice as a reader, editor, fellow writer. The interchange of purposeful comments between real people keeps the memos alive for both student and teacher, preventing them from becoming a dry, automatic activity akin to marking off boxes on some master checklist for revision" (184).

What I see myself doing here is describing the Writer's Memo in its ideal form: "Here's what it does when it works the way it's been designed to work." I recall being asked once by a participant at a workshop where I was presenting the Writer's Memo if the student examples I had presented were "typical." I was forthright in responding that I had selected really strong examples in order to convince the conference goers that the strategy was useful. Even then, I was well aware that not every Writer's Memo was equally insightful, but my 1989 essay was confident without qualification in the memos' effectiveness. In retrospect, the whole process seems positively idyllic.

CONFLICTING MOTIVES AND THE WRITER'S MEMO

But almost from its inception, the Writer's Memo had more than one intended function. Although I had not read Mary Beaven's work before I started assigning the Writer's Memo, when I subsequently read her article, I found it in a book devoted to evaluation and bearing a title that emphasized evaluation: "Individualized Goal Setting, Self-Evaluation, and Peer Evaluation" (Beaven 1977). One of my four 1980s publications about the memos was entitled "Enlisting the Writer's Participation in the Evaluation Process," making clear that whatever else they might do, Writer's Memos were intended to be a part of the teacher's response process. That essay focused primarily on how the memos could assist the instructor in responding. I wrote, "With the information provided by the student, the instructor need no longer be a 'dumb reader' [citing Walker Gibson]. The instructor becomes less likely to push the student into writing an essay the instructor wants instead of writing what the student wants" (Sommers 1985, 97), and a few pages later, I concluded that "the . . . memo allows instructors to ward off such comments [i.e., "I didn't know what you wanted"] by providing the insights necessary to offer useful commentary on student writing. Actually, as readers of student texts, writing instructors could just as often say to their students, 'I didn't know what you wanted me to respond to'" (102). The theme of memo as formative assessment tool has thus been present from the beginning of my work with reflection. I do not mean to suggest that there is anything wrong with asking students to participate in the formative evaluation of their own texts, but I do wonder how well asking students to focus on *my* response meshes with the idea of self-reflection about process and choices.

My early essays also employ language that focuses on the teacher's role as responder. Earlier I quoted this comment: "*My job* has become easier simply because I am listening" (Sommers 1984, 30; emphasis added). Other similar comments appear in my writing about the memos.

- "Students can be asked *to provide the instructor with needed assistance* in effectively responding to the draft" (1989, 176; emphasis added).
- "In short, the writer's memo *helps teachers to adopt a productive role as responders to* student writing" (180; emphasis added).
- "[Students] seek real results: *useful editorial comments from their reader*" (182; emphasis added).

I now see that the potential for conflict I am tracing was there from the outset. Initially, I named these reflections *Student-Teacher Memos*. One editor subsequently objected that the title suggested preservice teachers' writing notes during their student-teaching days, so I changed the name to *Writer's Memo*. The original label was intended to emphasize the transaction between student-writer and teacher-reader; the newer name makes the activity seem to be intended mostly for the writer alone, but the original name may actually be more accurate in its emphasis. Writer's Memos were never intended to be written by authors to themselves; they were never to be ruminations and insights of the sort kept in a writer's daybook. The very name *student-teacher memo* made clear that this writing assignment was to be a performance, a communication about a draft in progress between a writer and reader, not a writer to the self.

Where then is the conflict I have cited? Here is an excerpt from a student's memo about his personal observation of a high-school classroom discussion at his former high school; Mitchell, the student, is responding to this prompt: "What is the main focus of your draft? What is the most important thing you learned about the class you observed? Why?" Mitchell writes, "The point of my paper is to illustrate the fact that behavior is relative. Observing the class from an objective standpoint was really interesting because it made clear to me many of the points that [linguist Deborah] Tannen posits, especially those about quieter students. It also forced me to examine my own previous behavior in the class (Valery really reminded me of myself in that class), and try to figure out what it was that made me feel/ act in certain ways." As Mitchell explains that his interest was piqued as an observer when he recognized his own previous behavior in that same class, he is, I argue, engaged in metacognition, not only thinking about his observation as part of the invention phase of his project, but also reflecting on the causes of the observed student behavior, present and past, and thus perhaps gaining insight into his own writing experience in terms of generating ideas through observation and analysis. Later he concludes his memo by responding to another prompt asking him to pose questions for me as his responder. Mitchell writes, "Is my language consistently formal? Are any of my sentences awkward, and if so, where? Is the paper well structured, and do the subtitles effectively section the paper? If not, where, and what do you recommend?" In responding to the second prompt, Mitchell is no longer engaged, I contend, in reflection but instead is an author asking for feedback. Of course, that's a productive writerly behavior, but this behavior is not as much about reflection as it is about assessment, both by the student himself and subsequently by the teacher. What concerns me, then, is whether the Writer's Memo positions students in a much more complicated writing situation than it may seem at first glance. The question I am posing is, how compatible is helping the teacher with reflecting on one's own learning? I am troubled that the different purposes might at some point work against one another, reducing the possibilities that students will reflect in the way I hope they will because of interference from their understandable desire to produce an improved next draft, a draft that will please their evaluator.

A POTENTIAL RECONCILIATION

I believe Sarah Ash, Patti Clayton, and Maxine Atkinson's three-part model for effective reflection (Ash, Clayton, and Atkinson 2005) offers a reconciliation of the conflicting motives I have described. Their goal is to document learning in service-learning situations, and they begin by contending that "it is through careful reflection that service-learning—indeed any form of experiential education—generates meaningful learning" (50). I argue that first-year composition, too, is a form of "experiential education" in that students are asked to *do something by producing written artifacts*, whatever theoretical grounding may provide the course's curricular approach. Ash, Clayton, and Atkinson design a three-part reflection model that culminates in "articulated learnings" (51) or AL, as they call it. Their students regularly engage in "reflection sessions" designed to encourage them to describe their experiences and then to analyze them, using "a reflection framework, which is a series of questions designed to support students in *describing* (stage 1) and then *analyzing* (stage 2) their service experiences" (Ash, Clayton, and Atkinson 2005, 51). The goal of these sessions is to foster learning congruent with the course's stated learning objectives.

In stage 3, students are asked to consider four questions.

- What did I learn?
- How, specifically, did I learn it?
- Why does this learning matter? . . .
- In what ways will I use this learning? (Ash, Clayton, and Atkinson 2005, 51)

Answering these questions, Ash, Clayton, and Atkinson (2005) argue, leads to "articulated learning," the goal of the entire activity. These four questions are quite relevant to my deliberate use of the Writer's Memo: I would like my students to be able to articulate meaningful answers to these questions.

The Writer's Memo encourages both *describing* and *analyzing* through many of the questions it asks, as the emphasis on these two mental activities demonstrates in the following samples of Writer's Memo prompts (table 13.1).

Additional prompts ask the students to both describe *and* analyze: "What, specifically, did you change as a result of what you learned from our class workshop? What did you learn from reading the other rough drafts?" and the prompt to which Mitchell responded, "How did your observations of another class either surprise you or confirm your expectations? How was your reaction related to your own experiences in class discussions? In what ways did it resemble what you have experienced? In what ways was it different?"

Because the Writer's Memos are written in the heat of the moment, so to speak, while the composing is still in process, it seems to me unreasonable to expect students to manifest articulated learnings. The students are engaged at times in *describing* their writing processes and at other times in *analyzing* the shortcomings—and achievements—of their drafts in progress while keeping an eye on the future outcome of the drafting process. In other words, I think it unwise to expect the Writer's Memos themselves to lead the students through all three stages of the Ash, Clayton, and Atkinson model.

Table 13.1. Writer's Memo prompts and required mental activity

Description	Analysis
Describe how you went about analyzing the magazine issue you chose. What did you examine? Count? Notice? Question?	What was the biggest challenge in writing this draft? Why?
Describe how you decided on an effective organization for your paper. Why are the separate sections of the essay in this sequence?	Who is the ideal reader for your paper? If you could describe the kind of person who would get the most out of this paper, what would that person be like?
How did you select your pair of readings to synthesize in this assigned paper?	Have you done anything here to go beyond the ordinary on this paper?
Describe how you met the additional source requirement. How did you find a source? How did you evaluate that source to make sure it was reliable? What value did this additional perspective add to your draft? Why?	Remember that you are now part of the academic discourse community, and that will influence your writing decisions. Why did you choose this way to present your paper? (e.g., have you used subheadings or not? First-person writing or not?) What's the logic behind your organization—why are things in this order?

What is needed, I think, is a culminating activity that will afford the students an opportunity to reach the third stage in Ash, Clayton, and Atkinson's (2005) model: articulated learnings. So I now afford the students that opportunity in the redesigned portfolio letter I require at the end of the term.[1] The portfolio letter prompt reads in part: "Please write a letter in which you look back on your semester of writing in college. The point of writing this letter is to give you an opportunity to think about the writing you've done this term and reflect on its significance. I'd encourage you to write about what you're thinking currently that will be useful to you in the future as you look ahead to the rest of your career at West Chester." The encouragement to look ahead draws upon Ash, Clayton, and Atkinson's (2005) fourth question ("In what ways will I use this learning?"). I have argued that the Writer's Memos "create an ongoing semester-long conversation about their reflections on specific drafts, a conversation that forms a backdrop to the course experience for the students" (Sommers 2011, 60), so I am not surprised when students use their memos as a source for explaining in their final reflective assignments what they have experienced. In a recent semester, for example, 20 percent of my students referenced or quoted their own memos in their portfolio letter. One student wrote that the "writer's memos helped her to evaluate herself," and then related an anecdote about how she had come to see that at times she was articulating her ideas and arguments with more clarity and force in her memos, at which point she would substitute those reflections for "fuzzier phrasing in her drafts" (Sommers 2011, 72).

In passages such as this one, I can see that the student's *description* and *analysis* allow her to reflect upon her experiences. But I also see her *articulated learnings* in her recognition that what she wrote in her memos could inform her revision process. In addition, she seems to recognize the self-evaluation component in the memo writing, and it is also important to note that she never defers to the instructor's evaluation of her revision: she just asserts that she has replaced unclear writing with clear, forceful writing.

As illustrated in the previous example, the capstone reflective piece can provide evidence of articulated learnings through a student's reflections on the reflective nature of the Writer's Memos. In another capstone piece, a student, Ashleigh, claims she has learned a new appreciation for genuine revision and explains that

> the biggest reason for this adjustment would have to be the memos you assigned us to do. . . At first I assumed these memos were just more busy work attached to an already lengthy paper. Yet, once I started answering the questions, I began to see the point. The questions allowed me to understand what I was writing about. If I couldn't figure it out, how was the reader supposed to? In addition, sometimes when I answered these questions, I figured out a whole new point I didn't even realize I had made. It was a type of revising I had never heard or seen before. (Sommers 2011, 64)

In Ashleigh's commentary I can see that she has moved into the third stage of reflection by articulating what she has learned. In this case, the learning has been facilitated by the previous description and analysis she has employed in writing her memos, interestingly, in the service of revising—that is, improving—her draft. She seems to be experiencing no apparent tension between her need to reflect in the memos and her desire to improve a specific piece of writing.

Similarly, another student, Joyce, refers to the process of memo writing in her capstone piece, which she recognizes as a related reflective genre: "This entire letter is really just a memo in a letter's disguise, or a masked-meta-memo-cognitive piece of writing, if you will (cause I always will!). I am reflecting in writing about my thinking about my writing, all sandwiched between a salutation and closing. Only instead of one assignment that addresses the whole semester, I find that I have learned a great deal and had a great deal of fun doing it" (Sommers 2011, 63).

Joyce, in her playful way, demonstrates what she has learned about writing the memos, understanding the value of their metacognitive demands. Has she also demonstrated such learning in the memos themselves? Perhaps, perhaps not. The point she makes is that the reflections about her writing in which she engaged, even while perhaps focusing at times on the evaluation of her drafts, have been productive for her.

At this point, I accept that there is probably some tension caused by the design of the memos, setting up a potential conflict between questions that ask students to think about their writing process and questions that ask them to evaluate their own writing and, in a sense, focus on the impact it is likely to have on its evaluator, namely me. But perhaps that tension is not necessarily obstructive. The second motivation—improving the draft with the hope of raising its final grade—may fade away when the students take a retrospective look at their work as the term comes to a conclusion because the revisions are already complete. What may be left is the recollection of reflecting, of describing and analyzing their own writing processes, and that recollection can provide the students with evidence to substantiate their claims in their capstone reflections on the semester.

SCAFFOLDING THE WRITER'S MEMO

If the Writer's Memo, then, can serve both an immediate purpose as a student works on a specific writing project and a larger, semester-long purpose that will culminate in a richer portfolio letter, the question becomes one of how to prepare the students to write rich Writer's Memos worth rereading at the conclusion of the semester. Rachel Ihara (2014) suggests that an inadequate preparation for reflection may be the root cause of disappointing reflections, a point I now agree with: scaffolding is required to prepare students to write reflectively. In my own work on the Writer's Memo, I have always been aware that students require some preparation before making the best use of the opportunities afforded by the memos. Even my earliest presentations of the memos acknowledged the need for preparation; for example, I suggested that an analogue to the Writer's Memo is the consultation in which many writers engage by composing notes (or e-mails) to colleagues requesting feedback on a draft (Sommers 1989, 183–85). I provided a sample of a letter written by an author to her editor to illustrate how the Writer's Memo works (177), and I counseled that "two approaches . . . [that] . . . can stimulate students to write memos of substance are to write your own sample memos and to share provocative student memos with the class" (Sommers 1988, 79). Comments such as these, however, were hardly central in my publications at that time, nor in my classroom.

However, I have become much more strategic in my efforts to prepare my first-year composition students to write effective Writer's Memos (see Sommers 2011). I introduce the concept in the syllabus, and explain it more fully on the first assignment sheet for an essay in which they are to write about a memorable teacher. The description on the assignment sheet reads,

> Every time you submit a draft to me, I'll be asking you to complete a memo about that draft. I don't grade these, but I do expect you to complete them (it's part of earning credit for handing in a completed assignment on time.) Don't worry about your grammar/spelling, etc. You certainly shouldn't be writing a "rough draft" of a memo. Just free-write whatever comes to mind that answers the questions. Why am I asking you to do this? Is it just busy work? Actually, these memos can be very valuable in a couple of ways: To write a memo, you'll have to reflect on what you have written. Thinking about what we do after we do it is the beginning of self-awareness and self-evaluation. (That's why athletes watch game films and why performers watch videotaped performances.)
>
> • Rereading your own memos can help you remember what you were trying to do, which should be useful when you begin to revise your draft, particularly if you have to put work aside so that you can meet your other course obligations. When you return to the draft, the memo is a good place to start.
>
> • Sometimes writing answers to the memo questions actually generates information and ideas you can use in your draft.
>
> • The memos are very helpful to your readers (such as me or tutors at the writing center) because they provide background information. I know that I often feel lost in knowing how to respond to a student draft until I read the memo. Write a full page (250 words). If you only jot down a quick one-sentence answer, you don't get much exercise in reflecting on your own writing. (Short memos are like aerobic workouts that end as soon as you begin to sweat! There's no gain in that.)

Note that the multiple motivations I have analyzed are present here: the first three bullets emphasize the value for the student of the Writer's Memo, and the final bullet shifts to its value for readers (and/or, implicitly, evaluators).

I devote a full class meeting to a discussion of metacognition, scheduling the class for the day before the drafts and memos are due. I begin by projecting the word *metacognition* on the classroom screen along with this definition: "Awareness and understanding of one's own thought processes; thinking about thinking." At that point I ask the class a series of questions and request that they raise their hands and keep them aloft if they have had an athletic coach or drama teacher or music teacher or band director who has worked with them on developing a particular performance. I then ask how many have watched a recording of their performance and why. The students generally have much to say about the role of reflection in their various activities. That discussion leads to my sharing of Pat Belanoff's comment:

Am I saying that everyone needs to reflect to be educated? Yes, in a way I am—but at the same time I recognize that there are many ways to reflect. Watching a video together of a prior game can provide members of a football team the opportunity to integrate what they see into what's already stored in their heads. . . . Gymnasts study digital models of themselves in action created from videos, reflect on those, and work with their bodies to produce better configurations of their bodies in action. Certain diet plans require participants to keep a list of everything they eat during the day in order to create a record of their eating habits, which they can reflect upon and alter if necessary. Therapists ask patients to reconstruct past experiences and thoughts so they can be reflected on; reflection and discussion (in theory at least) lead to an improved sense of the self and one's relationship to others and to the environment. This (in theory) leads to improved performance and satisfaction. (Belanoff 2001, 416)

The class then engages in a discussion of their own prior experiences with reflection before we turn to an examination of a series of documents as I share a number of student memos with them so we can discuss their strengths and weaknesses. Then I share this excerpt from Barbara's memo, in which she answers a question about her current impressions of her draft: "This draft is not my most creative work, and I am not particularly proud of it. I really struggled to think of some substantial info without any type of primary source. This writing is very different from what I am accustomed to. I think it lacks creativity and is pretty boring. I guess that sounds strange—why wouldn't I just fix it? Well I suppose it has been a struggle to fix since I did not have much substance to begin with—I am really used to structured writing. Reading a novel, and then answering analytical questions about the characters or themes (i.e., *Heart of Darkness*—compare Kurtz and Marlow)." I ask the students why they think Barbara would confess to being so displeased with her own draft. Someone invariably points out that the memo is accompanying a draft, not a final paper to be graded, so the student is not risking her grade by being forthright about the paper's inadequacies. We note the different kinds of reflection Barbara has engaged in:

- She seeks an explanation for her own self-assessment.
- She looks back at her prior experiences as a writer.
- She poses a question for herself to answer.

We also examine reflective pieces written by professors, as I try to make the point that the Writer's Memo is not busy work I am foisting on them, but rather resembles the kind of reflection professional writers employ. I show the students two letters I received from a professor whose manuscript I was evaluating for *Teaching English in the Two-Year*

College, the journal I edit for NCTE.[2] In her letters, the professor writes about her revision process and uses sentences such as, "Overall, in this revision, I have tried to accomplish several tasks" and "As I have worked on this essay, I have felt a struggle between the pieces of data." She describes additions she has made to the text and language she either changed or excised. I also show them a two-paragraph e-mail I received from another writer in which she analyzes her attempts to respond to reviewers' critiques. This author concludes by writing, "OK, that's my memo to you." Even though it's an e-mail, her description of it as a "memo" seems to resonate with my students.

Finally, I share some reflective writing of my own. I explain that I had drafted a proposal to teach a seminar, and, being new to the university, I e-mailed it to a senior colleague with a note appended. My e-mail read, "My primary concern is whether I'm presenting the reading list in a suitable manner, and if it looks as if it will pass muster (it's rather eclectic, I'd say)." I then explain to the class that I realized how little my memo had revealed about my experience in writing the piece, so I revised it to read

> I've included more than the ten readings required because I don't think my list is perhaps what's expected. Some of the citations are from composition scholars, not literary critics. In fact, there's a pedagogical angle to some of them. I've also included two citations for articles of my own. I was thinking that I wanted to present readings that have impacted my teaching plans for the course. So here's my key question to you: how smart a strategy is that? I could replace some of the more pedagogical references with traditional literary critical material; that might make the list look more like other proposals. But my course is focused less on a literary genre or time period than it is on a way of teaching. What recommendations do you have about my reading list?

I am trying to make the point to the class that reflecting on one's writing has real value, sometimes assisting writers with invention and at other times providing insight into potential revisions. These examples by academic authors and me are focused both on describing and analyzing our own writing process and on eliciting useful feedback from a reader.

To conclude the class, I ask the students to write a brief anonymous comment on an index card I provide. I pose this question: "If a classmate who missed today's class were to ask you what it was important to know about the class session, what would you say?" I read through these and share a sampling at the next class, after which their first drafts and memos are due. I make sure to include at least one comment that is less than a full endorsement of the memos because there are always a few of those. Some representative comments include

- I learned that the memos are very crucial to making you a better writer. They allow you to see your strengths and weaknesses. It allows you to ask questions and get specific answers. Also these questions will help you for your writing in the future.
- Today in class I learned the real purpose of a memo. Before I thought that it was just busy work, but now I feel differently. I think it's a good way of asking essential questions that you really want to know the answer to.
- I feel like to be a serious, accomplished, and goal-oriented writer, I should take the memo more seriously and get used to including it on my own. I liked that you shared personal examples.
- I got that the memo is actually a really important part of the writing process and even though I already completed my memo, I thought of some things I would like to add to it.
- During this class we went over different examples of the types of things we should include in our memo. It was helpful to hear this because I had never written one before. However, the process was a bit tedious.

I note that the first two of the student commentaries focus on the memo prompt that invites them to participate in evaluating their drafts, which seems entirely understandable from a student perspective. Some students may focus on the evaluative aspects of the memo, but as long as they are answering all of the Writer's Memo prompts, they are engaging in the designed descriptive and analytical activities.

With about a month left in the course, I devote another day to the Writer's Memo, this time sharing some of the outstandingly detailed memos I have received from their class (with the students' permission, of course) by projecting them on the classroom screen and highlighting insightful moments in the memos. Throughout the term, I stipulate that only memos of at least 250 words earn credit for completion, but the most insightful ones are often much longer, and showing a few of them in class can remind everyone that I expect a serious effort at reflection in the memos. I have been pleased with the effects of these more focused efforts to prepare students to write useful Writer's Memos and to motivate them to continue to do so as the weeks go on. The additional scaffolding thus attempts to deromanticize the act of reflection by situating varied forms of reflection in different contexts and by showing that metacognition requires effort more than inspiration.

All of this preparatory work is designed to convince students that the metacognitive act will be useful to them as writers. When Susan Jarratt et al. recommend that "writing teachers might place more emphasis on preparing for learning, a manner of learning that acknowledges students' pasts . . . and gestures toward their writing futures" (Jarratt et al.

2009, 66), they are echoing the structured questions of Ash, Clayton, and Atkinson's (2005) articulated learnings strategy. Perhaps reflecting on one's thinking and asking a reader for help do conflict in the immediate context of writing a single Writer's Memo. Taking a longer view, however, I think the value of engaging in these regular acts of description and analysis constitutes preparation for learning and is worth any potential dissonance experienced by the student. The memo is something of a hybrid genre, serving multiple purposes at the time of writing. Because I am primarily interested in the students' progress toward articulated learnings, in Ash, Clayton, and Atkinson's (2005) phrase, I can live with the hybridity and the discomfort it might engender because of the rich sources of ideas and thinking that the memos can provide as the students write their culminating portfolio letters. In their study of transfer, Jarratt et al. cite one of their interview subjects as saying, "'I think every time I sat down to write a paper, I was thinking about what I learned the last time I sat down to write a paper'" (2009, 58). When students complete a Writer's Memo with every draft, they create a record of their experiences as writers in the course so that at the end of the term when they are asked to think about what they have learned, there is a valuable written record available to them.

CONCLUSION

In the prospectus for this collection, the editor has articulated three purposes for the book:

- to locate our observations about and research on reflection in very specific definitions
- to provide varying portraits of how we have designed reflection into curriculum and/or assessment and to what effect
- to raise the questions regarding reflection that should be researched

As I have written this essay, I have learned that my own definition of reflection in my first-year writing course has become more expansive in that it has grown clearer to me that the in-semester reflection required by the Writer's Memo is different from the end-of-semester reflection required by the capstone reflective letter I assign. The competing motivations of reflecting on their own experiences while also assessing their writing and seeking advice for improvement that define writing the memos seem potentially resolvable as students compose their final reflective pieces because those capstone pieces are, in fact, *final* drafts in a way that the Writer's Memos are not.

As for the book's second purpose, I think Rachel Ihara makes a very wise observation when she writes, "I do not think it makes sense to try to make students more 'reflective,' as if reflection were a singular thing. Nor would I suggest that we promote only one privileged view of self-reflection, whereby the instructor's particular aims and expectations for reflective writing, as evidence-based and thesis-driven, are reiterated and reinforced until students master this particular stance and approach. Instead, I would highlight the *different* ways one might write about writing, in different situations for different purposes and audiences" (Ihara 2014, 234). Those different ways might include Lindsey Harding's (2014) strategy of asking for a multimodal reflective response as a culminating project, or Hope Parisi's (2014) opening the final portfolio letter up to alternate audiences so students do not have to write directly to the instructor, or, perhaps, strategies offered in other pieces in this collection. My essay has attempted to present a narrative of a developing model for presenting reflection to my students, a narrative that has stretched nearly three decades and that continues to develop in response to my own greater understanding of what is happening in my classroom.

Finally, this collection's third purpose seems clear to me in terms of what I have written here. I need to learn more about my students' perception of the Writer's Memo as an assignment. What do they come to believe is its purpose? What considerations do they take into account as they write them? What conflicts do they experience as they compose the Writer's Memo? Rather than asking the students to write more reflections on the writing of the memos, I might employ Ihara's (2014) research methodology, I believe, and interview the students after they have completed the memos. Perhaps a think-aloud protocol would also be useful as students read their own memos and explain what they were thinking. The point, however, would be to learn more about what happens when reflection takes place in the rhetorical situation of the classroom because it has been assigned rather than engaged in voluntarily, as illustrated in the examples by professional writers I have shared with the students.

What I have learned is that the Writer's Memo may not *compel* the kind of reflection I value, but it serves as an affordance to engage in that kind of meaningful reflection. I have realized that the Writer's Memo is not a simple, straightforward assignment but may have its own internal conflicts students must learn to negotiate. Finally, I have learned that although I cannot legislate students' growth as writers just by assigning the Writer's Memo, I can continue to monitor the impact of the Writer's Memo and strive for better ways to prepare my students to take advantage of those multiple opportunities the Writer's Memo provides.

Notes

1.   This genre of reflection is both similar to and somewhat different from Kathleen Blake Yancey's (1998) reflection-in-presentation, both as explained in her *Reflection in the Writing Classroom* and as adapted for the Teaching for Transfer (TFT) composition curriculum: see Kara Taczak and Liane Robertson, this volume.

2.   The author was quite willing to grant me permission to share the letters.

References

Ash, Sarah L., and Patti H. Clayton. 2009. "Generating, Deepening, and Documenting Learning: The Power of Critical Reflection in Applied Learning." *Journal of Applied Learning in Higher Education* 1 (Fall): 25–48.

Ash, Sarah, Patti H. Clayton, and Maxine P. Atkinson. 2005. "Integrating Reflection and Assessment to Capture and Improve Student Learning." *Michigan Journal of Community Service Learning* 11 (Spring): 49–60.

Beaven, Mary H. 1977. "Individualized Goal Setting, Self-Evaluation, and Peer Evaluation." In *Evaluating Writing*, ed. Charles Cooper and Lee Odell, 135–53. Urbana, IL: NCTE.

Belanoff, Pat. 2001. "Reflection, Literacy, Learning, and Teaching." *College Composition and Communication* 52 (3): 399. http://dx.doi.org/10.2307/358625.

Bower, Laurel. 2003. "Student Reflection and Critical Thinking: A Rhetorical Analysis of 88 Portfolio Cover Letters." *Journal of Basic Writing* 22 (2): 47–66.

Flower, Linda S. 1981. "Revising Writing-Based Prose." *Journal of Basic Writing* 3 (3): 62–74.

Harding, Lindsey. 2014. "Writing Beyond the Page: Reflective Essay as Box Composition." *Teaching English in the Two-Year College* 41 (3): 239–54.

Ihara, Rachel. 2014. "Student Perspectives on Self-Assessment: Insights and Implications." *Teaching English in the Two-Year College* 41 (3): 223–38.

Jarratt, Susan C., Katherine Mack, Alexandra Sartor, and Shevaun E. Watson. 2009. "Pedagogical Memory: Writing, Mapping, Translating." *WPA: Writing Program Administration* 33 (112): 46–73.

Parisi, Hope. 2014. "Portfolio Reflective Writing and the Quandary of Disclosure: Toward a Dialogic Alternative for Basic Writers." *Teaching English in the Two-Year College* 42 (1): 7–26.

Sommers, Jeffrey. 1984. "Listening to Our Students: The Student-Teacher Memo." *Teaching English in the Two-Year College* 11 (1): 29–34.

Sommers, Jeffrey. 1985. "Enlisting the Writer's Participation in the Evaluation Process." *Journal of Teaching Writing* 4 (2): 95–103.

Sommers, Jeffrey. 1988. "'Behind the Paper': Using the Student-Teacher Memo." *College Composition and Communication* 39 (1): 77–80. http://dx.doi.org/10.2307/357824.

Sommers, Jeffrey. 1989. "The Writer's Memo: Collaboration, Response, and Development." In *Responding to Student Writing: Models, Methods, and Curricular Change*, ed. Chris M. Anson, 174–86. Urbana, IL: NCTE.

Sommers, Jeffrey. 2011. "Reflection Revisited: The Class Collage." *Journal of Basic Writing* 30 (1): 50–80.

Yancey, Kathleen Blake. 1998. *Reflection in the Writing Classroom.* Logan: Utah State University Press.

14

REFLECTION AND THE ESSAY

Doug Hesse

In their preface to a recent anthology, Carl Klaus and Ned Stuckey-French observe that "essayists themselves have not been reticent about the nature, form, and purpose of the essay, reflecting on it in columns, prefaces, introductions, letters, and reviews, as well as in essays on the essay and occasionally in book-length works about it" (Klaus and Stuckey-French 2012, xi). More than other genres, the essay embraces reflection, using it generatively in a way essential to its method and character, to the extent that in 1929, Hellaire Belloc (1955) waggishly published "An Essay Upon Essays Upon Essays." The eagerness of essayists to explain their genre simply manifests, in a broader frame, what they're doing as they practice it.

To be clear, I'm referring here not to the welter of short nonfictions that casually get designated as essays, chief among them school performances. Instead I'm pointing to the tradition from Montaigne through Addison, Lamb, Thoreau, Woolfe, Orwell, Dillard, Didion, and Wallace. I'm pointing to works that contrast sharply with such more "conventional and systematized forms of writing" (Klaus 2012, xv) as the article, the treatise, the report, the scholarly paper—works like this chapter, perhaps. In contrast to them, essays are "antimethodological," taking shape not from prefabbed structures but from ideas and experiences "organically" arising on the spot. They demonstrate "impressionistic rather than definitive thought" (Klaus, 2012, xvii), revealing truth not as it *is* but, rather, as it *seems* to a particular writer, who is crucially present in the work, either as a character/actor of narrated events or as a distinct voice or persona (Klaus, 2012, xxiv). Edward Hoaglund's precise formulation that "essays . . . hang somewhere on a line between two sturdy poles: this is what I think, and this is what I am" (Hoaglund 1976, 35) conveys this most precisely. In terms of reflection, the important consequence is that essays trace thinking as it occurs, the "display of a mind engaging ideas (Klaus, 2012, xxiii). Scott Russell Sanders puts it this way:

DOI: 10.7330/9781607325161.c014

The writing of an essay is like finding one's way through a forest without being quite sure what game you are chasing, what landmark you are seeking. You sniff down one path until some heady smell tugs you in a new direction, and then off you go, dodging and circling, lured on by the songs of unfamiliar birds, puzzled by the tracks of strange beasts, leaping from stone to stone across rivers, barking up one tree after another. Much of the pleasure in writing an essay—and, when the writing is any good, the pleasure in reading it—comes from this dodging and leaping, this movement of the mind. (Sanders 1988, 662)

REFLECTION EMBEDDED

Where does reflection come in? Essayists prominently mark these movements of mind by calling them out, ostensibly to themselves, but of course also in ways we overhear. A close look at how this happens in a contemporary work illustrates the strategy. Lia Purpura's (2011) "Jump" starts with a double mystery. One concerns a sign: "Last Death from Jumping or Diving from Bridge, June 15, 1995." What happened, at what bridge, where? The other concerns how the author came across the sign and why it matters to her and, ultimately, to us. In a familiar plot-thickening strategy, Purpura deploys the *fabula* of what happened in a disjointed *sujet*. Four paragraphs in, we learn that the location is Iowa City and that the essay's narrative present is 2007, twelve years after. Only six pages later do we have the facts: a newspaper story from the *Daily Iowan*, June 16, 1995, recounts a group of students hanging out, one diving into the river only to drown, his friends unable to help. If you're me, or a reader with my background, you know the *Daily Iowan* as the University of Iowa student newspaper. Further, if you've spent your undergraduate days four times a week crossing the Iowa River to music rehearsals, you recognize from the description of a beat-up dock and limestone boathouse that this is the Hancher footbridge. (If you're not like me, a few layers of mystery remain, though with Purpura's clues you could research if you cared.) Interposed between sign and solution are speculations and digressions, including a climb up 275 steps of a Cape May lighthouse. She knows, of course, from sentence one what happened; she just can't let us know.

The bigger mystery, of course, is why any of this matters, especially when the plain answer is, it really doesn't. Rather, the essayist's gift—or task, or indulgence, or delight—is to make something of the unremarkable by dint of extension and reflection. Guillermo Diaz-Plaja notes that "an essayist is produced when the period of acquiring information is allowed to develop into a personal understanding. Like wine left in a cask to acquire its appropriate character, the essay is the product of a long distillation of mental juices. It is the result of data received then analyzed at length from the sovereign vantage of a thinker" (Diaz-Plaja 2012, 99). The essayist, though, narrates the distillation. In her case, Purpura (2011) tells how she left her first view of the sign four months in the cask of memory, all that time "thinking it over, trying to figure out how to read the thing, trying to locate what's been lost and unsaid" (91). After all,

> Without a story, the fragments won't settle.
> Possibilities crowd in and distract.
> . . . .
> Conclusions assert.
> Stances take root. (87)

Throughout the piece, Purpura reflects on her attraction and motivation, on why the sign's ambiguity compels her. Partly, it's because falling from a bridge invokes her own fear of heights, which she documents by narrating her unwillingness, a year earlier, to join her husband and son on the deck of a lighthouse. But it's not completely some personal phobia. An insistent reflective urge, marked throughout the piece by questions, drives her on: "Why must I consider this daily" (Purpura 2011, 89)? Like most essays, "Jump" retains these plentiful reflective markers, the so what's and whys and what does it means, the partial answers found wanting but nonetheless useful for their incompleteness. They're heuristic but also structural to the piece itself, sort of like architect's sketches visibly laminated into trusses.

"Jump" performs the two countervailing dynamics of the essay: the extensive and the reflective. The extensive dynamic works by bringing as much as possible into the text through narrative—as when Purpura comes across the sign or climbs the lighthouse—and through association—as when she connects experiences in different places and times (in Iowa City twelve years apart and in Baltimore) with readings and interviews. Essayists often make the associative moves via a thin reflective bridge ("This got me thinking about the time" or "this reminds me of"), but essayists have also done so paratactically, as E.B. White (1944) does in a piece like "Spring," its twelve short isolated sections from 1941 wandering among a Superman marketing campaign, his tending a brooder stove for chicks, and the Nazi attack on the Balkans.

Complementing extension is interpretation and reflection, the essayist having reported something and now having to tell herself and her readers what it might mean. Purpura does this, for example, when she notes that the mysterious sign ("Last Death from Jumping or Diving from Bridge, June 15, 1995") could just as well be taken as celebratory (look how long we've kept safe!) as cautionary (so watch it!). Essays give the act of interpretation explicit attention through reflection; that is, they narrate the essayist's weighing possible meanings, letting readers behind the curtain of possible thought. The result is that "Jump," like many essays, is ultimately about the act of writing itself. For Purpura, the challenge is not simply figuring out what happened twelve years ago on the bridge, but also figuring out her own reaction and, finally, shaping event and idea into a text worth caring about. She does this through reflective moments that simultaneously undercut and impel. She declares, "I don't know why" (Purpura 2011, 89). Or, "All this time I've been thinking it over, trying to figure out how to read the thing" (91). Or, "The moments I've offered here, moments constituting this piece (my own foray into jumping), also remain ill-marked" (94). In the end, Purpura's self-evaluative reflection constitutes a sort of preemptive defense against critique. Commenting on all the remaining gaps in a piece "still largely unfurled," she declares, " You can stand before it and read, such a sign (memento mori-like, as in 'there is much work to do, Lia, keep at it') as I could come up with, here, Baltimore, MD, June 21, 2007, and I'd not be completely ashamed" (94). This gambit invites us to reflect.

Reflection overtly figures the author as the source of idea or speculation. This can take a couple of forms. One strategy is to give a comment a specific place within the narrative, presenting it as occurring at a particular time. An example is George Orwell's famous realization in "Shooting an Elephant" right before he pulls the trigger to kill an animal he knows doesn't need to die: "I perceived in this moment that when the white man turns tyrant it is his own freedom that he destroys" (Orwell 1946, 152). A second strategy is for writers to comment on themselves, often about their processes and decisions, often about the limitations of their insights or skills or even their writerly abilities. Montaigne's personal medallion asking "What do I know?" establishes this stance from the outset. Essayists weave comments overtly into their pieces, almost as if muttering to themselves, in a manner often reassuring in its diffidence.

For example, in "The Death of the Moth," Virginia Woolf narrates "a pleasant morning, mid-September, mild, benignant" writing at her desk by a window (Woolf 1992, 308). She watches a moth dancing at the glass, then settling on the ledge, and then, "It flashed upon me that he was in difficulties; he could no longer raise himself," and while she tries to help with her pencil, she realizes "nothing, I knew had any chance against death." The small drama, a "triumph of so great a force over so mean an antagonist filled me with wonder" (309). That wonder, of course, presented as reflection, is the impetus of the essay; without it, it might be published as a narrative sketch—but likely not.

E.B. White's essay "The Ring of Time" narrates a visit in March 1956 to a Florida circus grounds. A small crowd watches a rider practice tricks in a dusty ring, a barefoot girl of sixteen or seventeen swinging on and off a cantering horse, balancing, standing, kneeling. White is mesmerized by the nonchalant performance, which he describes in great detail, but the essay acquires depth—and becomes an essay—through reflection. He notes, "I became painfully conscious of the element of time" (White 1992, 181). Ostensibly, it's for the girl, who is "'at that enviable moment in life [I thought] when she believes she can go once around the ring, make one complete circuit, and at the end be exactly the same age as at the start,'" though White recognizes that "she was too young to realize that time does not really move in a circle at all" (182). His use of quotation marks and the bracketed insertion of "I thought" insist that he's exactly reporting a realization that occurred in that moment. The line between reflection and interpretation is dusty, but here it's marked by the explicit reference to the narrator's consciousness.

The crucial reflective move comes as he thinks not only about the girl's performance, but also about himself as watcher: "It has been ambitious and plucky of me to attempt to describe what is indescribable, and I have failed, as I knew I would. But I have discharged my duty to my society; and besides, a writer, like an acrobat, must occasionally try a stunt that is too much for him" (White 1992, 182). There's some preemptive false modesty in this comment, which claims ambition but confesses failure. But the real punch comes with White's casually conjoining writer and acrobat, writing and stunt making. After all, his plaintive pangs stem less from the girl's failure to appreciate how time is slipping away than from his own too-clear grasp of that very truth. As readers, we stand in the same relationship to this text, whose ring of words we can no more read precisely the same way twice than the sixteen-year-old performer can retrace each passing life moment.

One more example of how reflection turns article or account into essay: David Foster Wallace's "Consider the Lobster." *Gourmet* magazine had commissioned him to write a piece about the Maine Lobster Festival. Undoubtedly familiar with what Wallace had to say about the Illinois State Fair (Wallace 1997b) and a Celebrity Cruise (Wallace 1997a), the editor bargained for something other than a straightforward account—though almost not as much as they got. In the process of describing foods and festivities, Wallace is pulled to the problem of boiling lobsters alive. The matter takes him through fact finding (learning, for example, that it takes thirty-five to forty-five seconds for lobsters to die in boiling water), to philosophical questions (how does one determine if lobsters feel pain?), to ethical issues (what should he and readers do with any of this?). Each idea triggers another, often with a commentary. For example, at one point he reflects,

> I'm not trying to give you a PETA-like screed here—at least I don't think so. I'm trying, rather, to work out and articulate some of the troubling questions that arise amide all the laughter and saltation and community pride of the Maine Lobster Festival. The truth is that if you, the festival attendee, permit yourself to think that lobsters can suffer and would rather not, the MLF begins to take on the aspect of something like a Roman circus or medieval torture-fest. (Wallace 2006, 253)

Here and elsewhere, Wallace remarks on his writing process, seeming to check himself ("at least I don't think so") by naming what he's up to. Commenting on the term *torture-fest*, he asks, "Does that comparison seem a bit much? If so, exactly why" (Wallace 2006, 253)? The question is ostensibly posed to his readers, but it functions as much as a writerly heuristic, a way of plunging further. He acknowledges his own complicity as a meat eater, stating, "I'm . . . concerned not to come off as shrill or preachy when what I really am is more like confused" (253). These reflective statements display the genre's compact to generate tentative truths, the essayist's identity as explorer and confidant figuring things out as he goes, with modesty and deference. Of course, Wallace is ultimately assertive, even acerbic, but his method is to put readers in cold water and slowly bring us to a boil.

REFLECTION CONJOINED

In 2009, then-editor of *Fourth Genre* Marcia Aldrich announced a new feature of the magazine: "We readers want to know how the writers of nonfiction came to their material, how they felt a way through the experiential thicket, what artistic thing has been shaped from facts, feelings, thoughts, and anecdotes. To that end you will find in this issue the second in our new 'Essay and Self Reflections' series" (Aldrich 2009, x). Its first issue published in 1999, *Fourth Genre* was founded as a "literary journal devoted solely to works of contemporary nonfiction, extending from the personal essay—including nature, environmental, and travel writing—to memoir, literary journalism, and personal cultural criticism"

(Steinberg 1999, v). Founding editor Michael Steinberg invited works whose writers spoke "in a singular voice, as active participants in their own experience" in pieces that by turns might be "lyrical, expository, meditative, informational, reflective, self-interrogative, exploratory, analytical, and/or whimsical" (v). He emphasized the journal's intent "to emphasize the personal, autobiographical, and 'literary' impulses (discovery, exploration, reflection) that generate the kind of writing we call the 'fourth genre'" (vi).

From the outset, *Fourth Genre* published both examples of these writings and also works about them, not only reviews and interviews but also "roundtables," discussions among several writers about matters of craft, identity, status, and form. The first few issues, for example, featured roundtables on "Literal versus Invented Truth in Memoir" (1.1), "What Is Creative Nonfiction? Two Views" (2.1), "Character in Nonfiction" (3.1), and "The Art of the Personal Essay" (3.2). Ten years later, then, in announcing the Essay and Self Reflections series, Aldrich simply took these "works about" nonfiction a step further, inviting authors fully and separately to reflect on a short work they'd just published.

From the outset, the distinction in this feature between *essay* and *reflection* has been less pure than one might expect. While the original essay provides a pretext or occasion for the second piece, in practice the authors have pursued the latter fairly much either as continuations of the original or as self-standing pieces. Consider one of the first pairs, by Joy Castro, "Grip" (2009b) and "Getting Grip" (2009a). The former is a laconic essay in five shards of less than four hundred words total: a shot-up target hung above a baby crib, a vengeful stepfather out of prison, a mother who survived. The latter is five times as a long and divided into headings: Genre, Audience, Submerged, Synecdoche, Title, POV, Form, Patience. (Castro reflectively jokes, "It's funny to me that this essay is longer than 'Grip' itself" (Castro 2009a, 126).) Some of the headings correspond to the categories that arise in most every Q&A following an author's reading. In them Castro talks about process: how she revised "Grip" from poem to essay, how she incorporated the editor's suggestion to tell readers about her mother's fate.

But other headings clearly promise something else, and in part what they deliver is new material. Synecdoche begins, "My stepfather's sexual abuse of me has caused long-lasting damage, but I didn't want to go into all that in 'Grip.'" It explains that the part of the target hidden behind crib slats "stood in for my stepfather's abusive sexuality. It functioned as a synecdoche for all of it" (Castro 2009a, 124). There's no way a reader can pick that up from the piece itself, which suggests violence but nothing like sexual abuse. Castro concludes this section by reflecting that "my psyche accepted that line [not mentioning the abuse] as a reasonable compromise. . . . The reader doesn't need to know" (124). But now, of course, the reader does. Does reflection in the name of explaining authorial choices compel an author to disclose a fact she'd chosen to omit? No, though knowing does certainly both illuminate the writer's thinking and also recast the original essay. My point is that even in reflecting about her choices and processes in writing "Grip," Castro generates new material, producing what seems more like a two-part essay, theme and variation, what might in a different tradition have been melded and published as a single piece. More on that below.

A similar relationship exists between "Crush" (2014b) and "A Commentary on Crush: In Search of a Seamless Reflection" (2014a) by Michelle Pilar Hamill. "Seamless reflection" is an interesting aspiration. Does she mean a continuity between original and commentary so they seem of a single piece, or does she mean a relationship within the commentary essay between new materials and analysis? Actually, Hamill cites a third option, saying that in the original work she aspired toward "a seamless reflection, which fused with the action, so unobtrusive it would live inside the story like a wraith" (Hamill 2014b, 122). Indeed, "Crush" is almost pure narrative, with very few interpretive or reflective comments, following the aesthetic of "showing, not telling." Still, Hamill's comment indicates her understanding of the centrality of reflection, even if buried, to the essay form.

"Crush" (2014b) comes in four main scenes. Hamill is eight, living in New York City with her divorced mother, an actress. For her mother, she runs an errand to the dry cleaners, where she learns the definition of a term she's been seeing on posters around the neighborhood: *sodomy*. She runs another errand, by herself to a grocery store, where her thumb gets caught in an electric door (she's too light to trigger the sensor mat that controls it) and is rescued by three butchers, spending a long scene in their company listening to their patter, talking about her mother, and waiting for an ambulance. Drifting in and out of consciousness, she imagines the sodomizing criminal leaping from his wanted poster to be caught by the three butchers. Next, and brief, are the ride to the hospital, the doctor's treatment, and the next day at home watching old *Partridge Family* and *I Love Lucy* reruns, while her mother consults a Church of Religious Science manual for metaphysical healing solutions and declares they should start celebrating Father's Day because, she says, "After all, I'm not only your mother now, I'm your father, too" (Hamill 2014b, 119). In the last page she returns a few times to the grocery store, where the butchers tease her conspiratorially, though after some time, two of the butchers no longer work there.

Hamill's commentary invites/permits her to provide the reflection and interpretation she chose not to include in "Crush." After one observation, she states, "Now I've gone and told you something. But in writing 'Crush,' I set out to keep my analysis under wraps" (Hamill 2014a, 121). She asks, "What of the butchers and their paternal pull?" and then answers, "Today I can tell you: My father had all but faded from memory" (123). She says, "It struck me that the disembodied and overwhelming feelings I sometimes had, alone in the darkness watching my mother act, mirrored my state outside the theater" (123). All three lines—and there are many more like it—could have perfectly appeared in the context of the essay itself, consonant with the genre's tradition, but here they appear only in separate commentary. It's as if she'd pulled apart two traditionally constitutive elements of the essay, here the story, there the reflection, interpretation, and association.

"Commentary" (2014a) itself is an essay. Hamill begins with a paragraph explaining her reaction, just after high school, to a scene in *Crime and Punishment*, then a second paragraph on why she won't subject her infant daughter to long car trips. She's headed toward a point about her writerly sensibilities, in general and in "Crush," but why the oblique approach? After all, she could simply launch into processes and decisions made, her rationales and hopes for them. The answer—for Hamill and for all the *Fourth Genre* self-reflection authors—stems from the framework for these pieces; writing even a "service" piece for a journal dedicated to literary writing invites literary writing. After all, there's a scant gap, if any, between the first-person, mind-in-motion essay about *lived* experience and the first-person essay about *written* experience. The latter may, in fact, need or invite the narration of "new" experience to help both the writer and reader explain and understand the writing itself.

REFLECTION DEMURRED

These paired pieces from *Fourth Genre* are examples of recent genre shift within the essay in which the convention of explicit reflection is dwindling even as two essayistic traditions are ascending. Decades ago, Robert Scholes and Carl Klaus described a subgenre, "the essay as poem," referring to lyrical pieces trading heavily on image, descriptive and evocative (Scholes and Klaus 1969). These days, the lyric essay finds favor in academic creative writing, bridging the prose poem to nonfiction. Its aesthetic is impressionistic, emphasizing language, style, and mood, suggestive rather than declarative. And while lyric essays are often contemplative, they frequently lack overt reflective comment, as if to legitimize the essay's literary status as worthy for creative writing by going all in with showing. While "Grip" and "Getting Grip" might well have coalesced as a single piece in a different academic tradition, here the short, lyric work is published as the primary piece. In a separate reflection (which appeared on *Brevity's Nonfiction Blog* on January 29, 2014) on her essay "The Saigon Kiss" (2014), Kelly Morse notes that "the original draft was a prose poem." That piece describes a wheelchaired man in Hanoi traffic and the author on a motorbike stopped by a policeman and worried about burning her bare leg on a hot muffler. There's no room in "Saigon Kiss" (2014) for reflection.

Reflection is similarly scant in a related tradition, the segmented (or montage) essay, whose writers deploy short chunks of text separated by graphics or white space. This is the rhetoric of juxtaposed discontinuity. The technique is hardly new; earlier, I noted E.B. White's "Spring." But it's currently being embraced zealously, sometimes reduced to sparse fragments in list-driven essays like Jordan Wiklund's (2014), which consists of fifty-two sections, most of them but a sentence long.

> Ask him what growing up on the farm in Two Harbors was like.
> Ask him about what he learned on the farm, were he milked cows before going to school.
> Ask him about college in Duluth, that one time he stole a beer truck, the married woman who desired an affair.
> Ask him about those adventurous college days in the 70s!
> Ask him about fourteen job offers in the 70s!
> . . .
> Ask him about heart attacks.
> . . .
> Ask him about always referring to Steve as "his black friend."

Tracing the current enthusiasm for segmented essays is fairly impossible, but a significant signpost was the success of Joan Didion's "The White Album" and its collage of fifteen events, from a Doors recording session to the Charles Manson trial to Didion's own medical reports. Her reflections center on the elusiveness of coherence. Near the outset, Didion comments that "we live entirely, especially if we are writers, by the imposition of a narrative line upon disparate images," only to realize she is "talking here about a time when [she] began to doubt the premises of all the stories [she] had ever told [her]self" (Didion 1979, 11). After presenting several anecdotes, Didion comments, "In this light all

connections were equally meaningful, and equally senseless," concluding later that "quite often I reflect on the big house in Hollywood, . . . but
writing has not yet helped me to see what it means" (48).

Conventionally, the rise of fragmentation is ascribed to the rise of digital media. By this logic, we're living in an age of parataxis in which an
unlikely adjective, *longform*, now designates writings that merely would
have been articles or journalism not long ago. Screens invite brevity,
yes, but more significantly, they invite immediate and incremental publication. With readers at the ready *now*, onlookers to an endless textual
parade, what writer can bear not entering multiple floats—or affixing
streamers to floats passing by? Of course, we still read novels—books
aren't dead—but short forms, like the essay, are pressured to be even
shorter. Who has time for reflection in them?

Unconventionally, Didion's "White Album" suggests an explanatory arrow pointing in the opposite direction. In this logic, digital circulation isn't the cause of fragmentation but the manifestation of it.
Pursuing grand cultural narratives is naïve and unnecessary. Perhaps
the essay no longer needs the strategy of reflection. Perhaps the right
of writers to tell their own experiences and ideas, a campaign launched
by Montaigne five hundred years ago, has been fulfilled, and the diffi-
dent apology of reflection is now beside the point. Perhaps the idea of
truth as contingently measured by me—and by others like me (and for-
get those who aren't)—is now so widely embraced that reflection seems
downright quaint; either you carry a loaded AR15 into a Starbucks or
a Chipotle or you don't, and you seek like-minded company. Perhaps
multiple publishing channels have obviated the strictures of writing
for diverse readerships. To gain wide publics, earlier essayists may
have needed the rhetoric of reflection, the ethos of uncertain ponder-
ing, of hedging that their interpretation may be inflected and suspect.
Perhaps now that's all taken for granted—and the wide public is in any
event a fantasy.

That said, I speculate that we might need essayistic reflection as much
now as ever. We might need the modesty of authors leaving traces of
themselves in their writings, commenting on junctures encountered,
choices made and choices abjured. We might benefit both from less
narrow confidence and less lyric absence and from more authorial presence, albeit measured and self-critical. There are plenty of genres to fill
plenty of textual roles these days. The essay has its place among them
as writing that most directly figures making through reflecting, inviting
complexity and connection.

References

Aldrich, Marcia. 2009. "Editor's Note." *Fourth Genre: Explorations in Nonfiction* 11 (Fall): ix–x.

Belloc, Hellaire. 1955. "By Way of Preface: An Essay upon Essays upon Essays." In *One Thing and Another: A Miscellany from His Uncollected Essays*, ed. Patrick Cahill, 11–14. London: Hollis and Carter.

Castro, Joy. 2009a. "Getting Grip." *Fourth Genre: Explorations in Nonfiction* 11 (Fall): 121–27.

Castro, Joy. 2009b. "Grip." *Fourth Genre: Explorations in Nonfiction* 11 (Fall): 119–20.

Diaz-Plaja, Guillermo. 2012. "The Limits of the Essay." In *Essayists on the Essay: Montaigne to Our Time*, ed. Carl H. Klaus and Ned Stuckey-French, 99–100. Iowa City: University of Iowa Press.

Didion, Joan. 1979. "The White Album." In *The White Album*, 11–48. New York: Simon and Schuster.

Hamill, Michele Pilar. 2014a. "Commentary on 'Crush': In Search of a Seamless Reflection." *Fourth Genre: Explorations in Nonfiction* 16 (1): 121–24. http://dx.doi.org /10.14321/fourthgenre.16.1.0121.

Hamill, Michele Pilar. 2014b. "Crush." *Fourth Genre: Explorations in Nonfiction* 16 (1): 107–20. http://dx.doi.org/10.14321/fourthgenre.16.1.0107.

Hoaglund, Edward. 1976. "What I Think, What I Am." *New York Times Book Review*, June 27, 35.

Klaus, Carl H. 2012. "Toward a Collective Poetics of the Essay." In *Essayists on the Essay: Montaigne to Our Time*, ed. Carl H. Klaus and Ned Stuckey-French, xv–xxvii. Iowa City: University of Iowa Press.

Klaus, Carl H., and Ned Stuckey-French, eds. 2012. *Essayists on the Essay: Montaigne to Our Time*. Iowa City: University of Iowa Press.

Morse, Kelly. 2014. "The Saigon Kiss." *Brevity* 45 (Winter). http://brevitymag.com/issues /winter-2014/the-saigon-kiss/.

Orwell, George. 1946. "Shooting an Elephant." In *A Collection of Essays*, 148–55. Orlando, FL: Harcourt Brace.

Purpura, Lia. 2011. "Jump." In *Rough Likeness: Essays*, 85–94. Louisville, KY: Sarabande.

Sanders, Scott Russell. 1988. "The Singular First Person." *Sewanee Review* 96 (4): 658–72.

Scholes, Robert, and Carl Klaus. 1969. *Elements of the Essay*. New York: Oxford University Press.

Steinberg, Michael. 1999. "Editor's Notes." *Fourth Genre* 1 (Spring): v–viii.

Wallace, David Foster. 1997a. "A Supposedly Fun Thing I'll Never Do Again." In *A Supposedly Fun Thing I'll Never Do Again*, 256–353. Boston: Little, Brown.

Wallace, David Foster. 1997b. "Getting Away from Pretty Much Being Away from It All." In *A Supposedly Fun Thing I'll Never Do Again*, 83–137. Boston: Little, Brown.

Wallace, David Foster. 2006. "Consider the Lobster." In *Consider the Lobster*, 235–54. Boston: Little, Brown.

White, E. B. 1944. "Spring." In *One Man's Meat*, 231–37. New York: Harper & Brothers.

White, E. B. 1992. "The Ring of Time." In *Essays of E.B. White*, 178–87. New York: Harper Perennial.

Wiklund, Jordan. 2014. "When You Meet My Father." *Brevity* 45 (Winter). http://brevity mag.com/nonfiction/when-you-meet-my-father/.

Woolf, Virginia. 1992. "The Death of the Moth." In *Shaping Tradition: Art and Diversity in the Essay*, ed. Sandra Fehl Tropp, 307–309. Fort Worth: Harcourt Brace Jovanovich.

VI

In Conclusion

Reflection as Rhetorical

15

DEFINING REFLECTION
The Rhetorical Nature and Qualities of Reflection

Kathleen Blake Yancey

There is much to learn from the chapters within. As they demonstrate, it's clear that reflection as both process and practice is considerably more complex than the literature has suggested. In the early days of the process movement, in the first generation of reflection, its role was tightly circumscribed, focusing on writer and text; in a second generation, reflection was identified as a practice in both classroom and assessment contexts that would make visible student learning and in the process support learners as it also helped teachers. Today, in the third generation of reflection in writing studies, we understand reflection much more capaciously: among other defining features and characteristics, it is identified as a key move in transfer of writing knowledge and practice; is understood as culturally constructed; requires its own curriculum; takes different forms in different media, which bring with them different affordances; has distinctive characteristics as a genre; and, not least, is defined as rhetorical, that is, as an epistemological practice.

In this concluding chapter, then, I read across the earlier chapters in order to identify and define characteristics of reflection in writing studies as we currently understand it. These characteristics include its epistemological value and practice; its unsettledness; its location in community; its attention to vocabulary; its role in curriculum; its relationship to difference; and its fitness with more open genres. I then summarize our understanding of reflection in the current moment and provide questions that might guide our work in the future.

REFLECTION AS EPISTEMOLOGICAL PRACTICE

Overall, the claim of *A Rhetoric of Reflection* is that reflection is rhetorical: reflection is a process we use to make meaning and make knowledge,

DOI: 10.7330/9781607325161.c015

a kind of meaning and knowledge unique to reflection given its inter-sectionality, its insistence that only through bringing the human and the world together to theorize can a reflective knowledge and meaning be made. Such knowledge and meaning making is contingent, subject to change in a world also changing, a knowledge that, in philosopher Thomas Pfau's (2004) formation, requires, even demands, attention. According to Pfau, to make meaning, to make knowledge, we must attend: "Attention is solicited by our intuitive sense of a potentiality as yet undefined—some meaning or value that will only disclose itself in proportion to the attention we are prepared to bestow on the phenom-enon or person in question. Here, the underlying ethos is one of gener-osity rather than some claim staked in conceptual or quantifiable form" (Pfau 2004, 39). As a process, attention operates at the intersection of the mind and the "reality of what we attend *to.*" In this latter sense, attention, through an individual's "focused seeing," is at the same time a joining outside of the self with another—be it object, person, or event—a "participating in what gives itself to us" (38). From this perspective, a capacity for attending reveals—but also constructs—an "orientation toward the world, world . . . not as an inventory of impersonal objects and agendas, but rather as a realm of potentialities" (38).

Reflection, however, is also more than a process. In school contexts, as we have seen here, reflection can also refer to a product—a departmen-tal writing plan in biology; a video accounting for writing development in a reflective practicum; a reflection-in-presentation demonstrating transfer of writing knowledge and practice; notes on a document-based reflective interview. And in out-of-school contexts, as Doug Hesse observes, reflection informs the essay even when out of sight.

Cathy Leaker and Heather Ostman, studying both the process and the product of reflection in the context of prior learning assessment (PLA), bring an unusual perspective to the question of how reflection makes meaning given the stakes of the PLA exercise, the stakes not merely a grade on a single or multiple texts composed in school, but rather cred-its born of experience and explanation articulating a knowledge the academy will warrant. In their earlier article in *College Composition and Communication,* Leaker and Ostman (2010) put the point poignantly:

> It is within this context that PLA texts made manifest for us a series of issues central to composition research and practice: they foreground the "contact zone" between the unauthorized writer, institutional power, and the articulation of knowledge claims; they reinforce the central role of a multifaceted approach to writing expertise in negotiating that zone; and, finally, they call attention to new and alternative spaces in which learning

is gained and call for new forms in which it may be articulated. Ultimately, we want to claim that PLA as an emergent discourse compels composition-ists to re-imagine not only the students we all teach, but ways we might better—more explicitly, more reflectively, and more tactically—teach such students about writing as a mechanism for claiming and legitimating learning. (692–93)

Put another way, writing reflectively, *as a mechanism for claiming and legitimating learning*, provides a unique path toward making knowledge. As Leaker and Ostman comment, writing, "less than a neutral tool for asserting knowledge claims" (Leaker and Ostman 2010, 697), is the pre-ferred modality.

Such writing, writing reflectively, constitutes what writer Phillip Lopate (2005), echoing Sondra Perl (1980), refers to as "retrospective thinking on the page," a practice that, he concedes, is "difficult." Definitionally, writing reflectively is one part recording and one more important part the articulation of attending. Moreover, in defining such writing, Lopate notes that in reflective writing two intelligences, counterpointed in time, come into play, "one strand report[ing] on what happened, and another, equally important, speculat[ing] on the meaning of those events, through the ongoing dialectic between . . . prior and present intelligences" (Lopate 2005, 144). Such writing can also be oriented to the possible, the associative, the contingent, as Lopate suggests: "What I mean by thinking on the page is something more quicksilver and spon-taneous: to question all that might have been transpiring inside and outside themselves at the time, and to catch the hunches, doubts, and digressive associations that dart through their brains" (155).

To demonstrate, at least in part, what such knowledge making looks like, Leaker and Ostman, in this collection, cite iterative drafts com-posed by a student explaining his antique map-cleaning process. In Ralph's first draft, we learn about this process in an essay sounding very like what we read in first-year composition. "In this essay, I will describe the procedures for cleaning an antique map on paper. An antique map on paper is a printed image on paper that was made at least 100 years ago. When I first started at my company, I was just an art handler, which is just a glorified way of saying I was in charge of shipping all antique maps. But through my experience working with the maps, I began to learn there were special ways for cleaning paper—something I didn't even know before I started."

In a world where expertise can be developed outside of the school context—not unlike the situation during the Enlightenment when many, perhaps most, people developed expertise outside of any schooling context—what Ralph calls "doing" is academically credited only when the student can theorize the practice, the doing. Without losing his own role in the learning process or his own expertise, Ralph authors a new draft, one shifting from a prototypical first-year composition (FYC) process essay to an expression of knowledge located in personal experience crediting expertise intended to help someone without such expertise.

> In my ten years as a paper conservationist, I have learned through experience the best ways for handling an antique map, and many of these techniques are best learned through "doing," as opposed to being taught in a textbook or in a classroom. As the in-house paper conservator for an antique map and book dealer, I work with antique maps, which are maps that are printed image on paper made at least 100 years ago. Although I read advice from paper conservation websites, much of my knowledge about map cleaning comes from experience. Handling the paper, cleaning it, whether it is by dry cleaning or wet cleaning or a combination of both, is something no one can teach you in a classroom. Your hands need to be acquainted with the texture of the paper; your nose needs to be familiar with the smells of paper.

In this explanation, Ralph brings together attending to and doing through writing reflectively, which allows him to articulate what he now knows. He relies on both the specific and the general, toggling between them, defining, for example, the object of his specific area of expertise, "antique maps, which are maps that are printed image on paper made at least 100 years ago," and pointing to the general knowledge he has gained in "handling the paper, cleaning it, whether it is by dry cleaning or wet cleaning or a combination of both." Moreover, in explaining map conservation, Ralph operates from what we might call a *reflective stance*, one allowing him, in this case, to explain to those who don't know.

Such a reflective stance can be taken, as well, by those fully inside the academy, as we see in Pamela Flash's account of faculty collaborating to make explicit what is tacit and ambiguous as they inquire into their own writing and teaching practices. In this case, the materials helpful in making knowledge aren't maps and cleaning supplies, but rather surveys and responses eliciting student and faculty perceptions of critical writing abilities. The result, as Flash quite simply puts it, raises questions and calls into question assumptions: "Data reveal that abilities ranked highly by faculty are often not the most obvious to students." Reviewing these conflicting data together and reflecting on what they mean, faculty think aloud about how students' understandings have developed and what role, if any, the faculty themselves may have played in contributing to these understandings. In sum, this reflection, bringing together information and collective, conversational reflection, supports a making of knowledge otherwise not possible.[1]

Other reflective stances—as we see in Kevin Roozen's student Terri—are also tentative and exploratory. Terri's reflective interviews, for instance, allow her to trace the multiple, personal, and professional integrative connections—based in school, experience, and family life—contributing to her sense of, her knowledge of, the "whole patient." As Roozen explains, "What emerged from these reflective interviews was a sense that Terri's perspective of 'the whole patient' was occasioned by the connections she had forged among seemingly disconnected texts. Some of those texts, of course, were those readily associated with patient care, like the flowchart Terri used while recording at a patient's bedside. Other texts, though, included texts such as the cancer video she created for her family members and the many poems she wrote about patients and her experiences as a nurse." For Terri, the reflection, as for Ralph, is *enacted*, located in doing. In Terri's case, it's also highly textual and integrative, blurring the different contexts of "the 'official' world of the professional healthcare workplace and the various 'unofficial' worlds she inhabited," as Roozen puts it. It's through the bringing together of these worlds that Terri made meaning of the whole patient and the life of terminal disease.

THE UNSETTLED-NESS OF REFLECTION

Reflection, as we've seen, can serve different purposes. In Ralph's case, the purpose is to theorize what he knows so that it's more than idiosyncratic experience since such experience isn't what the academy credits; in the University of Minnesota's WEC program, to theorize writing and redesign curriculum; in Terri's life world, to make sense of life as of death. A *condition* for much reflection is what Christina McDonald calls "disequilibrium as exigence" and what Pamela Flash links to an "unsettling," a note of difference or point of departure providing a context for what is to be reflected upon, be it describing current methods for preserving an old map, articulating how writing works in a given discourse community, or understanding the life in dying. As Flash explains, "What [my faculty colleagues] may not have suspected is that unsettling is an initial goal of these conversations. When faculty members engage in active, dialogical reflection—when they effectively make the familiar strange—these discussions can catalyze a dismantling of entrenched and unproductive pedagogical thinking." Making the familiar strange thus seems a critical move in reflection: it is that un/familiarity that lies at the heart of Horner's translingualism, at the intersection of writing in FYC and in other disciplines, at the dissonance between what Kevin Roozen thought he understood about Terri's writing and what there is to understand.

Even where reflection is valued, it can become a practice too routinized, too familiar and thus not useful, as Naomi Silver suggests: "Even in the practices of an individual classroom, if reflective writing is perceived as routine, it may not lead students to engage the metacognitive cycle of learning so as to enable development of a 'theory' of self-understanding for their writing." In this sense, there seems to be a tension between a familiarity, based in routinization, functioning as a template reducing attention and the development of what we might call a *reflective habit*, one leading to insight, which for many is the goal of a reflective curriculum. Christina McDonald sees such familiarity playing out somewhat differently in the choices students make, more specifically in their playing it safe in a kind of routine descriptive reflective writing whose nature is all too familiar when the goal is for students to articulate a reflection oriented to the future, to the unfamiliar, and to significance.

> The first samples of randomly selected reflective essays (drawn across sections and departments) revealed the very dichotomies identified earlier: by and large, these early ePortfolios functioned as electronic repositories for completed assignments that had been uploaded at the end of the course as a showcase and were accompanied by a descriptive rather than reflective essay. Put another way, cadets were able to describe learning experiences illustrated by certain artifacts but seldom wrote about their significance or how the work prepared them for what lay ahead.

Elizabeth Clark makes the same point in commenting on a student's reflection. The student, commenting on her use of digital technology, was uncomfortable with and uninterested in such technology; she feels, she says, like "a child from another age." Clark observes that the student's reflection was important for her, moving her out of a comfortable stance into a site where she could "grapple," where she produced a kind of reflection whose messiness, Clark says, we should embrace: "Her reflection is not a neatly packaged, taut piece. Her reflection engages ambiguity and invention. . . . Reflection allows students space to think, to engage, to evolve. Reflection allows students to look uncertainty and change in the face and find in that growth and change a continuity that will follow them over time as they learn new things, have new experiences, and engage with the unknown." And sometimes the unsettling, the disequilibrium, is rooted not so much in contexts of time, but rather in contexts of space, such as the context of material conditions outside of school that set the stage for and shape what goes on inside school, as Asao Inoue and Tyler Richmond's student Nou explains:

> I remember as a child, I never got the experience of my parents reading to me before I go to sleep because my parents don't even know half of the English word that I know. Unlike most of the American parents, they tend to read to their children before they sleep; my parents gave me life lessons such as cooking, cleaning, caring for my siblings and lesson then is going to help me in the long run. I'm not saying that American parents are better or anything but what I'm trying to say is that although my parents did [sic] know English I still learn something from them and it's something that no one can take from me because I'm going to always remember those life lesson.

Here, through reflection, Nou articulates both what she's lost and what she's gained as she navigates the intersection between life and school. And more generally, what we see is that reflection occurs within multiple contexts, including time past and future and space; and with the increase in contexts comes an increase in ambiguity, which can contribute to invention.

THE ROLE OF COMMUNITY

A community helps set the stage for making meaning through reflection, be it the community between interviewer and interviewee, the discourse community of a given discipline, or the classroom community that so many writers here address. Jeff Sommers, for example, talks about writing to a senior colleague asking for advice, outlining possibilities but certain that help will come from another who knows more: here we see him summarizing what he has written in an effort to situate the text and ask for advice.

> I've included more than the 10 readings required because I don't think my list is perhaps what's expected. Some of the citations are from composition scholars, not literary critics. In fact, there's a pedagogical angle to some of them. I've also included two citations for articles of my own. I was thinking that I wanted to present readings that have impacted my teaching plans for the course. So here's my key question to you: how smart a strategy is that? I could replace some of the more pedagogical references with traditional literary critical material; that might make the list look more like other proposals. But my course is focused less on a literary genre or time period than it is on a way of teaching. What recommendations do you have about my reading list?

In reviewing Sommers's memo to a more experienced colleague about ways to reach a larger audience, we see how writing and reflecting within a small community works. Sommers outlines his thinking, identifies options, and asks for an evaluative response in a model of reflection he shares with students as they compose their Writers Memos intended to help them solicit the same kind of response.

In a larger community, that of the institution, reflection becomes a sustained activity over a longer period of time and is constructed through materials hosted in an electronic portfolio: Elizabeth Clark understands this model of community-based reflection as a socially supported, materially rich recursive process. Thus, less oriented to specific texts, reflection in the LaGuardia community is more oriented to a future that reflection, in concert with texts, helps shape. Reflection, according to Clark, "becomes a recursive process over time prompted by faculty, drafted by students, and revised through a community of faculty and staff readers who understand a student's goals through the materials and artifacts shared in the ePortfolio."

In a smaller community, that of the classroom, students in Fresno, California, and Lexington, Virginia, are reimagining how we learn, constructing classrooms as reflective semipublic spaces where learning is a communal process. Reading and writing in Fresno, for instance, Celina understands peer review not as a unilateral or competitive process benefiting individuals, but rather as a shared process helping all participants, a process in which *we're all in it together wanting to succeed*: "My peer Julie replied with some feedback that helped me know that I was doing something that was good and made sense. Her reply, 'I like the way you mentioned the problem and I also like how you mentioned everything that's going on and how you showed the examples. I really liked how you were informed with this information.' So I also try to give positive critical feedback that can help my peers rather than bring them down to hurt them because we're all in it together wanting to succeed."

At VMI, as at LaGuardia Community College, the portfolio provides the site of reflection, one that also is community based. As McDonald explains, "Cadets expect to join a community," here a very specific college community as signaled by the consistent use of the word *cadet* for student. In taking portfolio-based classes, cadets join a virtual community hosted by the portfolio extending the physical classroom, where students "interact and learn together": "Cadets we interviewed told us that they regarded the ePortfolio as an inherently social space and reflection as a more public than private enterprise. They expected to engage in dialogue with others about their own learning and to comment on the artifacts they posted to their ePortfolios during class, as well as afterward. In a digital space, these processes would be 'both individual and social' (Yancey 1998, 72)." Here, it's the faculty who are adjusting to the portfolio as inherently *social space and reflection as a more public than private enterprise*. Rather than space for iteration and dialogue, the portfolio, for faculty, was a static archive. What brings it alive, changes its status for students is, in part, what McDonald calls a "social pedagogy of reflective learning" documented in a reflective tag, in the portfolio, requiring cadets to reflect upon every submitted artifact though taking up three questions: "*What* is the artifact within the larger context of the course? *So what*, or why was this a meaningful learning experience? *Now what*, or what do I need to know or do for the learning that lies ahead?" The effect on cadets of tagging all artifacts, informal and unfinished as well as completed texts, was serendipitous.

> Tagging artifacts prompts cadets to reread, and thus *resee*, not only the artifacts in their ePortfolios and thus in another context but also the earlier reflections-on-action and constructive reflections that accompany them. Engaging in this iterative process—in community and in the digital space of the ePortfolio—also helps cadets address the problem of distance. Reflective tags prompt them, as one cadet put it, to "step away from the experience" of creating the artifact in order to try to understand it, for themselves and with their classmates, in a wider context. At the same time, working inside the ePortfolio diminishes the distance between cadets and their evolving body of work. . . . Writing reflective tags moves cadets through different stages of reflection, considering and reconsidering artifacts of their learning, so that when they arrive at the moment of reflection-in-presentation, they are better prepared for such a culminating assignment.

In sum, the portfolio supports an ecology of writing and reflection in dynamic relationship with each other. As McDonald describes it, the process cadets engage in is both iterative and recursive—the latter a word Clark uses as well—as they consider and reconsider "artifacts of their learning." Thus, the recursiveness and iteration we associate with writing has also become a feature of this reflective practice.

Similarly, Elizabeth Clark shows us another dimension of the writing-reflection ecology. Commenting on teaching voice to students, Clark says that allowing students to create videos unhitches them from preconceived notions about what academic writing is supposed to sound like, which to them is voiceless.

> In a course that emphasizes helping students to write in an authentic voice, I found that these video assignments were far more authentic and real than their written equivalent, in part because they literally captured students' pauses, facial expressions, and intonations. Put another way, their video voice was how I actually heard them talk and express themselves in

class. Moreover, as students worked on voice in their writing, the flattening of individual expression that often occurs in initial attempts at academic writing did not characterize the video reflections: each student's reflection sounded unique. What basic writing students were still attempting to master—style, tone, and voice in an effort to create an individual writing style—they were able to better communicate using their actual voices in how they presented their reflections. This was an important learning moment for me as I considered how I might continue to revise my basic writing assignment to include earlier videotaped reflective assignments as a way of teaching voice in writing: a concept that sometimes feels oblique in classroom discussion can be very transparent as we compare the written and videotaped versions of the same reflection.

The two media—composing in print and composing in video—provide different affordances, of course, for making meaning (a point taken up in the next section). But as important are the ways that the primary writing texts and reflections can inform each other: how, Clark wants to know, might her *basic writing assignment include earlier videotaped reflective assignments* as a mechanism for helping students understand voice in print? In an ecological model, working across media when composing reflectively can help students compose more felicitously in each; reviewing reflective writing can help us compose primary texts just as reviewing primary texts can provide material for reflection.[2]

VOCABULARY AND THE CURRICULUM

The vocabulary, or key terms, of a discipline or practice provide language we can use in articulating what we know and what we don't know. Sometimes the vocabulary of reflection is located in the content of the discipline, sometimes in the language of process, and sometimes in the intersection and interaction of content, process, and reflection. In working with faculty in many disciplines at the University of Minnesota, for example, Pamela Flash finds the WEC project itself provides a language helping faculty give the tacit a name. In asserting that the reflective conversation focusing on student writing "is changing the ways [the faculty] in turn teach and talk to students about writing," one of Flash's colleagues observes; "'We are . . . using our WEC language.'" Another points to how important language is for such reflection: "'I think [WEC] has helped many of our faculty be more thoughtful and self-reflexive about their teaching. It has helped others find language to talk with students about what they are doing in writing assignments.'" Likewise, addressing the readers of this book, Anne Beaufort too employs a specialized vocabulary, in this case of cognitive psychology, to help us understand some of what teachers should do to support transfer of writing knowledge and practice. Key terms and expressions like *mental models, deep-structure knowledge*, and *an inquiry process for learning* help us understand reflection's field of activity and the aims of a curriculum integrating reflection throughout.

A specific curriculum keyed to key terms is the TFT curriculum, one that has vocabulary as one of its three signature components. Like the curricula at both VMI and LaGuardia Community College, the Teaching for Transfer (TFT) curriculum is oriented to the future: its vocabulary is intended to help students understand current writing situations, but mostly to help them frame new ones in the future. In brief, key terms for TFT are crucial. As an example of how students use these terms, Kara Taczak and Liane Robertson cite the experience of Matt, who is completing an assignment for a psychology class that took place in a future the writing class anticipated, where "a situation in which writing itself was not specifically coached or directed as it was in the writing classroom." In describing his approach, Matt "mentions four of the key terms from the TFT course —*audience, genre, context,* and *purpose*— . . . using them as cornerstones to his conceptual framework as he reflects about his writing. . . . Through reflection, Matt is able to approach the writing situation, understand his role as the writer in the specific context of the assignment, develop a conceptual map for completing the writing task, and consider the implications for his writing on an audience other than the professor assigning it." For Matt, the combination of key terms—here, *audience, genre, context,* and *purpose*—and reflection help him understand and negotiate the new task.

For several of the authors in *A Rhetoric of Reflection*, the medium of reflection also matters: they ask, what does a curriculum located largely in digital media look like, and what role does reflection play? Michael Neal teaches a multimodal composition course, and his reflection, he explains, asks students to provide an account of what he calls "rhetorical decision making," that is, an explanation of why the student-composers made the choices they did. Thinking of a student who created a video, Neal comments on the contribution the reflection made to his evaluation, precisely because it helped him understand *why* a text is as it is:

> One student decided to develop her video on subjunctive moods (something I could tell through the video), but what I wouldn't have known is that her original plan was to include imperative and indicative moods as well. When she included that information in her reflection as well as a rationale for why she selected the subjunctive over the others, it provided insight for me on one of my assessment criteria: the ability to narrow in or

focus on a topic for the scope of the video. If I had watched the video and it included subjunctives, imperatives, and indicatives, I would have seen a disjuncture between her claims about focus and what she completed. How would I have known about that disparity if I hadn't read/viewed them both? Or on the other hand, if I had only viewed the video and not read any of her reflection, I wouldn't have known to look for that focus, and I wouldn't have known if the focus were intentional, planned, or otherwise. In the end I needed to read her reflection *and* view the video with the claims from the reflection in mind.

The reflection in this curriculum, keyed to rhetorical decision making, assists the teacher, much as do Jeff Sommers's Writer's Memos. It also requires that we read differently, putting the two texts in dialogue with each other for a fuller, more capacious understanding of text and a better informed assessment.

Naomi Silver is also interested in the role of digital media in composing; her class, she says, is something new, a digital reflective practicum. Silver's vocabulary for composing departs from the conventional language of writing process: terms like *draft* and *revise* compete with *versioning*, *histories*, and *metadata*, and the practicum itself is reflectively rich. Every version of all the major writing projects includes "self-reflective monitoring comments—using the Comments tool in their word processing or PDF-creation program for alphabetic and multimodal print documents or tools like VoiceThread or a screencasting program for websites or time-based digital media projects—that indicate bottlenecks, breakthroughs, or anything else they wish to draw to their readers' attention," prompting responses from both peers and Silver herself. In this classroom, then, reflection, much like digital composing, is ubiquitous.

> Reflection is not simply "threaded through" the curriculum . . . , an accompaniment to the three major writing projects, but in a very real sense it is the curriculum; it constitutes the warp and woof of the course. From analyses of their "go-to" sentence styles in previous writing assignments to interviews with their classmates exploring important writing experiences; from the major writing project examining "Why I Write" to planning activities, self-reflective marginal comments, and self-evaluations accompanying their Repurposing and Remediation projects; from the construction of their electronic portfolio with a reflective introduction and contextual reflections for each artifact to the blog on which all of this work is presented, shared, and dissected; and in both analog and digital media, students in the Gateway course are always reflecting on *something*.

As a result, Silver says, the reflective "act of describing, analyzing, and drawing some conclusions" isn't an act apart from composing but rather a part of it. And, much like Clark and Neal, Silver is rethinking her pedagogy. She notes, for example, that much of her response has become multimodal in response to the multimodality of the composing she has assigned as well as to a need to keep up with the students. Tools like VoiceThread and screencasting software are thus also now part of her pedagogical repertoire.

In the models of curricula presented here, vocabulary are integral to reflection, and reflection is integral to learning.

DIFFERENCE AND TENSION

Bruce Horner takes difference as the ordinary in teasing out a notion of reflection informed by, and contingent with, translingualism; Asao Inoue and Tyler Richmond consider difference in the context of material conditions that are invisible to outsiders but that necessarily frame reading and writing as well as reflection about both. As important, as Inoue and Richmond suggest, difference can contribute to tension and potentially to invention: the question is what we make of and do with it.

Horner begins with his strategy: "identifying in the seemingly different (exceptional) the ordinary, with an eye towards then redefining the ordinary" as we see it in language practice. Action-reflection, according to Horner, is "a feature of all language practice," but not one with a consensus yet, since "beliefs about language," Horner observes, "shape practice." At the heart of such language practice, he notes, is ambiguity, one that we should embrace: we need to develop "a willingness to engage ambiguity rather than using the experience of ambiguity as a reason for dismissing discourse." Given this context, and given the inherent ambiguity of translingualism, difference is to be expected. Ambiguity in this sense is Burkean, a site of invention and meaning making: "We are only beginning to explore," Horner argues, "how such a perspective can enable us to recognize difference as an inevitable outcome of all language practice, and with what consequences for ourselves and our students. One such consequence may be the recuperation of reflection as not only a crucial but also an inevitable, if often unacknowledged, constituent of the work we do in writing, and that we can put to better work through our teaching."

Inoue and Richmond take a somewhat different tack toward difference in their work with Hmong students developing college-level reading and writing practices, focusing not on a philosophy of language so much as on the multiple contexts of life. Much as in the case of Roozen's student Terri, these contexts include literacy and provide a frame for it, but in Inoue and Richmond's Fresno, the material conditions of life are problematic, making it difficult for students to read, write, and reflect: "Because these Hmong women see themselves, and have been seen by others, as racially other, as not the white norm in school, it is difficult for them to reflect upon their learning without references to a white norm, which causes tensions and contradictions. Through the dialectic between their material conditions and the words they use to understand and express their learning, these four Hmong women writers show how their racial and gendered subject positions form contradictions not easily resolved." Seen this way, reflection references a default whiteness at odds with the experience—and in some cases, the values as well—of Lina, Nou, Maiger, and Celina, a point not unlike that made by Ostman and Leaker in their account of PLA's neglect of lived experience that fails to conform to more prescriptive models of reflection. Ostman and Leaker thus recommend that faculty might "*stand under the student's discourse* in order to better respond to [student] learning and to [student] experiences of learning" (italics in original). In this model, the experience itself, as described and valued in the *culture* of the experience, is worthy of reflection and respect—quite apart from its value as material for reflective translation into school rewards. Like Inoue and Richmond, Ostman and Leaker also remind us that an "experience of Otherness both shapes [students'] relationship to dominant forms of knowledge and constitutes its own rich pool of knowledge. Standing under another's discourse urges us to attend to the crucial distinction between decontextualized prescriptions to reflect on learning and listening to what is elided when a student says that it's hard to claim her learning when she constantly sees herself devalued."

Another part of such otherness for Lina, Nou, Maiger, and Celina is related to the role of gender and culture; the women, constructing reflection as a collaborative activity, understand that the work of school is often in contradiction to the work they should be completing at home—not homework, but family work—and this conflict too provokes tension and ambiguity. As Inoue and Richmond observe, "Often their lessons are social in nature, benefiting those around them, not themselves, or reflective selves ambiguously moving between singular and plural subject positions, perhaps suggesting the ambiguity they feel in their school selves and the social structures that contextualize their agency." These women do reflect, however, seeing value in their collaborative learning, understanding the values of their families, and at the same time imagining a postsecondary future for themselves. Their success, in other words, "is accomplished despite their material conditions, not because of them, revealing how the struggles they have with reading and writing in English are less about the intellectual work involved and more about finding a space for that work in their complex lives." In so reflecting—if and when we make such space available—students can have the opportunity to name these contexts, to find a place for themselves inside them, and to articulate what that means. They benefit in this process, and we do as well.

GENRE

The genre we invite students to compose when reflecting also shapes what is articulated and what is shared. One genre for reflection is Jeff Sommers's Writer's Memo, a hybrid memo prompting Sommers's reflection on what he identifies as its conflicting motives. Is it chiefly to help students understand their writing, or to help faculty respond? In reflecting upon the memo, Sommers concludes,

> there is probably some tension caused by the design of the memos, setting up a potential conflict between questions that ask students to think about their writing process and questions that ask them to evaluate their own writing and, in a sense, focus on the impact it is likely to have on its evaluator, namely me. But perhaps that tension is not necessarily obstructive. The second motivation—improving the draft with the hope of raising its final grade—may fade away when the students take a retrospective look at their work as the term comes to a conclusion because the revisions are already complete. What may be left is the recollection of reflecting, of describing and analyzing their own writing processes, and that recollection can provide the students with evidence to substantiate their claims in their capstone reflections on the semester.

Here, Sommers places the Writer's Memo in another context, that of the capstone reflection, which like a reflection-in-presentation is a culminating reflection and which in this case draws from the earlier, scaffolded Writer's Memos. In addition, Sommers argues, we need to teach the Writer's Memo genre, design prompts for it, and provide feedback to it. Much like Silver, even if working in a different medium, Sommers, in expanding his understanding of the relationship between genre and reflection, creates a curriculum in reflection to support students' efforts, both short and longer term.

The essay, according to Doug Hesse, provides another hospitable genre for reflection: "More than other genres, the essay embraces reflection, using it generatively in a way essential to its method and character." The openness of the essay as genre, according to Hesse, speaks to what he calls the "eagerness of essayists to explain their genre," which "simply manifests, in a broader frame, what they're doing as they practice it." In this sense, the process of reflecting and the text itself are brought together in a single genre, the essay. And like Elizabeth Clark and others here, Hesse points to the relationship of ambiguity to reflection. Thus, citing one essayist, Hesse points to the reflective "incompleteness" characterizing her work: the essay "leaves in these plentiful reflective markers, the so what's and whys and what does it means, the partial answers found wanting but nonetheless useful for their incompleteness. They're heuristic but also structural to the piece itself, sort of like architect's sketches visibly laminated into trusses." Such reflection, which Hesse titles "essayistic reflection," is needed now, he says, more than ever.

SHARED PERCEPTIONS: A WAY FORWARD

Reflection, as we have seen here, is richly diverse and can look very different from one site to the next, from one perspective to another. At the same time, there are patterns, appearing here as defining characteristics.

- It is both practice and text; the practice is always implicitly in the text; and it is sometimes explicitly so.
- It is an epistemological practice based in experience and the theorizing of that experience.
- It is unsettled—and unsettling.
- It is located in community.
- It requires a vocabulary and is curricular: in some instances, reflection is itself a curriculum.
- It can be practiced in many media, each of which brings with it helpful affordances.
- It inherently values, and relies upon, difference.
- It often is located in moments of ambiguity.
- Operating in one context, reflection often points to another, sometimes unintended context; it brings such contexts together for a fuller, richer meaning.
- Certain genres, among them the Writer's Memo, the reflective tag, the reflection-in-presentation, and the essay, are especially hospitable to reflection.

It is also the case that we need to know more.

- Is it the case that we are developing a taxonomy of reflection? We certainly see that suggestion in several chapters, including in Christina Mc Donald's contrasting of descriptive reflection with analytical. And many authors here use the word *analysis*, in fact: what is the relationship of analysis to reflection?

- What is the relationship between reflection as a habit and the routinization that has been identified as at odds with reflection? What are the characteristics of reflection as a habit? Are there strategies we can use to assure and support reflection's habit?

- Ecology might provide a useful metaphor or framework for understanding reflection, especially in writing studies. If so, what are the parts of the system, what are their relationships, and what is the dynamic among them?

- Reflection is an important part of many writing curricula, but there is a suggestion now that reflection merits its own curriculum; that is one claim of the Teaching for Transfer curriculum as well of the projects at VMI and at the University of Michigan. If that is so, what are the outcomes, the readings, and the assignments for such a curriculum? How are they integrated throughout a course content? Or might we offer stand-alone courses in reflection, where students find their own field of application?

- How does reflection support transfer? The TFT curriculum posits three curricular elements, one of which is reflection; the claim is that it needs to be systematic. Do we know which points are optimal for reflecting? We know that students need practice in writing: what is the best balance between practice and reflection? Is it even the same for all students?

- The medium of reflection seems to make a difference, but precisely how? Are the observations and insights recorded in print, for example, substantively different than those narrated in video? Would students learn more about reflecting in one medium than another? Could that learning then support reflection in yet another medium?

- We seem to perceive competing values in reflection. On the one hand, we see it as providing an opportunity for faculty and students to uncover assumptions and to make the implicit explicit. On the other hand, we see reflection tapping, or even inhabiting, ambiguity. Is there a theory of reflection that can accommodate the tension in these understandings?

- Reflection is available to all people, but the version faculty know best is simply one construction, located in the values of the dominant culture. How do we widen reflective practice so that it supports writers but also welcomes observations speaking to material conditions and to power relations? How do we create assignments in reflection that accept, and allow us to learn from, personal, cultural, and disciplinary epistemologies other than those inherited from Western traditions?

- If humans are all, at some level, translingual, and if translingualism makes the different ordinary, how do we tap this acceptance of difference in our reflective assignments?

- The PLA rhetorical reflection project is premised on the idea that students can translate their experiences through reflection for course credit, a premise not unlike that underlying the reflection in much coursework. But there's also a question running throughout *A Rhetoric of Reflection* about how we might value the articulation of experience through reflection that surprises us or is just a bit too far outside of specified outcomes or that makes us uncomfortable. How do we value this reflection?

In *A Rhetoric of Reflection*, we don't have all the answers to these questions, but we hope that our observations, our analyses, and our own reflections can help provide contexts helpful for pursing them.

Notes

1. This process resembles the weekly reflective meeting surgeons attend: see Atul Gawande's (2002) *Complications: A Surgeon's Notes on an Imperfect Science.*
2. Writing ecologies, at least since the publication of Marilyn Cooper's (1986) "The Ecology of Writing," are not new; in fact, in the present moment, ecology seems to be a common, if not predominant, metaphor. Its utility for reflection, however, is promising but has yet to be explored.

References

Cooper, Marilyn M. 1986. "The Ecology of Writing." *College English* 48 (4): 364–75. http://dx.doi.org/10.2307/377264.

Gawande, Atul. 2002. *Complications: A Surgeon's Notes on an Imperfect Science.* New York: Holt/Picador.

Leaker, Cathy, and Heather Ostman. 2010. "Composing Knowledge: Writing, Rhetoric, and Reflection in Prior Learning Assessment." *College Composition and Communication* 61 (4): 691–717.

Lopate, Phillip. 2005. "Reflection and Retrospection: A Pedagogic Mystery Story." *Fourth Genre* 7 (1): 143–56. http://dx.doi.org/10.1353/fge.2005.0016.

Perl, Sondra. 1980. "Understanding Composing." *College Composition and Communication* 31 (4): 363–70. http://dx.doi.org/10.2307/356586.

Pfau, Thomas. 2004. "The Art and Ethics of Attention." *Hedgehog Review* 16 (2): 34–42.

Yancey, Kathleen Blake. 1998. *Reflection in the Writing Classrooom.* Logan: Utah State University Press.

ABOUT THE AUTHORS

KATHLEEN BLAKE YANCEY, Kellogg W. Hunt Professor of English and Distinguished Research Professor, teaches at Florida State University. She has served as the elected leader of several scholarly organizations, including NCTE, CCCC, CWPA and SAMLA. Cofounder and codirector of the Inter/National Coalition for Electronic Portfolio Research and immediate past editor of *College Composition and Communication*, Yancey has authored or coauthored over eighty-five articles and book chapters and authored, edited, or coedited twelve scholarly books—including *Reflection in the Writing Classroom*; *Delivering College Composition: The Fifth Canon*, recognized with the Best Book Award from the Council of Writing Program Administrators; and *Writing Across Contexts: Transfer, Composition, and Sites of Writing*, recognized with the CCCC Research Impact Award and the Best Book Award from the Council of Writing Program Administrators. She is the recipient of several awards, including the Donald Murray Writing Prize and Florida State University's Graduate Mentor Award.

***

ANNE BEAUFORT, Professor Emeritus at University of Washington Tacoma, earned a PhD in language, literacy, and culture at Stanford University with a specialization in postsecondary writing instruction. After a career in corporate communications and first-hand observations of smart people's struggles with writing, she sought to uncover some of the ways in which postsecondary writing instruction could be improved. She has published numerous articles and book chapters and two ethnographic studies of writers in university and workplace settings, *Writing in the Real World: Making the Transition from School to Work* and *College Writing and Beyond: A New Framework for University Writing Instruction*.

J. ELIZABETH CLARK shares her ideas about writing and technology at LaGuardia Community College, City University of New York, where, as Professor of English, she teaches a range of composition, literature, and creative-writing courses. She is particularly interested in the role of technology and how it is changing how and what we write. She has been a part of LaGuardia's award-winning ePortfolio team since 2002. She has published on a variety of topics such as ePortfolios, writing pedagogy, pedagogy and technology, digital rhetoric, assessment, women's studies, the poetry of HIV/AIDS, and NBC's *The West Wing*.

PAMELA FLASH directs the University of Minnesota's writing-across-the-curriculum program and codirects the campus's Center for Writing. She is the founding director of the Writing Enriched Curriculum (WEC) program, which offers academic departments a structured, faculty-driven model for strengthening relevant writing instruction. Her research, publications, consultations, and presentations focus on writing pedagogy, activity theory, academic discourse communities, and the use of qualitative research methods to enable pedagogic change in individual, departmental, and institutional practices.

DOUG HESSE is President of the National Council of Teachers of English and Professor and Executive Director of writing at the University of Denver. Previously he served as chair of CCCC and president of WPA. At Illinois State University, he directed the writing program, the Center for the Advancement of Teaching, and the university honors program. He's coauthored four books and published some sixty articles, mainly on creative nonfiction, writing pedagogy, and professional issues. He sings in the Colorado Symphony Chorus.

BRUCE HORNER is Endowed Chair in Rhetoric and Composition at the University of Louisville, where he teaches courses in composition, composition theory and pedagogy, and literacy studies. His recent books include *Rewriting Composition: Terms of Exchange*, *Reworking English in Rhetoric and Composition: Global Interrogations, Local Interventions*, coedited with Karen Kopelson; *Economies of Writing: Revaluations in Rhetoric and Composition*, coedited with Brice Nordquist and Susan Ryan; and *Cross-Language Relations in Composition*, coedited with Min-Zhan Lu and Paul Kei Matsuda and winner of the 2012 CCCC Outstanding Book Award.

ASAO B. INOUE is Associate Professor of interdisciplinary arts and sciences and the Director of University Writing at the University of Washington Tacoma, where he teaches writing courses and graduate courses on composition theory, rhetoric, and writing assessment. His coedited collection, *Race and Writing Assessment*, won the CCCCs Outstanding Book Award for an edited collection. His newest book, *Antiracist Writing Assessment Ecologies: Teaching and Assessing for a Socially Just Future*, theorizes and illustrates ways writing teachers can rethink assessment in their classrooms as a way to form antiracist projects.

CATHY LEAKER is Associate Dean of the Metropolitan Center of SUNY Empire State College. As a faculty member and administrator, Cathy is committed to developing inclusive strategies to help underserved and underrepresented students meet their educational goals. She advocates for equity mindedness as an educational principle that must be enacted materially, pedagogically, and discursively.

CHRISTINA RUSSELL MCDONALD is Professor of English and Institute Director of Writing at the Virginia Military Institute. Her participation in Cohort VI of the Inter/National Coalition for Research on Electronic Portfolios has resulted in numerous presentations on reflective learning and ePortfolios at meetings of the American Association of Colleges and Universities (AAC&U), the Conference on College Composition and Communication (CCCC), and the IUPUI Assessment Institute. Her publications include two books, *Teaching Writing: Landmarks and Horizons* and *Teaching Composition in the 1990s: Sites of Contention*.

MICHAEL NEAL is Associate Professor of English at Florida State University, where he explores intersections between composition, writing assessment, and digital technologies. He is the author of *Writing Assessment and the Revolution in Digital Texts and Technologies* as well as of articles and chapters on writing assessment, digital archiving, undergraduate research, and digital composing. Neal teaches undergraduate courses in the Editing, Writing, and Media major and graduate courses in rhetoric and composition. His current research includes assessment technologies, digital archives of everyday writing, ethical boundaries of intellectual property and multimodal composition, and writing assessment frameworks and practices.

HEATHER OSTMAN is Professor of English and Director of the Humanities Institute at SUNY Westchester Community College. She has collaborated with Cathy Leaker on the intersections of composition studies and prior learning assessment, and their work has also appeared in *College Composition and Communication*. She is the author of *Writing Program Administration and the Community College* and the editor and coeditor of two essay collections on the fiction of Kate Chopin. In addition to book chapters, she has written many articles, which have appeared in journals such as *Prose Studies*, *Philological Studies*, *Women's Studies*, and others.

TYLER RICHMOND is Assistant Professor of English at Bakersfield College. While serving as the assistant to the WAC director at California State University, Fresno, he helped to assess the effectiveness of supplemental writing instruction and the Early Start and Summer

Bridge programs. In addition, Tyler has traveled to numerous conferences to present on topics including online tutoring, student failure, and grading. His current work is focused on adapting critical assessment methodologies to a community college context as well as exploring the definitions, motivations, and effects of student resistance.

LIANE ROBERTSON is Assistant Professor at William Paterson University of New Jersey, where she teaches writing and directs the writing-across-the-curriculum program. Her research on writing transfer is specifically focused on the role of writing content in curricular design, particularly the efficacy of a transfer-based curriculum in repurposing knowledge about writing across different academic contexts. Currently, she is involved in a multi-institutional study exploring the adaptability of the Teaching for Transfer curricular model across a wide range of writing sites and student populations. Her recent work is featured in *Writing across Contexts: Transfer, Composition, and Sites of Writing; Naming What We Know: Threshold Concepts of Writing Studies; Composition Forum*; and a number of forthcoming edited collections.

KEVIN ROOZEN is Associate Professor in the Department of Writing and Rhetoric and Director of First-Year Writing at the University of Central Florida. Kevin's research examines the relationships among persons' multiple engagements with literate activity and the implications those linkages have for the extended development of literate persons and practices. Kevin's work has appeared in *College Composition and Communication*, the *Journal of Basic Writing, Kairos, Research in the Teaching of English, Written Communication*, and in a number of edited collections. With coauthor Joe Erickson, Kevin's current book project, *Expanding Literate Landscapes*, illuminates the dynamic interplay of multiple literacies that can inform disciplinary writing, learning, and socialization.

NAOMI SILVER is Associate Director of the Sweetland Center for Writing at the University of Michigan and Coeditor of the Sweetland Digital Rhetoric Collaborative book series with the University of Michigan Press. Her research interests include multimodal composing and pedagogies, electronic portfolios, and digital shifts in WAC/WID teaching and programing. She is coeditor of the book *Using Reflection and Metacognition to Improve Student Learning: Across the Disciplines, Across the Academy*.

JEFF SOMMERS, Professor of English at West Chester University and Professor Emeritus at Miami University, served two terms as editor of *Teaching English in the Two-Year College* and has written extensively about composition pedagogy, portfolio assessment, and response to student writing. He is also the proud husband of a professor of nursing (University of Pennsylvania) and an even prouder father of an associate professor of social psychology (Tufts University), an assistant professor of health policy (Harvard University), and a graduate teaching assistant in criminology (Northwestern U), all four of whom have won teaching awards at their respective campuses.

KARA TACZAK is part of the writing faculty at the University of Denver, where she teaches first-year writing courses and advises first-year students. Her research centers on the intersection of reflection and transfer of knowledge and practices. Taczak's current research project, which was awarded a 2014–2015 CCCC Research Initiative grant and a 2015 CWPA grant, inquires how a Teaching for Transfer curriculum supports students' transfer of writing knowledge and practice into other sites of academic writing on four very different campuses. This research is the second phase of research reported on in her coauthored book, *Writing Across Contexts*, which was awarded the 2014–2015 CCCC Research Impact Award. Taczak's publications have appeared in *Composition Forum, Teaching English in the Two-Year College*, and *Across the Disciplines*.

INDEX

64164767R00203

Made in the USA
Lexington, KY
30 May 2017